MANAGING THE
ORGANIZATIONAL
MELTING POT

Hi Debra,
Thank you for taking
soci 390 with me.
You enriched the class
discussions. I wish
you all the best in
applying your
knowledge in the
real world of
management.

Sept. 11, 2009.

Dedicated in loving memory of my mother
—Pushi Prasad

For Bert and Jill Mills—
and in loving memory of
Winifred (Pat) Mills, 1922-1995
—Albert J. Mills

To Anne, Katie, and Sarah
—Mike Elmes

Dedicated to my mother and
to the memory of my father
—Anshuman Prasad

MANAGING THE ORGANIZATIONAL MELTING POT

Dilemmas of Workplace Diversity

Pushkala Prasad
Albert J. Mills
Michael Elmes
Anshuman Prasad

editors

SAGE Publications
International Educational and Professional Publisher
Thousand Oaks   London   New Delhi

For information:

SAGE Publications, Inc.
2455 Teller Road
Thousand Oaks, California 91320
E-mail: order@sagepub.com

SAGE Publications Ltd.
6 Bonhill Street
London EC2A 4PU
United Kingdom

SAGE Publications India Pvt. Ltd.
M-32 Market
Greater Kailash I
New Delhi 110 048 India

Printed in the United States of America

Library of Congress Cataloging-in-Publication Data

Main entry under title:

Managing the organizational melting pot : dilemmas of workplace
   diversity / editors, Pushkala Prasad ... [et al.].
      p.   cm.
   Includes bibliographical references and indexes.
   ISBN 0-8039-7410-8 (acid-free paper). — ISBN 0-8039-7411-6 (pbk.:
   acid-free paper)
   1. Diversity in the workplace. 2. Multiculturalism. I. Prasad,
   Pushkala.
   HF5549.5.M5M365 1997
   658.3'041—dc20   96-35610

97 98 99 00 01 02 03 10 9 8 7 6 5 4 3 2 1

Acquiring Editor:	Marquita Flemming
Editorial Assistant:	Frances Borghi
Production Editor:	Michèle Lingre
Production Assistant:	Karen Wiley
Typesetter/Designer:	Danielle Dillahunt
Cover Designer:	Lesa Valdez
Print Buyer:	Anna Chin

Contents

Acknowledgments

Editing a book is often a long and difficult process involving the efforts of a host of people. As the editors of the book, we are the most visible or public element of the process and we would like to pay tribute to all those who gave of their time and energy. This project began as an attempt to examine the more challenging aspects of workplace diversity. With this end in mind, we organized a symposium, at the Eastern Academy Meetings in 1993. Much to our surprise and delight, our ideas provoked considerable discussion and excitement. Following the symposium, Harry Briggs of Sage Publications first planted the idea of an edited book in our minds. Many thanks therefore to Harry Briggs and to Marquita Flemming for their unstinting support and patience. Our thanks also go to Sandra Mahoney, Dianne Foley and her staff at computer services at Saint Mary's University, and to Julene Koslowski and Debbie Neilson at the Faculty of Management at the University of Calgary.

PART

I

INTRODUCTION

From Showcase to Shadow

Understanding the Dilemmas of Managing Workplace Diversity

PUSHKALA PRASAD
ALBERT J. MILLS

This chapter traces the recent interest in workplace diversity within management and organization studies. Despite the proliferation of research on discrimination, the value of diversity and multiculturalism in organizations, the literature fails to address the more serious dimensions of difference in organizations. In particular, we suggest that more attention must be paid to some common dilemmas of diversity, such as the backlash against any commitment to multiculturalism, the continuing anger and disappointment of women and minorities, and the systematic institutional resistance within organizations to difference. In general, this chapter also provides a rationale for the book and introduces the remaining chapters.

Few trends have received as much publicity or gained as much attention in managerial circles as the recent interest in managing diversity. It can be argued that much of this interest can be traced back to Johnston and Packard's (1987) influential report, *Workforce 2000,* which alerted organizations to the dramatic demographic changes that were in the process of transforming the North American workforce. Prior to that date, business educators had little or nothing to say on the issue (Mills & Hatfield, 1995). Confronted with the prospect of these major imminent changes, management practitioners, business educators, and organizational consultants quickly began preparing to meet the challenges of a new and diverse workforce in a number of ways. In contrast to this seemingly positive view, it has also been argued that the growing popularity of diversity management approaches among practicing managers is a reaction against affirmative action policies, which have proven unpopular among numerous U.S. companies (Agocs, Burr, & Somerset, 1992). The management of diversity, with its focus on internal control or management, may prove more attractive to affirmative action policies where the locus of control emanates from government agencies.

Broadly, the term *managing diversity* refers to the systematic and planned commitment on the part of organizations to recruit and retain employees from diverse demographic backgrounds (Thomas, 1992). Managing diversity also implies an active recognition and appreciation of the increasingly *multicultural* nature of contemporary organizations (Cox, 1991). Managing diversity has become an increasingly popular managerial philosophy employed by a wide variety of organizations, ranging from government bureaucracies and nonprofit organizations to Fortune 500 companies and educational institutions. In the last decade, the diversity movement has also attracted innumerable consultants and other training experts, becoming transformed gradually into a virtual *diversity industry* (MacDonald, 1993) dealing in training videos, multicultural workshops, cultural sensitivity seminars, diversity audits, and so on (Allen, 1991; MacDonald, 1993).

The concept of workplace diversity has also become tremendously popular in the mass media and has more recently entered the world of human resource and organizational behavior textbooks.[1] In all these sources, diversity is celebrated with the help of evocative metaphors such as the melting pot, the patchwork quilt, the multicolored or cultural mosaic, and the rainbow.[2]

All of these metaphors invoke enormously affirmative connotations of diversity, associating it with images of cultural hybridity, harmonious coexistence, and colorful heterogeneity. Overall, these metaphors tend to emphasize the cultural richness and socioeconomic contributions promised by the incorporation of diverse groups into North American society.

At one level, this celebration of diversity is to be applauded; it certainly stands in sharp relief to the recent period in North American history when race segregation and the exclusion of women from countless occupations was viewed as normal. However, there are persistent signs that the management of diversity is a Herculean task requiring much more than managerial enthusiasm, optimism, and good intentions. Managing diversity at the workplace presents as many dilemmas as triumphs, and is constantly fraught with innumerable tensions, conflicts, and contradictions. Metaphorically speaking, the melting pot may well have become a cauldron (Nash, 1989), the quilt may have been torn, cracks may have begun to appear in the mosaic, and the rainbow may have become twisted out of shape. Yet, much of the management literature on workplace diversity (with few exceptions) tends to ignore or gloss over these dilemmas while continuing to stress the potency of workshops and training to accomplish the goals of workplace diversity.

At the same time, we are also witness to a striking absence of serious scholarship on the process of managing diversity itself. Given the magnitude of the diversity movement, it is quite surprising to find that few scholarly attempts have been made to understand exactly what it offers and how it might be influencing organizational change (Comer & Soliman, 1994). Notwithstanding recent efforts by Jackson (1992) and Cox (1993), the academic interest in the process of managing diversity has actually been rather limited.

For the most part, management academics have adopted what might be described as an attitude of *distant cheerleading*. That is, although they continue to endorse the importance of managing diversity, they have rarely engaged the process itself as a serious research act. On the whole, the scholarly literature has restricted itself to emphasizing the urgency of the workplace diversity issue (Jamieson & O'Mara, 1991) and to proposing models and guidelines for managing the process (Burke, 1991; Jackson, 1992; Thomas, 1992). Workplace diversity remains, therefore, a significantly underresearched and undertheorized phenomenon in the management literature.

It is the goal of this edited volume to grapple with the more troublesome and disturbing aspects of workplace diversity, and to do so in a more theoretically informed fashion. We wish explicitly to focus on the cracks in the mosaic, the tears in the quilt, and the scalding temperature of the melting pot in order to illuminate what might be termed the shadow side of diversity. We believe that much of the diversity literature is characterized by an upbeat naiveté that averts its eyes from the rampant conflicts and ruptures that are endemic to a changing and diverse workplace. We also believe that focusing on the dilemmas of workplace diversity better prepares students, scholars, and managers for the turbulent challenges presented by a multicultural workforce.

In order to understand some of these dilemmas, the chapters in this volume adopt a diverse array of theoretical frameworks, which are, for the most part, striking departures from traditional and more functional perspectives on diversity. Theoretical perspectives employed by the different authors include intergroup relations theory, critical theory, Jungian psychology, feminism, postcolonial theory, cultural history, postmodernism, realism, institutional theory, and class analysis. The sheer multiplicity and potency of these frameworks provide very different and insightful understandings of some of the current dilemmas at the workplace.

Furthermore, the authors also examine a multitude of different workplace situations containing conflicts, problems, and concerns about diversity. Rather than comment upon the experiences of different ethnic, racial, age, and gender groups in organizations, we have chosen to look at a number of organizational situations in which complex predicaments of diversity surface. Many of these predicaments typically harbor conflicts that cross race, gender, ethnic, and other socially constructed demographic boundaries. Nevertheless, these dilemmas recur as constant motifs in contemporary workplaces and institutions. Some of the phenomena examined in the book include the problematics of gender construction at British Airways, unconscious resistance among women in academic institutions, the role of corporate masculinity in the Challenger space shuttle disaster, the crisis of organizational morality in the Tailhook scandal, and elements of imperialism in the corporate discourse of the Western petroleum industry.

With regard to the scope of this book, we define workplace diversity somewhat broadly. Although we principally examine the problems and practices of North American organizations in dealing with difference, we also believe that the increased globalization confronting contemporary organizations necessarily introduces an international element in our discussions of workplace diversity. This issue is dealt with to some extent by the geographical range of the collection—with examples drawn from the United States, Canada, Britain, and the Middle East. The issue is taken up more directly through chapters on the dilemmas raised within the field of international management (Chapter 14), as it prepares managers to encounter multicultural and transnational differences; the continuing impact of colonial discourse on the multinational corporation (Chapter 12), and the impact of immigration on women in the workforce (Chapter 13).

In focusing primarily on North America, we are referring specifically to the United States and Canada: Discussion of the situation in Mexico or the role of U.S. and Canadian corporations in Mexico is, sadly, beyond the scope of this collection. Nonetheless we do not mean to imply that substantial differences do not exist between Canada and the United States. They certainly do. The two countries have experienced different patterns of immigration, are regulated by somewhat different employment laws (notably greater mandatory protection of women's maternity benefits in Canada), and have officially espoused somewhat different multicultural policies, with the United States stressing assimilation through the melting pot metaphor and Canada emphasizing cultural pluralism via the metaphor of the mosaic. Canada has also not been directly subjected to the corrosive history of slavery that continues to cast its long shadows over the U.S. African American community, but it has to wrestle with its own unique problems over Francophone identity in Quebec. At the same time, however, both countries share a number of problems relating to workplace diversity. These include a growing hostility to preferential minority hiring, the persistent exclusion of nonwhite immigrants from managerial and professional positions, and an intensifying polarization between ethnic and racial groups within organizations and the broader society. Furthermore, both countries are also having to deal with these issues in a climate of economic contraction accompanied by chronic unemployment and shrinking resources. The chapters in this book speak somewhat broadly to many of these issues and are therefore likely to offer important if different insights to readers from both countries. Before discussing the contents of the book, this chapter will provide a brief discussion of the main themes found in the current diversity literature, highlighting some of the major dilemmas of workplace diversity.

MANAGING DIVERSITY:
THE SHOWCASE

Both Canadian and U.S. workforces have been targets of antidiscrimination legislation since the civil rights and student movements of the 1960s. Laws like the Equal Employment Opportunities Act (EEOA), the Age Discrimination Act, and the Pregnancy Discrimination Act in the United States and the Employment Equity Act and the Multiculturalism Act in Canada have attempted to curtail discrimination in the hiring and promotion practices of North American organizations.

The more recent diversity movement, however, can be sharply distinguished from these earlier antidiscrimination efforts in its focus and its philosophy. Although the term managing diversity does indicate a commitment on the part of organizations to recruit and retain employees from diverse demographic backgrounds (Thomas, 1992), it mostly implies the need for an active recognition and appreciation of the increasingly multicultural nature of contemporary organizations (Cox, 1991). Embedded within the philosophy of managing diversity is the notion that traditional monocultural organizations cannot function effectively in the context of today's and tomorrow's workforce. Thus, the main focus of managing diversity is cultural. Diversity programs consequently attempt to facilitate transformations by altering organization members' beliefs, values, and ideologies in dealing with difference at the workplace. Not surprisingly, managing diversity, as an organizational activity, is mainly to be found within the training and development domains of an organization (Betters-Reed & Moore, 1992).

The cultural nature of the diversity movement has meant that evaluating organizational attempts to manage diversity is difficult, because the desired outcomes are neither concrete nor easily measurable. Managing diversity is also not directly connected to the various employment laws that regulate different forms of discrimination at the workplace. In fact, the philosophy of managing diversity is entirely *voluntaristic,* calling for corporations and individual work organizations to take the initiative in responding to external demographic trends. It therefore places the onus of achieving workplace diversity squarely on the shoulders of managers in different organizations. Thus, managing diversity stands in contrast to anti-discriminationtory legislation in the United States, where the emphasis is on legal requirements and penalties for noncompliance, but it is an extension of employment equity policy in Canada, where the emphasis is on encouraging management to address broad policy changes.

Since its initial entry into the marketplace of managerial ideas, managing diversity has acquired a considerable following. It has been much publicized as a management technique and has been extensively covered in news magazines, the popular business press, trade journals, and academic publications. Both scholarly and popular depictions of the management of workplace diversity can best be encapsulated by the metaphor of the *showcase.* A showcase is defined as a setting that facilitates the most advantageous arrangement and display of certain objects. Organizational efforts at implementing workplace diversity have predominantly been showcased in the literature. In other words, workplace diversity has received enormously positive publicity in the literature, which has showcased it by highlighting its more striking accomplishments and attractive features. The showcasing of workplace diversity takes different forms and is accomplished in different ways.

The Economic Showcase

> One management challenge is to help people understand diversity so that they can establish productive relationships with people at work. . . .
>
> Organizations such as Arthur Andersen, Boeing, DuPont, Hewlett-Packard, Hoechst Celanese, and Xerox recognize the value of a diverse workforce . . . and they promote diversity in their organizations. For example, Hewlett-Packard conducts workshops for all employees in which the emphasis is on educating and encouraging managers to understand culturally different employees and *to create an environment that will foster productivity.* [italics added]
>
> *Hellriegel, Slocum, & Woodman (1995, pp. 7-8)*

Managing diversity is frequently represented as a viable long-term strategy likely to yield the firm some crucial economic benefits. The economic showcasing of diversity endows it with a tremendous pragmatic stature and gives it greater legitimacy than a purely moral imperative. The economic defense of diversity itself has three dimensions. First of all, diversity is framed as a valuable option because of the market forces behind it (Foster, Jackson, Cross, Jackson, & Hardiman, 1988; Fyock, 1990; Johnston & Packard, 1987). This argument proposes that the changing demographic profiles of the North American workforce leave organizations with few options but to actively embrace diversity. The suggestion is that changes in the market supply of labor constitute the fundamental driving force behind the diversity movement. By framing diversity initiatives as necessary managerial strategies driven by labor market conditions, the literature sounds an alarm bell, warning firms that they will be unable to find qualified and skilled employees unless they pay attention to managing their own diversity.

The economic value of diversity also comes through in discussions of enhanced organizational performance. Some writers argue that demographic and culturally diverse groups are likely to outperform more homogeneous ones ("How to Make," 1994; Kirchmeyer & McLellan, 1991; Loden & Rosener, 1991) because they bring diverse approaches to everyday organizational problem solving. An article in *Fortune* magazine showcased Ernest Drew's (chief executive officer of Hoechst Celanese) assertion that productivity in Hoechst began to surge in those plants with proportionately more diverse employees ("How to Make," 1994). Similar claims are constantly made by other proponents of workplace diversity. Diversity is thus conceptualized as a corporate *asset,* in terms of contributing indirectly to the performance of the firm. Interestingly enough, although academic support for this claim is actually somewhat mixed (Kirchmeyer & Cohen, 1992; Maznevski, 1994), the popular press continues to endorse the notion that greater workplace diversity translates into greater workplace productivity.

Third, the diverse workforce acquires economic legitimacy through arguments of *competitive advantage.* These arguments assert that a diverse workforce may actually provide an organization with a competitive edge because it ushers in greater awareness of the preferences and consumption habits of different groups in society (Fernandez, 1991; Thomas, 1992). As Foster at al. (1988) point out, "organizations that invite change and successfully manage diversity are more likely to detect and solve complex business problems that do not fit into orthodox business models of yesterday" (p. 39). Overall, this argument promotes the notion that diverse organizations are better prepared by virtue of their membership heterogeneity to assess and respond to the increasingly complex problems confronting organizations today.

The economic showcasing of diversity is both credible and persuasive to the public. It emerges from a long-standing intellectual tradition in North America, drawing upon the assumptions of *human capital theories.* Theories of human capital explicitly treat people as economic resources; their skills, qualifications, and characteristics are regarded as having potential value for the firms who hire them. Human capital theories tend to have enormous ideological appeal in Western capitalistic cultures on account of their overtly instrumental arguments; these eventually hold more sway than normative and value-laden positions. At the same time, the human capital underpinnings of the diversity discourse remain astoundingly blind to the conflict potential contained within diverse workforces, which results in dysfunctional rather than functional economic outcomes.

The Showcase of Guidelines

Managing diversity begins with valuing individual differences. . . . In one set of solutions, educational efforts are the common thread. The first solution is diversity training, which helps individuals understand their own and others' prejudices. At Honeywell, for example, diversity training focuses on four strategies:

- Management development—increase the visibility of, understanding of, and commitment to diversity throughout global Honeywell.

- Organizational development—promote an equitable work environment that values diversity.
- Talent development—obtain horizontal and vertical integration of diversity throughout all functions.
- Individual development—empower individuals to help reduce barriers to reaching their full potential.

A second alternative focuses on career training for minorities to assist them in advancement. A third solution rewards managers who create environments that foster individual growth, help develop minority employees, and mentor their advancement in the organization

Gordon (1993, pp. 95, 98)

The diversity literature also showcases ways in which managers can effectively introduce diversity into organizations. The literature does not entirely ignore problems likely to be encountered by managers of diversity. Rather, it presents them as minor hurdles that can be surmounted by following prescribed guidelines and directions (Jackson, 1992; Morrison, 1992). In fact, a large segment of the diversity discourse is preoccupied with building conceptual models (Morrison, 1992; Thomas, 1992), accompanied by sets of managerial guidelines and directions. Popular models include stage models that outline the various phases through which organizations pass in their transitions from monocultural to multicultural entities (Cox, 1991; Foster et al., 1988). Commonly prescribed actions include the involvement of senior management, the regular revisitation of diversity goals, and the constant advertisement of diversity efforts (Jackson, 1992; Jamieson & O'Mara, 1991). Overall, the discourse of diversity showcases the management of diversity by simultaneously anticipating problems in the process and proposing practical ways of dealing with them. Although the problems of diversity are not completely ignored, they are portrayed in a way that reduces their seriousness and emphasizes the fact that they can be dealt with. In a word, diversity becomes doable.

The Showcase of Exemplars

The extent to which organizations in North America are becoming multicultural can be seen in one Digital Equipment Corporation plant in Boston. . . . Its 350 employees come from 44 countries and speak 19 languages. Written announcements to plant employees are published in English, Chinese, French, Spanish, Portuguese, Vietnamese, and Haitian Creole. . . . .

Given this accelerating diversity within the workforce, it is unlikely that the nonwhite, non-Western part of the population will be assimilated as

fully into the dominant culture as in the past. . . . But at the organizational
level, managers are learning to build on the strengths of difference among
employees and customers.

Coffey, Cook, and Hunsaker (1994, pp. 26-27)

Above all, the literature showcases the "successes" of workplace diversity
by publicizing individual organizational attempts at incorporating difference
into the workplace. Both the popular press and the trade journals provide
glowing accounts of companies that have successfully implemented workplace
diversity. These lists of exemplars frequently read like excerpts from the Fortune
500 Who's Who. Among major companies whose diversity efforts are regularly
celebrated are Mobil Oil (Kleeb, 1989), Monsanto (Caudron, 1990), Honeywell
(Copeland, 1988), Corning Inc., and Kaiser Permanente (Allen, 1991). In
addition, consultants who are engaged in some of these organizational diversity
programs at companies such as Digital Equipment Corporation (Walker &
Hanson, 1992) and Xerox (Sessa, 1992) offer their own personal accounts of
these successes. In general, corporate exemplars are powerful testimonies of
both the value and virtue of workplace diversity programs. They serve as vivid
reminders that diversity can actually "work" in American and Canadian organizations. What remains interesting, however, is the superficial level of treatment
in these celebrations of corporate diversity efforts. Discussions of companies'
successful diversity programs rarely explore the subterranean domain of race
tensions, gender frustrations, and ongoing resistance. They present the happy
face of diversity without paying much attention to what lies behind it.

DILEMMAS OF WORKPLACE DIVERSITY:
THE SHADOWS

It is our contention that the elaborate showcasing of the diversity movement
has severely limited our understanding of the more problematic aspects of
multiculturalism at the workplace. A host of gender conflicts, race tensions, and
cultural frictions lie hidden in the shadows of the showcase. What kinds of
dilemmas are we, for the most part, neglecting, in our upbeat pursuit of diversity?
Some dilemmas surface in the more serious scholarship on race (Bolaria & Li,
1985; Brown, 1985; Painter, 1992), gender (Bannerji, Carty, Dehli, Heald, &
McKenna, 1991; Burnham, 1992; Malveaux, 1982), and ethnicity (Abu-Laban
& Stasiulis, 1992; Ford, 1994; Li, 1988; Nash, 1989). More recently, other
dilemmas have also emerged in reports on interracial hostility (Gates, 1993) and

minority frustrations ("The Hidden Rage," 1993) in the popular press. We would like to briefly enter this shadow land of dilemmas to understand the more complex problems facing the implementation of diversity in the workplace.

What Does Workplace Diversity Really Mean?

Despite the intense publicity surrounding the diversity movement, the process of managing diversity itself remains within something of a black box. How do organizations conceptualize workplace diversity? Do these conceptualizations differ from region to region and from industry to industry? How do organizations set goals and targets? How do they go about accomplishing them? How do managers evaluate the effectiveness of their diversity programs? These and other questions remain largely unaddressed by current discussions of diversity. Above all, the central hermeneutic question, what does diversity mean, is rarely addressed. As a result, we have a potpourri of popular views and opinions on what constitutes workplace diversity, without a serious consideration of the multiple and possibly conflicting meanings attributed to the term.

We suggest that the concept of workplace diversity itself may not hold uniform connotations, signifying different things to different groups and individuals within organizations and society. To some, diversity may be little more than proportional representation of various demographic and social groups in the workplace. To others, it may involve overcoming cultural prejudice and instilling new values about difference in the organization. To still others, it may connote changing the very fabric of work practices in keeping with the cultural influences of different social groups. At any rate, this more problematic reading of diversity deserves a closer examination by organization and management scholars.

Diversity Hype Over Diversity Substance?

Some authors (Comer & Soliman, 1994; MacDonald, 1993) are beginning to question the contributions of diversity programs by suggesting that many of them may be offering more hype than substance. Meanwhile, organizations themselves admit to not making serious attempts at evaluating the effectiveness of their diversity programs. Consequently, they have little awareness of how members of so-called diverse groups are actually affected by these organizational initiatives.

At the same time, we are faced with evidence of the frustration women and minority groups experience regarding persistent obstacles to career advancement (Blum & Smith, 1988; Collins, 1989) and the unchanging hostility of workplace cultures ("The Hidden Rage," 1993; Mansfield, Koch, Henderson, & Vicary, 1991). Experiences of marginalization, condescension, contempt, exclusion, and so on continue to surface in personal accounts of women, African American, and Asian organizational participants. Clearly, diversity programs are not having the far-reaching impacts they were meant to achieve. This brings us to some troubling questions. Are diversity programs organizational smoke screens concealing enduring patterns of discrimination and prejudice? Or are they merely enjoyable training interludes, after which managers return to unchanging realities of race hostilities and gender tensions in the workplace? This merely underscores the need for more in-depth examination of the more persistent patterns of organizational hostility and prejudice. Some of the questions might be: how does discrimination manifest itself in contemporary professions and organizations? What are the more "invisible" and less tangible forms of exclusion at the workplace? How do minority groups and women interpret their own workplace realities?

White Rage

The literature on managing diversity pays little attention to the growing hostility toward policies such as affirmative action and employment equity that actually promote workplace diversity, as well as the increasing anger directed by dominant groups toward practices of multiculturalism. Yet, one of the most disturbing trends in North America is the increasing antagonism being displayed toward the goals of diversity in both the larger society and within work situations (Gates, 1993). The growing neo-Nazi movements and white survivalist groups espousing overt ideologies of hatred are only caricatures of prevailing hostilities within North American culture. Products of a sense of intense alienation and disenfranchisement, the growing "white rage" is fueled by harsh economic conditions, increased immigration of non-European people, and the polarization of cultural differences within Canada and the United States.

White rage becomes manifested in a series of actions that oppose diversity within workplaces and public institutions, such as universities and museums. Recent outbursts of white rage have resulted in fierce battles over the literary canon in American universities, the assault on affirmative action, tougher immigration laws in California, the reversal of employment equity laws in Ontario, and "scientific" claims of superior intelligence of certain racial groups in controversial books such as *The Bell Curve* (Murray & Herrnstein, 1994). Within organizational contexts, acknowledging the presence of this anger and learning to deal with it needs to be made an important item in the agenda of managing diversity.

Organizational Monoculturalism

Despite the widespread rhetoric of diversity and multiculturalism, organizations are, in fact, extraordinarily monocultural entities. In other words, the premises undergirding organizational functioning are largely monocultural, composing a generic set of norms, values, and cultural preferences. The isomorphism of contemporary organizations has been extensively discussed elsewhere (DiMaggio & Powell, 1983), and it is well argued throughout the management literature that contemporary organizations actually share a number of cultural norms regarding the dress and demeanor of their employees, as well as cultural expectations regarding employee performance and commitment (Deal & Kennedy, 1984; Schein, 1985). More often than not, these norms and values do not easily accommodate multicultural preferences on a number of issues, including the boundaries between work and home, the role of work in society, and the conduct of interpersonal relationships within organizations (Martin, 1992; Mills & Simmons, 1995).

We are, therefore, also suggesting that even while the representation of diverse groups in the workplace may have improved, formal and informal organizational rules have hardly kept pace with the diversity of organizational membership. For example, informal rules governing interactions between men and women at work are often still rooted in the norms of the 1950s. As Caproni and Finley point out in Chapter 11, the moral codes of the corporation have invariably failed to keep pace with the changing values of the workforce, thereby resulting in serious cultural conflicts over issues such as sexuality and organizational justice.

More than anything, organizational monoculturalism leads to institutional resistance to workplace diversity. *Institutional* resistance can be distinguished from *individual* resistance by the structural potency of the problem. To illustrate, although individual managers may be sympathetic to the problems of parenthood and child care, institutional policies continue to treat motherhood as a barely tolerated form of organizational deviance. Organizational monoculturalism, therefore, results in innumerable routine workplace processes (such as reward systems) that are systematically hostile to the cultural values and lifestyles of different groups. The ultimate result is a structural failure to accommodate difference at the workplace.

Resistance to Acculturation

The "problem" of assimilation has always been present in the multicultural societies of Canada and the United States, but because of their different sociopolitical heritages, the problem of assimilation has developed in distinctly different ways. In the United States, early waves of Irish, Greek, and Polish immigration were accompanied by a certain resistance on the part of these ethnic groups to being completely absorbed by the broader American culture. Yet, in recent years, this problem has grown more acute with the rise of what Novak (1971) calls the "unmeltable ethnics."

Despite vast cultural differences, immigrants to the United States around the turn of the century were far more attracted to what was essentially a white Anglo-Saxon Protestant (WASP) ideal of the American way of life and were consequently more amenable to "becoming" American. Novak (1971) argues that since the 1960s, the obvious deterioration of the American dream has resulted in a reevaluation of the desirability of an American identity. In particular, the growth of black nationalism and black consciousness contributed to an acceleration among some groups of a search for ethnic identity (Du Bois, 1965; Jackson, 1971; Malcolm X, 1969). The powerful attraction of the notion of *ethnic identity* (Nash, 1989), which is rooted in shared constructions of kinship, a common language, and a common cultural heritage, has developed considerably up to the present. Today, ethnicity is worn proudly as a badge of honor (Nash, 1989), preventing the easy assimilation of different ethnic groups into something loosely defined as American. This resistance to acculturation has important implications for any discussion of workplace diversity because it raises issues of identity, style, and cultural preservation in organizations. The reluctance to "melt" or assimilate without question is already leading to controversial issues over language use in organizations in Florida and Quebec, as well as dress codes in more traditional East Coast organizations (Jenkins & Atkins, 1990).

In Canada, the issue of assimilation has gone through two broadly different stages. The first lengthy stage involved the establishment of the cultural and political dominance of the British founding groups and their successors over the French founding groups and their successors. Until fairly recently, this involved the suppression of French culture and language within Canada and fueled the strong nationalist feeling within Quebec, a feeling that remains a strong vibrant force today. Alongside this policy, immigration, with only rare exceptions in earlier years, was largely restricted to whites of European origin who could, by and large, be expected to fit in with the British cultural stamp of the nation. Simultaneously, successive Indian Affairs departments set about establishing reservations that effectively isolated native persons from mainstream society, while experimenting with assimilationist programs aimed at indoctrinating young native persons into mainstream religions and values. The pent-up anger— culminating in radical nationalist demands for Quebec sovereignty, and demands for native self-government and other requirements by various minorities and women's groups—encouraged a series of policy changes. This resulted in a series of laws focusing on bilingualism, multiculturalism, and employment equity. These new policies were designed to build a sense of integration through diversity. The declared intent of Canada's multiculturalism policy, for example, was to provide official recognition and support to those ethnic groups who sought to preserve their distinctive cultural heritage and ethnic identities within the framework of a pluralistic society. In recent years, backlashes against these various policies have threatened the very fabric of Canadian society, and they cannot simply be addressed through reference to diversity management (Mills & Simmons, 1995).

The Commodification of Diversity

The capacity of North American culture to transform any revolutionary idea or reform movement into a popular entertainment item and fashionable piece of memorabilia has been discussed in the context of social change in the 1960s by Roszak (1969). It is our concern that workplace diversity and multiculturalism may well be in danger of becoming trendy consumer items marketed in the form of executive seminars, T-shirts and mugs, museum exhibits and workplace training modules ("Capitalist Agenda," 1994). In other words, workplace diversity may have become little more than an organizational and educational buzzword, simultaneously signifying anything, everything, and nothing (Jacoby, 1994).

The problems with the commodification of diversity are varied. First, such an intense commodification of a change movement has transformed workplace diversity into little more than a fad, equally embraced by private businesses, federal agencies, universities, and nonprofit organizations. The trouble with fads is partly the fleeting nature of their impact. They rarely linger long enough to effect fundamental change, and even when they do, they are often not taken seriously. As a result, although a multitude of organizations are engaging in diversity programs, the latter's substantive and lasting impact remains somewhat questionable (MacDonald, 1993). Whereas the fashionable dimension of diversity programs exerts pressure on many organizations to implement them, their very trendiness may detract from a serious examination of the real and tumultuous problems presented by multiculturalism. Ultimately, as Jacoby (1994) points out, diversity remains popular mainly at the level of *consumption,* found in the proliferation of Thai restaurants and Moroccan rug stores and in the celebration of different cultural festivals. The monoculturalism of organizations and work practices remains relatively unchanged.

Our discussion of the dilemmas of diversity has clearly highlighted the complex nature of multiculturalism at the workplace. Common threads running through all the dilemmas are issues of individual and institutional resistance, the questionability of diversity change efforts, and the less visible ways in which exclusion and discrimination continue to be practiced in the workplace. It is our aim to examine these underlying themes more deeply in this book.

THEORIZING DIVERSITY

In the following six chapters, the question of workplace diversity is debated from a number of critical perspectives. J. Michael Cavanaugh (Chapter 2) draws upon institutional theory and ideological critique to argue that in order to understand why diversity management programs so often fail to live up to the promise of cultural plurality, we need to understand the process or character of the *framing* of organizational realities. He contends that any framing of the notion of diversity needs to take into account the demographic characteristics of those in positions of power (white males), the often silenced voices of the Other (i.e., women, people of color, the aged, etc.,), and the multitude of political interactions between dominant and nondominant groups within organizations. In other words, how workplace diversity is understood will, at any given time, depend on culturally relative, historically changeable, social interactions that are developed within contexts of political interaction and struggle. From this perspective, diversity is a representation of reality that needs to be understood in contexts of organizational power that have historically been dominated by white males; it is a privileged, discursive point. For Cavanaugh, diversity is "a site where the 'partial fixation' of political identity takes place—a nexus of political interaction and struggle where strategies of persuasion are brought to bear on the construction of modern racial and gender awareness and tradition" (p. 37). Thus, in a number of cases, workplace diversity programs may well serve to solidify the dominance, or hegemonic control, of organizations by white males.

By drawing our attention to the contingent, as opposed to fixed, nature of social representations, Cavanaugh attempts to encourage a strategy of change through a deeper appreciation of how things come to appear fixed, the political processes involved in the fixation of ideas, and the consequences of accepting ideas as unchanging. It is through the political process of including the voice of the Other in the considerations and framing of diversity that we can hope to change the discourse to one that is more receptive to cultural plurality in theory and in practice.

The themes of fixity, the political construction of diversity, the silenced voice of the Other, and the contingent nature of social relations are continued by Collette Oseen (Chapter 3). Whereas Cavanaugh uses these concepts as end points to draw attention to the *politically contingent* character of diversity, Oseen uses them as starting points to explore the *specific character* of politically contingent notions of diversity.

For Oseen, the problems of diversity are rooted in language structures and discursive practices. Drawing upon the work of the postmodernist philosophers Foucault and Irigaray, Oseen argues that existing notions of women are embedded in linguistic and organizational practices based on maleness as a point of departure; that hierarchical arrangements, discriminatory practices, and the linguistic practice of viewing difference as "less than" are all interrelated. She contends that the hierarchical structure of organizations, or the relation of domination and subordination, owes much to male-dominant linguistic practice whereby sameness is privileged and difference is denigrated. Women, for instance, are not simply seen as different from men but as somehow less than men. In a similar fashion, hierarchical structure privileges those seen to be similar in terms of level and position, while literally subordinating all those who are seen to occupy lower levels. Oseen argues, thus, that organizational and linguistic practices reinforce one another in ways that make it impossible to overcome gender differences simply by including the voice of the Other in any organizational reframing of diversity. She contends that change can only come by simultaneously reconceptualizing the notion of the Other and developing nonhierarchical or egalitarian structures.

Oseen challenges not only mainstream but some recent alternative theories of diversity in her view that a focus on sameness—or the appeal to a common humanity shared by all—as the condition for equality reinforces rather than obliterates discriminatory thinking. Instead, she argues, we need to develop an understanding of difference as contiguity, that is, difference without the normative anchor of the same to reestablish privilege. This can be achieved, according to Oseen, by a fundamental restructuring of relations among individuals, which involves a "reaching out rather than assuming either a dominating or subordinate role" (p. 54).

Issues of (racial and gendered) identity and power are central to Roy Jacques's reflections on white maleness (Chapter 4). Sharing Oseen's concern with exposing the linguistic character of discrimination, Jacques sets out to deconstruct the myths and processes that constitute a "commonsense" world that privileges white men. Informed by feminist postmodernist analysis, Jacques begins by arguing that dominance—which need not presume the conscious desire to dominate—resides in the structuring of social interaction, but that those with dominant identities must stop confusing privilege with personal intention. This viewpoint accords with Cavanaugh's (Chapter 2) in the contention that male-dominant political processes crucially frame understandings of diversity: Jacques addresses the issue by encouraging those who benefit from dominance to take responsibility for questioning the taken-for-granted, commonsense views (myths) and practices (strategies of dismissal) that keep dominance in place. Jacques ends by outlining a personal strategy of reflection designed to encourage himself and, by example, others in positions of dominance to resist discriminatory attitudes and behaviors.

In Chapter 5, Richard Marsden continues the theme of sameness that was introduced by Cavanaugh (Chapter 2), conceptualized by Oseen (Chapter 3), and reflected upon by Jacques (Chapter 4). Through the development of a theoretical framework informed by a fusion of the work of Marx, Weber, and Foucault, Marsden analyses the microprocesses of Industrial Relations (IR) and Human Relations (HRM) practices and their impact on the construction of "normal" or standardized behavior. His analysis leads him to conclude that the celebration of diversity is part and parcel of a process of individualism, which, far from tearing down discrimination, threatens to propagate substantive injustice. He makes the point through the argument that organizations are about regulatory mechanisms (disciplinary practices) involving the organization of time, space, and movement and that the effect of those mechanisms is simultaneously to totalize and to individualize. By comparing the individual to the collective, disciplinary rules regulate the performance, behavior, actions, and thoughts of those within organizations, detailing offenses and penalties, be they of time, activity, behavior, speech, the body, or sexuality. Quantitative differences among employees are equalized or averaged and translated into workplace norms governing behavior and performance. IR-HRM techniques, argues Marsden, are means to observe, examine, and normalize employees in accordance with this quantitative standard. This *normalizing* process—with its aim of reducing employees to knowable and thus manageable individuals—is at the heart of modern management and stands in sharp contrast to professed notions of diversity (with its implied commitment to difference).

Examining workplace diversity from a macro cultural-institutional perspective, Pushkala Prasad (Chapter 6) traces the influence of two cultural traditions on contemporary North American organizations: the Protestant ethic and the myths of the frontier. She begins with a discussion of some of the central values embedded in these cultural traditions, including the work ethic, utilitarianism, self-reliance, aggressiveness, and masculinity, and she goes on to show how these two ideologies have left strong *cultural imprints* on the everyday structures and practices in organizations through the enactment of work norms, expectations, and rules. Focusing on the imprints these ideologies have left on organizational expectations about managerial style, communication patterns, and orientations toward work and career, Prasad also shows how these expectations strongly favor traditional white men over women and many ethnic minorities. In essence, the conclusion she draws is that a major source of cultural tension in organizations may not take place entirely between privileged groups and others but is more likely to be the result of fundamental cultural clashes between the values of women and minorities on one hand, and the dominant cultural codes of the organization on the other.

Moving from meta- to meso-analysis, Elmes and Connelley (Chapter 7) use social identity and intergroup relations theories to analyze the barriers to the long-term effectiveness and sustainability of diversity in organizations. Shifting the debate to the area of group dynamics, Elmes and Connelley argue that three powerful social "resisting" forces are likely to hinder the emergence of truly pluralistic organizations—the proclivity for social groups, particularly dominant social groups, to preserve status differentials (this accords with Jacques's notion of common sense and strategies of dismissal in Chapter 4); social identity conflict among those who are supposed beneficiaries of diversity programs (see Oseen's argument in Chapter 3 about concepts of the Other); and the rise of ethnocentrism and intergroup aggression in an era of declining resources (this accords with Prasad's argument in Chapter 6 about the character of organizational work values). Analyzing the way these various forces hinder the potential for successful diversity management, Elmes and Connelley conclude that "change agents" need to (a) understand the impact that intergroup relations have on organizational processes, (b) acknowledge that subordinate groups may not share the same normative and value systems that the organization embodies; (c) become aware how their own social identities and group membership affect what they see; and (d) recognize that *structural* changes represent just the beginning of an effective diversity initiative by (e) addressing the underlying *emotions* and *group membership* issues associated with diversity.

Reading through this section, the reader will be struck by the number of similarities (i.e., the relationship between power and identity; issues of sameness, normality, etc.) as well as differences in focus (e.g., hierarchy, intergroup dynamics, self-reflection) and suggested outcomes (e.g., the use of organizational change agents and the development of nonhierarchical structures). In the third section of the book, the debate is continued through a series of analyses of diversity practice in the workplace.

Diversity in Practice

The section begins with an historical analysis of the development of corporate imagery in the British airline industry in the period 1945 to 1960. In Chapter 8, Albert J. Mills uses a feminist reframing of postmodernist theory to trace the development of gendered imagery over time. He argues that a deliberate corporate strategy of desexualization (an early attempt at equity image) was eventually overwhelmed and replaced by a strategy of eroticization (i.e., the use of female bodily sexuality to sell airline seats). Explaining that the policy of desexualization involved a limited and unformulated commitment to equity by the men at the top, Mills concludes that—even in its own limited terms—the early equity strategy failed because the top decision makers failed to address the values and practices that constituted the airline's culture, in particular the processes associated with the development of corporate imagery.

In Chapter 9, we move to current experiences of women in Canadian universities. In this chapter, Pat Bradshaw and David Wicks draw on Marxist/ radical and feminist postmodern positions to analyze the possibilities for female resistance to sexism. Using an approach that resonates with the theories of Cavanaugh (Chapter 2) and Oseen (Chapter 3), Bradshaw and Wicks challenge existing theories that encourage women to adopt appropriate strategies for "fitting in" with existing structures of power and achievement, arguing instead that the strategies for political action rest in the exploration of micropolitics, contests over meaning, counterdiscourses, and negotiations at the margins. From this perspective, they interview a number of female academics to identify forms of resistance and of compliance, and they conclude that women should adopt many forms of resistance that challenge the meaning systems while seeking out and challenging areas of women's disadvantage and compliance "in order to fuel strategies of resistance" (p. 199).

Chapter 10 finds us inside the corporate world of the U.S. National Aeronautics and Space Administration (NASA). Here Mark Maier explores the role of corporate masculinity in the events leading up to the 1986 Challenger disaster— when the space shuttle Challenger exploded, killing all seven crew members. Maier uses feminist theories of organizational culture to analyze NASA and other agencies (Morton Thiokol, Rockwell) associated with the Challenger disaster and concludes that a culture of masculinity played a crucial role in shaping and influencing the various processes that led to the fateful decision to launch the Challenger space shuttle in the face of evidence that it was unsafe to do so.

The problematic nature of organizational culture is also the theme of Chapter 11, Paula Caproni and Jocelyn Finley's exploration of the Los Angeles Police Department (LAPD) and the Tailhook Association of retired and active-duty Naval and Marine Corps aviators and defense contractors. Caproni and Finley explore the relationship between selected elements of an organization's culture and diversity through a focus on two (highly publicized) incidents in 1991: the Rodney King beating and the Tailhook convention. Looking beneath the surface of the cultures of the LAPD and the Tailhook Association, Caproni and Finley identify five organizational processes that contributed to the fostering of racist and sexist violence: organizational ideologies that promoted the moral exclusion of out-group members (see also Elmes and Connelley, Chapter 7); taken-for-granted rites and routines that reflected those ideologies (see also Maier, Chapter 10); and the use of language, rationalizations, and codes of silence (see also Mills, Chapter 8) that reinforced dominant cultures and values. Caproni and Finley conclude with two generalizable lessons for organizations, that managing multicultural organizations means (a) stopping systematic harm-doing toward out-group members, and (b) paying attention to how taken-for-granted ideologies and cultural practices promote the moral exclusion and harm-doing toward members of particular groups.

Chapter 12 returns to the theme of the social construction of the Other introduced in Chapter 6 (by Pushkala Prasad). In an historical analysis of the Western oil industry, Anshuman Prasad employs postcolonial theory to reveal the relationship between the language and practice (i.e., the discourse) of the petroleum sector and the social construction of the colonized peoples. In particular, the chapter analyzes the representation of difference in the discourse of oil with a view to elucidating the nature of the hierarchical system of binaries around which the colonialist construction of the Other seems to revolve. Using this approach, Prasad also offers the reader an understanding of the colonizing consciousness as it is revealed in the discourse of oil. His analysis shows the colonizing consciousness to be fundamentally characterized by ambivalence, contradictions, and schizophrenia. Arguing that colonial discourse (and the colonizing consciousness) continue to saturate the management of diversity in Western organizations, the chapter finds the diversity industry to be complicit with a system that hegemonically oppresses those at its margins. This chapter concludes with some brief practical suggestions for deconstructing the discourse of diversity.

Chapter 13 examines racial and gender discrimination in contemporary Canadian organizations. Through interviews with 14 immigrant women of color, E. Joy Mighty examines the complex reality of workplace diversity from the perspective of minorities with three distinct cultural identities based on race, gender, and ethnicity; what Mighty calls a "triple jeopardy" of discrimination. Her research leads her to a number of recommendations for change, including the need for organizations to (a) increase the representation of such women in the workplace; (b) avoid tokenism; (c) pay greater attention to educating and sensitizing all employees about valuing diversity; (d) develop an action plan for the structural and informal integration of organizational members with social identities different from those of the mainstream; (e) create formal mentoring programs targeted for marginalized employees, and (f) provide resources for the establishment and maintenance of identity-based support groups.

In the final chapter in this section (Chapter 14), Diana Wong-MingJi and Ali H. Mir return to the issue of Western values and organizational ideology (see Chapters 6 and 12) through an examination of what they call the sedimented parochialism in international management. Analyzing data from over 30 years of international management research, Wong-MingJi and Mir argue that, far from reflecting culturally diverse viewpoints, the field is constrained by the inertia of its own epistemic history. By revealing the persistent and limiting discourse of international management research, Wong-MingJi and Mir set out to challenge the cultural hegemony of the field and its impact on developing management thought.

Identifying Issues in
Diversity Management Research

In the fourth section of the book, Anshuman Prasad and Michael B. Elmes (Chapter 15) summarize the various issues raised and identify issues for further research.

NOTES

1. On the issues of race, ethnicity, and gender in the workplace, very few human resources management, organizational behavior, organization theory, or management texts had *anything* to say prior to 1990, and a sizable number have continued to remain silent on the issue since that date (Mills & Hatfield, 1995; Mills & Simmons, 1995). It can be argued that a commitment to diversity management by the American Assembly of Collegiate Schools of Business (AACSB), the central accreditation body for a large number of U.S. business schools, has influenced a number of business schools to include it in their curriculum and that this, in turn, is beginning to be reflected in textbook production (Mills & Hatfield, 1995; see also Chapter 2 of this collection).

2. In a partial recognition of the dilemmas of diversity, a recent text added the metaphor of the "tossed salad" (Moorhead & Griffen, 1995).

REFERENCES

Abu-Laban, Y., & Stasiulis, D. (1992). Ethnic pluralism under siege: Popular partisan opposition to "multiculturalism." *Canadian Public Policy, 18*(4), 365-386.

Agocs, C., Burr, C., & Somerset, F. (1992). *Employment equity: Cooperative strategies for organizational change.* Scarborough, ON: Prentice Hall Canada.

Allen, G. (1991). Valuing cultural diversity: Industry woos a new work force. *Communication World, 8,* 14-17.

Bannerji, H., Carty, L., Dehli, K., Heald, S., & McKenna, K. (1991). *Unsettling relations. The university as a site of feminist struggles.* Toronto: Women's Press.

Betters-Reed, B. L., & Moore, L. L. (1992). Managing diversity: Focusing on women and the whitewash dilemma. In U. Sekharan & F. T. L. Long (Eds.), *Womenpower: Managing in times of demographic turbulence* (pp. 31-58). Newbury Park, CA: Sage.

Blum, L., & Smith, V. (1988). Women's mobility in the corporation: A critique of the politics of optimism. *Signs, 13,* 528-545.

Bolaria, B. S., & Li, P. (1985). *Racial oppression in Canada.* Toronto: Garamond.

Brown, K. (1985). Turning a blind eye: Racial oppression and the unintended consequences of white "non-racism." *Sociological Review, 33,* 670-690.

Burke, R. J. (1991). Managing an increasingly diverse workforce: Experiences of minority managers and professionals in Canada. *Canadian Journal of Administrative Sciences, 8*(2), 108-120.

Burnham, M. A. (1992). The Supreme Court appointment process and the politics of race and sex. In T. Morrison (Ed.), *Race-ing justice, en-gendering power: Essays on Anita Hill, Clarence Thomas, and the construction of social reality* (pp. 290-321). New York: Pantheon.

Capitalist agenda fuels the "multiculti" fad. (1994, April 22). *Globe and Mail,* p. A18.

Caudron, S. (1990). Monsanto responds to diversity. *Personnel Journal, 69,* 72-80.

Coffey, R. E., Cook, C. W., & Hunsaker, P. L. (1994). *Management and organizational behavior* (annotated instructor's edition). Burr Ridge, IL: Irwin.

Collins, S. (1989). The marginalization of black executives. *Social Problems, 36,* 317-331.

Comer, D. R., & Soliman, C. E. (1994). *Organizational efforts to manage diversity: Do they really work?* (working paper). New York: Hofstra University.

Copeland, L. (1988, May). Learning to manage a multicultural work force. *Training,* pp. 49-56.

Cox, T. (1991). The multicultural organization. *Academy of Management Executive, 5,* 34-47.

Cox, T. (1993). *Cultural diversity in organizations: Theory, research, and practice.* San Francisco: Berrett-Koehler.

Deal, T. E., & Kenneedy, A. A. (1982). *Corporate cultures.* Reading, MA: Addison-Wesley.

DiMaggio, P., & Powell, W. (1983) The iron cage re-visited: Institutional isomorphism and collective rationality in organizational fields. *American Sociological Review, 48,* 147-160.

Du Bois, W. E. B. (1965). *The world and Africa: An inquiry into the part which Africa has played in world history.* New York: International Publishers.

Fernandez, J. P. (1991). *Managing a diverse workforce: Regaining the competitive edge.* Lexington, MA: Lexington Books.

Ford, Y. (1994). Who are the African Americans? In E. R. Myers (Ed.), *Challenges of a changing America: Perspectives on immigration and multiculturalism in the United States* (pp. 51-64). San Francisco: Austin & Winfield.

Foster, B. G., Jackson, G., Cross, W. E., Jackson, B., & Hardiman, R. (1988, April). Workforce diversity and business. *Training and Development Journal,* pp. 38-42.

Fyock, C. D. (1990). *America's workforce is coming of age.* Lexington, MA: Lexington Books.

Gates, D. (1993, March 29). White male paranoia. *Newsweek,* pp. 48-53.

Gordon, J. R. (1993). *A diagnostic approach to organizational behavior.* Boston: Allyn & Bacon.

Hellriegel, D., Slocum, J. W., Jr., & Woodman, R. W. (1995). *Organizational behavior* (7th ed.). Minneapolis/St.Paul: West Publishing.

The hidden rage of successful blacks. (1993, November 15). *Newsweek,* pp. 52-54.

How to make diversity pay. (1994, August 8). *Fortune,* pp. 79-86.

Jackson, G. (1971). *Soledad brother.* Harmondsworth: Penguin.

Jackson, S. E. (1992). Stepping into the future: Guidelines for action. In S. E. Jackson (Ed.), *Diversity in the workplace: Human resource initiatives* (pp. 319-338). New York: Guilford.

Jacoby, R. (1994). The myth of multiculturalism. *New Left Review, 208,* 121-126.

Jamieson, D., & O'Mara, J. (1991). *Managing workforce 2000: Gaining the diversity advantage.* San Francisco: Jossey-Bass.

Jenkins, M. C., & Atkins, T. V. (1990). Perceptions of acceptable dress by corporate and non-corporate recruiters. *Journal of Human Behavior and Learning, 7,* 38-46.

Johnston, W. B., & Packard, A. H. (1987). *Workforce 2000: Work and workers for the 21st century.* Indianapolis, IN: Hudson.

Kirchmeyer, C., & Cohen, A. (1992). Multicultural groups: Their performance and reactions to constructive conflict. *Group and Organization Management, 17,* 153-170.

Kirchmeyer, C., & McLellan, J. (1991). Capitalizing on ethnic diversity: An approach to managing the diverse workgroups of the 1990s. *Canadian Journal of Administrative Sciences, 8*(2), 72-79.

Kleeb, R. (1989). Mobil drills holes through the color barrier. *Business and Society Review, 70,* 55-57.

Li, P. (1988). *Ethnic inequality in a class society.* Toronto: Wall and Thompson.

Loden, M., & Rosener, J. B. (1991). *Workforce America: Managing employee diversity as a vital resource.* Homewood, IL: Business One Irwin.

MacDonald, H. (1993, July 5). The diversity industry. *The New Republic,* pp. 22-25.

Malcolm X. (1969). *Malcolm X on Afro-American history.* New York: Merit.

Malveaux, J. (1982). Moving forward, standing still: Women in white-collar jobs. In P. Wallace (Ed.), *Women in the workplace* (pp. 101-133). Boston: Auburn House.

Mansfield, P. K., Koch, P. B., Henderson, J., & Vicary, J. R. (1991). The job climate for women in traditionally male blue-collar occupations. *Sex Roles, 25,* 63-79.

Martin, J. (1992). *Cultures in organizations: Three perspectives.* New York: Oxford University Press.

Maznevski, M. L. (1994). Understanding our differences: Performance in decision-making groups with diverse members. *Human Relations, 47,* 531-549.

Mills, A. J., & Hatfield, J. C. H. (1995, December). *From imperialism to globalization: Internationalization and the management text—A review of selected U.S. texts.* Paper presented at the 6th Asia-Pacific Research in Organization Studies (APROS) International Colloquium, Cuernavaca, Mexico.

Mills, A. J., & Simmons, T. (1995). *Reading organization theory.* Toronto: Garamond.

Moorhead, G., & Griffen, R. W. (1995). *Organizational behavior: Managing people and organizations.* Boston: Houghton Mifflin.

Morrison, A. (1992, Summer). Developing diversity in organizations. *Business Quarterly,* 42-48.

Murray, C., & Herrnstein, R. (1994). *The bell curve: Intelligence and class structure in American life.* New York: Free Press.

Nash, M. (1989). *The cauldron of ethnicity in the modern world.* Chicago: University of Chicago Press.

Novak, M. (1971). *The rise of the unmeltable ethnics.* New York: Macmillan.

Painter, N. I. (1992). Hill, Thomas, and the use of the racial stereotype. In T. Morrison (Ed.), *Race-ing justice, engendering power: Essays on Anita Hill, Clarence Thomas, and the construction of social reality* (pp. 200-214). New York: Pantheon.

Roszak, T. (1969). *The making of a counter culture: Reflections on the technocratic society and its youthful opposition.* Garden City, NJ: Doubleday.

Schein, E. (1985). *Organizational culture and leadership.* London: Jossey-Bass.

Sessa, V. I. (1992). Managing diversity at the Xerox Corporation: Balanced workforce goals and caucus groups. In S. E. Jackson (Ed.), *Diversity in the workplace: Human resource initiatives (pp. 37-64). New York: Guilford.*

Thomas, R. R. (1992). Managing diversity: A conceptual framework. In S. E. Jackson (Ed.), *Diversity in the workplace: Human resource initiatives* (pp. 306-318). New York: Guilford.

Walker, B. A., & Hanson, W. (1992). Valuing differences at Digital Corporation. In S. E. Jackson (Ed.), *Diversity in the workplace: Human resource initiatives* (pp. 119-137). New York: Guilford.

PART II

THEORIZING THE DILEMMAS OF WORKPLACE DIVERSITY

(In)corporating the Other?

Managing the Politics of Workplace Difference

J. MICHAEL CAVANAUGH

I cannot tell the reader how much I would like to believe in this sunshine world. After the theatre lights brighten and I've found coins for a black beggar on the way to my car and am driving home through downtown Springfield, Massachusetts, the world invented by *Die Hard With a Vengeance* and America's highest court gives way only slowly to the familiar urban vision in my windshield—homeless blacks on trash-strewn streets, black prostitutes staked out on a corner, and signs of a not very furtive drug trade. I know perfectly well that most African Americans don't commit crimes or live in alleys. I also know that for somebody like myself, downtown Springfield in the late evening is not a good place to be.

Benjamin DeMott (1995, p. 33)

INTRODUCTION: WHERE'S THE BEEF?

This chapter evolved out of a growing concern that the formulation of *workplace diversity* is far too important a political project to leave to the unreflective

31

ministrations of diversity consultants and mainstream theorists. According to the burgeoning diversity literature, patriarchy's days are numbered. And despite a legacy of literally centuries of institutionalized discrimination in the United States, Otherness is soon to be history as well, due to the fortuitous intersection of two elements—the reconfigured demography of the American workplace and positive thinking (Buhler, 1993; Carnevale & Stone, 1994; Cox, 1991; Ellis & Sonnenfeld, 1994).[1] The polysemic reframing (Bartunek, 1988) ostensibly affirmed by this synergistic formula portends not only a historic step forward in reason's struggle to tame its Manichaean opposite, passion (Bauman, 1991), but also an enlightened pragmatic corporate realignment with the multicultural realities of the global marketplace (Esty, 1988; Johnston, 1991; McNerney, 1994; Napier, Schweiger, & Kosglow, 1993; Sims & Dennehy, 1993).

But step back with me for a moment. Let's set these earnest intentions against the following backdrop to see if we can't affect something approaching an (in vitro) ironic break (Vickers, 1994).[2] That is, in a society where politicians win elections by inveighing against the poor ("welfare queens") and illegal aliens (California's Proposition 187 referendum passes by a 2:1 margin); where the media routinely remind listeners of "massive immigrant invasions" and black street-gang violence; where both the Bush and Clinton administrations returned Haitian refugees to an uncertain fate at home; where "the race of the defendant and the race of the victim play a significant role in determining who is to live and who is to die in murder cases" (Ross, 1995, p. A19); where conservatives vigorously campaign against multiculturalism in teaching and research; where xenophobic tabloids and right-wing talk shows enjoy unprecedented popularity; where passage of the Equal Rights Amendment failed partly due to the opposition of women (Mackinnon, 1987); where a sitting U.S. President not so long ago employed the "quota" card to defend his veto of the 1990 Civil Rights Act; where despite "the incontrovertible evidence of the video camera" the police officers who bludgeoned Rodney King were set free by a white jury in April 1992 (van Dijk, 1993, p. 4); where it takes two and one half years to strip Oregon's senior senator, Bob Packwood, of his power; where no university campus is spared incidents of anti-Semitism and racial hatred; where senior offices of the U.S. Navy conspired to cover up the infamous Tailhook Affair at the Las Vegas Hilton; where "one out of every two black children lives below the poverty line . . . [and] the net worth of the typical white household is ten times that of the typical black household" (DeMott, 1995, p. 33); where "men . . . hold the levers of power, no matter what inroads feminism has made" (Carter,

1995, p. 26); *(Health, United States, 1994)*; where the near hysteria sparked by a decision to cease harassment of gay military personnel has shaken a presidency; where the Anita Hill-Clarence Thomas episode exposed viewers to an unforgettable lesson in gender relations; where unequal pay and career opportunities for women and minorities are still viewed as more or less natural; where determinist (biology over culture) tracts like that of Harvard's (no less) Richard Herrnstein and Charles Murray (1994; *The Bell Curve*) and Thomas Sowell (1994; *Race and Culture)* offer pseudo-scientific (and implicitly racist) justification for policies designed to punish the disadvantaged; and where by 5 to 4 margins a conservative Supreme Court has recently softened long-standing affirmative action *(Adarand Constructors v. Pena*) and school desegregation policy *(Missouri v. Jenkins)*; in short, in the present context of Howard Beach, Bensonhurst, the Los Angeles uprising, white male backlash, Proposition 209, U.S. Army sex scandals, former LAPD officer Mark Fuhrman, militias, the 104th Congress, and Ayn Rand WASP male-dominated organizations, the resonance produced by demography and the right kind of training, diversity's proponents claim, will do what decades of affirmative action, civil rights acts, the Equal Employment Opportunity Commission, countless judicial orders, legislation guaranteeing pay equality by law, and so on, have failed to do. And not least, exorcising the workplace of "perceptual distortions" (i.e., bigotry; Ragins, 1995, p. 103) will boost the corporate bottom-line as well (Fry, 1993; Laabs, 1993; McNerney, 1994).[3]

But it is not only the irony conjured up by the rhetorical tension (Hoy & McCarthy, 1994) we have wedged between diversity's "sunshine world" and the "familiar urban vision in my windshield" that justifies a critical second opinion, *but diversity's resonance among business academics and corporate leaders.* If, when located within a larger field, diversity begins to appear too good to be true, i.e., if the recontextualization above succeeds in planting the suspicion that diversity is at best a half-baked solution, to what then, do we attribute this magnetic appeal? If, as critical theory tells us, a discourse's adequacy is only as good as the truth it denies; and if we assume that as a rule, corporate executives demand value for their money, and that good intentions—no matter how genuine—sometimes create effects opposite from those intended; *what, then, are presumably bottom line-driven executives getting for their money* (see Cavanaugh & Prasad, 1994; Pfeffer, 1981)? Perhaps one way of coming to terms with this riddle is to decide just how to cope with the ambivalence conveyed by this question. If recontextualizing diversity's presentation leaves

us somehow unconvinced of its instrumental plausibility (Bolton, 1989), *how,
then, are we to comprehend its seriousness?* This is the question considered in
this chapter.

DIVERSITY MANAGEMENT:
CONSTRUCTING A COUNTERPOINT

These questions are meant to draw out diversity's *metaphoricity* (Jay, 1993),
its capacity to connote multiple images to different people. Otherwise, we are
left without a way to work through diversity's plausibility, save on its own
self-referencing terms. In this chapter, I are attempting in part to distance
ourselves from the literal meanings of diversity and to move our inquiry in a
direction that goes beyond an unquestioned acceptance of diversity's instrumental credibility. At the same time, I also suggest that although diversity
may not always appear to "work" at one level (the instrumental), it can still be
understood as smoothly operating on quite another (the symbolic). To gauge
diversity's resonance and seriousness—and at the same time, its seeming
incompleteness—requires that we redirect our attention to diversity's rhetorical functions.

In other words, entertaining the possibility of diversity's metaphoricity as a
fundamental condition for understanding its tenability creates a point of departure for the figure-to-ground inversion that I am attempting to work here. This
process of "metaphorphosis" if you will, allows us to redirect attention to
diversity's rhetorical contribution to the reproduction of organization (Alvesson &
Willmott, 1992; Battaglia, 1995; Burrell & Hearn, 1989) out of the suspicion
that diversity "management" may have more to do with affirming the given than
changing it. Dugger (1995) captures the gist of this with the warning that "the
theories we construct to illuminate the dynamics of social divisions organized
around race and gender have political effects that can abet or disable antiracist
and feminist struggles" (p. 1).

In short, engaging the diversity project as metaphor is key to gaining an
understanding of the resilience of the "dominant malestream" tradition in
organization theory and culture (Burrell & Hearn, 1989), and our own complicity in the denial of how profoundly race and gender affect our lives. As
Panglossian (overdetermined) as workplace diversity may at first appear, management may indeed be getting its money's worth.

DIVERSITY WITHOUT ILLUSIONS

Symbols, whether verbal or nonverbal, are wonderful things. They can
be shared widely, passionately supported, and also encompass
contradiction, fact and fancy, the possible and the impossible. They
serve as a means of avoiding the complicated and the delicate and of
evading the tests of logic and of data.

Judith Stiehm (1994, p. 140)

This chapter draws on aspects of institutional theory and ideological critique
to rethink the issue of diversity's seriousness (Pecheux & Gadet, 1991). Both
perspectives begin from the constructivist premise that the real business of
management is "mental production" (Greenfield, 1979; Smith 1975)—the management of meaning and legitimacy. Which also means that both, to varying
degrees, share an interest in modes of persuasion, active subjectivity, and
"cultural persistence" (Zucker, 1987).

Institutional theory (DiMaggio & Powell, 1983; Meyer & Rowan, 1977;
Meyer & Scott, 1983; Scott & Meyer, 1994), for example, adds conceptual
breathing room by stretching the traditional (instrumental) notion of management efficacy. A particular organization's legitimacy—its effectiveness—
depends on not only the success of its product line, but also the signals it sends
to important external and internal constituencies. To survive over the long haul,
management must perfect both its technical and legitimating functions (Child,
1969). As Intel corporation's senior management ("Intel Inside") discovered
recently, there are penalties to pay when this lesson is forgotten. Thus, managers
act not only for purely instrumental (economic and quantifiable) reasons, but in
ways that play up to the expectations of institutionalized audiences (Meyer,
1980; Scott & Meyer, 1983).

The institutionalist school also maintains that due to the accumulated weight
of institutionalized imperatives (the objectified norms embodied in reporting
requirements, embedded conventions, rules, tradition, and culture that dictate
the way things get done) over time, stability tends to eclipse an institution's
declared economic or social goals (Meyer & Rowan, 1977). And since legitimacy is tied to stability, managers often act in ways that defy immediate
instrumental explanation. Because what organizations look like and do is more
or less settled within a particular institutional field (Dowling & Pfeffer, 1975),
if it wants to avoid problematizing itself, management is largely condemned to
repeating "what's worked before." Organizations may fail as a result of this

self-productive process (e.g., when single-loop learning leads to collapse; Argyris & Schon, 1978) or never get off the ground; e.g., when banks refuse loan requests from collectivist or minority-run organizations (Rothschild-Whitt, 1979). Or, in order to comply with broader environmental expectations, organizations may import the form if not the substance of new practices and regulations (e.g., the corporate "greening" phenomenon). There are times when management acts in the absence of answers. Pfeffer (1982) observes that

> in the absence of the knowledge that would facilitate doing the work, institutionalized organizations develop in which ceremonies and symbols are used to ensure continued support and legitimacy from the social environment, while not actually impacting the organization's operations. (pp. 245-246)

There exists no reliable way to judge the impact of workplace drug-screening programs, for example. But major corporations continue to fund such efforts anyway, despite steep costs, risks of employee discontent and lawsuits, and unanswered technical and constitutional questions (Comer, 1994). From an institutionalist perspective, management screens not only for safety and productivity reasons, but to counter the potentially destabilizing symbolic resonance that drug use imports into the workplace (i.e., its connotative insubordination to the general rational will underwriting management's prerogative to govern) and society *writ large*. Whether technical answers are available or not (indeed, the more complex an issue, the more likely its symbolic resolution; Pfeffer, 1981), some problems are symbolically too important for management to ignore. The imperative of institutional stability demands that managers, as orchestrators of constancy (Bolton, 1989), devise a plausible (if purely symbolic) response in the name of instrumental rationality or risk losing irreplaceable face (Cavanaugh & Prasad, 1994).

By rescuing the symbolic from its epiphenomenal status, institutionalist theory illuminates the improvisational nature of management practice. But as Hall (1985) reminds us, "ideas (and 'improvisations') don't just float around in empty space" (p. 103) but operate within a field of constituting hegemonic formations where "each individual exists with produced identities placed in an already meaningful world" (Deetz, 1992b, p. 27; see also Deetz, 1992a, 1994; Greenfield, 1979; Hall, 1985; Mills, 1989; Mouffe, 1993). The institutionalist conceptualization of how advantage is reproduced, in other words, does not go far enough. It was left to critical theory to provide "a sense of how we, as members of particular social formations, are more readily able to accept some 'realities' than others and sometimes become imprisoned by these realities" (Mumby, 1993, p. 7). That is, until it was understood that the political "inherent to every humans society and . . . determines our ontological condition" (Mouffe, 1993, p. 3) it would not be possible to reconstitute workplace diversity as a theory of politics.

Working within a framework that acknowledges the centrality of language and the essentializing nature of social hegemony, critical theory supplies the missing conceptual muscle needed to reconnect diversity with its politics. In particular, critique's acknowledgement of the centrality of language and the problematic of "surplus meaning" (Laclau & Mouffe, 1985) that language brings in its tow, shifts the "conception of truth as discovery or product toward a view of truth as invention or process" (Brown, 1994, p. 29). Henceforth, the basic analytical question would be "not whether there is a truth, reality, or virtue independent of all possible accounts of it, but how such accounts are made adequate to their respective purposes and practices of poetic and political representation" (Brown, 1994, p. 33).

In effect, critique works to unveil the political nature of institutional accounts by focusing analysis on the day-to-day practicalities of "how one or more positions gain dominance" (Condit, 1994, p. 211). In this regard, our capacity to resist fixed or essentialized versions of reality hinge on a subjective ratio between what each of us considers "fixed" (that which exists "outside" and independent of us) and what is constituted (and therefore open to question and replacement) (Deetz, 1992; Raclau & Mouffe, 1985; Mumby, 1993). The greater our capacity to reorganize fixed meanings as "constituted" (to come to understand "business cycles" or "management" or "race," for example, not as autonomous "things" but as culturally relative and contingent social interactions) the deeper our appreciation of our own capacity to scrutinize and revise social convention.

The imagery of both institutional theory and ideological critique, then, warrants our problematization of the "gap" between diversity's seriousness and the entrenched politics of white male superiority. In an attempt to clarify what diversity means and what is at stake, the next section engages diversity as a "privileged discursive point" (Laclau & Mouffe, 1985, p. 112)—as one nodal point among many such signifying sites constituting the border between alienation (unity) and political involvement (contingency). Diversity, then, will be represented as a site where the "partial fixation" of political identity takes place (Laclau & Mouffe, 1985; Mouffe, 1993)—a nexus of political interaction and struggle where strategies of persuasion are brought to bear on the construction of modern racial and gender awareness and tradition. Perhaps this strategy will teach us something more about why bottom-line business executives find diversity so persuasive.

PUTTING THINGS INTO PERSPECTIVE

One must face written histories that erase and deny, that reinvent the past to make the present vision of racial harmony and pluralism more plausible. To bear the burden of memory, one must willingly journey to places long uninhabited, searching the debris of history for traces of the unforgettable, all knowledge of which has been suppressed.

bell hooks (1992, p. 168)

In their remarkable book, *Racial Formation in the United States: From the 1960s to the 1990s,* Omi and Winant (1994) urge us to make the effort to "understand race [and by extension here, gender, age, sexual preference] as an unstable and 'decentered' complex of social meanings constantly being transformed by political struggle" (p. 55). From biological concepts of race (species hierarchy), to eugenics, to melting pot theory, the construction of racial Otherness is fundamentally a political project (Omi & Winant, 1994, p. 65).[4] And it is an ongoing one. Beginning with the politics of "coddling" the poor introduced during Ronald Reagan's first term in office (DeMott, 1995) up to the present-day neoconservative racial project of "color-blind" racial politics and "hands off" policy orientation (Nkomo, 1992; Omi & Winant, 1994), few would argue that we are living in another such transformative period. To understand workplace diversity, then, is to understand the part it plays in this generalized rewriting project.

But it's not only that we live in an off-key period where someone with the xenophobic credentials of California's governor, Pete Wilson, can launch a presidential campaign under the shadow of the Statue of Liberty ("Give me your tired, your poor, your huddled masses, yearning to breathe free, the wretched refuse of your teeming shore. Send these, the homeless, tempest-tossed to me. I lift my lamp beside the golden door. [Emma Lazarus, 1883]"), or self-declared white separatist Randy Weaver can deny he is a "hateful racist" in testimony before a congressional committee; it is also a time when business finds itself on the defensive (Harwood, 1995; Mouffe, 1992; Scott, 1992). Management's legitimacy is based on how well it performs and achieves or is perceived to be doing so (Huczynski, 1993). However, economic trends dating from the early 1970s constitute grounds for concern (Madrick, 1995). In particular, the plateauing of real personal income, the growing gap between rich and poor, the exodus of decent-paying blue-collar jobs, plant closings, downsizing, a shrinking middle class, the decline of unionism, and so on documented in daily newspapers and the nightly broadcast news over the last three decades seem to have fed a vague but generalized "fear of decline" (Stiehm, 1994, p. 144), to which management, like everyone else, lacks an answer. The question is, will this chronic pessimism fuel suspicion that management itself is the problem? And if management is found inadequate, will it also be found unessential?

And, finally, there's the everyday problematic of ambiguity (Huczynski, 1993) that management must work around. Yes, managers are rewarded for performing and achieving, but they must do so "in a context where often they neither understand how their actions produce results, nor are able to influence the most volatile element in the organization—people" (Huczynski, 1993, p. 171). Given the polarizing potential of race and gender attitudes today, there is the Barnardian fear that celebrating an organization's multiculturalism may degenerate into "an ugly tribal negation of itself" (Hitchens, 1995, p. A1). Already some complain that a diverse workplace will add more uncertainty than it is worth (Sikula, 1995).

At the level of metaphoric discourse, then, diversity provides an answer to all of these concerns. That is, it provides management an effective way to reestablish its competency to three different audiences at once. One, diversity says to important outside groups that business is out in front of the multicultural question because the new diverse workplace (the positive erasure of irrelevant differences; DeMott, 1995) can be achieved without the conflict (and politics) associated with affirmative action.[5] In this way, workplace diversity aligns management thinking with the current "live and let live" policy orientation favored by powerful neoconservative interests (Omi & Winant, 1994). Second, the diversity project has raised hopes. Consequently, it is imperative that a new multicultural workforce be persuaded that management is serious about eliminating the politics of the Other. *Diversity,* accordingly, is a good noun because it has a "generous feel to it, it is welcoming, inclusive, embracing; like international or pluralist or ecumenical, it suggest a largeness of conception, a transcendence of sectional interest, an openness to the variety of human pursuits and achievements" (Caws, 1994, p. 381).

And possibly most relevant, diversity represents a neat solution to a complex problem (Stiehm, 1994). Thus, even if the issue of equality is sidestepped (Mackinnon, 1987), "resolving" the problem of Otherness functions to reassure management itself that it is still in the saddle. "Success," in other words, is a potent antidote for self-doubt (Huczynski, 1993). It also tends to deflect attention away from management's chronically unstable production.

BY DEMOGRAPHY AND
DIVERSITY WORKSHOPS ALONE?

I expect that "diversity" will soon acquire a negative connotation. This is because it is being used as a symbol with the purpose of avoiding the complex and sensitive.

Judith Stiehm (1994, p. 141)

It is diversity's near-fabulous quality that attracts curiosity and suspicion, not to mention disciples. From a critical perspective, what makes diversity problematic is its simplicity, and thus the suspicion of a conceptual quick fix that repositions the status quo (Huczynski, 1993). At the same time, simplicity (i.e., that difference is seated in our personal attitudes only, so let's wipe the slate clean and be friends)—by shielding us from a potentially painful "moral and psychological introspection" (Mura, 1992, p. 18) about the "discriminatory reality construction" (Mills, 1989, p. 44) we are all involved in (DeMott, 1995)—may explain diversity's wide appeal among corporate and academic elites.

Possibly, denial and self-absolution play important compensatory functions. Nonetheless, it is left to critique to ask how adequate can a discourse oblivious of power be? How much faith can be invested in a discourse that assumes away, and thereby exempts from critique, the systemic nature of racial and gender construction in the contemporary workplace and American society at large (Dyson, 1993; McIntosh, 1988; Ramsey, 1994; van Dijk, 1993)? In the end, it is not only diversity's easy pluralism that compels engagement, but a belief (based on the conviction that each of us must take responsibility for the realities our choice of language advocates; Summa, 1992) that we are capable of doing better. That is, because race and gender are not empty categories; that is, if we are serious about uprooting the discriminatory institutions that make gender, race, age, and sexual orientation opportunity-narrowing liabilities, we must speak to the political ramifications of diversity's simplicity (Cocks, 1989).

DIVERSITY FROM THE NECK DOWN

Individual acts can palliate, but cannot end, these problems. To redesign
social systems, we need first to acknowledge their colossal unseen
dimensions. The silences and denials surrounding privilege are the key
political tool here. They keep the thinking about equality or equity
incomplete, protecting unearned advantage and conferred dominance by
making these taboo subjects. Most talk by whites about equal
opportunity seems to me now to be about equal opportunity to try to get
into a position of dominance while denying that systems of dominance
exist.

Peggy McIntosh (1988, p. 81)

The corporate diversity movement grounds its case and final authority upon
recent census projections (Baytos, 1995; Cox, 1993; McKendall, 1994). To
diversity proponents, the numbers unequivocally demonstrate a market for
tolerance (Baytos, 1995; Cox, 1991; Jackson, May, & Whitney, 1993; McKendall,
1994). By the end of the century, that is, women will compose more than 47%
of the total workforce, blacks 12%, Hispanics 10%, and Asians another 4%
(Loden & Rosener, 1991). In addition, the U.S. workforce is graying due to a
surplus of older workers and a shortfall of younger ones. If current trends
continue, by the year 2000, 51% of the workforce will be 35 to 54 years old, up
25 million people from 1985. At the same time, the number of people between
16 and 24 years of age will decline by almost 2 million, or 8%. Census numbers
also reveal that immigrant populations represented one third of America's total
population expansion in the 1980s, and that white birthrates trail far behind those
of Hispanics, blacks, and Asians. No one expects these trends to deviate much
in the 1990s (Geber, 1990). Indeed, census trends in the conventional literature
figure as a kind of manifest destiny, a rendezvous with meritocracy represented
by a clean millennial break with prejudice and discrimination in the modern
workplace. In light of the numbers, tolerance ("color blindness") is not simply
an abstract ideal. It's now a quantifiable fact (Gallos, 1988/1989). The corporate
workplace is poised to enter a new era because fate has seen fit to compose a
"happy" (natural) ending; one unencumbered by identity politics or reverse
discrimination suits.

In short, the handwriting is on the wall. Whether we like it or not, the
multicultural complexion of the modern workplace can't be undone. At century's
end, if demographic forecasts play out as predicted, the meaning of the word

minority will have undergone a total inversion. Soon, the new politics of *practical tolerance* (Hage, 1994) will make male supremacy untenable. In the meantime, management's task is to face the facts (not buck the tide), and "manage" a smooth transition (Ferdman, 1992; Fine et al., 1990; Jackson et al., 1993; Ramsey, 1993).

This message has not fallen on deaf ears, of course. Since the publication of the Hudson Institute's *Workforce 2000* report (Johnston & Packer, 1987) documenting these trends, workplace diversity has generated considerable interest in the academic and business consultant literatures. Many companies have adopted diversity programs of various kinds (Galagan, 1991). And the American Assembly of Collegiate Schools of Business (AACSB) has endorsed diversity as essential subject matter in American business school curriculums (McKendall, 1994). In fact, "The Management of Diversity" was the theme of the Annual Academy of Management Meeting in 1992. Interpreted broadly, diversity is meant to sound a wake-up call to the primarily Caucasian male monoculture currently monopolizing positions of power in corporate suites around the globe (Cox, 1993; Fry, 1993; Greenslade, 1991; Jamieson & O'Mara, 1991; Thiedereman, 1991).

On a practical level, the realization of the pluralistic workforce compels a rethinking of traditional ethnocentric organizational designs and practices (Ragins, 1995; Thomas, 1995). Management's problem is to manage diversity so as to effect a fit between the demographics of business institutions and their surrounding societies. Those managements that succeed in raising their collective consciousness (by hiring expensive diversity consultants to train employees to manage their stereotypes; Wynter, 1994) and actually achieve the right mix of demographic fit(s) will reap the value-added benefits that a diverse workforce purportedly brings (harmony and creativity up, alienation and absenteeism down, etc.; Cox & Blake, 1991; Ellis & Sonnenfeld, 1994; Henderson, 1994; Herriot & Pemberton, 1995; Jackson et al., 1992, 1993; Laabs, 1993; Loden & Rosener, 1991; Miller, 1994; Powell, 1993; Thomas, 1994; Watson, Kumar, & Michaelson, 1993).[6] Diversity pays dividends when workers have been reeducated and when workforces reflect the demographic and cultural variety of domestic and international customer bases. Moreover, this return to utilitarian reason can be accomplished without the social justice tensions that have dogged affirmative action efforts (Kogod, 1993; Thomas, 1990, 1991).

But—and most revealing—for all the space devoted to divining the meaning of the census numbers, the diversity discourse remains excruciatingly silent on the enduring "demographic characteristics of those in positions of power" (Ramsey, 1994, p. 424; see also Brown, 1992/1993; Martin, 1992/1993). By themselves, census trends don't predetermine anything, certainly not workplace equality. After all, in a constructed world nothing *has* to happen. Women, for example, have always existed in roughly equal numbers to men in the United States. However, it took women 75 years of hunger strikes, marches, and jail time to win passage of the 19th Amendment (Horowitz, 1995). Moreover, the collective power of the "women's vote" was not felt until Eisenhower's first election in 1952. And 30 years of hiring minority police officers has not translated into black power in the management ranks of major urban police departments around the country. To quote the acting executive director of the National Association for the Advancement of Colored People, "We underestimated just how entrenched attitudes about race were in the police. We thought 30 years would be enough time to overcome it. Perhaps 30 years is not" (Kaufman & Gaiter, 1995, p. A1). Indeed.

VIRTUALLY NORMAL:
THE POLITICS OF SAMING

The tolerated Others are by definition present within our "sphere of influence." They are part of our "world" (society, nation, neighborhood) but only insofar as we accept them. That is, the tolerated Others are never just present, they are positioned. Their belonging in the environment in which they come to exist is always a precarious one, for they never exist, they are allowed to exist.

Ghassan Hage (1994, p. 28)

The quotation above stresses the political and interested nature of diversity. As we have seen, however, one of the implications of a language-based theory of knowledge is that this doesn't necessarily mean that diversity won't "work." The dialogical latitude (Pecheux & Gadet, 1991) that linguistic "surplus" warrants also serves to inform us that there is always more than one way to say something (Summa, 1992). It's time, therefore, to draw down some of the figurative leverage developed earlier and advance a counterinterpretation of the numbers.

To management, the census numbers represent a Pandora's box, if not a Trojan horse. Managing diversity, critically speaking, is really about managing the surplus meaning of the census figures. The numbers, the simple facts, diversity adherents contend, are reason enough to establish an authentic corporate meritocracy based on the liberal notion of a color-blind pluralism. Besides, the new global free market won't tolerate noneconomic discrimination. However, managing diversity takes on an altogether different flavor when power is considered. Add power and it is now possible to grasp the inherent ambiguity of the "facts" as a threat to politicize the hitherto apolitical (Mouffe, 1992), that is, the elite position of a select group of white males and the relations of subordination advantaging their interests. Thus, "celebrating workplace diversity" can be understood as a preemptive ideological project that aims to neutralize race and gender (the Other) before current demographic trends politicize them. Appeals for a more tolerant workplace today will possibly head off unsettling questions about the "persistence of male advantage in male organizations" (Acker, 1992, p. 248) tomorrow.

For this to work, not only must employee consciousness raising occur, but Others must undergo a head-to-toe reconstruction—a process of racial and gender undifferentiation through an abstracted disembodiment (Acker, 1992). Rendered body-less (universalized, race-less, gender-less; thus inoffensive because no longer a "woman" or "black" in an Ayn Rand man's world), generic men and women will finally gain admittance into the paradigmatic fraternity of universal masculine workers (Acker, 1992). Otherness is, in effect, dissolved by rising above differences and joining together in the solidarity of a common purpose, the organization's success. Having finally enacted this objectified (impersonal) state, henceforth, all workers will be judged by a uniform set of economic standards. By thus raising the corporation's public social space to the postconflictual level (achieved by consigning intolerance to the private realm), management's civilizing leadership is valorized (Bauman, 1993).

Nevertheless, a vexing fox-in-the-chicken-coop suspicion lingers on. Specifically, will the denial of the structural power imbalances that is called for in this thin psychological attempt to cure intolerance (Dyson, 1993) hasten the demise of racial and sexist hierarchies or operate to sustain them? Because of the suspicion that power-free discourses operate to separate the political and the economic (Giddens, 1991), it seems a bit premature to equate celebrating differences with celebrating equality (Mackinnon, 1987). Writing as a "consumer protection agent," Hage (1994) argues in this regard that

the very existence and social relevance of a discourse of tolerance implies the continuing presence of dominant and subjugated cultural/political formations.

In particular, I shall propose that multicultural tolerance should be understood as a mode of spatial management of cultural difference while reproducing the structuring of this difference around a dominant culture. (p. 19)

What results is a politics of "practical tolerance" (Hage, 1994), where the Other is accepted insofar as he or she enriches the center. Perhaps given the hegemonic instincts of the managerialist discourse, it could be no other way (Deetz, 1992a). For underneath this new sexual and racial modality lies the concern that diversity is too unstable, that it might actually backfire (Sikula, 1995). Diversity, then, must be managed because its heterodoxical implications pose an (albeit unintended) threat to the "imaginary unity" (Eagleton, 1991) of the Barnardian business place (Scott, 1992) and, hence, to those who sit at the pinnacle of privilege encoded within complex organizations.

In sum, what appears to be at stake is the glitchless reproduction of the managerialist discursive field itseclf (Bourdieu, 1977). Because of the figurative (contingent) signifying property of language—because the meaning of the *heterodoxical workplace,* for example, is open to interpretation, can't be "fixed" (Eagleton, 1991) along official lines—it represents a concept that threatens to introduce managerialism's sins of omission (Thompson, 1984), the socially constructed and therefore arbitrary nature of meritocracy, and along with it, the contingent notion of a rational (scientific) hierarchy. This offhanded potential to "discharge the threat of history" (Thompson, 1984, p. 31)—for transforming white male privilege itself into a political question—could place the reigning managerialist discourse in a very public and, therefore, untenable position. If the potentiality of meaning is not managed properly, so to speak, management elites might be compelled to "step out of (their) silence and produce a defensive discourse of *orthodoxy* [italics added]" (Thompson, 1984, pp. 49-50), which could be argued for today only in unfashionable terms, that is, a return to white patriarchy. As a "depotentiating" discourse (Battaglia, 1995, p. 9), diversity functions to prevent such a possibility from happening.

POSTSCRIPT:
HEGEMONY NEVER TAKES A BREAK

The pedagogical imperative here is to weigh cultural differences against the implications they have for practices that disclose rather than mystify, democratize culture rather than close it off, and provide the conditions for people to believe that they can take risks and change existing power relations.

Henry A. Giroux (1994, pp. 329-330)

What follows will unlikely win many new friendships, and it also runs the risk of attenuating old ones. But I feel it needs saying anyway. Some time ago, I presented a preliminary sketch of this chapter at a regional academic conference. A little into my talk, I was interrupted by a researcher of diversity. His exact words were, "Mike, you like to smirk, don't you." Taken off-guard, I'm afraid my reply was not equal to this person's show-stopping mockery. Afterward, I came to realize what a loss this was. Because his ad hominem represented a chance to explore the raw nerve I had evidently struck. And because his defensiveness seemed to confirm what I had come to speak about, hegemony at work. In effect, he was actually giving me my cue but, unfortunately, I failed to pick up on it. Specifically, his provocative question presented a golden opportunity to make discursive topic avoidance *the* topic. Actually, I'm probably being too hard on myself, because neither one of us, really, knew how to talk to the other.

It was pretty hard to miss his meaning, however, that is, when it comes to the issue of diversity, there's no room for a smirk. Interestingly, the word *smirk* or *smirker* echoes in sound and connotation the old management epithet *shirker.* By definition, shirkers and by extension smirkers lack seriousness. They therefore don't deserve to be taken seriously. Presumably, only serious experts—like this individual—are qualified to question. In essence, we, his audience, had been given front-row seats to expertise reproducing itself, reasserting its own privileged reality by asserting its self-elected prerogative to certify and signify when challenged (Deetz, 1992a). In other words, we were being "subjected" to a lesson in the micropractice of conflict suppression and discursive closure. But what wasn't mentioned was that in a world of excess meaning, we are allowed to deviate from the canon.

In finding an ironic voice, however, we must avoid returning snub for snub by, say, dismissing corporate diversity as merely another consultant-inspired oxymoron. I am afraid that Fitzgibbons and Steingard (1994), for example, do just that in a piece appearing in the *Journal of Management Education.* The authors score many cogent points with their postmodern analysis. However, the admonitory tone of their piece surely put their largely mainstream audience on the defensive. The result is that their incisive observations were unlikely to affect anyone save the faithful.

My complaint is that Fitzgibbons and Steingard (1994) failed to produce a *political* document—something encouraging of differences and cross-discourse dialogue (perhaps this chapter falls short of this goal, as well). Instead, their fundamentalist approach betrays (like my interlocutor above) a "nostalgia for hierarchical and binary order of their own" (Jay, 1993, p. 137). Indeed, this lapse may serve to reinforce the reproductive practices they intend to emancipate us from. At this stage in critique's development—and in light of the importance of the subject we are dealing with—we should make it a point to avoid surrendering to the logic of "hopeless polarity" (Coward, 1983, p. 7; see also Gergen, 1994). Our goal should be to find ways "to make the silences of discourses speak" (Coward, 1983, p. 3), not clam up (see Alvesson & Willmott, 1992; Jacques, 1992).

In other words, diversity is an opportunity not only to theorize about privilege, but also to take stock of the condition of our vaunted reflexivity, as well. Managerialism, critique claims, lacks the capacity to resist itself. It trips up on its own closure. Blind to the "radicalness of being" (de Man, 1986, p. xi), it is thus condemned to "constantly rediscover what we already know." Is it any wonder, then, that a diversity without political consequences turns up short of ecumenical? Moreover, should we be surprised that managerialism's incapacity "to apprehend the political" (Mouffe, 1993, p. 4) has left some conventional scholars concerned (and a bit touchy) about their own relevance (see Cavanaugh & Prasad, 1995)?

No need to follow with our own solipsistic example. Which means that we must be careful not to revert to the theoretical *ex cathedra* of the essentialist voice (Kerfoot & Knights, 1994). Cross-disciplinary engagement is hard enough as it is. Even if narrow scientism is on the run, there still remains an around-the-clock need for critical scholars to reflect on how our own representations contribute to the re-creation of hierarchy. With this caveat in mind, perhaps it is time to begin constructing a *political* dialogue premised on helping our mainstream colleagues "to explore *between* explanations" (Coward, 1983, p. 7; see also Fraser, 1989) so as to better understand how we *all* contribute to the maintenance of discriminatory realities (Mills, 1989).

NOTES

1. The diversity literature is literally mushrooming. However, one does not have to read very far before arriving at a consensus of concepts and format. For a solid start, see Baytos, 1995; Blank & Slipp, 1995; Chemers, Costanzo, & Oskamp, 1995; Cox, 1991, 1993; Fernandez, 1991; Geber, 1990; Ramsey, 1993; Thomas, 1991, 1994.

2. This author wants to make it clear from the outset that this critique is not meant to belittle the efforts of those who sincerely desire a more tolerant and culturally pluralistic workplace. In many organizations, diversity programs are doing some real good (DiTomaso et al., 1992). After all, a more tolerant workplace is an improvement over what came before. However, due to a number of factors discussed in this chapter, the relationship between intentions and outcomes is

not always as straightforward as it may first seem. That is, one of the self-perpetuating and paradoxical features of hegemonic discourse is that undesired or undesirable things may occur, regardless of whether people mean for them to happen.

3. Euphemism appears to be the *lingua franca* of the diversity literature. Terms such as apartheid, hate, bigotry, even racism, are assiduously avoided. It is this evasive vocabulary, among other features, that should clue us to the boundaries, that is, the basic euphemistic purpose, of the diversity literature as a linguistic structure.

4. If you are uncertain about the social construction of race in the United States, read Omi and Winant's *Racial Formation in the United States: From the 1960s to the 1990s,* or a recent piece in the *Wall Street Journal* by Leon E. Wynter (1995). For example, Wynter describes the debate brewing around the Bureau of Labor Statistics and Office of Management and Budget's decisions to modify racial categories for the next census.

5. Stiehm (1994) concludes that

> today, what may once have been a concept, "diversity," is rapidly becoming a symbol—a stimulus producing (at least for now) a positive response. I suspect that it has been carefully adopted as a replacement for the concept, "affirmative action," because the negative valence the latter acquired has made it no longer useful. (p. 140)

6. In essence, a diverse workforce catalyzes more organizational creativity and productivity because workers are drawn from a larger, more democratic, gene pool. The resemblance to the Olympic Games model of excellence is quite striking. For example, many experts in the field of exercise science have concluded that the reason modern Olympic records are so short-lived is not only better diets and training, but—unlike the upper-crust selection process that limited perform- ance in the inbred *Chariots of Fire* model—athletes are now drawn across all classes from nationwide samples (see Armenti, 1992). Olympic competition has become so stiff that no nation can afford to go with anyone short of the best that can be found, regardless of class or race. Like the Olympic prototype, diverse organizations are those in position to tap their full human and productive potentials. It is within the resonance of such familiar comparisons that the case for meritocracy is made.

REFERENCES

Acker, J. (1992). Gendering organizational theory. In A. J. Mills & P. Tancred (Eds.), *Gendering organizational analysis* (pp. 248-260). Newbury Park, CA: Sage.

Adarand Constructors, Inc. v. Pena, No. 93-1841 (U.S. filed June 12, 1995).

Alvesson, M., & Willmot, H. (1992). Critical theory and management studies: An introduction. In M. Alvesson & H. Willmot (Eds.) *Critical management studies* (pp. 21-45). Newbury Park, CA: Sage.

Argyris, C., & Schon, D. A. (1978). *Organizational learning: A theory of action perspective.* Reading, MA: Addison-Wesley.

Armenti, A. (Ed.). (1992). *The physics of sports.* New York: American Institute of Physics.

Bartunek, J. M. (1988). The dynamics of personal and organizational reframing. In R. E. Quinn & K. S. Cameron (Eds.), *Paradox and transformation: Toward a theory of change in organization and management* (pp. 137-163). Cambridge, MA: Ballinger.

Battaglia, D. (1995). Problematizing the self: A thematic introduction. In D. Battaglia (Ed.), *Rhetorics of self-making* (pp. 1-15). Berkeley: University of California Press.

Bauman, Z. (1991). Ideology and the *Weltanschauung* of the intellectuals. In A. Kroker & M. Kroker (Eds.), *Ideology and power in the age of Lenin in ruins* (pp. 107-120). New York: St. Martin's.

Bauman, Z. (1993). *Postmodern ethics.* Oxford, UK: Blackwell.

Baytos, L. M. (1995). *Designing and implementing successful diversity programs.* Englewood Cliffs, NJ: Prentice Hall.

Blank, R., & Slipp, S. (1995). *Voices of diversity: Real people talk about problems and solutions in a workplace where everyone is not alike.* New York: American Management Association.

Bolton, R. (1989). Introduction. In R. Bolton (Ed.), *The contest of meaning: Critical histories of photography.* Cambridge: MIT Press.

Bourdieu, P. (1977). *Reproduction: In education, society and culture* (R. Nice, trans.). London: Sage.

Brown, B. B. (1992/1993, Winter). Reporting and statutory refinements from DOL, OFCCP, and EEOC. *Employment Relations Today, 19*(4), 441-447.

Brown, R. H. (1994). Reconstructing social theory after the postmodern critique. In H. W. Simons & M. Billig (Eds.), *After postmodernism: Reconstructing ideology critique* (pp. 12-37). Newbury Park, CA: Sage.

Buhler, P. (1993, July). Understanding cultural diversity and its benefits. *Supervision, 54*(7), 17-19.

Burrell, G., & Hearn, J. (1989). The sexuality of organization. In J. Hearn, D. L. Sheppard, P. Tancred-Sheriff, & G. Burrell (Eds.), *The sexuality of organization* (pp. 1-28). Newbury Park, CA: Sage.

Carnevale, A. P., & Stone, S. C. (1994, October). Diversity beyond the golden rule. *Training and Development, 48,* 22-40.

Carter, S. L. (1995, June 25). Men aren't angry, just confused. *New York Times Book Review,* p. 26.

Cavanaugh, J. M., & Prasad, P. (1994). Drug testing as symbolic managerial action: In response to "A case against workplace drug testing." *Organization Science, 5,* 267-271.

Cavanaugh, J. M., & Prasad, A. (1995). Legitimation angst and the problematic of (ir)relevance: Or what management theory may have to offer to the practice of organizational change. *Journal of Organizational Change Management.*

Caws, P. (1994). Identity: Cultural, transcultural, and multicultural. In D. T. Goldberg (Ed.), *Multiculturalism: A critical reader.* Oxford, UK: Blackwell.

Chemers, M., Costanzo, M., & Oskamp, S. (1995). An introduction to diversity in organizations. In M. M. Chemers, S. Oskamp, & M. A. Costanzo (Eds.), *Diversity in organizations: New perspectives for a changing workplace.* Thousand Oaks: Sage.

Child, J. (1969). *British management thought.* London: Allen & Unwin.

Cocks, J. (1989). *The oppositional imagination: Feminism, critique, and political theory.* London: Routledge.

Comer, D. R. (1994). A case against workplace drug testing. *Organizational Science, 5,* 259-267.

Condit, C. M. (1994, September) Hegemony in a mass-mediated society: Concordance about reproductive technologies. *Critical Studies in Mass Communication, 11*(3), 205-230.

Coward, R. (1983). *Patriarchal precedents: Sexuality and social relations.* London: Routledge & Kegan Paul.

Cox, T. (1991). The multicultural organization. *Academy of Management Executives, 5*(2), 34-48.

Cox, T. (1993). *Cultural diversity in organizations: Theory, research, and practice.* San Francisco: Berrett-Koehler.

Cox, T., & Blake, S. (1991). Managing cultural diversity: Implications for organizational competitiveness. *Academy of Management Executives, 5*(3), 45-56.

de Man, P. (1986). *The resistance to theory.* Minneapolis: University of Minnesota Press.

Deetz, S. A. (1992a). *Democracy in an age of corporate colonization: Developments in commu-nication and the politics of everyday life.* Albany: State University of New York.

Deetz, S. A. (1992b). Disciplinary power in the modern corporations. In M. Alvesson & H. Willmot (Eds.), *Critical management studies* (pp. 21-45). Newbury Park, CA: Sage.

Deetz, S. A. (1994). The new politics of the workplace: Ideology and other unobtrusive controls. In H. W. Simons & M. Billig (Eds.), *After postmodernism: Reconstructing ideology critique* (pp. 172-199). Newbury Park, CA: Sage.

DeMott, B. (1995, September). Put on a happy face: Masking the differences between blacks and whites. *Harper's Magazine, 292,* 31-38.

DiMaggio, P., & Powell, W. (1983). The iron cage revisited: Institutional isomorphism and collective rationality in organizational fields. *American Sociological Review, 48,* 147-160.

DiTomaso, N., Farris, G. F., Barclay, D., Batten, E., Richards, S., Smith, T. J., & Watson, G. G. (1992, June). Diversity in the high-tech workplace. *IEEE Spectrum, 29*(6), 20-32.

Dowling, , & Pfeffer, , (1975). Organizational legitimacy: Social values and organizational behavior. *Pacific Sociological Review, 18,* 122-136.

Dugger, K. (1995). *Changing the subject: Race and gender in feminist discourse.* Unpublished manuscript.

Dyson, M. E. (1993). *Reflecting black: African American cultural criticism.* Minneapolis: Uni-versity of Minnesota Press.

Eagleton, T. (1991). *Ideology: An introduction.* London: Verso.

Ellis, C., & Sonnenfeld, J. A. (1994, Spring). Diverse approaches to managing diversity. *Human Resource Management, 33,* 79-110.

Esty, K. (1988). Diversity is good for business. *Executive Excellence, 5,* 5-6.

Ferdman, B. M. (1992). The dynamics of ethnic diversity in organizations: Toward integrative models. In K. Kelley (Ed.), *Issues, theory, and research in industrial/organizational psychology* (pp. 339-384). Amsterdam: North Holland.

Fernandez, J. P. (1991). *Managing a diverse workforce: Regaining the competitive edge.* Lex-ington, MA: Lexington.

Fine, M., Johnson, F., & Ryan, S. (1990). Cultural diversity in the workplace. *Public Personnel Management, 19*(3), 305-319.

Fitzgibbons, D., & Steingard, D. S. (1994, November). A postmodern analysis of "A course in work-force(d) divers(homogene)ity": Strategies and issues. *Journal of Management Edu-cation, 18,* 441-446.

Fraser, N. (1989). *Unruly practices: Power, discourse, and gender in contemporary social theory.* Minneapolis: University of Minnesota Press.

Fry, J. M. (1993, October). A firm diversity hiring action plan. *Public Relations Journal, 49,* 32-34.

Galagan, P. (1991). Tapping the power of a diverse workforce. *Training and Development Journal, 45*(3), 38-44.

Gallos, J. V. (1988/1989). Developmental diversity and the OB classroom: Implications for teaching and learning. *The Organizational Behavior Teaching Review, 13*(4).

Geber, B. (1990, July). Managing diversity. *Training Magazine, 27*(7), 23-30.

Gergen, K. J. (1994). The limits of pure critique. In H. W. Simons & M. Billig (Eds.), *After postmodernism: Reconstructing ideology critique.* London: Sage.

Giddens, A. (1991). Four theses on ideology. In A. Kroker & M. Kroker (Eds.) *Ideology and power in the age of Lenin in ruins* (pp. 21-24). New York: St. Martin's.

Giroux, H. A. (1994). Insurgent multiculturalism and the promise of pedagogy. In D. T. Goldberg (Ed.), *Multiculturalism: A critical reader.* Oxford, UK: Blackwell.

Greenfield, T. B. (1979). Organization theory as ideology. *Curriculum Inquiry, 9*(2), 97-112.

Greenslade, M. (1991). Managing diversity: Lessons from the United States. *Personnel Manage-ment, 23*(12), 28-32.

Gusfield, J. R. (1992). Listening for the silences: The rhetorics of the research field. In R. H. Brown (Ed.), *Writing the social text: Poetics and politics in social science discourse* (pp. 117-134). New York: Aldine de Gruyter.

Hage, G. (1994, Winter). Locating multiculturalism's other: A critique of practical tolerance. *New Formations, 24,* 19-34.

Hall, S. (1985, June). Signification, representation, ideology: Althusser and the post-structuralist debates. *Critical Studies in Mass Communication, 2*(2), 91-114.

Harwood, J. (1995, August 28). Sluggish "revolution" has voters thinking politicians are all alike. *Wall Street Journal,* p. A1.

Henderson, G. (1994). *Cultural diversity in the workplace: Issues & strategies.* Westport, CT: Greenwood.

Herriot, P., & Pemberton, C. (1995). *Competitive advantage through diversity: Organizational learning from difference.* London: Sage.

Hitchens, C. (1995, June 25). One nation after all. *New York Times,* p. A1.

hooks, b. (1992). *Back looks: Race and representation.* Boston: South End Press.

Horowitz, H. L. (1995, July/August). A man's and a woman's world. *Academe, 81*(4), 10-14.

Hoy, D. C., & McCarthy, T. (1994). *Critical theory.* Oxford, UK: Blackwell.

Huczynski, A. A. (1993). *Management gurus: What makes them and how to become one.* London: Routledge.

Jackson, S. E., & Associates. (1992). *Diversity in the workplace: Human resource initiatives.* New York: Guilford.

Jackson, S. E., May, K. E., & Whitney, K. (1993). Understanding the dynamics of diversity in decision making teams. In R. A. Guzzo & E. Salas (Eds.), *Team decision making effectiveness in organizations.* San Francisco: Jossey-Bass.

Jacques, R. (1992). Critique and theory building: Producing knowledge "from the kitchen." *Academy of Management Review, 17*(3), 582-606.

Jamieson, D., & O'Mara, J. (1991). *Managing workforce 2000.* San Francisco: Jossey-Bass.

Jay, M. (1993). *Force fields: Between intellectual history and cultural critique.* New York: Routledge.

Johnston, W. (1991, March/April). Global work force 2000: The new world labor market. *Harvard Business Review, 69,* 115-127.

Johnston, W. B., & Packer, A. H. (1987). *Workforce 2000: Work and workers for the 21st century.* Indianapolis: Hudson Institute.

Kaufman, J., & Gaiter, D. J. (1995, September 7). Shades of blue: Many minority police doubt that the force is really with them. *Wall Street Journal,* p. A1.

Kerfoot, D., & Knights, D. (1994). Into the realm of the fearful: Power, identity, and the gender problematic. In H. L. Radtke & H. J. Stam (Eds.), *Power and gender: Social relations in theory and practice* (pp. 67-88). Thousand Oaks, CA: Sage.

Knights, D., & Willmott, H. (1985, February). Power and identity in theory and practice. *Sociological Review, 33*(1), 22-46.

Kogod, S. K. (1993). *A workshop for managing diversity in the workplace.* San Diego: Pfeiffer.

Laabs, J. J. (1993, December). Employees manage conflict and diversity. *Personnel Journal, 72*(12), 30-35.

Laclau, E., & Mouffe, C. (1985). *Hegemony and socialist strategy: Towards a radical democratic politics.* London: Verso.

Levine, A. (1991, September/October). The meaning of diversity. *Change,* pp. 4-5.

Loden, M., & Rosener, J. B. (1991). *Workforce America: Managing employee diversity as a vital resource.* Homewood, IL: Business One Irwin.

Mackinnon, C. A. (1987). *Feminism unmodified: Discourse on life and law.* Cambridge, MA: Harvard University Press.

Madrick, J. (1995). *The end of affluence: The causes and consequences of America's economic dilemma.* New York: Random House.

Martin, L. (1992/1993, Winter). Glass ceiling initiatives. *Public Manager, 21*(4), 28-30.

McIntosh, P. (1988). White privilege and male privilege: A personal account of coming to see correspondences through work in women's studies. In M. L. Anderson & P. H. Collins (Eds.), *Race, class, and gender: An anthology* (pp. 70-81). Belmont, CA: Wadsworth.

McKendall, M. (1994, November). A course in "work-force diversity." *Journal of Management Education, 18,* 407-423.

McNerney, D. (1994, May). The bottom-line value of diversity. *HR Focus, 71,* 22-24.

Meyer, J. W. (1980). Organizational structure as signaling. *Pacific Sociological Review, 22,* 481-500.

Meyer, J. W., & Rowan, B. (1977). Institutionalized organizations:Formal structure as myth and ceremony. *American Journal of Sociology, 83,* 340-363.

Meyer, J. W., & Scott, W. R. (1983). *Organizational environments: Ritual and rationality.* Beverly Hills, CA: Sage.

Miller, E. K. (1994, Summer). Diversity and its management: Training managers for cultural competence within the organization. *Management Quarterly, 35,* 17-23.

Mills, A. J. (1989). Gender, sexuality, and organizational theory. In J. Hearn, D. L. Sheppard, P. Tancred-Sheriff, & G. Burrell (Eds.), *The sexuality of organization* (pp. 29-55). Newbury Park, CA: Sage.

Missouri v. Jenkins, No. 93-1823 (U.S. filed June 12, 1995).

Mouffe, C. (1992). Feminism, citizenship, and radical democratic politics. In J. Butler & J. W. Scott (Eds.), *Feminists theorize the political* (pp. 369-384). New York: Routledge.

Mouffe, C. (1993). *The return of the political.* New York: Verso.

Mumby, D. K. (1993). Introduction: Narrative and social control. In D. K. Mumby (Ed.), *Narrative and social control: Critical perspectives* (pp. 1-12). Newbury Park, CA: Sage.

Mura, D. (1992). Strangers in the village. In M. L. Anderson & P. H. Collins (Eds.), *Race, class, and gender: An anthology.* Belmont, CA: Wadsworth.

Murray, C., & Herrnstein, R. (1994). *The bell curve: Intelligence and class structure in American life.* New York: Free Press.

Napier, N. K., Schweiger, D. M., & Kosglow, J. J. (1993, Winter). Managing organizational diversity: Observations from cross-border acquisitions. *Human Resource Management,32,* 505-524.

Nkomo, S. M. (1992). The emperor has no clothes: Rewriting "race in organizations." *Academy of Management Review, 17*(3), 487-513.

Omi, M., & Winant, H. (1994). *Racial formations in the United States from the 1960s to the 1990s* (2nd ed.). New York: Routledge.

Pecheux, M., & Gadet, F. (1991). La langue introuvable. In A. Kroker & M. Kroker (Eds.), *Ideology and power in the age of Lenin in ruins.* New York: St. Martin's.

Pfeffer, J. (1981). Management as symbolic action: The creation and maintenance of organizational paradigms. In L. L. Cummings & B. A. Staw (Eds.), *Research in organizational behavior* (Vol. 3, pp. 1-52). Greenwich, CT: JAI Press.

Pfeffer, J. (1982). *Organizations and organizational theory.* Cambridge, MA: Ballinger.

Ragins, B. R. (1995). Diversity, power, and mentorship in organizations. In M. M. Chemers, S. Oskamp, & Mark A. Costanzo (Eds.), *Diversity in organizations: New perspectives for a changing workplace.* Thousand Oaks: Sage.

Ramsey, R. D. (1993, March). Dealing with diversity in the workforce. *Supervision, 54*(3), 9-12.

Ramsey, V. J. (1994, November). "Evenhandedness" in work-force diversity courses. *Journal of Management Education, 18,* 424-427.

Ross, M. B. (1995, September 7). End racism on death row—Abolish the death penalty. *Hartford Courant,* p. A19.

Rothschild-Whitt, J. (1979, August). The collectivist organization: An alternative to rational-bureaucratic models. *American Sociological Review, 44,* 509-527.

Scott, W. G. (1992). *Chester I. Barnard and the guardians of the managerial state.* Lawrence: University Press of Kansas.

Scott, W. R., & Meyer, J. W. (1983). The organization of societal sectors. In J. W. Meyer & W. R. Scott (Eds.), *Organizational environments.* Beverly Hills, CA: Sage.

Scott, W. R., & Meyer, J. W. (1994). *Institutional environments and organizations: Structural complexity and individualism.* Thousand Oaks, CA: Sage.

Sikula, A. (1995, May). Diversity: A good or bad idea. *Journal of Management Education, 19*(2), 254-262.

Sims, R. R., & Dennehy, R. F. (1993). *Diversity and differences in organizations.* Westport, CT: Quorum.

Smith, D. E. (1975). An analysis of ideological structures and how women are excluded: Considerations for academic women. *Canadian Review of Sociology & Anthropology, 12*(4), Part 1.

Sowell, T. (1994). *Race and culture: A worldview.* New York: Basic Books.

Stiehm, J. (1994). Diversity's diversity. In D. T. Goldberg (Ed.), *Multiculturalism: A critical reader.* Oxford, UK: Blackwell.

Summa, H. (1992). The rhetoric of efficiency: Applied social science as depoliticization. In R. H. Brown (Ed.), *Writing the social text: Poetics and politics in social science discourse* (pp. 135-153). New York: Aldine de Gruyter.

Thiedereman, S. (1991). *Bridging cultural barriers for corporate success: How to manage the multicultural workforce.* Lexington, MA: Lexington Books.

Thomas, R. R. (1990, March-April). From affirmative action to affirming diversity. *Harvard Business Review,* pp. 107-117.

Thomas, R. R. (1991). *Beyond race and gender: Unleashing the power of your total workforce by managing diversity.* New York: American Management Association.

Thomas, R. R. (1995). A diversity framework. In M. M. Chemers, S. Oskamp, & M. A. Costanzo (Eds.), *Diversity in organizations: New perspectives for a changing workplace.* London: Sage.

Thomas, V. C. (1994, January). The downside of diversity. *Training and Development, 48,* 60-63.

Thompson, J. B. (1984). *Studies in the theory of ideology.* Berkeley: University of California Press.

van Dijk, T. A. (1993). *Elite discourse and racism.* Thousand Oaks, CA: Sage.

Vickers, J. (1994). Notes toward a political theory of sex and power. In H. L. Radtke & H. J. Stam (Eds.), *Power and gender: Social relations in theory and practice* (pp. 174-193). Thousand Oaks, CA: Sage.

Watson, W. E., Kumar, K., & Michaelson, L. K. (1993). Cultural diversity's impact on interaction process and performance: Comparing homogeneous and diverse task groups. *Academy of Management Journal, 36,* 590-602.

Wynter, L. E. (1994, July 20). Business and race: The price of diversity varies by consultant. *Wall Street Journal,* p. B1.

Wynter, L. E. (1995, September 13). Business and race: Groups want census to expand race choices. *Wall Street Journal,* p. B1.

Zucker, L. G. (1987). Institutional theories of organization. In W. R. Scott (Ed.), *Annual Review of Sociology, 42,* 443-464.

3

The Sexually Specific Subject and the Dilemma of Difference

Rethinking the Different in the Construction of the Nonhierarchical Workplace

COLLETTE OSEEN

PART I: INTRODUCTION: RETHINKING DIFFERENCE AS CONTIGUITY IN THE RESTRUCTURED, NONHIERARCHICAL WORKPLACE

In this chapter, I want to consider how we might best work together if we are not all the same, and particularly if we are not all the same sex. I will argue that if we are different, or specifically sexed as Grosz (1990) puts it, a hierarchical structure cannot be the best way to organize because the processes that construct difference simultaneously construct hierarchy. Difference conceived as *other than* and as *less than,* I contend, is inseparable from the creation and maintenance of hierarchical relations, or relations of domination and subordination based on privileging sameness and denigrating difference.

However, does that mean that we must all be the same if we are to be equal, and therefore that women must be the same as men if inequality is not to be reconstituted? If we accept the premise that hierarchy requires difference, not only as other than but as less than, in order to both sort and rank, then must the assertion of sexual difference lead inevitably to hierarchy? Must this assertion of sexual difference necessarily operate within a hierarchical framework that itself depends on fixed categories like sameness and difference for its internal coherence, in the same way that a coherent meaning of a word depends on that which it both excludes and represses, but without which it cannot exist? Must this assertion of sexual difference necessarily be incompatible with the subject who can know and act in nonhierarchical ways?

In answer to these questions, I will argue two points. First, we can assert sexual difference without inevitably and simultaneously reconstructing hierarchy, by theorizing difference as contiguity, or difference side by side, without sameness as the norm or the anchor by which difference is constituted. Second, the acceptance of difference or diversity in the workplace cannot be achieved other than within a nonhierarchical or egalitarian structure. More precisely, it cannot be achieved other than as the (temporary, retrospective) product of nonhierarchical organizing activities. Without this context, difference will continue to be denigrated as the processes of domination and subordination in the form of hierarchy continue to reassert themselves, and criteria are continually reconstituted by which sameness, however defined, is continually privileged and difference, however defined, is continually denigrated.

Thus, instead of difference as other than the same and therefore lesser, a restructured, nonhierarchical workplace would subscribe to difference as contiguity, or difference side by side, without sameness as the norm or dominant term by which difference is hierarchically constructed. However, it is important to recognize that contiguity is not a relative position. It does not mean everyone is the same, which is the corollary to the notion that because we're all different, we're all the same in our difference, the relativism of which has been disputed. Without an absolute, there can be no relative, as Hekman (1990) among others has pointed out. Contiguity means difference without the normative anchor of the same to reestablish privilege. Moreover, contiguity also contains an inevitably political dimension that focuses on the restructuring of relations among individuals, a restructuring that involves reaching out rather than assuming either a dominating or subordinate role based on a position that has been already sorted and ranked. The notion of difference beside difference, or contiguity, is about strategic alliances, negotiated alliances, allegiances, networks. It is about power: not power as sovereign, but power as it resides in networks, alliances, allegiances, power as a productive force, not only power as inhibiting, repressive, juridical.

The advantage of difference as contiguity that focuses on strategies, alliances, allegiances, and networks has organizational implications in terms of how we think about power and thus how we structure our organizations in order to get things done. We can only work together with people who are different from us if we abandon hierarchy for the flattened organization. Thus, I maintain that we can't theorize difference or diversity in the organization without theorizing the hierarchical construction of sameness/difference, the construction of identity, and the construction of power—and here in my argument, I am going to draw on two contemporary French philosophers, Luce Irigaray and Michel Foucault. If we follow Irigaray, our identity—who we are, and whether we are the same or different—is constructed sociolinguistically, within the symbolic order; if we follow Foucault, we are constructed within capillary-like power relations, power everywhere and nowhere. Whether we are deemed to be the same, and privileged, or deemed to be different and not privileged, these categories of sameness, difference, and identity are all constructed within relations of power, or within regimes of truth, a phrase that nicely captures the inevitable intertwining of power and knowledge, the impossibility of innocent knowledge and the inescapability of power.

However, how, given the criticisms leveled against Irigaray, do we capture women's specific experiences with power without essentializing (cf. Grosz, 1993; Whitford, 1991)? And against Foucault, how is the construction of our identity within this capillary-like network of power relations sexually specific (cf. Deveaux, 1994; Diamond & Quinby, 1988)? How is our Otherness as lesser created and maintained within this capillary-like network of power relations? Finally, how might women act as and for themselves in organizations without reestablishing the very relations of domination and subordination that they first struggled against? How do we deal with difference without reestablishing hierarchical relations? These are the questions that face us.

PART II: THE HIERARCHICAL CONSTRUCTION
OF SAMENESS AND DIFFERENCE:
THEORIZING IDENTITY, SAMENESS, AND DIFFERENCE

In the literature on organizations, the focus has been on the universal or the same, rather than on "the different." Whatever the term used—the subject, the knower, the actor, the agent—the term has been deemed generic, universal, sexually indifferent rather than sexually specific. The different has not been theorized, an absence that has been justified through an appeal to equality as necessarily universalist, a universality that transcends the differences that mark us. The assertion of difference, and by extension sexual difference or sexual specificity, has been seen as fundamentally incompatible with the assertion of equality—to assert difference has been seen as an argument for inequality. Sameness, or the appeal to a common humanity shared by all, is the condition for equality, and transcendence, or the removal of oneself from one's bodily differences whatever they may be, is the condition that must be achieved if knowledge or justice applicable to all is to be discovered.

However, Frug (1992) points out that this suppression of difference results in the perpetuation of conditions of inequality. Contrary to the tenets of the Enlightenment, equality cannot be achieved by asserting sameness through transcending difference. Positing the universal "requires the suppression and/or denigration of difference" and "far from making us free, such approaches . . . generate and require relations of domination" (p. 115). Sameness is not the transcendent, neutral universal we have been lead to believe, but a sameness split and unacknowledged, difference set off and deemed lesser in order to create and define the category of the same. It is a process that structures in hierarchical relations, or relations of domination and subordination, privilege and denigration, and in a similar argument, allows for the projection onto the Other the unwanted characteristics of the same.

Feminist theorists in particular—and particularly those who draw on the arguments of Freud and the French postwar theorists such as Derrida, Foucault, Lacan, and Irigaray—have been concerned with exploring the construction of this universal subject—the subject as the same—in terms of sexual specificity. To them, this supposedly universal neutral subject, this subject as the same, this subject without a body, is sexed—but as male. This construction of the subject as a male subject depends on the exclusion and repression of the Other, the different, the woman, to maintain its internal coherence, just as reason depends on the exclusion of the body, a construction that rests on the Cartesian equivalencies of the male/female, mind/body dualisms, dualisms that leave the female subject untheorized and the male subject disembodied, and dualisms that create the conditions for hierarchical regulation and control. Within these dominant modes of representation and systems of knowledge, the subject as male is left unacknowledged, the male claim of mind and the evacuation of the male body left uncommented upon, the structural involvement of these dualisms in the creation and perpetuation of relations of domination and subordination overlooked. The female subject is submerged, her sexually specific representation effaced, under the rubric of (male) universalism, her female body inscribed "as a negative, dependent, lacking object" (Gross, 1986, p. 134), her subjectivity and self-representation denied within a system that depends for its coherence on the female body while systematically denying its difference.

It was Freud who called into question the Western ideal of the knowing, autonomous, conscious rational subject by his positing of the unconscious—how can we fully know ourselves if we cannot ever fully know our unconscious, if our needs and desires remain beyond us, inexplicable in terms of reason? With that move not only the conscious sovereign subject, but innocent knowledge, and power separate and sovereign, are put into play. The subject of the Enlightenment, unified, stable, transcendent in its all-knowingness, is called into question, and a breach in the wall of the fixed categories of sameness, difference, identity, and power is made.

This position is further elaborated by Derrida. He takes up the subject who cannot completely know, and focuses, like Foucault and Lacan, on language. To Derrida, the subject is produced within language, an effect of the repressive dualisms of Western metaphysics, which attempt to ground the limitless instability of language, but where both meaning and subjectivity can be nothing other than a temporary, retrospective fixing (cf. Weedon, 1987). Derrida deconstructs the subject to reveal the subject as a text, "to reveal the necessity with which what a text says is bound up with what it cannot say" (Grosz, 1990, p. 97). He takes apart the subject to show how this term hangs together; he shows how this term must repress the necessary Other in order to maintain its coherence; he shows how it works in order to "unveil the political commitments of various prevailing discourses" (p. 101). He shows the "precarious dependence of dominant forms on repressed, subjugated, or subordinated terms" (p. 110).

With Derrida, everything is the text. However, it is not a helpful position to feminist theorists, who need a way of analyzing power that allows for resistance and change. If the subject is not fixed, if it is an outcome of the play of the text, then how can power be adequately theorized? Conceptualizing power as sovereign, as something held, unified, and fixed, the city on the hill which can be overcome, does not fit with Derrida's notion of prevailing discourses. Nor does power as sovereign fit with the Freudian subject who cannot know, the subject who cannot transcend the unknowable self to achieve the objectivity that innocent knowledge requires and through which justice is obtained.

In search of a more adequate conceptualization of power, many feminists turned to Foucault, with his sophisticated analysis of power everywhere and nowhere, capillary-like, like the body, no part untouched by the silent running of blood. To Foucault, the subject is constructed as the effect of strategies of discourse, where power and knowledge intertwine to produce a disciplinary regime of truth focused on the body. Unlike Derrida, who admits of no place outside of discourse, Foucault does: There is both discursive and nondiscursive power, although there is no place outside the relations of power.[1] Agonistic power, or the final development of his analysis of power everywhere (cf. Deveaux, 1994), is viewed as multiple, interweaving, and "inherently contested" (Deveaux, 1994, p. 223). Unlike Marxist notions of power, it is "not located exclusively or even primarily in state apparatuses or in prohibition" (p. 231); it is not equatable to structures, institutions, practices, ideologies, or hegemonies (cf. Grosz, 1990); it is not only or primarily repressive and dominating. Power is exercised. It exists in actions, it is productive, it enables, it produces things (cf. Grosz, 1990, p. 87). It is separate from knowledge, or social relations, but it is "their condition of existence" (Grosz, 1990, p. 89); it enables these knowledges and social relations to exist, and not others. Foucault asks not what do Marx or Freud have to say about women, but what makes it possible for Marx or Freud to say or not to say what they do about women. He questions how the conditions for existence of certain knowledges came about, and not others. He allows us to ask why do we think in the way that we do, and what does it mean?

In Foucault's analysis of the subject and its relationship to power (cf. Grosz, 1990), the body is the place where power is connected to the social order; the body is the mediator between the endless circulation of power and the social order. And it is at the site of this body that feminist theorists find difficulty with Foucault.

His body is, ultimately, a male body, and a body where the mind rules, where rationality takes its place once again as separate and superior to the body and the feelings and emotions that are relegated to it. As sophisticated as his analysis is, he repeats the hierarchical construction of the Enlightenment in its separation of the mind from the body, and its association with the mind and man, the body and woman.

Without a sexually specific body, he neutralizes power. If power is everywhere and nowhere, he has no way of dealing with or analyzing women's sexually specific experiences of power, such as male violence directed at women's sexually specific bodies. Nor does he have a way of dealing with systemic oppression in its various and specific forms. With power endlessly circulating, how can we deconstruct the specific contexts of women's oppression? For example, Bartky's (1990) use of shame is a way of looking at how "unreciprocated emotional labor, nurturing, and caregiving" (Deveaux, 1994, p. 234) are sources of both power and powerlessness for women. Given Foucault's stress on the institutional and on the rational, how can these forms of power be unpicked, and how would Foucault's theories help to unpick them? Foucault's analysis of power lies on the side of reason, and he leaves the emotional side as a source of inequality unanalyzed. These areas of nurturance—the inseparability of loving mother and good servant, "the managed heart" of the smiling stewardess in Hochschild's (1983) memorable phrase—are

> easily obscured by Foucault's agonistic model of power, because it reflects neither outright domination nor the intersubjective play of power between two free agents. Feminists need to look at the inner processes that condition women's sense of freedom or choice in addition to external manifestations of power and dominance. (Deveaux, 1994, p. 234)

In neglecting to look at sexually specific experiences of power, he reinforces the association of women with the body and men with the mind in the very act of theorizing power. Foucault's notion of power is itself one that both privileges (male) rationality and excludes emotionality from consideration; it is this privileging of male rationality that is the condition of existence for Foucault's notion of power.

Nonetheless, feminists find the notion of no place existing outside of relations of power liberating. It allows them to focus, not on the sterile defense of an innate identity—the construction of a truth defended by power sovereign, the moated castle—but on strategy, allegiances, shifting alliances. It allows them to use Derrida and the idea of a coherent term inevitably repressing and suppressing the necessary Other, but without seeing everything as a text: It allows them to look for the conditions of existence of that way of thinking. It allows them to ask if the focus on language is only a rewrite of Descartes' focus on reason, the mind still privileged. Most important, it allows them to remember that this condition of existence for these particular knowledges is itself sexually specific, to remember that "all theory, all knowledge is produced from sexually specific positions and with sexually specific effects" (Grosz, 1990, p. 109).

What is useful for us, then, about Foucault is that we can theorize power as networks, as capillary-like, as everywhere and nowhere, as the impetus for shifting and strategic alliances; we can use this theory as a condition for our strategic assertion of the right to act as more than either isolated sexless bodies or as only sexed bodies. Just as Derrida's deconstruction of the totalitarian impulses underlying the position of either/or alerted us to the dangers of advancing dualistic positions, Foucault's notion of shifting alliances alerted us to the advantages of the notion of both/and as a strategy. Power everywhere frees us from advocating fixed essentialism but doesn't preclude us from advancing the notion of strategic essentialism. We can use the notion of strategic essentialism as a way of building alliances; we can reappropriate and subvert "an identity while maintaining an understanding of its historical contingency" (Deveaux, 1994, p. 241). Or as Grosz (1990) puts it, "strategy involves recognizing the situation and alignments of power within and against which it operates" (p. 59). We may be inevitably complicitous, but that position never precludes resistance.

However, as helpful as Foucault's notion of power everywhere and nowhere is in allowing feminist theorists to focus on the construction of strategic allegiances, his inability to conceptualize a sexually specific subject is not. Thus, in search of a way to conceptualize a sexually specific subject without essentializing, a number of feminist theorists have drawn on the psychoanalyst and linguist, Luce Irigaray. She herself has drawn on Lacan and his rereading of Freud for her notion of the subject constructed within the symbolic order, but unlike Lacan, she focuses on both the possibility and the necessity of change within the symbolic order in order to create a place for women, a place they do not yet have.

To Lacan (cf. Grosz, 1990), it is through the naming role of language that the subject becomes the subject. He argues that if Freud had read de Saussure, a linguist writing about the same time as Freud, he would have recognized that the unconscious is structured like a language. It is through language that we are named, through language that we take our place in the social order, through language that we are constituted "as an ego or unified self (the imaginary) and as a social and speaking subject (the symbolic)" (Grosz, 1990, p. 72). As we are constituted in this act of naming, we enter into the social or symbolic order, an order that for Lacan hinges on the phallus, "the signifier of signifiers" (Wright, 1992, p. 319). It is within this symbolic or social order, or the law of the father, that "the phallus as the preeminent signifier provides the stability through which the subject is constituted, and through which the sexes are distinguished and positioned as opposites" (Grosz, 1990, p. 79). There cannot be a "sexually neutral model of subjectivity"; our sexuality is not "contingent or incidental" (Grosz, 1990, p. 79). In taking up our place in language, we become who we are and who we may be; this is a symbolic code that dictates our place in the social order.

However, although the use of the phallus as the signifier of signifiers consigns women to the "negative or supplementary side," rendering "the structures and power relations between the sexes eternal and universal, conditions of the very existence of language and sociality" (Grosz, 1990, p. 105), feminists have argued that Lacan's rereading of Freud remains helpful because he focuses on "the powerful subjective effects of language and systems of signification in producing the sociosymbolic subject" (p. 106). He links "the individual to the social" through his materialist understanding of language (p. 107); he points out that language has "primacy over experience," and that "what is not spoken is as significant as what is said" (pp. 106-107). And through his theory itself, with its focus on the phallus and its elaborate theorization, we gain insights regarding "male fantasies about women that are actively imposed on women" (p. 107). Lacan theorizes male desires, giving feminist theorists an ambivalent insight into the intersection of power and desire dressed as reason.

Irigaray, the French philosopher, psychoanalyst, and linguist, takes from Lacan his focus on the subject as a creation of the symbolic order, but she analyzes Lacan's focus on the phallus as the preeminent signifier as an expression of power and desire and moves from there. She asks, in a way that neither Derrida, Foucault, nor Lacan could, how we might account for and theorize the sexually specific body, the body that is not the same. Irigaray insists that the sexually specific body must be theorized, that a subject position for the specifically sexed female body must be articulated within a symbolic order that recognizes sexual difference. She analyzes man the subject as a man who cannot see himself as sexually specific, a man who simultaneously relies on and disavows the role of the sexually specific, concretely sexed body in the production of knowledge within which his subjectivity is also understood, confusing himself with the universal. To Irigaray, patriarchy is a

> symbolic order which is sexually indifferent, that is to say, which does not recognize sexual difference; in this hom(m)osexual economy, there are only men, either men possessing a phallus/penis, or castrated and defective men. The other sex is defined in terms of its relation to men: as mother, virgin, or whore, for example, but not in relation to itself. Women have no identity as women. This sexual indifference is far reaching: it is embodied in language, in representation, in theory, in scientific knowledge, in philosophy, and in psychoanalysis, yet it remains unrecognized, because women's difference is never symbolized. (Wright, 1992, p. 180)

Within the present symbolic or social order that we inhabit, we are what men do not want themselves to be, or to have; we are their rejected parts of themselves, we are their necessary but disavowed bodies, disavowed to maintain the purity of reason, the mind unsullied by immanence. We are ourselves unsymbolized, unarticulated, and inarticulate; we are a blank screen for men's projections, a state of nature, a condition of dereliction, lost and abandoned. We need a "home in the symbolic order," our own "house of language" (Whitford, 1991, p. 156), we need to speak in a language that speaks of and to us, in the symbols and myths that "indicate representationally how that society is structured and organized at other levels" (p. 170), myths that resonate far beyond those we have available to us now, where only the "maternal function" speaks, not the woman, where the mother-son of the Pieta presides, but never the mother-daughter. What Irigaray wishes to construct are "new fictions, to anticipate and perhaps assist the birth of a new social order" (p. 170).

As an undutiful daughter, Irigaray undertakes to use the same tools as Freud and Lacan to creatively imagine a place within the symbolic order that women might inhabit as women, not as men with a lack, the metaphysics of Freud and Lacan. We wish not to reveal our innate being, but to create a female symbolic—a place in the language—where one has never existed, to symbolize the relations between women, to find a place "distinct from the maternal function" (Whitford, 1991, p. 109). In so doing, we wish to construct an Other as distinct from the Other of the same, where "there is only one sex, . . . that sex is male, and . . . therefore women are really men, in a defective, castrated version" (p. 120).

Our goal is not merely invention, or new terms for a place in the symbolic order where before there was none—it is also redistribution. In this total symbolic redistribution (cf. Whitford, 1991, p. 165), men would reclaim not only their disavowed bodies on which the myth of transcendence depends, but those parts of themselves—the disavowed emotionalism that serves to support the rationalism they alone claim is only one example—that they have rejected, and in rejecting, gave to women; and women creatively imagining what it means to be a woman. Here "Lacan, notoriously conservative, emphasizes the [symbolic] code . . . the domain of constraint. . . . Irigaray emphasizes the context, the possibility of limitless combination, a new syntax of culture which is creative and open-ended. . . . The metonymic allows for process" (pp. 179-180). Irigaray calls this the contiguous or "metonymical subject-to-subject relation between women" (in Whitford, 1991, p. 184), which stands for "women's sociality, love of self on the women's side, the basis for a different form of social organization and a different economy" (p. 180). In this creative imagining and reimagining of the symbolic order, Irigaray proposes for both a space to be free, for both to exist in contiguity, side by side, not in opposition, one over the other, within the hierarchical dualisms that structure our thoughts, our relations, and our organizations.

PART III: MANAGING DIVERSITY:
THE ORGANIZATIONAL LITERATURE

Given difference as contiguity, and power everywhere and nowhere, how might we understand the organizational literature on diversity or difference in the workplace? In this next section, I will look at four examples from the literature, all of which approach this question in slightly different ways: Thomas's (1991) *Beyond Race and Gender,* an American analysis that focuses on the management of diversity and the shift from doing to enabling; Stewart and Drakich's (1994) short monograph on using the rules to achieve diversity in Ontario universities; Semler's (1993) book-length analysis of the transformation of his Brazilian factory through restructuring and the minimizing of difference; and, *Women Organising,* Brown's (1991) account of the struggles facing feminist organizations in the 1980s in Britain, as they tried to organize in nonhierarchical ways by minimizing difference through sharing work activities.

Thomas (1991) expresses a widely held view in the literature on management and difference in the workplace. Like many others, he stresses two points: first, the manipulation of organizational culture is the key to the successful management of diversity—only if a culture is made more inclusive will diversity succeed. Second, because a more diverse workforce assures that there are more ways of doing things, it's also more efficient. Diversity is not less efficient because of greater difference, but more efficient because of greater choice. It's the principles of consumerism applied to the workforce.

To Thomas, the organizational culture is both the unexamined milieu in which we work and the unifying force—the glue—that holds the organization together. Only by manipulating the culture to produce the view that greater choice is all to the good, and that narrowing the types of people who work there means less choice because there's less access to differing views, will managers be able to achieve the harmony they desire. Only then will people understand why there has to be change because this type of change is in the best interests of all.

Affirmative action, or managing by numbers, is a necessary step, albeit only the first step, toward managing diversity. The second step is education, or valuing diversity. But the third step, and to Thomas the most important and the most overlooked, rests on changing the core culture by changing the way we manage, or in Thomas's metaphor, changing the roots of the tree. We must change the roots—the management style—not just graft on branches, or graft diverse peoples onto the organization, leaving the culture of the organization unchanged. We have to go beyond achieving diversity—numbers—and valuing diversity—education—to managing diversity, if we are to move beyond the problems engendered by those actions: the view that special treatment is unfair and that some groups are special interest groups, and others are not. In other words, it is through managing diversity, not just adding different people, and then educating the others about the value of working with different people, that the backlash can be avoided.

To succeed, because changing the organizational culture won't happen without both a knower and leader, an outside consultant and an inside change agent are absolutely necessary. Outside consultants are invaluable for their ability to analyze the organization and for their advice on how to manipulate the culture to achieve the desired ends. An outside consultant can provide both the necessary distance from the organization and the necessary insight to rethink metaphorically how people of diverse backgrounds might best work together.

Inside change agents are equally necessary, if this knowledge is to be used to advantage. This person is someone, and not only someone in the human resources department, who can clarify the motivations and concepts, insist on consistency, foster a pioneering spirit and a long-term perspective, and conduct diagnostic research. It is also someone who can emphasize education rather than training, because "training builds specific skills; education changes mindsets" (Thomas, 1991, pp. 36-38), although education is only the last step toward managing diversity, not the thing itself.

Change agents can, for instance, ensure that the definition of diversity is wide rather than narrow—by including everyone, opposition is muted. And most important, they can focus on the necessity of simultaneously rewarding a different management style, those who enable rather than those who do for. It is enabling that is the key to managing diversity, because enabling is the only management style that can deal with a diverse workforce. However, as Thomas (1991) underlines, doing for is far more common than enabling, and thus "the number one barrier to acceptance [of managing diversity] . . . is the way 'managing' is defined in most corporations. . . . In spite of recent trends towards participatory management styles," most managers want a clone of themselves, people who do things just like them. They are doers, taking charge; "taking care of people [is] secondary" (p. 46). Cloning prevents diversity; it also prevents any focus on managing people as a legitimate purpose within the organization. But according to Thomas, most managers in organizations aren't interested and aren't very good at managing people because they don't see managing people as contributing directly to the bottom line. What does contribute to the bottom line is ensuring that people do it right, and that can only be ensured by either doing it for them, or by having someone in charge who does it just the way they would have done it. Enabling, in that context, is a foreign concept.

That's why the enabling or empowering model of management is much better: Enabling helps people find the best way for them to achieve their goal; cloning demands that one way be followed. Not everyone is going to be a white male; if people are different, they are going to be different in how they work, how they work together, and how they achieve the goals of the organization.

Enabling, rather than cloning, is the only answer to the successful management of a diverse workforce, but if enabling is going to be successful, it must operate on two levels. Not only does enabling allow for different ways of doing things; enabling must also include how white males do things, which points out, of course, that no one group acts in one, stereotypical, way.

As Thomas (1991) points out, managing a diverse workforce by enabling does not mean excluding white men; it means including everyone. For diversity to work well, managing diversity must be broadened "to include multiple dimensions" (p. 81), which means white men, but it also means that the many different styles of working and leading on the part of everyone are to be encouraged. Paradoxically, the focus on assimilation has meant that white men have had many routes to the top, but others found that imitation of the stereotypic (white, male) managerial style was necessary for advancement. As one woman pointed out, if you're part of the majority, you can act in a number of ways, but if you're part of the group labeled different from the same, you have to act in a way that closely emulates the stereotype:

> The women who have been promoted . . . share a common style. They are extremely aggressive and appear to subordinate their personal lives for the laboratory. Many are not married. In contrast, men . . . have all kinds of styles—from aggressive to quietly competent. (Thomas, 1991, p. 108)

To Thomas, if the routes to upward mobility are based on cloning the stereotype, the glass ceiling remains, because "no amount of mentoring or adaptation will result in women becoming men" (p. 109), or anyone black becoming white, or any other characteristic that belongs to the privileged group, and that the less privileged group, by definition, does not have and cannot achieve.

Although they do not take a Foucauldian stance, the approach of Stewart and Drakich lends itself to a Foucauldian analysis. They are concerned with the subversion of the existing rules and regulations, the interstices of power, not the who of power, but where power lies, in "performance evaluations, audits, selection and promotion procedures, tenure mechanisms," in the "routinization of procedure," in the "many minute forms" that characterize the regimes of power and knowledge that are our organizations (Jermier & Clegg, 1994, pp. 3, 4).

In their discussion of diversity in Ontario universities, the intent of Stewart and Drakich (1994) is to show the process by which rules and regulations, the minutiae of any large organization, can be turned inside themselves to reveal the repression that is at their heart, and to use that revelatory process to advance those whom the rules and regulations were supposed to keep out. Their study of Ontario universities indicated very little progress toward increasing the percentage of women as full-time professors over the last two decades, so they were particularly concerned with detailing how the barriers to hiring and retaining women could be overcome. Although they take a standard approach to organizational analysis, in that organizations are understood to have both a formal and informal structure, they point at the rules of the organization as both the place of resistance and the place of advancement. If power is everywhere and nowhere, it is most likely resisted everywhere and nowhere, in the rules, procedures, and mechanisms that are the university. Those same nodes of power that keep women in their place can be used to advance women, the process turned against itself, a feudal bureaucracy predicated on the exclusion of women liberated for emancipatory ends.

Rather than endless study—they point out that employment equity officers often have their time used for endless and purposeless data collection—they recommend action. A full-time equity officer is a necessity, but not for research purposes. Instead, the equity officer helps to ensure that due process is indeed followed, from the initial discussions of the wording of the advertisement, to ensuring that the advertisement itself is widely distributed, to ensuring that the interviewing questions are vetted and that the interviewers are taught how to read letters of reference. What is theoretical to Stewart and Drakich is made practical through equity officers who do more than monitor numbers, interviewing committees that are called to account at every step, and finally and most important, hiring that can be refused at the vice president's level if all the steps are not followed, monitored, and justified in terms of fairness applied to ensuring demographic diversity.

They recognize that an *equity culture* must be put in place if people who are different from those already there are to be welcomed, but they are most concerned with numbers and with process. In that sense, theirs is an excellent reply to Thomas's account of diversity in the workplace. To Thomas, reason and a more enlightened form of domination in the form of enabling will work to bring together people who are different to get work done. Stewart and Drakich recognize that at a university, reason has been dressed in a number of ways to maintain privilege. Rather than argue the more esoteric points, they focus on strict adherence to the rules, which in the classical move of work to rule, subverts them.

However, they do point out that in order to begin this process of subversion, universities must have a committed group of feminists and men sympathetic to feminism—in other words, a body to lobby—and someone in the administration with clout who is committed. They point to one Ontario university with a committed president and successful implementation of the process of strict adherence to rules of fairness, and to one Ontario university with a president who stated that he found this focus on increasing diversity reverse discrimination. At that university, the process failed. It is a sobering insight into hierarchical relations constituting and reconstituting relations of domination and subordination, and how easily difference is squashed in the absence of a commitment to egalitarian relations.

How might Ricardo Semler's notion of restructuring as empowerment and difference or identity as tribalism be understood from the point of view of Irigaray's notion of difference as contiguity and Foucault's notion of power as capillary-like networks, or power everywhere?

Semler understands the minimalization of difference in the workplace in structural terms—as fixed and unified—in the way he understands power, the way he understands organization, and the way he understands diversity. As a very practical example of how the flattened hierarchy and worker empowerment is achieved, Semler is instructive: Only by minimizing difference among workers by restructuring the hierarchy can success be achieved, and success is making your workers want to come to work in the morning. To accomplish this, he eliminated most supervisory and management positions; allowed the workers to decide how, when, and where they would do the work, to hire those they would work with and those they would work under; instituted profit sharing and bonuses; and allowed the workers to decide, after reading the balance sheet, how much those would be. In the interests of keeping supervision and coordination to a minimum, he also spun off satellite units from the main company, creating positions for outside entrepreneurs who sold materials and services not only to his company but to others. To maintain flexibility and creativity, he eliminated any rules for innovators within the company, the only criteria imposed a 6-month renewable contract, but no other guidelines, timelines, or supervisors.

Power in the form of rules is an anathema to Semler; workers freed from the stifling net of rules are free to be responsible, to be motivated, to be creative, to be involved—to want to get up in the morning to come to work. Hierarchical ways of organizing are not innate, nor are they necessary to get things done. Instead, they stand in the way, inhibiting workers and turning them into children, obeying with reluctance as father hoves into view.

But if hierarchy is not innate, tribalism is. To Semler, the need for like to associate with like is nothing the organization can change; it might as well learn to live with this need for "identity," to accept this need to define the different and the same. Workers were allowed to hire whomever they liked, and one of the few policies in an organization that banned policy manuals focused on promoting from within: those with 70% of the qualifications wished for would be hired in preference to outsiders with a 100% match. Semler pays very little attention to the construction of the different and the same. What intrigues Semler is one aspect of power in the organization, and that is power as it resides in rules and regulations.

This is precisely the problem Brown (1991) struggles with in *Women Organising*: power and the construction of ranked differences among people who work together, and the hierarchical structures that ensue. To Brown, dealing with diversity or difference in the workplace cannot be separated from restructuring the workplace in order to minimize hierarchy, as Semler does. She argues that power exists not only in the structure of the organization, but in the differences among workers, however those differences are defined, and that those differences must be minimized. Brown's solution to this problem is to minimize hierarchical relations among workers by focusing on organizing as a process or as a series of activities, none of which can be ranked, including the activity of leading. By stressing the necessary involvement of everyone in everything, she hopes to provide a way for organizations to get things done with a minimum of domination.

Brown's (1991) analysis rests on negotiated order theory, a theory which maintains that the social order is negotiated and as such always involves struggle. She takes pains to point out, however, that although negotiating is not something bereft of struggle or conflict, it is not only antagonistic. In the process of negotiating, decisions are made "through a process of consensus which encourages dissent" (p. 16), a process of decision making that is repetitive, reflective, and political. It is not a process that is complacent or innate, spontaneous, or natural. It is work and struggle, not a happy anarchy that just emerges, thus requiring no analysis. Most important, it is in these organizing activities, none of which are ranked, that we have to find a way of "managing a priori differences between individuals" (p. 17), however these differences might be described and categorized. The question then becomes how do we figure out how to deploy these differences so that hierarchy is not constructed and reconstructed on the basis of those differences?

To Brown, the answer lies in understanding organizing as a process. It is not the organization that exists, but the organizing activities that give it the temporary retrospective fixing that allows us to define a structure that is itself a construct of meaning, a taken-for-granted set of assumptions that allow us to act within the illusion of a structure. But this structure, as illusionary as it is, can be hierarchical or nonhierarchical; this set of assumptions is both literally and figuratively the outcome of our organizing activities, which are either kept separate or shared among us. In her discussion of these organizing activities, Brown is careful to make no real distinction other than to use the names already familiar to us, of doing, working, managing, and leading—all are activities which can be exchanged, learned, negotiated, and shared.

Brown points out, however, that leading, because it has occupied such a central place in the literature, needs to be dealt with in a way that demystifies its separateness and its individualization, as something that in order to get things done, must ideally reside in one person alone. In what comes close to a parody of the 1950s lament for any marriage that strayed from *Father Knows Best*— "But somebody has to be the boss!"—the assumption is that individualized leadership is the only effective way of getting things done. But according to Brown, leadership, like the notion that families could not function without a (male) boss, must be rethought if organizing nonhierarchically is going to succeed. As long as the activity of leading is individualized or confused with the position, nonhierarchical relations among workers will not be possible. Leading, just like all the other organizing activities, must be shared and exchanged to ensure that it does not reside either with one person or in one position for long.

To Brown (1991), leading, although a particularly skillful kind of organizing activity, is the purview of every worker. To accomplish this, every worker must be involved, an involvement requiring constant negotiating; no one can be left out. As she stresses in her analysis, and particularly in her analysis of leadership and how it is usually presented, she wishes to differentiate between the usual elision of leadership with management and its behaviorist and positionalist focus. She proposes that we separate our study of management from leadership, or from "status position or delegated task management" (p. 64), and recognize that the activity of leading is far more sophisticated than a simple analysis of positional responsibilities and how well they are carried out. What we need to do instead is to teach more people to be skillful organizers so more can be leaders. Thus, we should focus not on what people are, or the traits they exhibit in particular positions, nor on what they do in particular positions, but

> rather on leadership as process, and specifically processes in which influential acts of organizing contribute to the structuring of interactions and relationships, activities and sentiment; processes in which definitions of social order are negotiated, found acceptable, implemented, and renegotiated; processes in which

interdependencies are organized in ways which promote the values and interests of the social order. (Brown, 1991, p. 69)

Leading, then, becomes a political process in which everyone must be involved; the only way to achieve order without hierarchy is if every member "has both the right and the responsibility to contribute" (p. 163). If we are to get things done, everything must be shared, which includes any activity termed leading.

To Brown, this is the key to understanding how we organize nonhierarchically. It is a constant process of organizing, a constant process of negotiation, involvement, teaching, and sharing. Nothing is individualized in the sense that not one of these organizing activities is left to any individual for long. And of course, as we are involved in these organizing activities we ourselves are shaped: We become what we do. Nonhierarchical organizing activities construct us as confident, autonomous, innovative, and creative individuals bound together by these collective, consensual, negotiated activities, activities in which leading is an intrinsic—and shared—part.

CONCLUSION

How have these five authors approached diversity in the workplace? What have they used as their analytical framework, and how helpful has this analytical framework been for understanding how we can all work together in our difference, in our infinite human variety?

In their analyses, Thomas, Stewart and Drakich, Semler, and Brown have all assumed some version of power as fixed and sovereign, a notion that has had a direct impact on their theorizing of diversity and hence on how to attain and maintain diversity in the workplace. Power as diffuse, ambiguous, capillary-like networks, as enabling, not only prohibiting, has not been considered. Nor has difference been considered in any other semblance than in its relationship to the same. In this conceptualization of difference, women lack symbolization, except as the Other which must be excluded and repressed in order that the category of the same might maintain its internal coherence—what Irigaray calls "the economy of the same."

Roosevelt Thomas uses metaphor as a unifying trope that prevents any analysis of how power circulates to construct difference or diversity as lesser at the same time as it constructs organizational hierarchy. He focuses on realigning the organizational culture to account for organizational diversity, substituting one form of management style, enabling, for another form, doing for. Paradoxically, diversity among employees is to be marshaled to achieve harmony in the organization, and Thomas has no way to account for the relentless processes that construct and reconstruct both sameness and difference and their hierarchical relations. Culture and change are manipulable variables, agency is separate from structure, the outside consultant and the internal change agent are indispensable, and difference as a category can easily be expanded to extend to everyone. Power everywhere and difference as difference side by side, and not as sameness suppressing difference, are not part of what is, to him, an equation.

In his analysis, organizations are understood as "relatively homogeneous, integrated, and unicultural" (Jeffcutt, 1994, p. 243), meaning that the culture of the organization is understood as a coherent category, as something that both acts as the glue unifying the organization and symbolizes the organization. Thomas uses the metaphor of the tree, its roots and branches, in order to both exemplify the culture of the organization and to indicate what can be done—changing the roots rather than grafting strange fruit onto the existing branches. However, the use of metaphor is problematic. As a literary trope, it is unifying and fixing. Nor does the use of metaphor allow for a sophisticated analysis of power: Shifting discourses of power and knowledge that create the conditions by which a tree with roots is an appropriate representation are not admitted. There's no way of analyzing why this metaphor is used, what its use silences, how it fixes a particular representation to the benefit of some and not others, or how it is completely inapplicable for analyzing how women and men are differently situated in the organization. Where are the sexually specific subjects who exist and work there? Where are the discourses of power and knowledge that position them differently, construct them differently, that are impossible to pin down, that circulate as silently and efficaciously as blood in the body?

In Thomas's analysis, culture as a fixed and unifying category is also something that can be revealed by the neutral and dispassionate observer/ consultant who is able to strip away the layers to show the truth of the organization to itself, and thus provide a guide to what needs to be done. But that this guide is also an orientalizing discourse, that the outside consultant is also the professional stranger who interviews and then decides the truth that the natives are not privy to, is not admitted. Or that this guide, in the interests of presenting a unified truth, suppresses "division and disharmony" in order to privilege the "epic and romantic narrative" that the hero on the quest for truth requires, is not admitted (Jeffcutt, 1994, p. 250). Nor is it admitted that the outside consultant who knows, the professional stranger who constructs the orientalizing discourse, the romantic hero: All require the presence of women as the Other in order that knowledge as it is constructed in Western thought (cf. Hekman, 1990), the idea of the Orient (cf. Said, 1978), and the romantic quest itself, may maintain their internal coherence. Difference as other and as lesser is structured into Thomas's analysis.

However, if culture is not something which we can reveal, show, or interpret through the inspired use of metaphor, if it is a way of representing the world to ourselves that we ourselves create, it is then a recursive process from which transcendence is not possible. If organizational culture is "relatively heterogeneous, diffuse, and multicultural" (Jeffcutt, 1994, p. 243), if the observer stance is not possible and there is no truth to be revealed, discerned, or correctly interpreted, where is the outside consultant? What happens to the change agent if change is not to be pinned down, if it, like culture, is diffuse and ambiguous, if agency and structure both disappear into capillary-like networks of power and knowledge, if organization can be read like a text constructed within these networks of power and knowledge where meaning is only temporary and retrospective; where, then, is managing diversity, enabling, and efficiency?

If we follow Derrida (cf. Grosz, 1990), texts inscribe order through suppression and repression, and nothing can be separated from anything else, not the author from the text, the reader from either. If we follow Foucault, organizations themselves are discourses of power and knowledge; the point is not to ask, what is this truth, but what are the conditions that enabled this truth to be labeled as such. We might ask ourselves, then, if what Thomas postulates is even possible, or if it is inherently contradictory. For difference to be labeled as such, it depends on sameness. Neither could exist without the other. Thomas's analysis depends on reason freeing the organization from the bonds of power that determine difference as lesser; his faith in education—in the triumph of reason—and in enabling, which is still power as domination, only with the sharp edges less apparent, indicate that. However, he fails to grapple with the inherent contradiction of his analysis: without confronting the processes that construct difference as both other and as lesser, and thus which continuously create and re-create hierarchical relations, his focus on enabling will come to naught. The criteria that create difference remain, and humanist organizational theory becomes merely manipulative.

In their analysis of how diversity might be achieved at universities, Stewart and Drakich recommend that the rules and regulations of a hierarchical institution like a university be turned inside out and used against themselves: first, to show that the explicit intent of these rules to ensure fairness in the hiring and retention process can be doubled over to ensure diversity, and second, to show that this doubling over can expose the old boys' network embedded in these rules to reveal the contradiction at their heart: affirmative action for men. Although Stewart and Drakich use a version of the formal versus the informal structure for their analysis, this strategy of using the rules and regulations against themselves can be more usefully analyzed using Derrida and the pleasures of the text, but embedded in Foucauldian notions of organizations as networks of power and knowledge, and extended to include Irigaray's focus on creating a space in the symbolic order for women. That rules can be overturned to reveal the repression and exclusion of the subordinate term that allows the whole edifice to stand—as Irigaray points out the same dualistic structure that creates the domination of men and the subordination of women—is ultimately a more useful way to analyze how diversity can be achieved in organizations.

Thus, these rules and regulations, the minutiae of power, are both the place of resistance and the place of advancement; they both keep women in their place and can be used to free women; they are contradictory in intent and ambiguous. It is in these rules that the coherence of the organization is most clearly revealed to be based on the necessary exclusion and repression of women through the interstices of power, the what and where of power, not the who; the rules and regulations, not the people. Using the rules against themselves rather than focusing on the people who hold the position seems to be the more successful approach to achieving diversity, and perhaps more permanent. But these rules and regulations are also nodes in the networks of power and knowledge that are our organizations. These networks enable some to advance feminist goals, for example, the top administrators and others sympathetic to feminism, as well as feminist lobby groups; and they enable others to oppose these goals, like the university president who saw equity proposals as reverse discrimination.

However, just as Weedon (1987) has pointed out that Derridean analysis lacks a theory of power, Smith (1990) points out that Foucault's analysis lacks an ontology, a bodily presence, a point that a large number of other feminist theorists have reiterated (cf. Deveaux, 1994). Without a bodily presence, Foucault is incapable of analyzing either specific sexual oppression, or systemic oppression, like the lack of demographic diversity in the institution of the university.

The Irigarayan analysis directly confronts that lack of specific bodily presence in both Derrida and Foucault. If women are not symbolized, if they lack symbolic representation, if we lack ways of understanding what women might do or how they might act because women still exist in the state of nature, it is only in creating that symbolic representation for women—not discovering, but creating—that we may have a place for women as women in institutions without demanding either that women be the same as men—Irigaray's economy of the same—or the same as all other women, a fixed, unified, and ultimately confining category of woman. Instead it is contiguity, in metonymy, in symbolizing in new and creative ways our incredible human variety, that we find a place for women. It is not enough to overturn the rules and regulations of an institution to be used against itself, not enough to understand how discourses of power and knowledge are both the organization itself and that which enables us to think about the organization in the way that we do. Only in symbolizing women differently, and not as the necessary Other that enables man to achieve its coherence, can we find a place for ourselves in the organization.

Ricardo Semler wishes to negate the effects of power by removing power from the structure of the organization, from the position held or the credentials required. To Semler, power as domination is effectively negated by restructuring alone. Without an oppressive structure, workers are free. His notion of power is similar to Baumann's description of the dentistry state (cf. Jermier & Clegg, 1994); power is intrusive and violent but can be avoided; the king and his troops are not always out. But to follow Foucault and his dispute with the notion of power as sovereign, if power is everywhere and nowhere, if power is disciplinary and normalizing, power does not disappear in the act of restructuring. Power simply assumes a different guise, amorphous, ambiguous, reappearing in the self-policing subject, the subject who disciplines himself[2] and who has internalized the capitalist goals. The workers police themselves and each other, they become stand-ins for the absent boss. As Stewart Clegg points out, we can use the notion of the self-policing subject as a way of theorizing power in organizations; we can see these subjects who constantly regard "themselves, their labor processes, their products and practices, from the singular auspices of zero defects as a discourse organizationally implanted into them" (Jermier & Clegg, 1994, p. 7). To Jermier and Clegg, it is a form of "neurotic subjectivity" (p. 7), an analysis that is similar to Bartky's (1990) linking of self-policing, women, and shame of. In Semler's theorization of power, the boss never really disappears, and mutual policing is no substitute for mutual cooperation.

Semler's theorization of power extends to his categorization of identities as merely tribal. Identity is irrelevant because the goal is the flattening of organizational hierarchies. Differences in status or position are bad, rules and regulations as sites of power are bad, but people, grouping or being grouped or categorized is irrelevant. However, categorization as a site of power that interpolates identities is not irrelevant, as Semler would have it. It is another site where difference as lesser is constructed, and through which hierarchical relations are created and sustained. Semler, for all his discussion of hierarchy, overlooks the most obvious of all, the domination of men and the subordination of women, apparent even in his own factory. His analysis rests on the elimination of difference among men by understanding difference as encased in credentials, in position, in status. That this lacunae in his theorization of eliminating power differences among people working together does not extend beyond eliminating the differences between father and son, the rule of the church replaced by the Enlightenment, where equality is presumed among all men but the women are left out, means that hierarchical structuring will inevitably reappear. The son freeing himself from the omniscient and omnipresent father may be an easily discernable subtext, but the role of a sister and what restructuring might mean for her in the absence of any notice of how sameness/difference is constructed, is left unattended. Although Semler points out that the metaphor of one big happy family forces everyone into either parental or children's roles, he does not attend to any of the different roles occupied by mothers as opposed to fathers, sisters to brothers, and what a rereading of tribalism might necessitate in order to grapple with that.

Brown's stance on minimizing difference is neither Foucauldian nor Irigarayan, although negotiated order theory, in its emphasis on flux and indeterminacy and on meaning as temporary and retrospective, is similar to the concerns of Derrida, as well as to Habermas and his theory of communicative action (cf. Brown, 1991; Burrell, 1994). In that focus on the negotiated social order, both deconstruction and particularly critical humanism share a concern with the unifying nature of culture (cf. Jermier & Clegg, 1994). As Jeffcutt (1994) points out, in critical humanism,

> Culture is . . . theorized as a creative expression of the inhabitants of a particular setting, a symbolizing process which is amorphous, transient, and sensual . . . a communal possession, a meaning system through which disintegrative forces are mediated and negotiated order pursued. (p. 244)

However, in this theorization of culture, power, and diversity, if culture is unifying it is also and at the same time exclusionary and repressive. Something must be both excluded and repressed so that the dominant term may attain and maintain its coherence. And in that process of exclusion and repression, in that projection onto the excluded and repressed Other, that which we most hate and fear in ourselves and by which we create difference, lies the means by which hierarchy continually reasserts itself. In this analysis of culture, power, and diversity, there is no room for discord, for ambiguity, for flux. Culture as a unifying force suppresses the "heterogeneity" (Jeffcutt, 1994, p. 256) that characterizes organizing activity and suppresses conflict between those who are different from the most privileged, however the most privileged are defined. The fixity that underlies this idea of culture is inevitably repressive, not the least to the diversity Brown wishes to encourage.

Brown attempts to deal with the inherent contradiction between the unifying nature of the negotiated social order and diversity or difference in the workplace by focusing on the notion of distributed power, or power shared in the form of shared skills, including the skill of leading. By distributing leading, Brown is attempting to ensure that leading cannot reside in one person or in one position, and that hierarchy cannot reconstitute itself through the privileging of one particular position or person associated with leading. To Brown, organizing is an ongoing process composed of organizing activities. These organizing activities must be distributed or shared: All are skilled, and leading is an organizational skill that is just somewhat more skilled than others. Decision making, which is part of leading, is a process of negotiating, hence the term negotiated order. By all taking part, all negotiating, all making decisions, all leading, we construct the social order or the organization in which we work.

However, as Blackmore (1989) and Calas and Smircich (1989) have pointed out, although in different ways, the reconstitution of hierarchy and the concommitant—and seemingly paradoxical—demand that everyone be the same is a subtle process. To Blackmore, theories about leadership are embedded in notions of how men should act and are based on men's experiences, whether they are trait or behavioral; there is no place for women other than as subordinate. To Calas and Smircich, leadership is based on the exclusion and repression of seduction, a denial of the female, which allows an exclusionary male-dominated form of leadership to stand defended. What exists in both analyses is the economy of the same: The coherence of leadership depends on the exclusion of women.

Although Brown attempts to rectify that exclusion by focusing on the notion of distributed leadership, because it continues to depend on the idea of power as sovereign, as fixed and therefore divisible into parts—distributed—her argument is undercut both by Foucault's notion of power everywhere and Irigaray's idea of the necessity of symbolizing women, that we might understand women as other than only the nurturing mother, that women might relate to each other not only as mothers and daughters, but in other ways in which men do not play a part. The skill of leading, shared among many, cannot overlook the necessity of creating new myths through which women might talk about leading in order to lead in ways that have not yet been thought.

I have argued that power operates to construct and reconstruct hierarchy in organizations through the construction of hierarchical relations among the different, not only as other than the same, but as lesser than the same. I believe that instead of the inevitable suppression of difference that is the outcome of hierarchical relations, difference as something other than lesser is possible only if difference is constructed as contiguity, or as difference side by side. Hierarchical relations in organizations, then, could not exist along with difference side by side; conversely, hierarchical relations in organizations will inevitably reconstruct difference as lesser. Organizing activities, including the activity of leading, that do not construct and reconstruct hierarchical relations are only possible if they are put into play by sexually specific subjects who exist in contiguity, side by side, where difference is symbolized rather than suppressed so that we may maintain the masquerade of the same. Contiguity also contains an inevitably political dimension, in that contiguous relations are not hierarchical. Just as contiguity is about difference in relational form without rank, without suppression, so can power be relational rather than hierarchical as it takes form in capillary-like networks, allegiances, alliances, enabling contiguous relations among people who are infinitely variable. Rather than denying difference, or privileging difference, we need to rethink difference if we are ever going to work together, where getting things done can be an actual goal rather than a mask for power held by a few.

NOTES

1. Unlike Derrida, Foucault does not see everything as discourse; he sees discourse, nondiscursive events, and effects. In terms of discourse, "power utilizes strategies for the production of truth and the disqualification of non-truths"; at the level of nondiscursive events, power establishes technologies "that inscribe themselves on the bodies and behaviors of subjects"; "at the level of events, power establishes programmes, forms of extraction of knowledge and information that help constitute at particular moments in time, overarching more global systems" (Grosz, 1990, p. 89).

2. For both Foucault and for Semler, I use that pronoun advisedly; neither of their analyses has a place for women.

REFERENCES

Bartky, S. L. (1990). *Femininity and domination*. New York: Routledge.
Blackmore, J. (1989). Educational leadership: A feminist critique and reconstruction. In J. Smythe (Ed.), *Critical perspectives in educational leadership* (pp. 93-129). New York: Falmer.
Brown, H. (1991). *Women organising*. London: Routledge.
Burrell, G. (1994). Modernism, postmodernism, and organizational analysis 4: The contribution of Jurgen Habermas. *Organization Studies, 15*(1), 1-20.

Calas, M. B., & Smircich, L. (1989, August). *Using the "F" word: Feminist theories and the social consequences of organizational research.* Paper presented to the Academy of Management annual meeting, Washington, DC.

Deveaux, M. (1994). Feminism and empowerment: A critical reading of Foucault. *Feminist Studies, 20,* 223-247.

Diamond, D., & Quinby, L. (Eds.). (1988). *Feminism and Foucault: Reflections on resistance.* Boston: Northeastern University Press.

Frug, M. (1992). *Postmodern legal feminism.* New York: Routledge.

Gross, E. (1986). Philosophy, subjectivity, and the body: Kristeva and Irigaray. In C. Pateman & E. Grosz (Eds.), *Feminist challenges: Social and political theory* (pp. 125-143). Sydney: Allen & Unwin.

Grosz, E. (1990). Contemporary theories of power and subjectivity. In S. Gunew (Ed.), *Feminist knowledges: Critique and construct* (pp. 59-120). London: Routledge.

Grosz, E. (1993). Bodies and knowledges: Feminism and the crisis of reason. In L. Alcoff & E. Potter (Eds.), *Feminist epistemologies* (pp. 187-215). London: Routledge.

Hekman, S. (1990). *Gender and knowledge: Elements of a postmodern feminism.* Cambridge, UK: Polity Press.

Hochschild, A. (1983). *The managed heart: The commercialization of human feeling.* Berkeley: University of California Press.

Jeffcutt, P. (1994). From interpretation to representation in organization analysis: Postmodernism, ethnography, and organisation symbolism. *Organization Studies, 15,* 241-274.

Jermier, J. M., & Clegg, S. R. (1994). Critical issues in organization science: A dialogue. *Organization Science, 5,* 1-13.

Said, E. (1978). *Orientalism.* New York: Random House.

Semler, R. (1993). *Maverick.* New York: Warner.

Smith, D. (1990). *The conceptual practices of power: A feminist sociology of knowledge.* Toronto: University of Toronto Press.

Stewart, P., & Drakich. J. (1994). *Employment equity in Canadian universities.* Canadian Association of University Teachers SWC Employment Equity Workshop, Vancouver, BC.

Thomas, R. (1991). *Beyond race and gender: Unleashing the power of your total workforce by managing diversity.* New York: Amacom, American Management Association.

Weedon, C. (1987). *Feminist practice and poststructuralist theory.* London: Basil Blackwell.

Whitford, M. (1991). *Luce Irigaray: Philosophy in the feminine.* London: Routledge.

Wright, E. (Ed.). (1992). *Feminism and psychoanalysis: A critical dictionary.* Oxford: Basil Blackwell.

The Unbearable Whiteness of Being

Reflections of a Pale, Stale Male

ROY JACQUES

I am man; hear me roar. My dream of providing a better living for a family has been blasted over the last 20 years by inflation, stagflation, Japan Incorporated, and the world economy. I have been plateaued, downsized, and reengineered into perdition. In corporate cubicles, well-paid trade and factory jobs, and the professions, my job is now reserved for a woman or person of color. The ideals of freedom, individual self-determination, and democracy that I learned in school are now attacked as a white, male, Western conspiracy to oppress others. My father fought Hirohito and Hitler and saved the world for democracy. My friends fought shadows in Vietnam and defended cheap gasoline in Kuwait. I try to help around the house and be sensitive to my wife's career in ways that hurt my own, but she complains about having to do the "emotional labor" and manage the relationship. She resents my not getting ahead *and* she resents my doing the hard work necessary to get ahead.

Pity me?

The above is autobiographical, not in a personal, but in a generational sense.[1] Straight white men are stigmatized for embodying the very beliefs socialized into us. As traumatic as it has been to begin to recognize that we are not people, but *white* people; not people, but *male* people; not people, but *Western American* or even *modern(ist)* people, we are still said to have taken too much and given too little. On the one hand, this is like lung cancer; the fact that cigarettes were sold to you as a good thing doesn't change the fact that you have the disease. On the other, in a white male world, if the white males are threatened, *everyone* suffers. As I send this manuscript off for review, the headline in the *San Francisco Chronicle* lying in my doorway trumpets the decision of the University of California system to eliminate affirmative action. In the words of governor and presidential wannabe, Pete Wilson, "The adoption of [these measures] says California's diversity should be achieved naturally rather than through preferences" (quoted in Yoachum & Epstein, 1995, p. 1). Naturally?

Throughout this chapter, I will speak of *dominance* and *marginality.* Some will object to these terms. I find them appropriate. By the dominant, I mean those who can look at their identity as fitting the social norm. By the marginal, I mean those who are judged with reference to their deviance from or conformity to another identity. As a straight white man, I find that the norms I encounter in terms of social expectations about the "good" scientist, the "good" manager, and so on conform closely to the norms of the identities within which I have been socialized. Were I a woman, gay, African American, and so on, learning to take a position in society would involve a cross-cultural experience of sorts, requiring that I learn to be judged by norms originating in a group different from mine. Tannen (1990) is referring to this difference when she makes the point that "conversation between women and men is cross-cultural communication" (p. 47). *Dominance need not—and most often does not—presume the conscious desire to dominate. The dominance resides in the structuring of social interaction.* We of dominant identities must stop confusing privilege with personal intention. Having been born with dominant identities is not an ethical issue. Failing to acknowledge the consequences of moving through society bearing these identities is.

This chapter has two primary goals. The first is to establish that diversity is a defining problem of managing in today's multicultural business environment, not merely a peripheral issue. The second is to identify some of the ways the "common sense" of day-to-day thinking functions to reinforce dominance and marginality. The focus is on structural, not individual issues. The concluding thought of the chapter is that we of dominant identities must actively work to identify and resist these dynamics, in part because social equity demands it, but also because, in a multicultural organizational world, such resistance is a defining problem of effective management. The following sections will

1. Use gender research as an example of what has been missed in diversity research.
2. Argue that dominant identities are indeed a form of privilege by debunking the logic of five commonly stated objections to that view.
3. Illustrate how common sense reinforces dominance and marginality by discussing a number of what I term *strategies of dismissal,* through which buried assumptions reinforce the dominant view as the only sensible possibility.

The concluding thought is that we of dominant identities are obligated to identify and resist the operation of this structural dominance in theory and practice. Although this chapter addresses the general dynamics of dominance and diversity, specific examples are mostly related to gender. This is an artifact of my having worked primarily with gender issues in my research. It is also related to the fact that, because women are a nonminority marginal identity, gender issues are somewhat more deeply integrated into the mainstream of academic theorizing and organizational practice than are other diversity issues.

IDENTITY POLITICS AND GENDER RESEARCH: THE UNREALIZED PROMISE OF THEORIZING DIVERSITY

This chapter will attempt to deal with some of the issues of straight white maleness with a degree of sympathy for what is, after all, my identity group, but without attempting to dodge our obligation to continue to work toward a social order that may make us even less comfortable than we are at the moment. Elsewhere in this book, Mark Maier will suggest that changing the social construction of masculinity may even benefit those in dominant positions. I agree, but I also recognize that change for the privileged, by definition, means giving up privilege. Whether such privilege was deserved or not, this will often be difficult; it will often seem unfair to those losing it, and there will be situations where what is gained does not compensate for what is lost, at least within the value system of those losing.

This has major implications for research and practice. Consider the example of gender and organizational theorizing. Within the mainstream of organizational studies, issues of gender have been narrowed to issues of women in management, reflecting its point of emergence in the 1960s. In the United States, an interest in blacks in management appeared in the research literature in the wake of equal opportunity legislation of the early 1960s. This was followed in the early 1970s by the coalescence of a women in management research stream (Calás & Jacques, 1988). As can be seen from recent reviews of the literature (cf, Powell, 1993), this research has continued to focus on (a)

TABLE 4.1 Possibilities for Gender Research

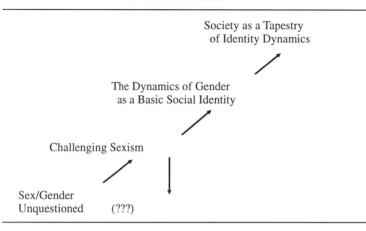

Society as a Tapestry
of Identity Dynamics

The Dynamics of Gender
as a Basic Social Identity

Challenging Sexism

Sex/Gender
Unquestioned   (???)

sex differences at the individual level and (b) women who manage.[2] This has left largely unexplored the areas of:

- Women in *non*management (the majority)
- Men as gendered organizational (and social) agents[3]
- The gendered quality of organizational norms and values
- The gendered quality of organizational *research* norms and values

If these issues were central themes of research on gender in organizations, it would be possible to understand that gender is not merely a form of inappropriate power exercised by individual men against women. It is a basic identity, pervasively shaping the structure of social reality.[4] As indicated in Table 4.1, one might hope this to be a step toward theorizing society as a tapestry of interacting social identities. The present danger, however, is that, having reached the level of criticizing sexism, public discourse will now retreat to denial of the role of gender. That is why we men cannot be permitted to declaim that if we are not personally and intentionally sexist, we are then neither gendered in any relevant way nor implicated in sexually oppressive interaction. Such a view is dangerously inadequate.

This is a specific case of the more general problem of valuing diversity. To my mind, the central shift represented by the emergence of diversity as an issue is that equal opportunity/affirmative action thinking merely expected women and minorities to bring different *bodies* to organizational life. Diversity thinking is an argument for bringing the *norms and values* of those bodies into the workplace, as well. This raises another level of resistance perhaps equivalent to that encountered by civil rights marchers in the United States, yet one that is less easy to identify. When white supremacy was defended by turning fire hoses and attack dogs on marchers in Selma, Alabama, the nation watched in horror. When the supremacy of white cultural *values* is defended by the appointment of a Clarence Thomas,[5] the implications are less clear; many would even consider it a step forward for African Americans. Similarly, recent years have witnessed the emergence of "feminists" such as Camille Paglia, Christina Hoff Sommers, and Katie Roiphe, whose feminism consists largely of bashing other feminists for the benefit of the media and to the advantage of the status quo (cf. Faludi, 1995).

This tension is reflected in research circles, as well. The central finding of women-in-management research is that there is not much difference between the sexes. Thus, a woman cannot be argued to be inherently inferior to a man. This supports progress women have made in gaining entry to formerly all-male positions in organizations, but it also bounds their condition of entry with the mandate that they not express any needs based socially or biologically on their experiences as women. Organizational reality can continue to be made up of "real men," male and female; only the faces change. To argue for difference based on identity threatens to undercut these gains. For the optimistic, arguing difference can be a way of challenging the norms and values of organizations. For the more skeptical, it can be a fast track back to the world of separate spheres, where women's experiences will be discovered to make them "naturally" suited for supporting and nurturing men.[6]

Similarly, most of the core values underlying organizational behavior and organizational development reflect a liberalism that (at least nominally, but often sincerely) values inclusion of diverse people but accepts as explicitly or tacitly universal an ontology of instrumental realism, an epistemology of individualist rationality, an explicit ethos of participative democracy, and an implicit ethos of organizational hierarchy.[7] Diversity arguments are doubly threatening to this position because it has positioned itself as a force for progressive thought. One cannot criticize it because it presumes to have *already* dealt with issues of identity. Proponents of diversity issues are likely to be characterized as unnecessarily politicizing debates for personal gain and as sowing unnecessary dissension.[8]

BUT ENOUGH ABOUT US;
LET'S TALK ABOUT ME

So, as a straight white male, what sense do I make of this? I am, frankly, uncomfortable in many ways with a diverse future. I grew up learning to be Ward

Cleaver.[9] I know how he responds to things. Dark skin does not automatically make me uncomfortable, but African American cultural values (be they a group of men on a street corner or interacting with an Afrocentric colleague) make me conscious of my whiteness, and I don't know what to do with that. People from other countries remind me of my provincialism. What can I know of global management when I speak one language and have lived in one national monoculture? How can I even dare to claim profeminist status when, after years of studying and trying to live feminist values, I can *articulate* the surprising amount of gender-typical baggage my wife and I carry into our disagreements, but have little ability to *change* it. I know that portraying women as available sex objects promotes patriarchal oppression; why is my visceral response to sexist advertising inconsistent with my espoused beliefs?

Dealing with these issues requires a sort of double consciousness. I have to stay in touch with my spontaneous feelings and to acknowledge their existence, but I don't have to value them and act on them. The converse of this experience has been discussed by Collins (1991) as the *outsider within* phenomenon of the marginal group member working within the dominant group. Perhaps I am talking about an *insider within* phenomenon of the dominant group member who both acknowledges that membership and attempts to deal openly and progressively[10] with the conflicts it creates. Engels, whose capitalist fortune subsidized the "specter haunting Europe," is one possible example of such a dual consciousness.

LISTENING TO THE OTHER

Female friends have sometimes asked me why so much of my personal work on gender has been informed by feminists and feminist theorizing—women speaking to women—rather than by men and the men's movement. My answer has been that feminists make me deal more scrupulously with my discomfort. Even if I focus on the element of the men's movement that is genuinely profeminist (don't even get me started on Robert Bly[11]), a group of men will, on the whole, push ourselves only as far as we are comfortable pushing. In a group of women, I must inquire as far as *they* expect me to go. I have not always found this immediately rewarding, but, on the whole, it has been growth inducing. It has also made me somewhat comfortable with patriarchy as something of which I am a part, but which does not make me a bad person. However, there is also a danger of identity denial. One feminist friend and colleague reacts with particular delight every time she catches me referring to men in the third person.

There is a paradigmatic aspect to this listening as well. As people coalesce around different identities, they do not simply develop different *positions* on the questions of the day, they also tend to ask different *questions,* and in different *ways.* For instance, in a recent doctoral seminar on gender and organizations, I asked students who had reviewed Powell (1993), a very good overview text on women in management, to take home one of my back issues of *Ms.* magazine to reflect on the question, what issues have been underrepresented or unrepresented in organizational gender research. Their general reaction was amazement at how little had been discussed in "the literature." Especially among the women, there was some preference voiced for both *Ms.*'s choice of topics and for their construction. For instance, what might be expressed in the organizational literature as a problem of mentoring might appear in *Ms.* as a problem of ethics and political identity—the price of advancement being conditioned on leaving one's identity group and its values behind.

This has also been impressed upon me in my studies of nursing. For several years, I struggled to be able to articulate the problems of that group in a way that would be validated by nurses themselves. By the time I had achieved this, however, I found that I could *only* talk to nurses about the issues important to me in that field. The assumptions of non-nurses about health, medicine, and the role of nursing diverged so fundamentally from those I had learned from nurses, that any question non-nurses posed had the form of the old cliché, are you still beating your wife. Without challenging the question, there is no possible way to offer a meaningful answer.

One of the benefits of listening to the Other is that this is necessary in order to look at diversity issues from a balanced perspective. We who fit the demographic profile expected of those in positions of authority can often be the victims of distorted expectations. It is as though you and I had gone for a very long time with me earning $8 and you earning $2 for the same job. If the balance were shifted to $7 and $3, I would still be inordinately privileged, but if my baseline were $8 and my life were adjusted to that baseline, I might see even the reduction from $8 to $7 as infringing on my rightful reward.

For instance, I was recently in a meeting with a middle-aged, white male senior executive of a West Coast computer company known in the industry for its progressive policies. He was seen as relatively progressive even within that environment. In fact, the meeting was about things he could do to expand opportunities for women. Before we got started, however, he wanted to share his frustration with the problems of being a white male today. His son, it seems, had not been able to get into medical school in California and had to matriculate at an Eastern school away from home and family. The executive paid lip service to diversity but noted that almost 40% of the student body at the desired school was Asian. Of course, this number is not surprising. The Asian population in

California is high, and Asian American families send their children to college at higher rates than do other Americans. In my area of the state, an entering class that was about 20% white and male would reflect the demographics of the area. But there is a more fundamental issue surfacing here: *The executive was not complaining that his son could not get into medical school, but that he could not get into the school of his choice.* Such is the sense of entitlement among those of us with dominant identities that we are likely to judge *any* failure to achieve our goals as evidence of structural inequity.

KEEPING A BALANCED PERSPECTIVE

The general fallacy from which this executive was reasoning is a tacit and seldom challenged assumption regarding dominant/marginal relationships in society. It has two components:

- The success or failure of the dominant group is judged by the incidence of failure within members of that group.
- The success or failure of the marginal group is judged by the incidence of success within members of that group.

Thus, it is considered a good thing that the number of women managers has grown to something like 40% in the last 30 years, even though this is still less than proportional representation and the 40% are clustered at junior levels.[12] It is seen as a good thing that two women and a black man sit on the Supreme Court, even though the panel is still predominantly white and male. Yet, it is considered evidence that the system is flawed, that affirmative action has gotten out of hand, when *anyone* offers an anecdote of a white male failing to get a job in a context sensitive to race, gender, or other identity issues. Among academics, it is easy to externalize this attitude as characteristic of the stereotyped "Joe six-pack," but this flies in the face of my experience. First of all, we professionals don't frequently talk to Joe six-pack (we talk *to* managers *about* him), so we have little idea what "he" is thinking. This blatant, but routine classism silences the many blue-collar stories of men who have wrestled with the difficulty of seeing their jobs downsized, globalized, or reengineered and while still resisting scapegoating women and minorities.[13]

More to the point is the readiness with which scapegoating can be found among the "enlightened." Last year, I became engaged in an E-mail debate regarding affirmative action in which more than one white male Ph.D. job seeker posted his story of not getting a job as evidence that an inordinate portion of positions were reserved for women and minorities. Note the logic operating here. Failure to get a job, in a market where there were several applicants for every available job, was the only data the author required to document "reverse discrimination." The implicit assumption this reflects is that there is injustice unless *every white male finds an appropriate job*. I applaud the ideal of a society that has a meaningful place for all its members, but I greatly doubt that this same criterion will be applied soon to women or minorities. We should also remember that, 30 years after Equal Employment Opportunity legislation, few U.S. management academics work in departments where the senior faculty are not at least 80% white and male. The barricades may have been breached, but they have hardly fallen. We who are white and male often forget this as we fall into one of several frequently voiced laments.

WHITE WHINE; IT'S INTOXICATING

I would like to briefly touch on five myths often expressed as verities by angry white males:

1. I'm not responsible for the past.
2. Every person deserves to be judged on his [*sic*] merits.
3. All the good jobs are now being held for women and minorities.
4. Qualified white males are being passed over for unqualified Others.
5. *I'm* not dominant; I'm just as powerless as you.

1. *I'm Not Responsible for the Past.* Quite true, but remember also that the past is not past. Past events trace a trajectory through the present whose intersection defines places of relative privilege and exclusion. Our lives are the medium through which these trajectories travel. We can sometimes influence them, but we are powerless to evade them. Slavery forms a context for black/white race relations in the United States; a century after its eradication, slavery shapes social action and social policy in a way incomprehensible to even our parent society, England. There, however, the Raj forms a context for race relations with immigrant Indians and Pakistanis dramatically different from the experiences of those groups in the United States.

The past conditions *expectations*; those who see themselves modeled in the media, who encounter their group in positions of authority, and who are socialized to take charge are more likely to do so. Those who see themselves defined as a problem are more likely to become one. The past conditions the *normal*. I can walk into a board room, a symposium, or a town meeting and the skills that will make me effective there are absolutely congruent with the skills socialized into me from birth as a member of the dominant culture. I have the skin color and sex people have been taught to associate with authority. I have also been given a sense of self that makes me most comfortable at the center of attention. Women and minorities may possess these skills, but only if they have become bicultural, since being a good member of their group and being an effective authority figure in the dominant culture are two separate scripts. And, of course, the past conditions how we are *received by others*. When I was a graduate student, teaching Introductory Organizational Behavior along with colleagues, some of whom were female, black, and Asian, I was continually struck by how much it aided my teaching to fit student expectations of what a management teacher looked like. While my friends spent much time fighting to achieve and to hang on to credibility, I had credibility by default unless I grossly defaulted on student expectations.

2. *Every Person Deserves to Be Judged on His [Sic] Merits*. Good point. If we accept this and look at the demographic distribution of people in positions of authority, two conclusions are possible. One is that straight white men are superior to others, because they (whoops, "we") have a disproportionate number of senior positions.[14] If one rejects this explanation (even most straight white men publicly claim only equality), the only alternative is that people are not being judged on their merits unless it is meritorious to be a straight white man. The status quo constitutes, in effect, "affirmative action for white men."[15]

What is difficult is that social policy must be made at an aggregate level, and this will indeed result in cases where qualified white men are passed over for jobs because they had the misfortune to need them at a time when the system was correcting for past injustices by hiring mostly or entirely women and minorities. Unfortunately, social policy cannot be judged by this criterion because *any* conceivable policy will result in injustice for some individuals. At the societal level, one can only minimize the aggregate damage and maximize the aggregate good. If we take seriously the claims of disenfranchised white males, what their complaints should direct us toward is not returning to affirmative action for the dominant, but questioning the pyramid logic of a social system where a few get satisfying and remunerative jobs, many get undesirable jobs, and a significant number have no place in the system at all. As long as this is the structure of the job market, a rhetoric of merit, work ethic, and individual achievement cannot effect *whether* injustice is done. It can only effect the *distribution* of injustice among society's constituent groups.

3. *All the Good Jobs Are Now Being Held for Women and Minorities*. Perhaps this has been occasionally true in a department of critical literary theory or in a civil service appointment where there are 1,000 applicants and three jobs, but there is ample evidence that the roughly 35% to 40% of the society who are straight, white, and male have at least 35% to 40% of the good jobs. It is easy to muster statistical evidence, but I think that would be a mistake. A Sommers (1994) could come along and endlessly defer interpretation with a pharisaical exegesis of methodological foibles. Rather, I say merely, *look around*. What sex/color is the police officer or fire fighter? Do you notice when the construction crew has even one woman on it? Is she the flag "man"? Count the race/sex of the next hundred people you see on the evening news. Is the only female senior manager in your company the head of human resources? Five years out of school, did the income of your graduating class rise as fast among the women as the men? Conversely, how many clerical workers in the office are women? Why are 97% of nurses female? Among the physicians who are women, why are there more, proportionately, in general practice than in surgery? What is the average income of white men ages 20 to 30 compared to women and minorities? Why does men's disposable income rise after divorce while women's plummets? Proportionately, are more people of color or more white people living in poverty? Who takes care of the vast majority of single-parent children, men or women?

4. *Qualified White Males Are Being Passed Over for Unqualified Others*. Do you have solid evidence that the women and minorities selected are unqualified? This question boils down once again to the logic that there should be a place guaranteed in society for every qualified white man, but others can compete for what's left. When an individual loses credibility, he or she must win it back over time; this is equally true of societies. The evidence prior to the 1970s suggests that when the only criterion for jobs was merit, those seen to have merit were overwhelmingly straight (or closeted), white, and male. To accept this as an adequate explanation is no less an act of white male supremacy than is joining a skinhead group. Classism gives this form of hate-group behavior a veneer of respectability, but to accept the perpetuation of structural violence is not ethically superior to skull cracking. At least, Aryan Nation provides a concrete enemy to honestly oppose.

5. *I'm Not Dominant; I'm Just as Powerless as You.* In an excellent and widely cited article entitled "White Privilege: Unpacking the Invisible Knapsack," McIntosh (1990) writes of her racial identity as "an invisible package of unearned assets that I can count on cashing in each day" (p. 31). These include such easily taken for granted privileges as being able to live in any neighborhood one can afford, not being followed or harassed as a potential thief[16] when shopping, and seeing one's race represented widely in the news media. There are certainly straight white men less powerful than Colin Powell, Oprah Winfrey, or Barbara Walters, but this may not be the best way to frame the question. I would ask, *given your present circumstances,* would it assist or hinder you to be a woman and/or person of color? Apart from the relatively rare circumstance of a job being awarded to a person based on marginal identity, in the overwhelming preponderance of social situations, it is advantageous to be seen as straight, white, and male.

This was pointed out to me in a very effective, if poorly monitored, experiential exercise. While I was walking to a professional meeting in Santa Fe, two men in a car attempted to start a conversation by yelling: "hey faggot!" I avoided eye contact and ignored the remarks that followed. Somehow, correcting them on the error of their observation seemed a secondary issue. Between that encounter and my arrival at the conference hotel, the world was a changed place for me. What had been a charming city became a threatening landscape and a pleasant walk became a gauntlet. I was most impressed by my sense of helplessness. Unless I could beat up two larger and stronger men, I was on my own. I know that nobody gets too upset by a little fag bashing. What I realized during that walk, which has powerfully remained with me, is that if I were gay, a woman, or any person who is casually accepted as the legitimate butt of such encounters, *my whole life would be lived within this hostile reality.* It would change my perspective on everything. Perhaps being straight, white, and male is not an advantage, but if so, being anything else is a distinct *dis*-advantage. My sense that I am free to walk in the world is, itself, a privilege.

STRATEGIES OF DISMISSAL:
TOWARD THEORIZING IDENTITIES AND DIVERSITY

In Table 4.1, I suggested that if gender research were rescued from the current backlash danger, it might be used as a vehicle for understanding gender as a basic social identity and, eventually, for moving toward a more general theoretical understanding of social subjectivity as a tapestry of interacting identities. As a small step in that direction, I would like to look at one aspect of social common sense through which privilege and marginality operate. I call the processes I will present here strategies of dismissal. Although I have been keeping a list of these strategies for several years, it is far from complete. Much could be done to expand and refine these concepts in future work. I invite you, the reader, to seize the opportunity.

What is a strategy of dismissal? It is a linguistic convention whose taken-for-grantedness permits it to function as though it were a neutral, or even laudable, reflection of competent thinking, but which also contains embedded cultural assumptions that act to reinforce the values of the dominant and to devalue the marginal. The most insidious aspect of these strategies is that they operate within common sense. Thus, their effects are not available for scrutiny or discussion. Those who benefit from their operation frequently use them unreflectively, perhaps believing that they are merely thinking "clearly," or rationally. Even those who are marginalized by their action may often take for granted the logic through which they are dismissed.

For this reason, I thought seriously about the appropriateness of calling these tropes strategies. Can one be executing a strategy unconsciously? Would *dynamics of dismissal* be a more appropriate term? Perhaps. This is a matter for further debate. My provisional choice to retain the term strategy rests on the observation that even if these are not conscious strategies, they can be, and the choice to use them or not should be a decision one makes rather than a result of habit. The term strategy reminds us that, whether desired or not, our use of these tropes is a value and power-laden activity. There are alternatives to using them, and there are consequences. Table 4.2 lists the strategies of dismissal I will discuss in this chapter.

1. Dismissive Naming

Would any sensible person give credence to "a motley crew of post-Marxists, radical feminists, and other 'antis' . . . [including the] new nihilists, 'the Deconstructionists'!" (Drucker, 1993, p. 211)? What is the difference between a religion and a cult? Between a freedom fighter and a terrorist? The words with which we name things are not mere labels. They contain embedded values that do much to determine our reactions to that which is named. Based on recent popular media reporting, I have decided that I must be a victimizing, radical, lesbian, feminazi—odd identities for a white male heterosexual. When did it become incorrect to be politically correct? There is a logical inconsistency here that is masked by unexamined common sense.

TABLE 4.2 Strategies of Dismissal

1. Dismissive naming
2. Dismissal as self-evidently wrongheaded
3. Reference to a presumed objective reality
4. Pseudo-middle ground
5. Dichotomize-and-dismiss
6. Red herring
7. Semantic eclipse
8. Slippery-slope theory
9. Empirical filibuster
10. The "necessity defense"
11. Egalitarian fallacy
12. Maximization fallacy
13. Hearsay fallacy
14. Reliability fallacy
15. Consistency fallacy
16. Everyone-can't-do-that fallacy
17. Clarity fallacy
18. Laissez-fairness
19. Excellence fallacy
20. Inoculation/ Seeing the "good" Other
21. Invisibility or valuation of flaws of the dominant

My current favorite is the label *victimizing feminist.* This is effective as a term for disempowering whoever is tarred with such a label, but it has an even more pernicious effect. Many women, understandably reluctant to label themselves as victims, distance themselves from positions labeled as victimizing. As a result, they agree to compete without special favor in a system in which men start with many advantages. The effect of the label is that *systemic inequality* is invisibly protected and strengthened.

Imagine that I am in a meeting to discuss affirmative action. As a white male, my identity group is already disproportionately represented in the most highly compensated positions. Still, I am further insulated by a rhetoric in which maintaining the status quo is defended with terms such as *fairness, merit,* and *promotion based on qualifications.* Nobody identifies the status quo as affirmative action for white males, even though demographic data show it to be just that. Those seeking to advance the interests of women and people of color will have to survive a rhetorical handicap of being labeled advocates of "special treatment." To brand their views "PC" or feminist is as good as to disqualify them. Meanwhile, there is no equivalent brush with which to tar me. I need not fight against these advocates in order to protect the system that will give me disproportionate opportunity. It is sufficient that I permit the asymmetrically value-laden terms of debate to operate without my active resistance.

2. Dismissal as Self-Evidently Wrongheaded

In casual and formal discourse, some things are presumed true until shown to be false. Other things are presumed false until shown true. But proof is a scarce commodity. The presumption of falsity or truth is seldom reversed. But by what mechanism does an idea's truth value receive this provisional acceptance or rejection? Belief in the self-evidently wrongheaded nature of certain beliefs may be a necessary element of sense making in that it helps one simplify the overwhelming surplus of interpretations social life offers. The problem is that when combined with power asymmetries, the prejudices of the dominant group become the prejudices of public discourse in general. For instance, in a recent *New Yorker* article entitled "PC Cheesecake," Wolcott (1992) writes, "According to Naomi Wolf's 'The Beauty Myth' (which I intend to read someday), women feel tyrannized by these stick-figure space zombies with pouting lips and pouting breasts" (p. 117).

Because he expresses a dominant view, Wolcott can offer his ignorance of the book as support for his views—dismissing in caricature an argument he admits to not knowing. Similarly, the poet Nuala Ní Dhomhnaill (1995), who writes in the Irish language, recently wrote of encountering a fellow Irish citizen whose disparaging manner toward the official, but minority language of the Irish state convinced her that he "obviously thought it was an accomplishment to be ignorant of it" (p. 3). Try using this logic to dismiss *Administrative Science Quarterly.*[17] Yet, when women criticize men, when people of color criticize Anglo culture, when the postcolonial world criticizes the West—even when critical organizational theorists criticize the narrowly held dominant views of neopositivist scientism—the first requirement of the critic is that she or he be able to show comprehensive knowledge of that which she or he intends to challenge. The truths of the marginal can only be voiced within the reality of the dominant.

Or consider reactions to the recent book, *The Bell Curve* (Herrnstein & Murray, 1994). Measured differences between racial groups are cited, but what those differences mean is predetermined by one's basic assumptions. Those willing to accept difference will view this as evidence of that difference. Those believing in the basic equality of all human groups will question the methods and attribute any remaining difference to social inequity. Note the passivity of the data. It willingly serves any master. This condition also informs my position on inherent differences between people of differing identities. For instance, I am resistant to explanations of gender difference grounded in biology, not because I doubt such differences exist, but because the "objective" interpretation of these differences within a patriarchal society has consistently been to the detriment of women's social position and the aggrandizement of masculine norms (cf., Ehrenreich & English, 1978). More or better data will not contribute to a resolution of issues such as these. This is a problem of politics and power with which research is inextricably linked. Until an environment of equal voice can be created between dominant and marginal parties to the debate, open inquiry into the existence, sources, and consequences of difference will be restricted.

3. Reference to a Presumed Objective Reality

The marginal cannot use "let's get realistic" as a communication strategy. On the other hand, if one is in a dominant position the appeal to common sense can dismiss an argument without a hearing. Debates abound with terms such as "the reality is . . . ," "realistically . . . ," and "let's get real here . . . ," but if one digs into situations with an open mind, one invariably finds that what may constitute reality is by no means clear. For instance, in some recent consulting, I have noticed senior executives attempting to bound discussion of glass ceiling and work\family issues with the disclaimer, "we have to be realistic"—but everyone's reality differs from everyone else's. Reality *would* be important to heed if it were discernible. Because we do not know what it is, realism boils down to accepting the biases of the most powerful participant.

4. Pseudo-Middle Ground

Several years ago, I participated in a conference panel in which a man and a woman presented a paper suggesting that men and women are equally responsible for gender problems. The presenter (the man) appeared intent to acknowledge men's share of the responsibility in this area. To his surprise, the mostly female audience attacked the paper in an exchange that became very emotional on both sides. What the paper had failed to account for in claiming male responsibility was *asymmetric power* and *past gains*. Men may not be inherently worse than women, but our more prominent social position permits our failings to do more damage than women's failings do. Past dominance means that the positions in society are already filled predominantly with men. This both limits opportunities for women and creates the likelihood that the opinion of the average manager, average scientist, average legislator, and so on will correspond to the opinion of the average *male* in that position. For we who reap the passive benefits of dominant identity-group membership, *sharing* responsibility is not enough. We must accept the *preponderance* of the responsibility. Women, to paraphrase Chairman Mao, do not hold up half the sky. They hold up the sky, period. We men move around under it, calling our actions his-story. One cannot change history, but if we of the dominant groups accept its passive gifts (and this is unavoidable), we must accept accountability for the inequity that produced them.

5. Dichotomize-and-Dismiss

There is a basic two-step movement in the dance of modern Western knowledge. The first step is to simplify a complex situation into two functional (not necessarily logical) opposites. The second step is to dismiss the validity of one option, leaving the other as the only reasonable option, belief, or course of action. When the Soviet empire imploded in the late 1980s, this news was widely interpreted in the American press as a victory of democracy over communism. We were doing the two-step. Raised on the rhetoric of the Cold War, many Americans can actually imagine only two political systems. One pole is the parliamentary-bureaucratic Western system often confused with democracy. The other is the (not so) opposite state party-bureaucratic system often confused with communism. The plethora of other options existing in countries around the world are unknown and thus unsuspected. The failure of one system is not a vindication of the other unless those two are the only possible options, but such thinking protects the Western status quo by deflecting debate from the successes and failures of that system in its own right.

One way I have seen this in operation is when executives back away from gender and work/family issues with the disclaimer that "there are no final solutions to these problems." Perhaps, but does this preclude attempting to take a step in the direction of improvement? This is the reductio ad absurdum version of dichotomizing and dismissing—because the extreme is unattainable, it is useless to try to move at all.

Another example of this thinking comes from a sales team with which I have worked. The goal of the discussions was to envision a new model for the sales process in an environment where profit margins are decreasing, material and human resources are being reduced, and sales goals are being raised, but where new virtual office technologies also permit new ways of working. What pre-vented new thinking in this situation was dichotomize-and-dismiss logic that directed the group to focus on one piece of the current model at a time and to explain—in terms of the current model—why it could not be changed. Thus, the fact that no individual piece of the current model could be changed prevented recognition that in an entirely new model, the piece would have very different constraints. A system that currently favors male sales people and seriously unbalanced work/family lives was thus "shown" to be a necessity.

6. Red Herring

The basic move of this trope is to credit or discredit something that has been substituted for the underlying issue. Any academic who has been exposed to debates regarding the "validity" of qualitative research has encountered a red herring strategy of dismissal. More than 15 years ago, Morgan and Smircich (1980) warned the field that the issues of contention in the paradigm debates were not centered on method but on more fundamental differences regarding assumptions about reality, truth, and core social values. Despite constant reit-eration of this point in the ensuing years, it is still widely believed that one can resolve this disagreement by showing the compatibility of qualitative and quantitative methods (cf, Hunt, 1994)—which *any* trained researcher knows is not a problem to begin with.

How might this operate with respect to gender? One subtle shift is the substitution of glass-ceiling issues for more complex issues of gender dynamics. Focusing on *either* the progress or lack of progress made by women in achieving representation within the status quo makes it more difficult to question the status quo itself. Thus, two decades of research have centered on women (but not men) in management (only), with little attention being given to the gendered aspects of organizational practices themselves. This parallels a red herring dynamic of first-wave U.S. feminism. The Seneca Falls convention of 1848 produced a mani-festo questioning the patriarchal structuring of society. As the century wore on, this radical energy was gradually co-opted into the red herring issue of suffrage, so that, when women won the vote, a total victory for women was declared by society, despite the fact that its patriarchal structure had survived nearly intact.

7. Semantic Eclipse

In a lunar eclipse, observers on Earth see a small body blocking the view of a much larger one. In a semantic eclipse, a relatively small subset of

meanings comes to block sight of a broader set of potential meanings.
For instance, when a mode of rationality normative to Western culture,
masculine behavior, and the modern era is simply called rationality, the
only category remaining for the reasoning of other cultures, women, and
other historical periods is *ir*rationality or *non*rationality. Only a small area of
the domain of rational behavior is visible; the rest is eclipsed by it.

Roy Jacques (1996, p. 159)

Examples of semantic eclipse supporting white masculine norms are pervasive. If the mode of thought valorized by the dominant results in a failure to
consider multiple options, this is clarity. What is left for thinking that is more
appreciative of ambiguity and complexity except to be unclear? A logic is simply
called logic, leaving no room for other logics. A reality is simply called reality,
and so forth. Semantic eclipse creates the equally unfortunate options for the
marginal of accepting the dominant definition of the world or appearing to be
reasoning poorly. Either way, an alternative mode of understanding is discredited without having been heard.

In the interests of brevity, I will simply give a brief description and an
example of the following strategies of dismissal:

8. Slippery-Slope Theory

One cannot change at all because one cannot change to the extreme. *If we let
people leave work whenever they say they have a problem with their kids, they'll
never be at work.*

9. Empirical Filibuster

This is the "show us the data" defense; despite the fact that no social
phenomena are ever proven or disproven (do cigarettes cause cancer? Ask the
Tobacco Institute). What *hard* evidence is there that fear of sexual harassment
limits women in this company? How do we *know* that having a stay-at-home
spouse is an asset for reaching top management?

10. Hearsay Fallacy

This is the opposite of the empirical filibuster. It dismisses existing data as
hearsay, "soft," or otherwise not valid. This is what Christina Hoff Sommers and
Katie Roiphe have done with women's stories of sexism, harassment, and rape

(cf, Faludi, 1995). If 25% of my female friends were really being raped, wouldn't I know it? Her samples were inadequate and not randomized; the data were anecdotal; the study failed to control for [fill in the blank]; experts question the design.

11. The "Necessity Defense"

We have no choice; it's the market, the environment, reality. Diversity and affirmative action are good ideas, but in our downsizing and reengineered environment, the *reality* is they're too expensive.

12. Egalitarian Fallacy[18]

If we can't act on objective truth, any value statement is as valid as any other. What do you mean women's realities? I'm open to others' opinions as long as they can express them clearly and logically.

13. Maximization Fallacy

Blind striving to maximize one criterion instead of balancing all criteria. We have to be open to the issues of women and minorities, but we also have to be responsible to the shareholders; our job is to maximize ROI.

14. Reliability Fallacy

To avoid the hearsay fallacy argument, phenomena must be dependably repeatable. Thus, anything that can be construed as idiosyncratic can be dismissed. Yes, my secretary needs our child-care programs, but she's unusual. Marilyn was offered a vice presidency and had to refuse for personal reasons, but she's the only example I can think of.

15. Consistency Fallacy

Those upholding the status quo are judged more leniently than those fighting for progressive change. If I espouse self-interest and am inconsistent, it means I have been caught in a selfless act. This is inconsistent, but only adds to my stature as a credible person. If I espouse the interests of others, it is another story. The alleged affairs of Martin Luther King, Jr., are used to discredit his efforts on behalf of racial justice. Paul De Man's anti-Semitism as expressed in the

1940s was used to discredit his work against the dominant canon of Western knowledge in the 1980s.

16. Everyone-Can't-Do-That Fallacy

This trope has two steps. The first is interpreting equity narrowly to mean giving the same thing to everyone, regardless of their varying needs. The second is imagining a scenario in which everyone actually receives it. We can't permit managers who are single parents the option of job sharing; what if all our managers job-shared?

17. Clarity Fallacy

Clarity can mean one has thought one's position through thoroughly. It can also mean one has artificially eliminated counter opinions, ambiguity, and contradiction. Women in this culture, and males or females of many other cultures, are socialized to think and speak in a more diffuse manner appreciative of multiple interpretations and ambiguity. To require clarity as a condition of credibility is to permit the system to force these people to speak in the terms in which I was socialized as an American white male—the bias of my interest group becomes an "objective" criterion of goodness.

18. Laissez-Fairness

Equality of opportunity is interpreted to mean lack of interference. This assumes a level playing field to begin with, an assumption that is often not met with women and minorities. We just want to judge people on their merits. The marginal are often co-opted into accepting this view: I just want to be judged on my merits.

19. Excellence Fallacy

Speaking to a college undergraduate audience at the University of Massachusetts a few years ago, the African American scholar Stella Nkomo was challenged with the allegation that there are opportunities today for African American men and women who excel. Her response did not challenge this observation but instead reframed the question. What she was waiting to see, she said, was a society in which there were opportunities for *mediocre* men and women of color, as there are opportunities for mediocre white men. To display a few prominent women and minorities in an organization as evidence of diversity constitutes an illustration of this fallacy in action.

20. Inoculation/Seeing the "Good" Other

Many business school departments have a "house radical" who dissents, but not vehemently enough to rock the boat. Meanwhile, his or her presence creates the image that dissent is fostered and prevents the emergence of more vigorous and effective dissent. The person who carries appropriate demographic traits (race, gender, ethnicity, etc.) while embodying the dominant cultural values is an effective inoculation against people who refuse to leave their culture at the door.

21. Invisibility or Valuation
of Flaws of the Dominant

Are you a workaholic? You can brag about it in *Fortune* magazine. Did you neglect your family while working obsessively on a book? You can put it into the acknowledgments, and it will reinforce your stature with most business readers. A female friend and I once spent a conference lunch trying to think of words for flaws typical of men in organizations, and every one we could come up with sounds like a compliment (he doesn't take any s**t; he always has to get his way). Conversely, any word stereotyped as feminine—words connoting domesticity or emotion—are insulting to men *or* women[19] (she's so nurturing). *So what?*

Why bother to identify these tropes? Because the first step in addressing power differences is to *name power as power*. As a straight white middle-class American male, I do not have to assert myself to claim privilege relative to others in similar circumstances. I need merely permit the operation of business-as-usual. Both formal knowledge and informal common sense will operate to create a world within which those who get ahead are those equipped with values and skills congruent with my identity groups. This does not guarantee my success, but it gives me an advantage. The "good" manager, the good consultant or technical expert, and the good citizen all exhibit qualities I do not have to relearn as an adult because they have been hard-wired into me by my socialization; an illustration of this asymmetry formulated by Jacobson and Jacques (1990) is given in Table 4.3. True, identity is not destiny—I could never be as much of a "real man" as Maggie Thatcher—but it goes very deep. For instance, my wife and I both consider ourselves to be somewhat cross gender-identified in terms of our values and personas. We have also done much work to resist falling into

TABLE 4.3 Gender Values and the Values of Science

Stereotypic Male/Masculine Characteristics	Characteristics of "Good" Science	Stereotypic Female/ Feminine Characteristics
Independent/Individuated/ Autonomous Self	Atomism/ Reductionism	Dependent "self-in-connection"
Unemotional/Objective	Objectivity	Emotional/Intuitive
Analytical/ Math-science skills	Statistical power/Hypothesis testing	Interpretive/"story telling"
Dominant	Validity (Control)	Submissive
Logical/Rational	Inductive/Deductive cycle	Expressive/Nonlinear
Decisive	True/False judgments	Sensitive to complexity/Feelings
Ambitious/"gets ahead"	Progress/Cumulation of knowledge	Supportive/Nurturing
Leader	Rigor/Supremacy of scientific knowledge	Follower
Global/Worldly	Generalizability	Context sensitive
Abstract	Parsimony/Elegance, universality	Concrete

SOURCE: Jacobson & Jacques (1990).
NOTE: Please note that this chart is not intended to represent the way men and women are, or should be. On those questions, there is immense disagreement. We are representing what most people believe constitutes dominant, Anglo-American social expectations regarding appropriate female and male behavior. It is these social norms, not individual views or traits, we wish to compare.

traditional gender roles. Nonetheless, we can open Tannen's (1990) *You Just Don't Understand* at random and there is about a 90% probability we will identify in a gender-appropriate way with the male-female communication dynamics being described.

TOWARD ACTION: "UNFREEZING" IDENTITY DEBATES AND DIVERSITY WORK

Table 4.1 noted the danger that instead of moving toward a diverse future, organizational life might regress in the direction of entrenched but outdated gender roles. To date, the bulk of gender research has been driven by women and the bulk of race research by people of color. White men are present, but underrepresented. Only a few years ago, I attended an Academy of Management session on race and gender and found myself the only white male in the room.

In other forums, I am part of the problem. For instance, I am a participant in a small E-mail network that espouses resistance to racism and sexism, but this is easier said than done. We still find the exchanges dominated by about a quarter of the participants—mostly white males. A part of this problem is a failure to recruit diverse members, but even where diversity is represented, as it is with gender, the dynamics are difficult to change. It is a start to acknowledge this situation's existence and power-ladenness and to engage in dialogue about how to change it, but that is a small and inadequate step.

We who experience social life from dominant positions—male, straight, white, dominant culture, middle class, middle age—must come to better understand that the problem is structural as well as personal. Of course, it is a personal ethical imperative not to discriminate against individuals based on work-irrelevant criteria, but this is not nearly enough. Conversely, when others point to the existence of asymmetrical power and voice, relative privilege and marginality, or even outright oppression, we must learn not to personalize the charge (yes, we have sometimes been inappropriately stigmatized by the marginal. So what? cf, the Consistency Fallacy above). Even if every individual were to root out his or her discriminatory attitudes and behaviors, *systemic* factors would still result in our society being deeply skewed in favor of those possessing dominant identities. Critics of this structural problem are not reflecting on my goodness as a person or on my masculinity.[20] I must accept that, as a producer of research, as an organization member, and as a citizen, *to fail to resist these systemic forces is as much an act of dominance as is face-to-face discrimination.* The following are some of the points I try to bear in mind:

- I *am* responsible for history; the past acts through me and everyone else in every social interaction.
- The problem is primarily and pervasively systemic.
- There is no position outside of power; objectivity is as political a stance as advocacy.
- The misfortune of one white man is not evidence of injustice in the system.
- I am not a bad person because I passively receive privilege, but it is a moral and ethical act to fail to question and resist that privilege.

- There is no final solution, but there is the possibility of making things incrementally better or worse.
- If there is a problem, those with more power have more responsibility, regardless of what we have done or not done to produce the problem.
- What I will learn about myself and about others is a valuable area of growth closed to me unless I accept and work with these issues.
- The journey is endless. I will always have to work with my socialized baggage; I will always embody my ideals imperfectly.
- Most women and minorities do not expect me to have finished this work; they will usually be supportive of the fact that it is occurring at all.

It would be fatuous to close this chapter acknowledging only the win-win aspect of diversity. Change involves pain. Giving up privilege cannot always be construed as a gain, even if the privilege was bestowed passively and inappropriately in the first place. But, unless I can sustain the myth that I am inherently superior to the marginal, I have to admit that I have more than my share of social space. This is an ethical issue, a pragmatic issue of organizational effectiveness, and an issue of personal growth and development.

Ward Cleaver is dead.

NOTES

1. The "generation" old enough not to worry about acne and young enough not to worry about Alzheimer's.

2. McQuarrie (1992) provides a trenchant critique of this narrow focus.

3. Collinson (1992) is a rare example of research that, although conducted in an all-male environment, continually notes the ways that enacting masculinity shapes the values and behaviors of the men studied.

4. This conceptualization parallels the narrow and minimally useful way *power* has been operationalized in organization studies as the conscious action of Individual A against Individual B. Hardy (1989) provides a review and critique of this attitude and suggests the value of considering more comprehensive theories of power as a pervasive social force. I find the work of Foucault valuable in this respect.

5. A conservative, African American U.S. Supreme Court justice.

6. The implications of this conflict for gender research are discussed in Jacobson and Jacques (1990).

7. Many would argue that they are antihierarchical, but they are generally content to argue merely for *less* hierarchy. The role of managers as the constituency to whom one speaks remains unquestioned. Anarchist theorizing, labor process theorizing, and workplace democracy continue to be marginalized as radical. On the cultural and historical specificity of "universal" management values, compare Jacques (1996).

8. Although I do not have a convenient citation for this comment, it reflects numerous recent experiences I have had within academic professional societies and is certainly easy to encounter firsthand.

9. Father figure on the 1950s television sitcom *Leave It to Beaver,* an icon of postwar suburban normativeness.

10. Those who question modernity may object to terminology valorizing progress, but I am at a loss for a better term to signify movement in a direction one considers an improvement over the status quo. It is in no way intended to support the modernist ideal of the progressive perfectibility of society.

11. Under the nominal label of profeminist values, Bly and the movement he inspires attempt to recapture an increasingly irrelevant warrior, "red in tooth and claw," who is prepared for (admittedly metaphorical) combat. In so doing, this ideology perpetuates worse-than-industrial sex roles, harking back to a man-the-hunter/woman-the-gatherer past that may never have existed in that form to begin with (cf. Gimbutas, 1987; Moore, 1988). What would be more useful in today's world is a man whose masculinity can be constructed in a manner that makes it central to his identity to be relational in ways that have been stereotyped as feminine, but that more closely reflect the dynamics of masculine relationships in professional/postindustrial economies than does a warrior mythos. Such a mythos implicitly gives men permission to value aggression, individuation, and "heroic" thinking—all qualities we should work to *de*-emphasize. Our heroes should not be those who went to war, but those who stayed behind to make a home in a war-torn world.

12. The now-familiar glass ceiling is once again headline news in the wake of a report that "at a time when more than half of the nation's master's degrees are awarded to women, 95% of the senior-level managers in the Fortune 1000 industrial and Fortune 500 companies are men, and 97% of them are white" (Swoboda, 1995, p. A-9).

13. It requires little imagination to see why academic experts, whose lunch is bought by senior managers, might find it expedient to permit the flourishing of a myth that focuses the worker on the dangers posed by coworkers rather than promote a myth that credits the disappearance of jobs to senior management policies.

14. And let's not raise the "change takes time" argument. The average tenure of Fortune 500 or *Business Week* 1000 chief executive officers is less than the 30 years since equal opportunity became the law of the land in the United States, and a negligible number of these individuals are women or minorities. The average income of women relative to men is stagnant at roughly 70%. About 5% to 10% of the population is gay or lesbian. How many openly gay or lesbian managers do you personally know?

15. I thank CSPP student Renato Almanzor for this phrase.

16. I recently saw an article in which the African American movie star Denzel Washington stated that this still happens to him, despite his commercial success.

17. I regularly encounter this in "discussions" with mainstream colleagues who dismiss my views in caricature, saying, "I don't know anything about philosophy (poststructuralism/feminism, etc.), but . . . ," then proceed to explain why my position could not possibly make sense even though they have just professed not to understand it. Simultaneously, their self-professed ignorance of the philosophy of empiricism, which would explain the limitations of their position as described by adherents of that position, functions to bolster their argument by removing from discussion anything that might constrain it with knowledge.

18. This term and concept are elaborated in an essay by Smith (1987).

19. For a discussion of the absence of language to represent work coded as feminine, and the role of that absence in the devaluing of relational work in organizations, compare Fletcher (1993).

20. I think it says something about the inappropriately fragile nature of masculinity that there is no feminine equivalent to the word *emasculate*. Is femininity a condition, but masculinity an achievement? Why do we fear loss of this dubious achievement?

REFERENCES

Calás, M. B., & Jacques, R. (1988, August). *Diversity or conformity: Research by women on women in organizations.* Paper presented at the Seventh Annual Conference on Women and Organizations, Long Beach, CA.

Collins, P. H. (1991). *Black feminist thought: Knowledge, consciousness, and the politics of empowerment.* London: Routledge.

Collinson, D. L. (1992). *Managing the shopfloor: Subjectivity, masculinity, and workplace culture.* Berlin: de Gruyter.

Dhomhnaill, N. N. (1995, January 8). Why I choose to write in Irish, The corpse that sits up and talks back. *New York Times Book Review,* pp. 3, 27.

Drucker, P. F. (1993). *Post-capitalist society.* New York: Harper Business.

Ehrenreich, B., & English, D. (1978). *For her own good: 150 years of experts' advice to women.* New York: Anchor Doubleday.

Faludi, S. (1995). I'm not a feminist, but I play one on TV. *Ms., 5*(5), 31-39.

Fletcher, J. (1993). *Toward a theory of relational activity in organizations: A feminist reconstruction of "real" work.* Unpublished doctoral dissertation, Boston University.

Gimbutas, M. (1987). *The language of the goddess: Images and symbols of old Europe.* New York: Van der Marck.

Hardy, C. (1989). *What do we really mean by power and politics? A review of the literature.* Paper presented at the Academy of Management annual meetings, Washington, DC.

Herrnstein, R. J., & Murray, C. (1994). *The bell curve: The reshaping of American life by differences in intelligence.* New York: Free Press.

Hunt, S. H. (1994). On the rhetoric of qualitative methods: Toward historically informed argumentation in management inquiry. *Journal of Management Inquiry, 3*(3), 221-234.

Jacobson, S. W., & Jacques, R. (1990). *Of knowers, knowing and the known: A gender framework for revisioning organizational and management scholarship.* Paper presented at the annual meeting of the Academy of Management, San Francisco.

Jacques, R. (1996). *Manufacturing the employee: Management knowledge from the 19th to 21st centuries.* London: Sage.

McIntosh, P. (1990, Winter). White privilege: Unpacking the invisible knapsack. *Independent School,* pp. 31-36. (Reprinted from *Peace and Freedom,* July/August 1989)

McQuarrie, F. A. E. (1992). *Elitism or diversity?: "Women in management" reconsidered.* Paper presented at the Academy of Management annual meeting, Miami.

Moore, H. L. (1988). *Feminism and anthropology.* Minneapolis: University of Minnesota Press.

Morgan, G., & Smircich, L. (1980). The case for qualitative research. *Academy of Management Review, 5*(4), 491-500.

Powell, G. (1993). *Women and men in management.* Newbury Park, CA: Sage.

Smith, B. H. (1987). Value without truth-value. In J. Fekete (Ed.), *Life after postmodernism: Essays of values and culture.* New York: St. Martin's.

Sommers, C. H. (1994). *Who stole feminism?* New York: S&S Trade.

Swoboda, F. (1995, November 26). Most senior-level managers still white, male, panel finds. *San Francisco Chronicle,* p. A-9.

Tannen, D. (1990). *You just don't understand: Women and men in conversation.* New York: William Morrow.

Wolcott, J. (1992, October 5). P.C. cheesecake. *The New Yorker,* pp. 117-118.

Yoachum, S., & Epstein, E. (1995, July 21). UC scraps affirmative action: Regents' vote gives Wilson major victory. *San Francisco Chronicle,* p. 1.

Class Discipline

IR/HR and the Normalization of the Workforce

RICHARD MARSDEN

This chapter questions the "diversity" of the workplace approach by rethinking the concept of class. This is done by exploring the similarities between the work of Michel Foucault and Edward Thompson. Challenging the belief that Marxian and Foucauldian social theory are fundamentally incompatible, the chapter argues that far from being a "retreat from class" (Meikins-Wood, 1986; Miliband & Panitch, 1990; Palmer, 1990), Foucault's work provides the means of understanding in greater detail "the way the machine [of class] works . . . the friction of interests—the movement itself" (Thompson, 1978, p. 295). Foucault's work is used to rethink the relationship between industrial relations and human resource management and to show how their apparently apolitical techniques, so important to managing diversity, are central to the operation of class. The message of this chapter is that the same techniques that organize labor into a productive force within the workplace, atomize civil society, rip people from their communities, *reduce* diversity, and make employees more and more the same. Diversity is not a rich tapestry of individuals (to be sustained by enlightened management techniques), but a loose and dangerous collection of increasingly atomized and privatized monads.

INTRODUCTION

Recent years have witnessed recognition that the diversity of people that constitute the broader society should be reflected in the composition of workforces. Diversity refers to the multitude of differences—gender, sexual orientation, race/ethnicity, physical and mental capacities, age, religion—that constitute the identity of individuals and affect their workplace behavior. Increasingly, these differences are recognized and protected in employment law, collective agreements, arbitral jurisprudence, and industrial relations legislation, although the degree of protection varies enormously across jurisdictions and within and between countries.

Measures that celebrate and protect the diversity of human beings should be applauded. But in much the same way that one can support quality but have reservations about Total Quality Management, so one can support diversity but reserve a degree of circumspection toward the particular conception of the workplace to which it has become attached. What is interesting about advocacy of diversity is the way in which it meshes with the individualism fostered by the "new" Industrial Relations and Human Resource Management (henceforth referred to as IR and HRM). In the name of flexibility, management worldwide is fragmenting the collectivism of workers and re-creating it as the collectivism of companies. Good management, according to this approach, can be an effective substitute for trade unions by obviating employees' need for them. In practice, of course, flexibility for the employer tends to mean the creation of a relatively secure and well-compensated core group of workers and a much larger and much worse off peripheral group of part-time and short-term workers, many of whom are women.

Advocates of diversity claim that it is not only a way of introducing more fairness into the workplace, but also an essential component of organizing and managing employees in an age of global competition. To compete globally, employers need to create workplaces that tap the full potential of every employee. Thus, working with and managing diverse employees is a strategic imperative because it can bring competitive advantage and be profitable (although the specific links between diversity and competitiveness are rarely explained). This celebration of diversity, however, is part and parcel of an individualism which, whatever it contributes to procedural fairness, through its association with flexibility, threatens to propagate substantive injustice.

A notable feature of this individualism is the way in which the relationship between IR and HRM is being recast. HRM focuses on individual employees, how they are recruited and selected, appraised and compensated, trained and developed. IR focuses on collective labor issues, particularly the negotiation and administration of collective agreements. HRM is traditionally regarded as the social work or nursing of industry, dealing with the human casualties of the modern organization of work. IR is often regarded as a war zone contested by managers and trade unionists, sometimes the trench warfare of the First World War, sometimes the guerrilla warfare of Belfast. The contrast between the soft female HRM nurse/social worker tending to the hard male IR soldier is striking and pervasive.

IR academics tend to regard HRM techniques as worthy and necessary, but innocuous and uninteresting. For this reason, they are downplayed in importance in the IR literature and often neglected altogether. If they are considered at all, it is usually as the velvet glove on the iron fist of control. It is uncommon, for example, to find job analysis and performance appraisal examined in IR text-books. The neglect of HRM by IR academics parallels their neglect of the nonunionized in favor of the unionized employee. Perhaps because of its implicit pluralism, IR research and teaching has, until recently, tended to focus on collective bargaining between the union and the employer and has treated nonunionized workplaces as an anachronism or an aberration, as "not-yet-but-soon-to-be-unionized." As the economy develops, they will disappear beneath the expanding collectivism of the smoke stack, the rising tide of trade unionism, and the widening scope of collective bargaining. If this stance toward the nonunionized ever made sense, now it certainly does not. Unions everywhere are on the defensive. In the United States, union membership has declined by nearly 50% during the past two decades. In the private sector, just 12% of nonagricultural workers are unionized (Hoerr, 1991). In the United Kingdom, where trade unionism has its roots, just over 11% of the private-sector workforce is unionized (McLaughlin & Gourley, 1994). Unions in Canada have fared better. About 36% of the Canadian labor force is unionized. But most union members work in the fast-shrinking public sector, and large parts of the private sector are nonunionized and will probably remain so. The stark fact is that in most countries the majority of employees must face their employer alone. Moreover, the old argument linking the expansion of unionism to economic development has been turned on its head. Far from being anachronistic, the nonunionized individual is now presented as the postmodern employee: responsible, flexible, motivated by performance-related pay, committed to quality, and integrated into the culture of the organization. By this argument, the traditional blue-collar unionized worker in the manufacturing industry is a relic in the postmodern world of knowledge workers.

During the past 10 years or so, a remarkable transformation has occurred in the relationship between IR and HRM. The most striking characteristic of the much heralded new IR is that it is called HRM. The global trend is toward renaming IR positions, practices, and departments—in academia and in industry—HRM. As IR is increasingly subsumed to HRM, the boundary between the practices and the study of these once discrete areas is blurred. For this reason, henceforth I will refer to them as IR-HRM.

In this chapter, I examine the practices of IR-HRM in light of the challenge that individualism poses for explanations of the workplace based on class. In the process, I want to introduce some ideas that may be unfamiliar to students of workplace diversity. I begin by reflecting on the roots of class in Marxist thought and then consider some criticisms of this approach, particularly those of the historians Edward Thompson and Michel Foucault. On this basis, I present Foucault's concept of *disciplinary power* and indicate how it can be used to rethink the practices of IR-HRM. I conclude that, far from contributing to diversity, these techniques render individuals more and more the same.

CLASS AND MARXISM

Class is an emotive and controversial topic, in part because it forces us to think about the relationship between what we do and who we are. For this reason, one's stance toward the "labor question" is usually a litmus test of one's broader political position. A common reaction is to deny the existence of classes and to construe the very idea as an unhelpful description of society. Many North Americans, for example, have long thought that class is inapplicable to their societies. Another reaction is to reluctantly admit the existence of classes but to regard them as an unfortunate historical legacy that will wither away provided class consciousness is not whipped up. The harmonious coexistence of groups is best facilitated by providing working-class people with a channel for airing their grievances in the expectation that they will accept their allotted role.

Whether one realizes it or not, understanding of class has long been shaped by debates with the ghost of Marx. Because of the symbolic fall of the Berlin Wall in 1989, the subsequent disintegration of the Soviet Union, and the wave of commodification and privatization currently sweeping Eastern Europe, it is now widely thought that Marxism was wrong and is now dead. Witness the Western management consultants and teachers flocking to the old Soviet bloc to teach former Marxists how the market works. Indeed, these events are often taken to have ushered in a new, post-Fordist and postmodern society, of which diversity is part, characterized by flexibility within both the workplace and the marketplace: "Only with the collapse of Marxism as an ideology and of Communism as a system did it become completely clear that we have already moved into a new and different society" (Drucker, 1993, p. 7). Given the close association between Marxism and class, if the first is dead does this mean class analysis is anachronistic? Are we all individuals now?

Although class is certainly identified with Marxism, remarkably, neither Marx nor Engels ever systematically explicated the concept. Indeed, the impetus to Marx's life's work was provided by the problem of explaining the atomization of society into monads, not its organization into classes (Marsden & Townley, 1995). The only section devoted to classes in *Capital* appears at the very end of volume 3, Chapter 52, "Classes"; but this is little more than a page long and ends with the tantalizing editors' note: "Here the manuscript breaks off." Marxism's understanding of class, however, is not drawn from *Capital,* it is drawn from Marx's two most widely read texts, written before and after the revolution in Paris during 1848, the *Communist Manifesto* (Marx & Engels, 1962) and the Preface to *A Contribution to a Critique of Political Economy* (Marx, 1970).

Let us first consider the Manifesto, which Marx and Engels were commissioned to write for an international association of workers known as the Communist League. It stands today as one of the finest pieces of Communist propaganda, eloquent and full of dramatic force. Under the subtitle "Bourgeois and Proletarian," the Manifesto declares, "The history of all hitherto existing society is the history of class struggles" (Marx & Engels, 1962, p. 34). In a footnote to the 1888 English edition, Engels clarifies what is meant by *classes:*

> By bourgeoisie is meant the class of modern Capitalists, owners of the means of social production and employers of wage-labor. By proletariat, the class of modern wage-laborers who, having no means of production of their own, are reduced to selling their labor-power in order to live. (Marx & Engels, 1962, p. 34)

This is the basis of the common belief among Marxists that the tendency of capitalism is for society to split up into two great hostile camps facing each other (bourgeoisie and proletariat) and that class struggle is the motor of social change. We should note, however, that the fragment in *Capital* is more circumspect and draws attention to three classes, wage-laborers, capitalists, and land owners, not two. These are the "three big classes of modern society based upon the capitalist mode of production" (Marx, 1967, p. 885). Many of the class conflicts mentioned in the *Communist Manifesto* are, in fact, conflicts between status groups, not classes. Indeed, in the chapter on classes, Marx concludes by noting "the infinite fragmentation of interest and rank into which the division of social labor splits laborers as well as capitalists and landlords—the latter, e.g., into owners of vineyards, farm owners, owners of forests, mine owners and owners of fisheries" (Marx, 1967, p. 886). But such subtleties of the little-read *Capital* have generally lost out to the clarity of Marx and Engels's most widely read text, the *Communist Manifesto.*

The second source of the traditional Marxist conception of class is the Preface to *A Contribution to a Critique of Political Economy* (Marx, 1970). The book itself has never attracted much of a readership, but its Preface is one of the most cited of Marx's texts because its few pages are widely taken to provide the definitive summary of his concept of history. Here we find these much-quoted words:

> In the social production of their life, men enter into definite relations that are indispensable and independent of their will, relations of production which correspond to a definite stage of development of their material productive forces. The sum total of these relations of production constitutes the economic structure of society, the real basis, on which arises a legal and political superstructure, and to which correspond definite forms of social consciousness. (p. 20)

These two sentences are the source of the famous base-superstructure metaphor that generations of people have used to make sense of Marx. According to this view, society consists of an economic base and an ideological, political, and legal super-structure. Class is a given thing located within the economic base, but consciousness of class is obscured by an ideological superstructure. Thus, one can distinguish between the objective situation of a class and subjective awareness of this situation. This distinction fuels a political strategy aimed at dissolving the false consciousness of workers. When and if subjective perception is matched with objective reality, a "class-in-itself" is transformed into a "class-for-itself." This normally requires the intervention of revolutionary theorists who will disclose class consciousness not as it is but as it ought to be, and a political party that will help overcome intra-working class conflict, short-termism, and trade union consciousness in the interests of the larger common interest. This base-superstructure approach is implicit in studies of the workplace based on the control of the labor process (Knights & Willmott, 1990). Marxian analysis construes the interests of employers and workers as contradictory and imputes a motive for the first to control the behavior and performance of the last and a motive for workers to resist this control.

The twin influences of the Manifesto and the Preface have done much to shape what is usually referred to as traditional or classical Marxism: a focus on classes, their economic interests, the role of ideology and the State in suppressing working-class interests, a belief that class struggle is the motor of history, and a political strategy that focuses on the need for intellectuals to help remove the mist from workers' eyes so that they can recognize and act on their real interests. This set of beliefs was handed down from generation to generation, under the watchful eye of the custodians of this tradition (the editors of the Marx-Engels *Collected Works*), and this interpretation of Marx's key concepts acquired the authority of tradition.

This is not the place to critique traditional Marxism or to comment on its present crisis and attempts at its reconstruction, but three points are worth heeding. First, when considering the content of political tracts such as the Manifesto, the circumstances behind their creation should be considered. The Manifesto is a call to arms written on the eve of an anticipated revolution, hardly a reasoned discourse on the nature of class directly applicable 150 years later. Second, when considering the Preface, written in London a year after the Manifesto, it is important to note that the book itself was written by Marx mainly for a German audience, to keep his name in the public eye there in expectation of his returning home to play a leading role in a renewed revolution. But Germany was in turmoil and employed censors whose purpose was to prevent the publication of politically dangerous material. Prinz (1969) argues, persuasively in my view, that knowing that the preface of a book was often the only part censors bothered to read, Marx wrote the Preface in code, with a wary eye on the censor, "to ward off the danger of confiscation" (p. 447). This suggests that it should be treated with great circumspection. Finally, perhaps because of this last influence, it is interesting to note that this supposed definitive statement of Marxism never as much as mentions the word *class,* let alone *struggle*.

Long before its present crisis, Marxists themselves recognized the inadequacies of the base-superstructure approach and have tried, so far with little success, to develop a systematic and coherent alternative. This remains an active and pressing project. I am interested in the ideas of one particular critic—Edward Thompson—for I believe his conception of class offers insights into rethinking the nature of IR-HRM. Thompson, who died in 1993, was an adult educator, historian, an activist for nuclear disarmament, and, above all, a socialist intellectual and writer. He was also an early, stalwart, and consistent critic of traditional Marxism, his criticisms galvanized in opposition to the Soviet suppression of the Hungarian revolution in 1956. Thompson's influence is not in doubt; he "was cited more frequently than any other historian in the twenti-eth-century world, and [was] one of the 250 most frequently cited authors of all time" (Palmer, 1994, p. 184).

Thompson is, perhaps, best known for *The Making of the English Working Class* (Thompson, 1968), a book widely acknowledged for reconceptualizing how class is regarded. It inspired and energized a generation of historians of working-class life and broke the stranglehold of institutional labor history. In the Preface to this work, Thompson indicates that the book was written against the "weight of prevailing orthodoxies," of both institutional history, which construes the working class as passive victims of laissez faire, and traditional Marxism, which construes class formation as a mechanical reflection of change within the economic base. He objects to both orthodoxies because "they tend to obscure the agency of working people, the degree to which they contributed by conscious efforts, to the making of history" (p. 13). It is for this reason that he aims to rescue working people "from the enormous condescension of posterity" (p. 13). Class formation, for Thompson, is an active process: "The working class did not arise like the sun at an appointed time. It was present at its own making" (p. 9).

Thompson is also well-known for his polemics directed at fellow members of the Left. Of particular interest are the four essays, written over a period of 20 years, published in *The Poverty of Theory and Other Essays* (Thompson, 1978). Each essay addresses issues posed by traditional Marxism. Of these, perhaps the best-known is his 1978 polemic against the then influential interpretation of Marx developed by the French social theorist Louis Althusser, "The Poverty of Theory." "Biting satire, hyperbole, flights of rhetoric, and refusal to let the seemingly squirming subject off the hook of relentless punishment, all made the text unique in the annals of contemporary Marxist criticism" (Palmer, 1994, p. 118).

Thompson's (1978) critique of Althusser broadens into an indictment of traditional Marxism. He complains of a Marxism characterized by the "trans-mutation of analogies into concepts, and of analytical categories into substantive descriptions" (p. 114). Regarding the base and the superstructure,

> I found that law did not keep politely to a "level" but was at *every* bloody level;
> it was imbricated within the mode of production and productive relations
> themselves (as property-rights, definitions of agrarian practice) and it was

simultaneously present in the philosophy of Locke; it intruded brusquely within alien categories, reappearing bewigged and gowned in the guise of ideology; it danced a cotillion with religion, moralizing over the theatre of Tyburn; it was an arm of politics and politics was one of its arms; it was an academic discipline, subjected to the rigor of its own autonomous logic; it contributed to the definition of the self-identity both of rulers and of ruled; above all, it afforded an arena for class struggle, within which alternative notions of law were fought out. (p. 96)

Of particular interest to me are his thoughts on class contained in his essay, "The Peculiarities of the English." Here Thompson (1978) notes that

when, in discussing class, one finds oneself too frequently commencing sentences with "it," it is time to place oneself under some historical control, or one is in danger of becoming the slave of one's own categories. Sociologists who have stopped the time-machine and, with a good deal of conceptual huffing and puffing, have gone down to the engine-room to look, tell us that nowhere at all have they been able to locate and classify a class. They can only find a multitude of people with different occupations, incomes, status-hierarchies, and the rest. Of course, they are right, since class is not this or that part of the machine, but *the way the machine works* once it is set in motion—not this interest and that interest, but the *friction* of interests—the movement itself, the heat, the thundering noise. (p. 295)

The time-machine in question is the capitalist mode of production; class is the movement of this machine, the way it works, the way production is organized.

The thing to note is that Thompson's understanding of class is the reverse side of his criticism of traditional Marxism. In *The Making of the English Working Class* (Thompson, 1968), his very practice of historiography refutes the determinism of Marxism and its compartmentalization of life into the analytical boxes *base* and *superstructure*. In *The Poverty of Theory* (Thompson, 1978), using Althusser as a foil, he engages with the theory of Marxism. In the course of this critique, he comments,

Marxism has for decades been suffering from a wasting disease of vulgar economism. Its motions have been enfeebled, its memory fading, its vision obscured. Now it has swiftly passed into a last delirium of idealism, and the illness must prove terminal. (p. 168)

This assessment seems to have been proven true.

The difficulty for Marxism posed by Thompson's conception of class is that when it comes to explaining how the machine works—the capitalist mode of production—Marx has notably little to say. He presents a compelling explanation of the *why*: The *primus mobile* of capitalist production, for Marx (1976), is the creation of surplus value by developing "the productive forces of social labor" (p. 990). This, he says, is "the absolute motive and content" (p. 990) of the capitalist's activity. Marx also gives a persuasive historical account of how labor is priced off the land and whipped and branded, as he puts it, onto the road that leads to the labor market, and how labor is reduced to the status of a thing, or "hand," by the relentless movement of machinery. But when it comes to explaining what happens to labor when it enters the "hidden abode," how it is organized into a productive power, and how the conditions that make possible the introduction of machines are created—beyond allusions to "barrack-like discipline" (p. 549) and "factory codes" (p. 550)—Marx has remarkably little to say. He nowhere gives an adequate account of how this organization is achieved.

No one who follows Marx's progress in painstakingly presenting his model of the dialectic that drives production relations can fail to be struck by the ambiguous language of causation in those sections of *Capital* that address the transition to the capitalist mode of production. For example,

> *After* the various operations have been separated, made independent, and iso-lated, the workers are divided, classified, and grouped according to their pre-dominant qualities. (Marx, 1976, p. 469)

> The technical subordination of the worker . . . *gives rise to* a barrack-like discipline which is elaborated into a complete system in the factory. (Marx, 1976, p. 549)

> The organization of the capitalist process of production, *once it is fully devel-oped,* breaks down all resistance. (Marx, 1976, p. 899)

> *There now arises* a transformation of the labor process and its actual conditions. (Marx, 1976, pp. 1034-1035)

> The relations of production *themselves create* a new relation of supremacy and subordination. (Marx, 1976, p. 1227)

The question is, to take the third quotation, what develops the organization of the capitalist process of production in such a way as to break down all resistance? Some have interpreted this in technological determinist terms: Social organization is materialized in machines, and these break down resistance.

Certainly there is evidence in Marx to support this position. But this overlooks the fact that it is changes in production relations that bring about developments in technology, and begs the question of what brings about new forms of social organization in the first place? It is in response to the last question that the work of Michel Foucault is valuable, in particular his concept of disciplinary power. It provides a basis, I contend, for rethinking those apparently innocuous techniques of HRM so important to managing diversity.

FOUCAULT, MARX, AND POWER

Michel Foucault was Professor in the History of Systems of Thought at the Collège de France until his death in 1984 at the age of 57. He is widely regarded as one of the most influential intellectuals of the 20th century. The diversity of his work defies categorization, but its common thread is a concern with the nature of power and a dissatisfaction with existing liberal and Marxist concepts of power. The failure to analyze how power is exercised, "concretely and in detail," in favor of deducing its existence from a motive, is a criticism Foucault levels at "traditional" Marxists who, he says, worry more about the definition of class than the nature of the struggle. Foucault's concern is less with the why, and more with the how of power. Although Foucault seldom directly criticizes Marx in his books, his interviews make clear that his work is an implicit critique of the traditional understanding of the main categories of Marxism, and there seems little doubt that Foucault was "violently anti-Communist" (Eribon, 1991, p. 136).

Foucault is a very concrete writer about power. He prioritizes empirical detail over conceptual precision and consistency. He is no theorist. His model of power is, therefore, implicit, in need of explication; and exploratory, in need of criticism and development. Although Foucault never directly addresses production, his work illustrates how the logic or rationality of power is transferable across different domains. That Foucault's work is seldom applied in analysis of the organization of production is due to the widespread belief that it is philosophically incompatible with that of Marx—the postmodern idealist versus the modern materialist. Establishing that this belief is mistaken is a work in itself. Suffice it to note here that I believe the ontology of critical realism (Bhaskar, 1989) mediates their work and makes possible a rapprochement and the deployment of a synthesis between them in analysis of the practices of IR and HRM. The following introduction to Foucault's concept of disciplinary power is limited to pointing out some points of agreement between Marx and Foucault.

Foucault's general concern is to deconstruct what Marx (1976, p. 168) refers to as the "natural, self-understood, forms of social life"—those ingrained, taken-for-granted social forms whose very familiarity and obviousness blind us to the fact that they are historical social constructs. More specifically, he is concerned with the relationship between forms of experience (madness, illness, delinquency, sexuality), forms of knowledge (psychiatry, medicine, criminology, psychology), and institutions of incarceration (asylums, hospitals, prisons). In this way, he shows how "madness," for example, is no given datum, but something constituted historically as both an object of knowledge and a target of institutional practices. Foucault, in tracing the histories of the production of knowledge in psychiatry (1971), medicine (1973), the human sciences (1972), and the penal system (1977), shows how the exercise of power simultaneously generates forms of knowledge: "knowledge follows the advances of power, discovering new objects of knowledge over all the surface on which power is exercised" (Foucault, 1977, p. 204). These institutions are both architectures of power and apparatuses of knowledge; discipline is both a system of correction and a system of knowledge.

Although a concern with power permeates all of Foucault's work, it is the particular concern of *Discipline and Punish: The Birth of the Prison.* Despite its title, the book is less a history of the prison and more an account of the creation of a new form of power—a disciplinary power—which was stimulated by the privatization of property in the late 18th and early 19th centuries. The change in the forms of power is graphically illustrated in the book's opening pages. The description of the gruesome details of that very public and violent form of punishment—hanging, drawing and quartering—is contrasted with the private and silent punishment of the timetabled regimen of the prison, with which it had been replaced 80 years later. The exercise of disciplinary power had replaced public spectacle as a means of securing social control. This illustration is a metaphor: The prison is a laboratory of power and microcosm of a disciplinary society.

Disciplines are simply organizing devices, but they are central to the operation of power. Through the organization of time, space, and movement, disciplines operate simultaneously on the population and the individual, enabling both to be directed (Foucault, 1980). Their effect is simultaneously to totalize and to individualize. They are "tiny, everyday, physical mechanisms," methods of controlling the operation of the body that work through exploring, breaking down, and rearranging its operation (Foucault, 1977, pp. 137-138). As Foucault points out, the body has been a neglected dimension of work on power. Marxists, in particular, have a "terrible tendency to occlude the question of the body, in favor of consciousness and ideology" (Foucault, 1980, p. 59).

Disciplinary techniques developed from isolated and diverse origins. Many, however, originated in the rules of monastic life; in many ways, the monastery is the prototypical rational organization. Foucault shows how the logic and operating principles of disciplinary mechanisms gradually dispersed throughout society, constituting a variety of organizational forms—barracks, hospitals, asylums, workhouses—where their techniques were perfected. For example, the monastery contributed the art of organizing time and movement (the timetable); the army contributed the art of distributing people in space (the rank and the file) and the close supervision of the bodies, movements (army drill); the school contributed the system of organizing activity in time (the temporal sequence of knowledge through grades) and methods of comparing the individual to the collective whole (the examination). These disciplinary rules regulate the performance, behavior, actions, and thoughts of those within organizations, detailing offenses and penalties, be they of time, activity, behavior, speech, the body, or sexuality. "What is specific to the disciplinary penalty," says Foucault (1977), "is nonobservance, that which does not measure up to the rule, that departs from it" (p. 178). These rules provide what Foucault terms a counter- or infra-law to the liberties and rights enshrined in law. As he puts it, liberty was discovered as discipline was invented: "the 'Enlightenment' which discovered the liberties, also invented the disciplines" (Foucault, 1977, p. 222).

Foucault's conception of power has several consequences. First, by showing how mechanisms of disciplinary power are simultaneously instruments for the formation and accumulation of knowledge, Foucault dissolves the traditional, positivist distinction between power and knowledge. We should, says Foucault (1977), "abandon a whole tradition that allows us to imagine that knowledge can exist only where the power relations are suspended and that knowledge can develop only outside its injunctions, its demands, and interests" (p. 27). Power and knowledge, conceived by positivism as independent, are internally related, sides of the same social relations, and known by the conceptual shorthand, "power-knowledge."

Second, just as for Marx capital alienates while it produces, for Foucault power represses while it creates and enables. Foucault's concept of power is, then, an implicit critique of conceptions of power solely in terms of negation and repression of the actions of others. Marxist and liberal conceptions share an economism, says Foucault. Liberals regard power as a property of rights that are bestowed by a protective state and that one can possess like a commodity.

Marxists simply replace the benign with the malign state, juridic with economic subjects. Liberal and Marxist conceptions are, therefore, mirror images. The aim, for Foucault (1981), is to

> try and rid ourselves of a juridical and negative representation of power, and cease to conceive of it in terms of law, prohibition . . . power is not an institution, and not a structure, neither is it a certain strength we are endowed with . . . power is not something that is acquired seized or shared, that one holds or allows to slip away. (pp. 93-94)

Like Marx (1976, p. 990), Foucault views power as a machinery in which everyone is caught, "those who exercise power just as much as those over whom it is exercised." This redirects attention toward the everyday, the normal: "Rather than *A* getting *B* to do something *B* would not otherwise do, social relations of power typically involve both *A* and *B* doing what they *ordinarily* do" (Isaac, 1987, p. 96).

Like Marx, Foucault is concerned not with what people imagine or conceive, but what they actually do—with practice. Foucault's (1977) empirical inquiries revealed to him that power relations "go right down into the depths of society . . . they are not localized in the relationship between the state and its citizens or on the frontier between classes" (p. 27). Thus, he urges us to study power at "the point where power reaches into the very grain of individuals, touches their bodies, and inserts itself into their actions and attitudes, their discourses, learning processes, and everyday lives" (Foucault, 1980, p. 39). We should adopt an "ascending" analysis. Starting with the infinitesimal mechanisms of power and showing how they have been incorporated and colonized by more general, state mechanisms and cloaked in its theory of power and system of rights. Thus, we should study techniques rather than institutions; practices rather than intentions; webs of power rather than classes or groups; knowledge rather than ideology. In short, the way power is exercised, concretely and in detail.

Reconceptualizing power in this way has implications for how it is studied. The focus shifts to the regulatory mechanisms that make a domain manageable. Managing, or ruling, highlights points of intersection between power and knowledge. To make something manageable or governable requires knowledge, vocabularies, ways of representing that which is to be governed; for example, methods of observation, techniques of registration, mechanisms for the supervision and administration of individuals and groups. To know is "to be aware of (a person or thing) as being or doing *what is specified*." To be in the know is to be at "the utmost of one's power" (*Concise Oxford Dictionary*). This places the focus on governmentality (Foucault, 1991): the processes of inventing, promoting, and installing mechanisms of rule: "the apparently humble and mundane mechanisms which appear to make it possible to govern . . . the indirect means of action and intervention" (Miller & Rose, 1990, p. 8). Disciplinary rules represent systems of power-knowledge which, through rendering a sphere knowable, make it governable.

DISCIPLINARY PRACTICES:
IR AND HRM

In this section, I explicate Foucault's disciplinary practices and then indicate their relevance for reevaluating the traditional concerns of IR-HRM. They can, I suggest, be used to explain how labor is organized into a productive power or force (Marx, 1976, p. 440). Briefly, my argument is that quantitative differences among employees are equalized or averaged and translated into workplace norms governing behavior and performance. IR-HRM techniques are means to observe, examine, and normalize employees in accordance with this quantitative standard. They make individuals and their activities knowable and governable. They constitute a microphysics of power, serving to bridge the gap between promise and performance in the employment contract. They are means by which individualized labor is organized into an intelligible whole, to create, in Marxist vernacular, a "collective worker," or, more familiarly, an "organization."

Disciplinary practices comprise four types of organizing devices, each consisting of several interrelated elements. The first is the art of distribution, that is, the division, distribution, and arrangement of people in conceptual, temporal, and geographical space. Distributing or locating individuals uses a series of techniques that focus on dividing individuals from one another. Foucault (1977) identifies three methods through which this is achieved: *enclosure,* the creation of a space closed in upon itself; *partitioning,* in which "each individual has his own place and each place an individual"; and *ranking,* the hierarchical ordering of individuals. Essentially what Foucault identifies is the process involved in knowing through establishing classificatory tables, or taxonomies. The organization of space through categorization enables individuals to be classified and ranked; they are arranged vertically (by rank) and horizontally (by column and file).

Another disciplinary device is the control of the body through time. This is effected in two ways. First, time is divided into segments through the operation of the timetable. It is budgeted, that is, measured precisely in order to eliminate idleness and waste: "In mature capitalist society, all time must be consumed, marketed, put to *use*; it is offensive for the labor force merely to 'pass the time'" (Thompson, 1974, p. 64). The second element, allied to this, is what Foucault labels the control of activity: the prescription of how bodies should act; defining and coordinating the gestures that should be used; specifying how the body should engage with physical objects. The combination of these two disciplinary operations produces what Foucault (1977) calls the *temporal elaboration of the act:* "The act is broken down into its elements; the position of the body, limbs, articulations is defined; to each movement are assigned a direction, an aptitude, a duration; their succession is prescribed" (p. 152).

The detailed articulation of activity and time is the *capitalization of time:* the ability to organize activity in a series or in a temporal sequence, each one successfully graded from the other and leading to a seemingly logical progression. In this way, both time and activity are rendered productive. "The disciplines which analyze space, break up and arrange activities must also be understood as a machinery for adding up and capitalizing time" (Foucault, 1977, p. 157).

These disciplinary practices combine in the *composition of forces:* the recomposition of individuals in space and through time to form an organization with a productive power greater than the sum of its elementary forces. "Discipline is no longer simply an art of distributing bodies, of extracting time from them and accumulating it, but also of composing forces in order to obtain an efficient machine" (Foucault, 1977, p. 164). Through these techniques, the body is confined within a triangle, with time, space, and movement as its sides. They impose order through codifying, defining activities, fixing scales, determining rules of procedure, and defining roles.

It is important to recognize two simultaneous functions of these processes of situating the body. First, they function as a penal mechanism, making the slightest departures from correct behaviors subject to punishment. They give a punitive element to the apparently indifferent elements of organizing time, space, and activity. They allow for the identification of nonobservance, that which does not measure up to the rule. They simultaneously impose and enforce an order. Ranking, for example, organizes individuals around two poles, one negative, the other positive: "the distribution according to ranks or grades has a double role; it marks the gaps, hierarchizes qualities, skills, and aptitudes, but it also punishes and rewards" (Foucault, 1977, p. 181). Judging individuals according to comparative, scalar models, however, not only acts as a disciplinary process (in both senses of the word) but also as a *normalizing* process. As Foucault (1977) puts it, "disciplines characterize, classify, specialize; they distribute along a scale, around a norm, hierarchize individuals in relation to one another and, if necessary, disqualify and invalidate" (p. 223). The second function of the disciplines is that they "make" individuals (Foucault, 1977, p. 170). By referring individual actions to a whole in a field of comparison, it enables individuals to be known through being differentiated from one another. It measures and hierarchizes according to the value, the abilities, the level, the nature, of individuals. Implicit within such judgmental processes are socially constructed definitions of the *norm.*

Through these effects, the disciplines are incorporated into a *technology of power:* hierarchical observation, normalizing judgment, and the examination. Effectiveness is based on the internal relationship between power and knowledge. The limits of power are delineated by the field of vision, which must, therefore, be increased incessantly. Individuals must be rendered "visible." The observation of conduct must be meticulous; the political awareness of small things must be heightened. This is achieved through hierarchical observation mechanisms that allow those at the apex or the center of an organization to observe those at the base or the periphery while themselves remaining unseen. This architecture of power is exemplified in the panoptican. Although this was originally a model for a prison, it is employed in the design of a variety of organizations and is evident today in the shape of information systems and the practices of IR-HRM (Townley, 1994).

Once a population is known, demarcated, or categorized, deviations from this may be noted. Once isolated, mechanisms may be introduced that bring deviant behavior in line with the norm. Normalizing judgement refers to those processes through which the norm is enforced. The examination is a technique by which both hierarchical observation and normalizing judgement are fused. A moment's thought about the school examination illustrates the point. Individuals' abilities and knowledge are made known, they are placed in a hierarchy, and norms of performance are calculated which students then try to attain or surpass.

This outline of disciplinary power provides a framework for understanding the day-to-day practices of IR-HRM. Competition among corporations—that great flywheel of capitalism—dictates that labor be regulated, organized, made "socially necessary." Bodies must be subjected, used, transformed, and improved. They must operate at a predetermined speed and efficiency. Work organizations, therefore, require systems to inspect workers, to observe their presence and application, to inspect the quality of their work, to compare workers to one another, and to classify them according to skill and speed. Foucault's account of the operation of disciplinary practices describes the division of labor in the typical factory and office. Labor is productive, in large part, because each worker performs a well-defined, limited task and because the relationship between individual tasks is precisely calculated. This is achieved in two ways. First, disciplines detail and coordinate movement within the labor process and, second, they determine the nature of the labor to perform the work. Thus, they articulate two dimensions: the nature of work and the nature of the worker (Townley, 1994).

Disciplines begin with the distribution of individuals in space. Most fundamentally, *enclosure* polices the boundaries between work and nonwork. People are classified according to their location on either side of this division: housewife, retired, unemployed, part-time employee, and so on. Within the enclosed sphere of work, there are further mechanisms of enclosure: for example, the operation of internal labor markets; gendered definitions of work; the operation of closed or union shop provisions, and the enforcement of union jurisdictions.

Partitioning refers to the horizontal and vertical divisions of labor, which are created internal to the work organization. Divisions of labor necessarily incorporate specific loci of domination, they are all "embodied, gendered, departmentalized, hierarchized, spatially separated" (Clegg, 1989, p. 197). Thus, we find divisions of white-collar and blue-collar; core and periphery; productive and unproductive labor; craft, industrial, skilled, and semiskilled labor. These partitions may be reinforced by the legal sphere. For example, in North American certification procedures, managerial employees are excluded from union certification, thus requiring judicial clarification of the definition of management. The right of a union to exclusive representation of an appropriate bargaining unit, in addition to reinforcing vertical divisions within the workforce, prompts further calls for judicial clarification.

Ranking is the process of creating a hierarchical ordering among employees. Several IR-HRM practices operate to ensure that individuals become classified, specialized, and hierarchically ordered along a scale. Job classifications and job ladders, for example, are systems designed to create a hierarchy of jobs based on skill, responsibility or experience, time, and effort. Seniority systems and "bumping" rights are other mechanisms through which ranking is materialized. So too are salary administration and job evaluation schemes. These determine the relative value of a job in terms of education, skill, experience, and responsibility. Although classification schemes are often presented as simply techniques to analyze labor, they are very much disciplinary techniques. Classificatory or ranking systems designate individuals to their own space. In establishing their presence and absence within them, the calculability of individuals is enhanced.

The above are examples of how the disciplines are applied to a population, in this case, the labor force. They are active also in the division and articulation of the labor process through the control of bodies through time. Examples of the articulation of time in IR-HRM are legion. Most obviously, the working day itself is segmented and work assigned within discrete time periods—day shift, night shift, split shifts, overtime, and so on—and regulated through the time card and the time clock. Activity is then articulated through time: rates of pay per hour of work, call-in pay, call-back pay, idle time, "quality" time, slow down, and speed up. Activity itself is codified. Work rules, for example, limit the production work of supervisory personnel; limit the assignment of work outside an employee's classification; and stipulate the minimum number of workers on a job, and so on. Attempts at removing some of the effects of disciplinary practices—such as the proliferation of job classifications and general rules of managing (Kochan, Katz, & McKersie, 1994)—are reflected in the Japanization of IR-HRM and in the introduction of QWL. This is especially the case in North America, with its highly contractual—and disciplinary—approach to IR-HRM. These attempts do not remove the disciplines, however: they simply redesign them.

The articulation of activity can also be seen in the technology of personnel systems, for example, in job categories, tasks and skills specifications, and job analysis. These define skills, apportion responsibilities, justify hierarchies and create the "internal state" (Burawoy, 1979). Job analysis, for example, is the systematic process of collecting data and making judgments about the content of a specific job. In essence, it is a "nonindividualized impersonal definition" of the nature of the work, which provides the basis for other aspects of personnel activity: recruitment and selection, job evaluation, performance appraisal, training, and career planning. It operates, however, to inscribe activities of workers and thereby creates a visibility that ultimately becomes the basis for constructing norms and trends.

Making activities more visible necessarily renders the individual "known." Early factory organization had little knowledge of, or interest in, the individual. But systems quickly developed that classified workers on the basis of their skill, age, performance, and behavior. More sophisticated techniques elaborated more aspects of the individual. Because supervision involves assessing and judging workers, they must be compartmentalized according to their identifiable features, such as speech, attitudes, behavior, bodily characteristics, or sexuality. Personnel discourse, through the use of behavioral science and occupational psychology in particular, provides the basis for this.

The coordination of large numbers of people, and the ability to differentiate between them—the rational and efficient deployment of a population—requires the development of techniques that enable people to be managed en masse. What is required is the elaboration of a vocabulary that provides both a means of knowing and a means of managing employees (Rose, 1988). Selection testing— the systematic procedure for observing an individual's behavior, ability, and personality, and describing it with the aid of a numerical scale or category system—is one means of fulfilling this function. The familiar tools of personnel management—skills inventories, performance appraisal systems, assessment and evaluation methods, attitude measurements—are further means. As systems of classification, partitioning, and ranking, they contribute to the detailed enumeration of the capabilities of organizational members. All represent technologies that attempt to codify and enumerate time, space, and movement as closely as possible. They reach their zenith in Human Resource Accounting, which epitomizes the attempt to provide a detailed articulation of these elements, wherever possible reducing them to a numerical equivalent. As Flamholtz (1985) notes of its potential, it "represents a type of balance sheet of the potential services that can be rendered by people at a specified time" (p. 244).

Conventional interpretations of personnel are that its traditional concerns lie with the "human" side of the organization. Its role in the control of labor has usually been seen as the provision of a suitable labor supply, and "helping to motivate or at least prevent its insurrection once it is there" (Armstrong, 1985, p. 144). These motivational concerns are seen as personnel's human relations and social skills stock-in-trade, and, as such, are thought to be in diametric opposition to the concerns of accountants and engineers. But this interpretation, both of the behavioral school of psychology and the techniques of human resource management generally, is unduly influenced by personnel's welfare ideology. To the contrary: personnel comprises a nexus of disciplinary practices driven by capital's desire to know and to manage. It is a technology aimed at making employees' behavior and performance predictable and calculable. In a word: manageable.

CONCLUSION

I began this chapter by noting the challenge that the individualism at the heart of diversity poses to explanations of the workplace based on class. The import of my argument is that if class is the way the machine works, as Thompson puts it, then those apparently apolitical techniques of IR-HRM are central to its operation. Far from encouraging diversity, these techniques render workers more and more the same. This approach stresses the practical, day-to-day activities of IR-HRM practices, which seem innocuous precisely because they make the organization of production seem normal. Although there are political struggles over these forms of rule at the margins, for the most part, people live within the categories and social spaces that constitute Marx's "natural, self-understood forms of social life." Conflict—that preeminent pluralist concept—is not the phenomenon to be explained: but its absence. This Foucauldian account of IR-HRM finds power in what seem apolitical techniques and procedures. Through their insidious nature, they attempt to squeeze the politics out of production (Burawoy, 1985).

REFERENCES

Armstrong, P. (1985). Changing management control strategies: The role of competition between accountancy and other organisational professions, *Accounting, Organizations, and Society, 10*(2), 129-148.

Bhaskar, R. (1989). *Reclaiming reality: A critical introduction to contemporary philosophy.* London: Verso.

Burawoy, M. (1979). *Manufacturing consent.* Chicago: University of Chicago Press.

Burawoy, M. (1985). *The politics of production.* London: Verso.

Clegg, S. (1989). *Frameworks of power.* London: Sage.

Cohen, G. A. (1978). *Karl Marx's theory of history: A defence.* Oxford: Clarendon.

Drucker, P. F. (1993). *Post-capitalist society.* New York: Harper Business.

Eribon, D. (1991). *Michel Foucault.* Cambridge, MA: Harvard University Press.

Flamholtz, E. (1985). *Human resource accounting* (2nd ed.). San Francisco: Jossey-Bass.

Foucault, M. (1970). *The order of things: An archeology of the human sciences.* London: Tavistock.

Foucault, M. (1971). *Madness and civilisation.* London: Tavistock.

Foucault, M. (1972). *The order of things.* London: Tavistock.

Foucault, M. (1973). *The birth of the clinic.* London: Tavistock.

Foucault, M. (1977). *Discipline and punish.* London: Penguin.

Foucault, M. (1980). *Power/knowledge: Selected interviews and other writings by Michel Foucault 1972-77* (C. Gordon, ed.). Brighton: Harvester.

Foucault, M. (1981). *The history of sexuality,* Vol. 1. London: Penguin.

Foucault, M. (1991). Governmentality. In G. Burchell, C. Gordon, & P. Miller (Eds.), *The Foucault effect.* London: Harvester.

Hirst, P. Q. (1985). *Marxism and historical writing.* London: Routledge & Kegan Paul.

Hoerr, J. (1991, May-June). What should unions do? *Harvard Business Review,* pp. 30-45.

Isaac, J. C. (1987). *Power and Marxist theory: A realist view.* Ithaca, NY: Cornell University Press.

Johnson, R., McLennan, G., Schwarz, B., & Sutton, D. (1982). *Making histories: Studies in history writing and politics.* Minneapolis: University of Minneapolis Press.

Kaye, H. J., & McClelland, K. (1990). *E. P. Thompson: Critical perspectives.* Oxford: Polity.

Knights, D., & Willmott, H. (Eds.). (1990). *Labor process theory.* Basingstoke: Macmillan.

Kochan, T., Katz, H. C., & McKersie, R. B. (1994). *The transformation of American industrial relations.* Ithaca, NY: ILR Press.

Kritzman, L. D. (Ed.). (1988) *Michel Foucault: Politics, philosophy, culture: Interview and other writings, 1977-1984.* London and New York: Routledge.

Littler, C. (1990). The labor process debate: A theoretical review 1974-88. In D. Knights & H. Willmott (Eds.), *Labor process theory.* Basingstoke: Macmillan.

Marsden, R. (1992). The state: A comment on Abrams, Denis, and Sayer. *Journal of Historical Sociology, 5,* 358-377.

Marsden, R. (1993a). *Marx, realism, and Foucault: An enquiry into the problem of industrial relations theory.* Ph.D thesis, University of Warwick.

Marsden, R. (1993b). The politics of organizational analysis. *Organization Studies 14*(1), 93-124.

Marsden, R. (1995). *Marx's method: The 1857 introduction and the 1859 preface.* Centre for Economics, Industrial Relations and Organization Studies, Athabasca University, mimeo.

Marsden, R., & Townley, B. (1991, June). *Deconstructing industrial relations: Power, rules and Foucault.* Paper presented at Canadian Industrial Relations Association Learned Society, Queen's University.

Marsden, R., & Townley, B. (1995). Power and postmodernity: Reflections on the pleasure dome. *Electronic Journal of Radical Organization Theory, 1*(1). http://www.mngt.waikato.ac.nz/leader/journal.ejrot.htm

Marx, K. (1967). *Capital: Vol. 3. The process of production as a whole.* New York: International Publishers.

Marx, K. (1970). *A contribution to the critique of political economy.* Moscow: Progress Publishers.

Marx, K. (1976). *Capital: Vol. 1. The process of capitalist production.* Harmondsworth, UK: Penguin.

Marx, K., & Engels, F. (1962). Manifesto of the Communist party. In *Karl Marx and Frederick Engels selected works.* Moscow: Foreign Languages Publishing House.

McLaughlin, I., & Gourley, S. (1994). *Enterprise without unions: Industrial relations in the nonunion firm.* Buckingham: Open University Press.

Meikins-Wood, E. (1986). *The retreat from class: A new "true" socialism.* London: Verso.

Miliband, R., & Panitch, L. (Eds.). (1990). *The retreat of the intellectuals.* London: Merlin.

Miller, P., & Rose, N. (1990). Governing economic life, *Economy and Society, 19,* 1-31.

Palmer, B. D. (1990). The eclipse of materialism: Marxism and the writing of social history in the 1980s. In R. Miliband & L. Panitch (Eds.), *The retreat of the intellectuals* (pp. 111-146). London: Merlin.

Palmer, B. D. (1994). *E. P. Thompson: Objections and oppositions.* London: Verso.

Prinz, A. M. (1969). Background and ulterior motive of Marx's 'preface' of 1859. *Journal of the History of Ideas, 30,* 437-450.

Rose, N. (1988). Calculable minds and manageable individuals. *History of the Human Sciences, 1,* 179-200.

Sayer, D. (1987). *The violence of abstraction: The analytic foundations of historical materialism.* Oxford: Blackwell.

Thompson, E. P. (1968). *The making of the English working class.* London: Penguin.

Thompson, E. P. (1974). Time, work-discipline, and industrial capitalism. In M. W. Flinn & T. C. Smout (Eds.), *Essays in social history.* Oxford: Clarendon Press.

Thompson, E. P. (1975). *Whigs and hunters: The origin of the black act.* London: Penguin.

Thompson, E. P. (1978). *The poverty of theory and other essays.* London: Merlin.

Thompson, E. P. (1980). *Writing by candlelight.* London: Merlin.

Thompson, E. P. (1993). *Customs in common: Studies in traditional popular culture.* New York: New Press.

Townley, B. (1993). Foucault, power/knowledge and its relevance for human resource management. *Academy of Management Review, 18,* 518-545.

Townley, B. (1994). *Reframing human resource management: Power, ethics, and the subject at work.* London: Sage.

The Protestant Ethic and the Myths of the Frontier

Cultural Imprints, Organizational Structuring, and Workplace Diversity

PUSHKALA PRASAD

In an article commenting on the intense homogeneity of contemporary North American organizations, DiMaggio and Powell (1983) coined the term *institutional isomorphism* to refer to the amazing uniformity characterizing organizational structures today. It is the contention of this chapter that certain prominent cultural and ideological features shared by contemporary isomorphic organizations limit the enactment of diversity by instilling a rigid form of *institutional monoculturalism* that is rooted in the cultural myths of the American historical experience.

In analyzing common barriers to workplace diversity, the tendency is to focus on the role of stereotypes and prejudices (Cox & Nkomo, 1986), the "glass ceiling" (Morrison & Von Glinow, 1990), institutional sexism and racism (Blum

AUTHOR'S NOTE: This chapter was made possible in part by a grant from the Social Science and Humanities Research Council of Canada to study workplace directly.

& Smith, 1988; Howitt & Owusu-Bempah, 1990), and the more overt forms of discrimination (Ilgen & Youtz, 1986). Although all these areas are undoubtedly key to understanding dilemmas of diversity at the workplace, what remains somewhat neglected is a cultural-historical examination of the common values and assumptions undergirding work organizations and their role in constraining diversity. Because organizations themselves are cultural artifacts, they are extraordinarily influenced by dominant cultural ideologies that (directly and indirectly) shape organizational rules, values, taboos, and practices. It is therefore worthwhile to examine some prominent ideological forces that have, over the past few centuries, influenced the *structuring* of American organizations and that continue to guide their present-day actions.

Two major periods characterize the initial economic expansion of America. The first is the rise of economic enterprise in the original colonies leading to the development of eastern centers of commercial activity in Boston, New York, and Philadelphia. The second is the sweeping movement westward entailing the acquisition, settlement, and conquest of new lands. Both economic movements were rooted in comprehensive ideologies justifying their emergence, celebrating their successes, and providing coherent cultural explanations emphasizing their significance in American history. The first ideology can broadly be designated the *Protestant ethic,* a system of thinking derived from the common worldviews of Calvinism, Quakerism, Presbyterianism, and Puritanism, which developed in unique ways in colonial and industrial America. The second ideology is best characterized as the *myth of the frontier,* a worldview that explained, legitimated, and celebrated the entire westward expansionary movement and that developed a unique set of legends, heroes, and symbols around it. Both ideologies revolved around prominent economic movements: the growth of commercial and industrial activity in the East, and the agricultural and prospecting enterprises that moved westward. Historians have consistently argued that both these ideologies have exerted and continue to exert significant influences on various social and cultural arrangements in American life and to shape American conceptualizations of self, Other, and society (Bellah, Madsen, Sullivan, Swidler, & Tipton, 1986; Billington, 1966; Marty, 1970). Yet these ideological influences on contemporary American *organizations* remains a remarkably undertheorized domain.

ORGANIZATIONAL MYTH AND IDEOLOGY

Few terms have generated as much debate over their meaning and definition as myth and ideology. Both terms, have, moreover, been employed differently by many different scholars and consequently carry multiple and sometimes conflicting connotations. Although this chapter does not propose entering into minute theoretical examinations of these concepts, it will provide a brief and concise summary of their usage in contemporary scholarship.

Both myth and ideology are extraordinarily complex concepts, fraught with ambiguity and often used interchangeably. There is no doubt that they also remain highly interrelated concepts, as well. Ideology, in general, can be thought of as comprehensive in scope, broadly defining what exists, what is good, and what is possible (Therborn, 1980, p. 18). Ideology is thus often treated as an overarching mind-set comprising an interrelated and coherent system of values, beliefs, assumptions, and prescriptions. Ideologies determine individual and collective beliefs about the nature of culture and society, as well as their normative directions. Ideologies are often discussed with respect to societal levels (Geuss, 1981; Therborn, 1980), organizational levels (Czarniawska-Joerges, 1988; Weiss, 1986), and occupational and managerial levels (Bendix, 1956; Larson, 1977).

Myth is used both similarly and differently from ideology. To Strenski (1987),

> Myth is everything and nothing at the same time. It is the *true* story or a false one, revelation or deception, sacred or vulgar, real or fictional, symbol or tool, archetype or stereotype. . . . Myth . . . is charter, recurring theme, character type, received idea, half-truth, tale, or just a plain lie. (p. 1)

To Campbell (1988) and Barthes (1957), myth is primarily a *message*. But whereas to Campbell, the mythic message provides guidelines to living one's life, to Barthes, the comprehensive and influential messages of myth are capable of immense distortion on account of their taken-for-granted and self-evident appeal. Myths frequently symbolize a society's ideology and dramatize its moral consciousness (Slotkin, 1992). Myths furnish us with heroes, salutary lessons, aphorisms, and cultural codes. The power of myth lies in its capacity to express ideology as *narrative* rather than as a logical and argumentative structure. Above all, myths are emotional and metaphorical, although often undergirded by a particular form of rationality. In sum, ideologies are often expressed in symbolic and mythic forms, whereas myths and symbols themselves need to be understood within their ideological content (Alvesson, 1991).

Organizational scholars have long recognized that ideologies and myths play pivotal roles in shaping organizational level action. Ideologies are seen as affecting styles of organizational decision making (Beyer, 1981), constraining organizational planning and practice (Starbuck, 1982; Torbert, 1988), influencing responses to technological change (Prasad & Prasad, 1994), and indirectly controlling employees' beliefs and actions (Bendix, 1956; Merkle, 1980; Weiss, 1986). To begin with, the concept of myth was mainly of interest to researchers of organizational culture. However, the influence of myth on organizational structuring has been most acutely grasped by institutional theorists, notably Meyer and Rowan (1977), who argue that the myths in an organization's institutional environment eventually become *reflected in its formal structure.* Furthermore, Meyer and Rowan (1977) stipulate that myths come in multiple guises and emanate from multiple sources including laws, public opinion, ideologies, credentialing bodies, and so on. Institutional theorists have commented on how different ideologies and myths including rationality (Meyer & Rowan, 1977), professionalism (DiMaggio, 1991; Prasad & Prasad, 1994), and standardization (Olshan, 1993) shape varying organizational structures. Collectively, these studies have alerted us to the wide variation and cultural persistence (Zucker, 1983) of these myths, once they have been institutionalized in the everyday life of the organization.

In order to fully grasp the complex relationships between organizations, myths, and ideologies, Scott (1991) suggests that organization theorists turn their attention to the sociology of culture and make the study of cultural systems a field in its own right. And this chapter does precisely that. It takes a detailed look at two powerful American ideologies and shows their *cultural imprint* on contemporary organizational structuring. The idea of the cultural imprinting of organization first received extensive attention from Stinchcombe (1965), who showed how certain social and cultural conditions became reflected or imprinted in an organization's formal and informal functioning, and then became taken for granted as they were institutionalized in the organization's routine practices. As the chapter will also show, these cultural imprints have far-reaching consequences for many dimensions of organizational life, in particular, for the way in which cultural and demographic differences are received in the workplace.

THE PROTESTANT ETHIC
IN NORTH AMERICA

Following the initial conflicts with the Native Indians and the establishment of permanent settlements, the founding colonies in the United States became sites of substantial economic activity. The southern colonies, notably Virginia and the Carolinas, turned primarily to the cultivation of cash crops and soon developed prosperous plantation economies, whereas the Northeast rapidly became the center of flourishing trade and commercial enterprise. These burgeoning businesses in New York, Philadelphia, and Boston were primarily run by different Protestant groups, including the English Puritans, the Quakers, and the Dutch Calvinists. The strong connection between these successful commercial ventures and the Protestant religious experience cannot be sufficiently emphasized (Schneider, 1958). Countless commentators (Marty, 1970; Miller, 1963) have stressed the inseparable nature of the relationship between Protestant religious ideals and the conduct of everyday life. Furthermore, whereas Protestant religious doctrine in America was drawn from the teachings of Europeans such as John Knox, Calvin, Zwingli, and others, historians also point to the unique appropriation of Protestant theology in colonial America (Schneider, 1958).

To understand Protestant ideology in North America, one needs first of all, to appreciate how the notion of *providence* operated to secularize the Protestant faith, linking it to the "moral" conduct of commercial activity (Marty, 1970). According to early Calvinist doctrine, certain individuals were chosen or selected by providence to be blessed by the grace of God. These chosen individuals were clearly identifiable through their success in the material world, which, in effect, was a clue differentiating the chosen few from the rest of the population. In other words, those who succeeded materially were marked by *divine grace.* In this way, the Protestant creed "linked the probation of self, work in the world, and eternal salvation" (Jackall, 1988, p. 8). The first thing this ideology did was to sanctify the accumulation of material wealth, because it treated worldly success as a mark of divine grace (Marty, 1970; Miller, 1954). The second thing it did was to identify characteristics that contributed to the acquisition of wealth and to eventually treat them as godly virtues in their own right (Jackall, 1988; Schneider, 1958). This creed, which eventually developed into what we now call the Protestant work ethic, implicitly shaped the worldviews and actions of individuals in parts of America from the 16th century to the present day.[1]

Too often, the Protestant work ethic is regarded solely as an endorsement of the value of hard work itself. And certainly, the moral stature of hard work was central to the Protestant creed (Rodgers, 1978). Prominent Protestant preachers, even up to the 19th century, proposed biological theories showing that nature herself had fashioned man for a life of hard work (Beecher, 1844), and they spiritualized toil by suggesting that *work itself was prayer* (Rodgers, 1978; Tawney, 1926). Nevertheless, it is also important to remember that hard work, although central to the doctrines of Protestantism, was only one element in the entire ideological configuration. As Rodgers (1978) suggests, what we refer to as *the work ethic* is largely a simplified label referring to an entire *ethos.*

Other prominent features of this creed are worth exploring if we are to understand its mythic appeal. Alongside hard work, the ideology elevated *frugality, sobriety,* and *temperance* to a level of high moral virtue, thereby shaping a cultural consciousness that produced the austere and disciplined individual as a mythic hero. Certainly, reputed community leaders and local heroes of colonial and early industrial America were men like John Winthrop (first governor of Massachusetts), Benjamin Franklin, and Henry Ward Beecher (theologian and abolitionist), all of whom exemplified these core values.

The ideology of American Protestantism also extolled a level of *self-reliance* and *rugged individualism* not found in Europe. Early settlers in the colonies were confronted with a largely untamed land and native people with practices so different from the Europeans that they very quickly were seen as "savages." Confronted with a savage wilderness and a savage people, early settlers interpreted the Protestant doctrines in order to prepare members of their community for a relatively isolated and adversarial existence in which self-sufficiency played a major role (Miller, 1963). Nothing fostered self-sufficiency as much as the myth of rugged individualism, which ensured that values such as sobriety and hard work were underscored by a drive toward self-reliance. Early colonial encounters with the Indians also left their permanent mark on American Protestantism (Marty, 1970). To early settlers, the savage Indian was constantly in need of taming and subjugation, and not particularly deserving of civilized treatment, either. Eventually, the brutality of colonial encounters with the Indians triggered the enunciation of new doctrines justifying this brutality, in which Indians were categorized as *inferior races,* often in alliance with the Devil (Schneider, 1958). These early depictions of the Other prepared the ground for later race-based worldviews representing non-Anglo Saxon groups in America as evil and inferior.

The Protestant ethos also celebrated *detachment* and *impersonality* by systematically devaluing passion and emotionality in every aspect of social interaction (Leverauz, 1980). Romantic love was regarded as excessively hedonistic and sanctioned only for the purpose of bearing children, while all artistic expression was frowned upon unless it had some tangible instrumental value (Kasson, 1976; Rourke, 1942).

Protestant colonial attitudes toward women are also interesting, reflecting a high level of complexity and ambivalence. The Puritan cultures of the Northeast regarded women as adults, responsible for the development of their own souls, while simultaneously viewing them as dangerously close to forming alliances with the Devil through the practice of witchcraft (Barstow, 1994). The early settlements of New England were in fact, constantly overshadowed by accusations of witchcraft, usually leveled against single women who were economically independent, and with reputations for being outspoken and self-willed (Demos, 1982). It is interesting to note that although American Protestantism treated women as independent adults, it also defined their social and economic roles rather narrowly, emphasizing their subordinate positions in family and community, and prescribing relatively harsh punishments for women who tried to break these norms (Karlsen, 1987).

Altogether, the Protestant ethos in North America helped produce a cultural mind-set that valued austerity, hard work, rugged individualism, and impersonality as virtues that were essential to leading a blessed life. It regarded the Native Indians as unquestionably inferior and harbored ambiguous attitudes toward the role of women in society.

THE MYTHS OF THE FRONTIER

The second major period of American expansion took place in the 19th century and coincided with the vast geographic expansion westward through the conquest, settlement, and purchase of new lands. This westward movement was strongly linked to a developing industrial economy in the East and was therefore seen as a source of ongoing material prosperity (Hine, 1980). Like the earlier Protestant experience, the American westward movement also generated its own mythology influencing generations of Americans with respect to their cultural identity, social arrangements, and choices of action (Slotkin, 1985). The myths of the frontier were disseminated through innumerable vehicles of popular culture, including popular histories of the West (Roosevelt, 1907), the classic novels of James Fenimore Cooper (1826, 1841), the dime novels or "penny dreadfuls" of the 19th century, the spectacular stage performances of shows like Buffalo Bill's Wild West, and the more recent genre of the Hollywood Western.

Nothing characterizes the ideology of the frontier as much as the themes of *conflict, conquest,* and *violence.* As Slotkin (1992) suggests, "violence is central to both the historical development of the frontier and its mythic representation" (p. 11). Violence in the form of uncontrolled aggression and savage ruthlessness permeates the entire ideology of the frontier. Above all, violence toward the Native Indians is celebrated and justified on the grounds that it was instrumental in making North America a civilized place, free from the primitive savagery of the Indians (Roosevelt, 1907; Slotkin, 1992).

In much the same way as the work ethic framed the Protestant ethos, violence was a fulcrum around which many frontier myths were woven. In all these celebrations of violence, what often emerges is the theme of *rugged individual-ism,* which is emphasized much more strongly than within the Protestant ethos. The heroes of the frontier, Buffalo Bill, Davy Crockett, and John Wayne, are always rugged individuals who exhibit astounding capacities for *self-reliance* and *savage ruthlessness* (Gard, 1949; Green, 1979; Slotkin, 1992). The ideology of the West also constructed new notions of *masculinity* (Mangan & Walvin, 1987), highlighting personal isolation and a unique form of ruthlessness as hallmarks of manly men (Atherton, 1961). Frontier heroes are always remark-able for the degree of *emotional self-reliance* they exhibit. Whether engaged in fur trapping, homesteading, prospecting, or any other pioneering adventure, cowboy heroes have few family ties, rarely develop permanent romantic rela-tionships, and inevitably ride out alone into the sunset once their work is done. Certainly, the overall mythical cowboy figure signifies personal isolation and emotional detachment, with few strong bonds to either community, family, or any specific individual.

Not surprisingly perhaps, women emerge as shadowy and unsubstantial figures in Western lore. Never at the heart of western myths, women usually play roles typifying innocent maidens in need of rescue by cowboy heroes or saloon keepers with hearts of gold (Slotkin, 1992). Similarly, families rarely appear as significant entities in frontier myths. Families are either completely absent from cowboy lives or play marginal roles in the stories of the West.

Two other features of the ideology of the frontier are worth noting. One is the construction of *lawlessness* as a virtue, and the second is a tendency to interpret events in singularly *simplistic* and straightforward ways. In other words, ambiguity is not a part of the frontier mind-set. Legends of the West present extremely clear-cut visions of society with good and evil, right and wrong, being clearly spelled out (Elson, 1985). Moral issues are rarely depicted as troubling or complex in frontier mythology. Typically, the cowboy hero represents the forces of good, and the cowboy villains represent the forces of evil. What is interesting is that cowboy heroes are not necessarily law-abiding individuals either. Law-lessness in the service of "good" causes is seen as a virtue in its own right and is responsible for the emergence of countless outlaw heroes such as Deadwood Dick and the fictional Jesse James (Ellis & Wheeler, 1966). Frontier justice is therefore often quite arbitrary (Gard, 1949) and involves the same savage ruthlessness that characterizes most mythic actions of the western hero.

Overall the ideology of the frontier shaped a cultural consciousness that affirmed a particular form of masculinity demanding aggression, violence, and ruthlessness. It pushed family ties and intimate relationships into the background, celebrated a unique brand of lawlessness, and provided a simplistic schema for the interpretation of the world.

CULTURAL IMPRINTS ON
CONTEMPORARY ORGANIZATIONS

That the Protestant ethos and myths of the frontier have significantly affected different aspects of American life is accepted by historians and social scientists alike. Beginning with Weber's (1958) influential thesis, in which he held the Protestant ethic primarily responsible for the development of Western capitalism, countless writers have commented on the enduring influence of both these ideologies on American politics (Shain, 1994; Slotkin, 1992) and on American culture (Bellah et al., 1987; Lasch, 1979). The Protestant ethos and frontier mythologies have been vividly portrayed as playing key roles in shaping American foreign policy (Baritz, 1985; Slotkin, 1992), American systems of government (Shain, 1994), American attitudes toward technology (Kasson, 1976), and the development of American national character (Bellah et al., 1985). Few writers, however, have attempted to trace the influence of these ideologies on the formal and informal structures of contemporary North American organizations.

It is the contention of this chapter that the Protestant ethos and the mythologies of the frontier have left lasting cultural imprints on the structure and functioning of current organizations. In other words, the values inherent to these two ideologies pervade and shape countless organizational practices in such fundamental and taken-for-granted ways that they remain largely unquestioned and invisible. Obviously, not all organizations are identically imprinted upon by these two ideologies. Furthermore, occasionally, legacies of the frontier mythology clash or conflict with legacies of the Protestant ethos. Neither of these ideologies are, moreover, imprinted on organizations in their exact original form. Rather, organizations, while profoundly influenced by them, continue to transform these imprints in different ways within different institutional contexts.

Cultural imprints of these two ideologies are embedded within routine organizational practices and unquestioned organizational thinking. Both the Protestant ethos and the frontier ideology have left clusters of values that are constantly reproduced through everyday organization-level actions. The rugged individualism of early colonial America and the ruthlessness of cowboy legends have jointly left their mark on organizational values such as *individualistic competition* and the endless striving toward success. These values have turned organizations into locations filled with intense interpersonal competition, severe managerial battles, and the "masked politics" (Jackall, 1988) of executive intrigue. Underlying the organizational reverence toward competition is a dogmatic belief in individualistic self-reliance and a sense that employees can shape their own career trajectories and are ultimately fully responsible for their own organizational destinies.

Early Protestant values of detachment and objectivity, along with frontier preoccupations with personal isolation, also linger in American organizations. In discussing the *technocratic rationality* of contemporary organizations, countless commentators (Alvesson, 1991; Denhardt, 1981) have also highlighted the central role of detachment and objectivity in organizational systems. Organizations themselves are upheld by notions of purposive rationality and neutrality, whereas managers within these organizations are expected to embody a careful detachment that excludes emotional displays and value-laden decisions. In fact, rationality and neutrality are embedded in the fundamental structures and functioning of organizations. Organizational policies are ostensibly *impersonal* in nature, carrying no hint of value preferences, while management styles are expected to reflect a self-controlled detachment and deliberation, free of any emotional attachment to subordinates, colleagues, or supervisors.

Some writers also point to the pervasiveness of *masculinity* in organizations. In many ways, contemporary ideals of organizational masculinity echo the masculinity of the 19th century frontier. Organizations value *tough-minded approaches* in managers and admire both aggressiveness and ruthlessness. Overall, it is easy to argue that specific ideals of corporate masculinity influence most spheres of organizational decision making, a phenomenon perhaps best illustrated by Maier's (1993) discussion of dysfunctional decision making leading up to the NASA space shuttle Challenger disaster. Elsewhere, Young (1993) and Fitzpatrick (1980) have also proposed that ideals of masculinity shape the acceptance and enactment of violence in a variety of workplaces, including coal mines and oil rigs.

These cultural legacies of masculinity also prescribe the roles to be played by women and families in the workplace. Women's roles as peripheral and background figures in the Protestant ethos and the myths of the frontier continue to be reproduced in today's organizations. Families too have no place within the structure and discourse of contemporary organizations, which frequently treat emotional attachments to families as unwelcome distractions from work. Other cultural imprints can be found in organizations' open violation of laws, their repeated public endorsements of hard work, and their adulation of aggressive and ruthless corporate leadership styles.

CULTURAL IMPRINTS AND
MULTICULTURAL CLASHES

Cultural imprints are fundamental to the structure and functioning of all organizations. They systematically shape organizational values and organization-level action, and they are intensely ideological in the sense that they implicitly prescribe what an organization should look like and be like. In so doing, cultural imprints inevitably favor individuals from certain demographic and social groups over others. Cultural imprints left by the Protestant work ethic and the myths of the frontier reflect a particular worldview and set of *cultural preferences* with which some groups (notably white, male Anglo-Saxon) are far more comfortable. Furthermore, cultural imprints influence organizational definitions of appropriate workplace behavior and professional competence. Put differently, remnants of dominant American mythologies continue to define contemporary notions of the "ideal employee" and desired organizational action. Above all, these cultural imprints also dictate who "fits" into accepted modes of organizational practice and who does not. Cultural imprints, therefore, often reproduce *experiences of marginalization* among individuals from specific social groups (notably women, minorities, and homosexuals) whose cultural values and lifestyles come into repeated conflict with the cultural codes of the organization. Some specific sources of such cultural tensions are discussed below.

Cultural Imprints on
Managerial and Leadership Styles

How have cultural imprints influenced managerial and leadership styles in contemporary organizations? By valuing and perpetuating interpersonal and communicative styles found in the mythological representations of the Yankee entrepreneur and the frontiersman. Managers and executives are expected to be confident and aggressive, intensely competitive and tough-minded, and consistently impersonal and detached. They are expected to demonstrate the rugged individualism of the early pioneers and the savage ruthlessness of the cowboy, especially when it comes to making tough decisions in organizations (Maier, 1993). Twentieth century organizational heroes have included men like Donald

Trump and Henry Ford, who exemplify self-reliance, ruthless individualism, and an intense zeal for work. However, this brand of leadership style can be exclusionary toward women, Hispanics, and African Americans (to name only a few), whose own managerial styles are likely to be shaped by different cultural myths and experiences (Eagly & Johnson, 1990).

Several writers have systematically highlighted different cultural assumptions and values undergirding the communication styles of different cultural groups in America (Harper & Hirokawa, 1988). Basing his discussion on a study of Cuban Americans, Delgado (1981), for instance, suggests that Hispanics value work itself and abstract organizational goals less highly, while simultaneously valuing connections with colleagues over and above task considerations in leadership situations. This can result in intense cultural clashes when Hispanics have to work in organizations that are structured to value social distance and the work ethic over consideration for organizational members. Similar issues have been raised by Foeman and Pressley (1987) in their discussion of problems faced by African Americans in contemporary organizations. They and others argue that Black Americans' strong sense of community and reliance on collective responsibility (Sitaram & Cogdell, 1976) can be an enduring source of cultural tension in organizations that are primarily structured to endorse *individual* decision making and accountability.

At a more microlevel of managerial communication, legacies of the Protestant ethos call for *restrained* speech styles, while cultural imprints of frontier ideologies demand functional simplicity and brevity in language. Neither the Yankee entrepreneur nor the cowboy are famed for expressiveness in language. Both are reputed for their directness and simplicity of speech patterns. American managerial communication is ideologically driven by these values of restraint and functional simplicity. Right from the first day of business school, incipient managers are socialized to express themselves tersely and directly, with a minimum of creativity in both spoken and written language. Again, these implicit and explicit rules favoring direct communication styles can clash with the cultural codes underwriting Hispanic and Black forms of expression, in which language is often more colorful, ambiguous, and inventive (Kochman, 1981).

Cultural imprints also affect organizational rules about employee *appearance.* Contemporary organizations actually hold extremely narrow definitions of what constitutes *acceptable professional appearance,* definitions that are predominantly influenced by myths of the Protestant work ethic. Sobriety is at the cornerstone of what constitutes acceptable organizational appearance. In a study of college recruiters' preferences, Jenkins and Atkins (1990) found that conservative dress styles were overwhelmingly preferred and eventually influenced the recruiters' selection of candidates. Despite the growing diversity of the workforce, organizations continue to uphold dress codes and requirements about physical appearance that are more in keeping with the aesthetic preferences of early East Coast enterprises and that are less inclusive of diverse cultural influences. Organizational rules about physical appearance can thus become a source of cultural tensions because they stifle a multitude of cultural inclinations and associate images of unprofessionalism with those employees who deviate from traditional organizational norms.

In extreme cases, organizations have been known to exhibit tremendous *cultural hostility* toward individuals who look and dress "differently" from dominant organizational expectations. Both men and women who are judged to be overweight have repeatedly experienced this form of organizational discrimination, especially in industries where the individual directly interacts with the public and the media. Other extreme cases include decisions like the one made by a leading Fortune 500 company to discipline one of its employees for braiding her hair in a style commonly worn by many African American subcultures. In both situations, organizations were merely endorsing structural preferences about how organization members should look like. These structural preferences however, are so deeply embedded in contemporary culture that their normative influence is usually taken as a given.

Cultural Imprints on the
Discourse of Work and Career

Mythic values of the Protestant work ethic and the frontier influence the discourse of career and work in organizations. The term *discourse,* which has been introduced and popularized by postmodern and post-structural thinking (Best & Kellner, 1991; Roseneau, 1992) refers to the entire ensemble of ongoing enunciatory practices including writing, everyday speech and conversation, media representations, and electronic text. If we examine the discourse of work and career, we can easily locate the legacies of early Protestant notions of work as salvation lingering today, especially in the preeminent place accorded to work and career in our everyday lives. It is possible to argue that individual identities are substantially shaped by occupational linkages, and social status is largely dependent on career success. Not only has the Protestant work ethic shaped ideas about the value of hard work, it has also given work and career a central position within the American cultural experience (Perin, 1990).

Both the frontier mythologies and the Protestant ethos have also left behind intensely individualistic orientations toward the performance and evaluation of work. Current teamwork fads notwithstanding, American attitudes toward work continue to be dominated by ideas of individual merit, effort, and competitiveness.

Formal performance appraisals usually search for signs of individual effort and assertiveness, and informal organizational mechanisms encourage the same values. Overall, images of the hard-working and disciplined Yankee entrepreneur combine with those of the ruthless cowboy to produce an *ideology of career* that is underwritten by assumptions of providence and the survival of the fittest.

These discourses of work and career negatively affect individuals whose cultural socialization is at odds with these values. Those whose dominant cultural experiences have been in community-oriented groups are often quite uncomfortable with both the omniscient place of career and its individualistic flavor. For decades, feminists have been stressing that women are frequently alienated by such strident orientations toward competitiveness, leaving them sometimes adrift in the corporate jungle. In sum, the mythic values of individualistic careerism can clash with different sets of values held by women, African Americans, individuals from Latin and Eastern European cultures, and so on, and this can prevent many minority group members and women from making "correct" career moves and decisions.

Similarly, the ideology of meritocratic career advancement can often be at odds with cultures like several Asian American ones that strongly revere age, experience, and wisdom in the workplace. In organizations that regularly edge out senior members to make way for younger and presumably more cutting-edge "pioneers," cultural groups that hold strong attitudes about the value of age and wisdom can experience considerable discomfort and have a hard time developing professional relationships with individuals in these positions.

It is also interesting to note how career discourses that bear the imprint of frontier and Protestant mythologies of masculinity prevent women from articulating and enacting a different notion of career. As discussed earlier, both work and career have been historically constructed as exclusively male domains calling for a particular masculine orientation. Organizational career legends in America are rarely about women. Henry Ford, Lee Iacocca, Donald Trump, Steve Jobs, Bill Gates, and countless other male career successes endorse the sense that career success is a masculine affair conducted in a predominantly masculine domain in which women are by definition intruders. Not only are these career heroes invariably men, they also radiate the values of the Calvinist and the cowboy. By their discursive associations with career success, a whole exclusionary domain is created with respect to women, minorities, and others who do not fit the image.

Finally, the discursive absence of families in the myths of the Protestant ethos and the frontier are reproduced today in the discourse of organizational careers. Career is discursively constructed as an exclusively *organizational* sphere requiring single-minded devotion and commitment to work. The subtext of this discourse can be read as treating children and families as an unwelcome distraction that organizations can ill afford. My contention here is that the mythic neglect of the family in two culturally prominent discourses combines today with specific political and economic conditions to structure organizations that are *culturally hostile* to the notion of women (and perhaps men) raising children, nurturing families, and simultaneously pursuing organizational careers. Certainly, maternity laws and policies in America are among the most backward in the industrialized world with respect to accommodating family concerns into career ones. For both men and women whose family orientations are rapidly changing, tensions around career and family accommodations have been on the rise over the last decade and continue to contribute to an overall sense that diversity is still an undervalued condition in the workplace.

CULTURAL IMPRINTS AND DILEMMAS OF DIVERSITY

Discussions of workplace diversity invariably revolve around formal mechanisms of inclusion of historically disadvantaged groups in organizations. Since the publication of *Workforce 2000,* organizational scholars have addressed the diversity question mainly by examining hiring and promotion figures and by emphasizing the need for valuing different styles and cultures. However, as discussed in the opening chapter of this book, these endorsements of diversity have not mitigated the frustration and anger felt by women and minority groups in organizations. This chapter suggests that this phenomenon can perhaps be best understood as a form of *cultural tension* that is produced as a result of clashes between cultural codes governing various societal subcultures on the one hand, and the dominant cultural codes of contemporary organizations on the other.

This chapter thus shifts attention away from a narrow perspective that regards the problems created by an increasingly multicultural workforce as resulting solely from uneducated stereotypes and intergroup conflicts. Rather, it suggests that we look to the culture and structure of organizations themselves as sources of enormous potential cultural conflict. This analysis also suggests that the problems of fit experienced by women, ethnic minorities, homosexuals, and others may not always be with respect to specific members of the majority group as much as with the underlying rules of organizational life.

This view has important implications for how we engage the diversity issue. By pinpointing structural-cultural sources of tension, it suggests that diversity education/training is a far from adequate response to the problems of multicultural inclusion.

By adopting a historical perspective, it also shows how fundamental taken-for-granted assumptions in organizations are products of specific mythological moments and are therefore open to change. This kind of analysis permits us to see organizational values such as impersonality, masculinity, assertiveness, the work ethic, and so on, as not necessarily pragmatic or moral in themselves, but as reified cultural imprints of earlier ideologies. This in turn suggests that a whole spectrum of alternative values and cultural codes may be more relevant to organizations that operate in increasingly multicultural societies.

It is hoped that this chapter has introduced the notion that contemporary American organizations are structured in ways that may be culturally irrelevant. Bureaucratic organizations are very much the cultural products of a specific set of economic movements and ideologies. Given the strongly institutionalized nature of most of their practices and values, however, they continue to retain much of their original form and shape. However, their institutionalized practices may be rapidly becoming less meaningful to different groups of people who conceptualize the nature of work and life very differently. By suggesting that much of what passes for organizational realities are in fact leftover cultural imprints of the Protestant ethos and the myths of the frontier, we are also encouraging the idea of conceptualizing organizations in different ways and using different cultural experiences. For organizations to become multicultural, their rules and values will also have to change in diverse directions.

NOTE

1. This is not to say that the Protestant ideology remained static and fixed over time. Countless commentators, including Lasch (1979) and Marty (1970), emphasize the shifting nature of this ideology from the early colonial writings of Cotton Mather to the sharper and more secularized visions of Benjamin Franklin and Henry Ward Beecher. Nevertheless, most writers also argue that certain features of the Protestant ethic have remained constant and continue to guide beliefs and actions, even as they undergo changes in meaning and definition.

REFERENCES

Alvesson, M. (1991). Organizational symbolism and ideology. *Journal of Management Studies, 28,* 207-225.

Atherton, L. (1961). *The cattle kings.* Lincoln: University of Nebraska Press.

Baritz, L. (1985). *Backfire: American culture and the Vietnam war.* New York: Ballantine.

Barstow, A. L. (1994). *Witchcraze: A new history of the European witch hunts.* London: Pandora.

Barthes, R. (1957). *Mythologies.* St. Albans: Paladin.

Beecher, H. W. (1844). *Seven lectures to young men.* Indianapolis: Thomas B. Cutler.

Bellah, R. N., Madsen, R., Sullivan, W. M., Swidler, A., & Tipton, S. M. (1985). *Habits of the heart: Individualism and commitment in American life.* New York: Harper & Row.

Bendix, R. (1956). *Work and authority in industry: Ideologies of management in the course of industrialization.* Berkeley: University of California Press.

Best, S., & Kellner, D. (1991). *Postmodern theory: Critical interrogations.* New York: Guilford.

Beyer, J. M. (1981). Ideologies, values, and decision making in organizations. In P. C. Nystrom & W. H. Starbuck (Eds.), *Handbook of organizational design* (pp. 166-202). New York: Oxford University Press.

Billington, R. A. (1966). *America's frontier heritage.* Albuquerque: University of New Mexico Press.

Blum, L., & Smith, V. (1988). Women's mobility in the corporation: A critique of the politics of optimism. *Signs, 13,* 528-545.

Campbell, J. (1988). *The power of myth.* New York: Anchor.

Cooper, J. F. (1826). *The last of the Mohicans: A tale of 1757.* New York: Penguin.

Cooper, J. F. (1841). *The deerslayer.* Philadelphia: Lea & Blanchard.

Cox, T., & Nkomo, S. M. (1986). Differential appraisal criteria based on race of the ratee. *Group and Organization Studies, 11,* 101-119.

Czarniawska-Joerges, B. (1988). *Ideological control in non-ideological organizations.* New York: Praeger.

Delgado, M. (1981). Hispanic cultural values: Implications for small groups. *Small Group Behavior, 12,* 69-80.

Demos, J. (1982). *Entertaining satan: Witchcraft and the culture of early New England.* New York: Oxford University Press.

Denhardt, R. (1981). *In the shadow of organization.* Lawrence: University of Kansas Press.

DiMaggio, P. J. (1991). Constructing an organizational field as a professional project: U.S. art museums, 1920-1940. In W. Powell & P. J. DiMaggio (Eds.), *The new institutionalism in organizational analysis* (pp. 267-292). Chicago: University of Chicago Press.

DiMaggio, P. J., & Powell, W. (1983). The iron cage revisited: Institutional isomorphism and collective rationality in organizational fields. *American Sociological Review, 48,* 147-160.

Eagly, A. H., & Johnson, B. T. (1990). Gender and leadership style. *Psychological Bulletin, 108,* 233-256.

Ellis, E. S., & Wheeler, E. L. (1966). *Seth Jones and Deadwood Dick on deck.* New York: Oddessy.

Elson, R. M. (1985). *Myths and mores in American best sellers, 1865-1965.* New York: Garland.

Fitzpatrick, J. (1980). Adapting to danger. *Sociology of Work and Occupations, 7,* 133-159.

Foeman, A. K., & Pressley, G. (1987). Ethnic culture and corporate culture: Using Black styles in organizations. *Communication Quarterly,* 293-307.

Gard, W. (1949). *Frontier justice.* Norman: University of Oklahoma Press.

Geuss, R. (1981). *The idea of critical theory.* Cambridge: University of Cambridge Press.

Green, M. (1979). *Dreams of adventure and deeds of empire.* New York: Basic Books.

Harper, N. L., & Hirokawa, R. Y. (1988). A comparison of persuasive strategies used by female and male managers: An examination of downward influence. *Communication Quarterly, 36*, 157-168.

Hine, R. V. (1980). *Community on the American frontier: Separate but not alone.* Norman: University of Oklahoma Press.

Howitt, D., & Owasu-Bempah, J. (1990). The pragmatics of institutional racism: Beyond words. *Human Relations, 43*, 885-895.

Ilgen, D. R., & Youtz, M. A. (1986). Factors affecting the evaluation and development of minorities in organizations. In K. Rowland & G. Ferris (Eds.), *Research in personnel and human resource management* (Vol. 4, pp. 307-337). Greenwich, CT: JAI Press.

Jackall, R. (1988). *Moral mazes: The world of corporate managers.* New York: Oxford University Press.

Jenkins, M. C., & Atkins, T. V. (1990). Perceptions of acceptable dress by corporate and noncorporate recruiters. *Journal of Human Behavior and Learning, 7*, 38-46.

Kasson, J. F. (1976). *Civilizing the machine: Technology and Republican values in America, 1776-1900.* Harmondsworth, UK: Penguin.

Karlsen, C. (1987). *The devil in the shape of a woman: Witchcraft in colonial New England.* New York: W. W. Norton.

Kochman, T. (1981). *Black and white styles in conflict.* Chicago: University of Chicago Press.

Larson, M. S. (1977). *The rise of professionalism: A sociological analysis.* Berkeley: University of California Press.

Lasch, C. (1979). *The culture of narcissism: American life in an age of diminishing expectations.* New York: Warner.

Leverauz, D. (1980). *The language of Puritan feeling: An exploration in literature, psychology, and social history.* New Brunswick, NJ: Rutgers University Press.

Maier, M. (1993). "Am I the only one who wants to launch?" Corporate masculinity and the space shuttle Challenger disaster. *Masculinities, 1*, 34-45.

Mangan, J. A., & Walvin, J. (Eds.). (1987). *Manliness and morality: Middle-class masculinity in Britain and America, 1800-1940.* New York: St. Martin's.

Marty, M. (1970). *Righteous empire: The Protestant experience in America.* New York: Dial.

Merkle, J. (1980). *Management and ideology.* Berkeley: University of California Press.

Meyer, J. W., & Rowan, B. (1977). Institutionalized organizations: Formal structure as myth and ceremony. *American Journal of Sociology, 83*, 340-363.

Miller, P. (1954). *The New England mind: The seventeenth century.* Cambridge, MA: Harvard University Press.

Miller, P. (1963). *The Puritans.* New York: Harper & Row.

Morrison, A. M., & Von Glinow, M. A. (1990). Women and minorities in management. *American Psychologist, 45*, 200-208.

Olshan, M. A. (1993). Standards-making organizations and the rationalization of American life. *The Sociological Quarterly, 34*, 319-335.

Perin, C. (1990). *Some cultural properties of careers.* Paper presented at the annual meeting of the American Anthropological Association, New Orleans.

Prasad, P., & Prasad, A. (1994). The ideology of professionalism and work computerization: An institutionalist study of technological change. *Human Relations, 47*, 1433-1458.

Rodgers, D. T. (1978). *The work ethic in industrial America, 1850-1920.* Chicago: University of Chicago Press.

Roosevelt, T. (1907). *The winning of the West.* New York: G.P. Putnam's Sons.

Roseneau, P. M. (1992). *Post-modernism and the social sciences: Insights, inroads, and intrusions.* Princeton, NJ: Princeton University Press.

Rourke, C. (1942). *The roots of American culture and other essays.* New York: Van Wyck.

Schneider, H. W. (1958). *The Puritan mind.* New York: Holt.

Scott, R. W. (1991). Unpacking institutional arguments. In W. W. Powell & P. DiMaggio (Eds.), *The new institutionalism in organizational analysis* (pp. 164-182). Chicago: University of Chicago Press.

Shain, B. A. (1994). *The myth of American individualism: The Protestant origins of American political thought.* Princeton, NJ: Princeton University Press.

Sitaram, K. S., & Cogdell, R. T. (1976). *Foundations of intercultural communication.* Columbus, OH: Charles E. Merrill.

Slotkin, R. (1985). *The fatal environment: The myth of the frontier in the age of industrialization, 1800-1890.* New York: Atheneum.

Slotkin, R. (1992). *Gunfighter nation: The myth of the frontier in twentieth-century America.* New York: Atheneum.

Starbuck, W. H. (1982). Congealing oil: Inventing ideologies to justify acting ideologies out. *Journal of Management Studies, 19,* 3-27.

Stinchcombe, A. L. (1965). Social structure and organizations. In J. G. March (Ed.), *Handbook of organizations* (pp. 142-193). Chicago: Rand McNally.

Strenski, I. (1987). *Four theories of myth in twentieth-century history: Cassirer, Eliade, Levi-Strauss and Malinowski.* London: MacMillan.

Tawney, R. H. (1926). *Religion and the rise of capitalism.* New York: Harcourt, Brace & World.

Therborn, G. (1980). *The ideology of power and the power of ideology.* London: Verso.

Tolbert, P. S. (1988). Institutional sources of organizational culture in major law firms. In L. Zucher (Ed.), *Institutional Patterns and Organizations,* (pp. 101-113). Cambridge,MA: Ballinger.

Weber, M. (1958). *The Protestant ethic and the spirit of capitalism.* London: Charles Scribner's Sons.

Weiss, R. M. (1986). *Managerial ideology and the social control of deviance.* New York: Praeger.

Young, K. (1993). Violence, risk, and liability in male sports culture. *Sociology of Sport Journal, 10,* 373-396.

Zucker, L. (1983). The role of institutionalization in cultural persistence. *American Sociological Review, 42,* 726-743.

7

Dreams of Diversity and the Realities of Intergroup Relations in Organizations

MICHAEL ELMES

DEBRA L. CONNELLEY

An explosion in the availability of workshops, videotapes, training, and books on managing diversity (Chemers, Oskamp, & Costanzo, 1995; Cox, 1993; Fagenson, 1993; Gudykunst, 1994; Haight, 1990; Jackson, 1992; Powell, 1993) implies not only strong demand but also abundant supply of expertise on the topic. Much of this material suggests that diversity training will lead to improved organizational performance; by "transitioning" from homogeneous, hegemonic, white, male-dominated organizations to consensus-based, merito-cratic, multicultural ones, we are led to believe that market share will increase, costs decrease, and productivity improve (e.g., Morrison, 1992).

Although the eradication of racism, sexism, elitism, and ageism, among others, from organizations is a worthy goal irrespective of its economic value, from an intergroup relations perspective, we doubt that the transition can occur quickly or easily. Furthermore, we doubt that an economic utility narrative built around "diversity for improved organizational performance" can bridge the strong and often highly contentious differences that exist among groups in organizations. Just as Nord (1978) raised doubts about humanizing the workplace in light of the realities of power, we question whether managers and change agents can succeed in creating and sustaining organizations that truly embrace diversity much less "celebrate differences," to use a popular term. The basis for our argument is that the way that members experience themselves and behave toward others in organizations is shaped, in part, by psychological processes that drive people to favor members of their own in-group and discriminate against members of out-groups. For this reason, we believe that any discussion of managing diversity must take intergroup dynamics into account.

In this chapter, we propose that three powerful social "resisting" forces are likely to hinder the emergence of truly pluralistic organizations:

- The proclivity for social groups, particularly dominant social groups, to preserve status differentials
- Social identity conflict among those who are the supposed beneficiaries of diversity programs
- The rise of ethnocentrism and intergroup aggression in an era of declining resources

We discuss how each of these forces represents a potent barrier to the long-term effectiveness and sustainability of diversity programs in organizations.

THEORETICAL BACKGROUND: INTERGROUP RELATIONS AND SOCIAL IDENTITY THEORY

Much of the current thinking in the area of managing diversity is based on assumptions that we consider to be flawed. These assumptions are rooted in the work of Allport (1954), who argued that expressed hostility toward people of different racial or ethnic groups was simply a matter of prejudice, "ultimately a problem of personality formation and development" (p. 41). In this view, prejudice arises from a preference for what is familiar over what is alien. Negative attitudes, stereotypes, and discriminatory behavior can therefore be diminished by increasing the familiarity of the "alien Other" through social interaction. Person-to-person contact, it is argued, will lead individuals to realize that they have much in common with those against whom they have been biased, increasing interpersonal attraction and reducing hostility.

We believe that this view is naive. There is no guarantee that contact between members of dissimilar groups will lead to the discovery of similitude. It is equally plausible that such contact could confirm negative stereotypes or even reveal additional differences. In addition, empirical study has failed to support the claims made by the *contact hypothesis*. While contact under certain conditions may improve attitudes toward individuals, there is no evidence that positive evaluations reliably transfer to the group as a whole (Hewstone & Brown, 1986). For contact to generalize to the group, the change in attitudes toward the individual must also be associated with the group. It is essentially an issue of level of analysis. Discrimination toward a group or class of people must be understood at the level on which it occurs—the level of intergroup dynamics.

When viewed from an intergroup perspective, individuals in organizations relate to others as members of social groups and categories within those organizations. Although individuals might be identified as members of any number of specific categories or groups, essentially people are classified as either "like me" or "different from me." What seems to determine the nature of the relationship between people is the perception of similarity or difference—over and above the characteristics of a particular group.

The minimal group studies[1] have demonstrated this concept conclusively. In these studies, even individuals who are randomly assigned to meaningless groups behave differently toward others who they think are members of their own group (in-group) than they act toward people who they think are members of another group (out-group). Specifically, individuals will judge themselves to be similar to people who are said to be in the same group. They will also express feelings of liking toward in-group members and report a desire to cooperate with them on a variety of tasks. The opposite is true concerning members of different groups. Toward out-groupers, individuals will express feelings of dislike and dissimilarity, adopting a competitive orientation. These reactions occur even when the people involved have *never met and know nothing about each other* except group membership.

These findings are especially powerful because it is the simple act of categorization itself, even without interaction or anticipated contact, that seems to create in-group bias. This bias manifests itself in perceptions of similarities between the in-group and the self and differences from the out-group. These perceptual biases, in turn, produce differential attitudes and behaviors (Doise, 1978). The overall conclusion from the minimal group studies was that in-group/out-group distinctions trigger a psychological process that "tends to create discriminatory social relations" (Turner, 1981, p. 77). Therefore, we submit that intergroup dynamics are essential drivers of prejudice in organizations.

As important as minimal groups were to demonstrate the strength and pervasiveness of intergroup bias and discrimination, real groups in organizations do interact. Therefore, in this chapter, we adopt the definition of a group proposed by Alderfer and Smith (1982), who define a group as: a collection of individuals

1. who have significantly interdependent relations with each other,
2. who perceive themselves as a group by reliably distinguishing members from nonmembers,
3. whose group identity is recognized by nonmembers,
4. who, as group members acting alone or in concert, have significantly interdependent relations with other groups, and
5. whose roles in the group are a function of expectations from themselves, from other group members, and from nongroup members. (p. 38)

Categorizing individuals according to social groups serves several important psychological functions, including assisting in sense making and contributing to self-esteem. Recent theory in social cognition maintains that people categorize others according to group membership because it simplifies the process of sense making and allows them to easily distinguish between people. Categories are useful insofar as they allow the user to make inferences (e.g., between ethnicity and traits such as aggressiveness), evaluations (good or bad), or diagnoses (relationship between group membership and behaviors). In other words, categorization helps to anticipate or predict the behavior of others (albeit not always accurately) and determine an appropriate response. For example, information gained by categorizing another person into a social group would help you choose a topic of conversation with a Baptist minister—or a rock star.

Identification with a social group also has profound implications for the way the individual perceives the self. Social groups or categories may include, for example, race, gender, hierarchical rank, profession, and so on. Individuals define themselves in terms of in-group stereotypes of status, prestige, needs, goals, attitudes, behavioral norms, and so on (Turner, 1982). Therefore, the act of social classification and identification assists individuals in defining themselves and others within the social environment, in answering the question, who am I? (Ashforth & Mael, 1989), and in providing a positive view of themselves (Turner, 1982), contributing to self-esteem.

Several factors influence whether individuals are likely to group themselves or others in a given social category. In their review of the literature on social identity theory, Ashforth and Mael (1989) identify four factors that increase the probability that individuals will experience themselves as "psychologically intertwined with the fate of (a particular) group" and feel at a personal level the "successes and failures" of the group (p. 21). Note that these four factors involve both conscious, or behavioral, and nonconscious, or psychological, processes.

First, identification with a group is more likely to occur when characteristics of the out-group are salient. A theoretical construct for determining salience is the *meta-contrast ratio* (Turner, 1987), which describes just how much dissimilarity exists between members of one's own group and others. If the ratio is high, the separateness and disparity between groups is conspicuous to the individual. For example, if an inexperienced male is named vice president of marketing over a woman with 25 years of experience, gender may be quite salient to the female employees.

Second, individuals are likely to identify with a group when it has distinctive characteristics in relation to comparable groups (Oakes & Turner, 1986). Distinctive groups have qualities that are unique from other groups, for example, the traditional garb for Islamic women versus the standard business suit worn by American professional women. However, there are bases of distinctiveness that have served as a focus of discrimination in many cultures over time, namely gender, race, and ethnicity. McGuire's (1984) Distinctiveness Theory suggests these are potent identity groups because rare, atypical, or novel traits are noticed more readily due to their "greater informational richness and value for discriminating self from others" (Cota & Dion, 1986, p. 770). Presumably, the novelty of the trait draws the person's attention to it (Oakes, 1987), causing comparisons of similarity and differences between the observer and the trait. Not surprisingly, then, ethnicity is more salient for minority groups than for majority groups (e.g., being white is not atypical in most organizations). Recent studies confirm (Fiske, 1993) that the three most frequent categories used to group people are gender, age, and race.

Individuals are also likely to identify with a group that they perceive as being prestigious and successful in the organization, because self-concept is inextricably tied to in-group status. When membership is based on physical characteristics, such as age, race, or physical disability, the status of the group is enhanced by comparing the in-group to other groups on dimensions that cast the in-group in a positive light (Hogg & Abrams, 1988).

Finally, competition between groups increases the potential for hostility. Competition accentuates we/they differences between groups, clarifies group boundaries, and makes group identification more likely (Brewer, 1979; Doise, 1978). Greater identification with social groups from any combination of these four factors invites comparisons of similarities and differences and sets the stage for discriminatory behavior.

On the basis of social identity and intergroup relations theories, we propose that the transition to a truly diverse organization—one in which differences in the physical, social, cognitive, and emotional orientations of various groups are accepted and valued in the organization—will be far from smooth. As group values and practices become more distinctive, as group status is elevated (or threatened), as features of out-groups become more salient, and as competition among diverse groups increases, relations among members of various groups are likely to become increasingly polarized and combative. This is in marked contrast to the popular, romanticized version of diversity in which, like a peaceable kingdom, harmony among diverse groups (presumably leading to improved organizational performance) is achieved by preaching the benefits of a diverse workforce and occasionally, usually quite publicly, promoting "diverse" individuals into positions of responsibility.

In our view, this impoverished narrative for diversity serves more to defend against the fear, uncertainty, and hostility that already exist among groups than to bridge the deep differences that separate them. Below we discuss in detail some of the social forces that, from an intergroup relations perspective, are likely to impede the development of genuine diversity in organizations. We also discuss the implications for theory and practice.

INTERGROUP RELATIONS AND
THE MAINTENANCE OF STATUS DIFFERENTIALS

One barrier to the evolution of a diverse organization is the power of social identity to define group (and, subsequently, group members') status relative to other groups. Because of the importance of identification with a social group to self-definition, group members come to believe that the status they have—high or low—is the status they are supposed to have, and they often enact roles and behaviors that are consistent with their groups' relative status. Specifically, groups possessing high status will attempt to institutionalize their position, often by enacting and enforcing rules for behavior that preserve the status quo. For example, during the past 10 years, of the women and minorities who now make up more than 50% of the U.S. workforce, only 2% have been promoted into senior executive positions among America's 1,000 largest companies (Dominguez, 1990). A recent study of promotion and pay practices by the Office of Federal Contract Compliance Programs (OFCCP) unexpectedly found that women had plateaued at entry-level and middle management positions in nine Fortune 500 companies (Simpson, 1991). From an intergroup relations perspective, this career plateauing, commonly referred to as the "glass ceiling" effect, can be explained by the dominant group's success in maintaining its higher status standing in the organization as well as the social and emotional conditioning of lower status groups to "know their place" in the organization (Gery, 1977).

It is no surprise that access to the upper level positions in most organizations is limited to members of the dominant group. We agree with social theorists who argue that the social order is largely constructed by those who dominate it. Hence, the definitions of competency and determinants of success reflect the characteristics of the dominant group. Accepting women and minorities into senior management positions is not compatible with the social identity of what is primarily a white, male bastion. A heterogeneous population at that level would therefore lead to varying levels of discomfort among the people working at that level.[2] People who were once thought of as lower in status would now become working peers, yet they would not, by definition, "fit." For example, one senior executive described an intelligent, articulate woman who was being considered for a promotion into an executive position: "I always think of her as . . . I mean, she could be married to my brother" (Gallese, 1991). Apparently, this executive did not relish the thought of interacting professionally with a woman who reminded him of his sister-in-law—a category of person that diverged sharply from the executives with whom he normally (and comfortably) interacted. Because individuals tend to stereotype out-groupers, contributing to a misleading notion regarding the homogeneity of out-group members, it is likely that this executive (and many others like him) would find it difficult to see women as colleagues—viewing them instead as mothers, sisters, wives, and daughters (Connelley, 1993).

Members of dominant organizational groups are likely to deny that the exclusion of members of lower status groups occurs due to social categories rather than to ability: to do so would raise doubts about their own success in the organization. They need to believe that their ascendancy (as well as the plateauing of women and minorities) is attributable to their competence and skill—internal factors—rather than to their gender or race—situational or external factors.

Indeed, Hewstone and Jaspers (1984) argue that individuals enhance their own self-image by making category-based social attributions that are based on stereotypes held by other members of their in-group. The "ultimate" attribution error (Pettigrew, 1979) is the propensity for attributing causes to people's behavior that confirm our biases. Specifically, when a member of an out-group engages in positive or desirable behavior, the tendency is to attribute that behavior to situational factors. However, when an out-grouper engages in negative or undesirable behavior, the tendency is to attribute the cause to dispositional factors, chiefly group membership.

The social and emotional conditioning of women and minorities into lower status roles also contributes to the maintenance of status differentials. As Gery (1977) notes,

> Women and minorities have had so few role models and such limited amounts of personal sponsorship in the system that is necessary for success. . . . In the past, only the truly exceptional have been able to succeed, and there has been almost no tolerance for mediocrity and/or failure by minorities and women that has not resulted in negative generalizations to most other women and minorities who might follow. (p. 373)

In addition, by virtue of their training and the reward systems they have had to deal with in the past, many women and minorities have come to believe that they are not sufficiently capable or entitled to the same kinds of roles and positions that their white male counterparts enjoy.

There is evidence that gender, race, and ethnicity affect perceived self-efficacy, thereby contributing to the maintenance of status differentials. Whites, particularly males, have been found to have a significantly stronger perception of personal control and self-determination than African Americans (Gurin, Gurin, & Morrison, 1978) or Mexican Americans (Mirowsky & Ross, 1983). Similarly, males have been found to have a greater sense of control, mastery, and self-efficacy than females (for a review, see Block, 1983). Gecas (1989) argues that power differences in society are at the root of these differences in self-efficacy, which, we argue, are preserved in status differentials in organizations.

Social identity theory predicts that under conditions where groups are evaluated negatively and assigned inferior status, out-groups will act to counter the negative effects on self-esteem produced by social stratification. Tajfel and Turner (1979) suggest three possible strategies. The social mobility strategy involves an attempt by the individual to leave the negatively valued group and join the higher status group, thereby improving his or her personal status. In terms of demographically based identity groups, this is difficult, if not impossible to accomplish. In order to effectively execute a mobility strategy, the boundaries must be permeable. Becoming white, or becoming male, is simply not an option. When boundaries are unbreachable, social change strategies may be adopted. There are two types; the first is social creativity, which involves three possible tactics:

1. The out-group can find new criteria by which they compare themselves with the dominant group (e.g., men may have more personal power, but women are better at empowering others).
2. Out-group members can redefine their attributes so that they are given a positive value (e.g., the development of a more Afro-centric definition of beauty as a result of the "black is beautiful" movement). This allows the out-group to "feel superior in terms of their most valued characteristics" (Hogg & Abrams, 1988, p. 57).
3. The out-group can select alternative out-groups with which to compare themselves. Lower status groups are chosen, thereby creating the opportunity for positive evaluation of one's own group. (An American-born minority group may look down on immigrant workers because of their accents.)

The final strategy for overcoming negative evaluations in out-groups is social competition. Here, the very legitimacy of the position of the dominant group is challenged by direct confrontation (e.g. riots, open conflict, or war).

Although not addressed by Tajfel and Turner, yet another option is to "cannibalize" one's own group. Research suggests that to lessen their discontent as members of lower status groups, some individuals are likely to compare themselves to each other rather than to members of higher status groups (Hyman, 1942). The so-called "black sheep effect" describes the tendency of individuals to reject or derogate members of their own group who adopt objectional positions or who do not exemplify the characteristics that provide the group with positive differentiation from other groups (Marques, Yzerbyt, & Leyens, 1988) In our view, this phenomenon of within-group differentiation among members of lower status groups only perpetuates the belief in their subordinate status and weakens any possibility of community.

Given that mobility opportunities often turn out to be illusory, and it is socially desirable to avoid the extreme of competition strategies, the previously mentioned creativity strategies may have some merit for managing diversity and reducing organizational conflict. Research on minority-majority relations suggests that if lower status groups try to effect social change on their own—to "integrate their sectional claims into the very structuring of the organization" (Mumby, 1987, p. 116)—they will be effective to the degree that they are cohesive as a group, unified behind a common vision, and able and willing to articulate that vision with persistence and consistency over time (Nemeth, 1986). Although this strategy may force members of higher status groups to rethink their assumptions and beliefs about organization practices, it also assumes that the dominant group is going to encourage or at the least simply accept the efforts of the out-group to establish a positive identity. This may not always be in the dominant group's self-interest, threatening the higher status group's sense of identity and privilege. The lower status groups' rhetoric of injustice may accentuate the threat because, as suggested earlier, members of dominant groups often feel little responsibility for inequities as they currently exist; in fact, they may see themselves as agents of change who are trying to rectify past injustices. Not surprisingly, when lower status groups try to broaden generally accepted beliefs and practices, they usually encounter strong resistance from members of the dominant group (Elmes & Wynkoop, 1990).

Assuming that groups are more or less invested in maintaining status differentials, we are somewhat skeptical of the idea that organizations can quickly embrace diversity in ways that reduce these status differentials. This is particularly true given the underlying frustration, blame, defensiveness, and cynicism that members of both dominant and subordinate groups often feel about each other and about the prospects for real change.

SOCIAL IDENTITY CONFLICT IN
THE TRANSITION TO DIVERSITY

Social identity conflict is another potential barrier to the emergence of diversity in organizations. Ashforth and Mael (1989) note that, "Given the number of groups to which an individual belongs, his or her social identity is likely to consist of an amalgam of identities" that are activated at different times under different conditions. These different conditions often "impose inconsistent demands" upon the person in terms of the "values, beliefs, norms, and demands inherent in [their various] identities" (p. 29). For example, a woman design engineer in charge of a project team in a high technology company is not only a project manager who identifies herself with the category, project manager, but also a design engineer and a woman. Social identity conflict is likely to arise when, as a design engineer, she feels compelled to recommend further testing to improve product quality but, as a project manager, she recognizes the importance of meeting project deadlines. Either choice also has implications for her as a woman in a male-dominated role and profession.

We argue that social identity conflict makes it particularly difficult for women and minorities—the alleged beneficiaries of diversity—to succeed in a system which, although emphasizing the importance of diversity, is still dominated by traditional norms and values. Unlike most senior management, a homogeneous, well-educated group of white males who seldom face identity conflict, minorities and women each day experience the dissonance of social identity conflict. A seemingly routine decision for a manager in a profit-driven enterprise can be quite complex, even strategic, to a woman or minority working in a hierarchical organization dominated by traditional norms and values. As Du Plessis (1985) points out, "For women, then, existing in the dominant system of meanings and values that structure culture and society may be a painful double dance, clicking in, clicking out—the divided consciousness" (p. 149).

Consider Alex's (1969) ethnographic study, *Black in Blue,* of African American policemen in the 1960s. In it, he discusses the dilemma that black policemen face when dealing with black protestors during civil rights demonstrations. As one officer notes,

> I am in a ticklish situation. How so? Let's say I have to decide if I am going to be a policeman first or a [black] first. If I am a policeman first, I ostracize the other [blacks]. If I am a [black] first, there goes my job. So I don't know. (p. 163)

Another officer spoke about being tough with African American offenders, particularly if they tried to embarrass him in the presence of other white policemen:

> Yes, under certain circumstances I'm more tough. If I feel I can do more to help him [the offender] by being harsh. But I'm even more tough if they try to embarrass me. I have been embarrassed by [black] offenders, by their behavior and calling me names in front of white police officers. If I am with a [black] cop and they call me names, it doesn't bother me. But with a white cop it is embarrassing. (pp. 154-155)

In both instances, African American officers were forced to reconcile being black with being police officers who worked in both white and black communities with white policemen.

Similar kinds of identity conflicts occur in many corporations today. In a 1992 *Wall Street Journal* article on codes of silence and race in organizations (Kotlowitz & Alexander, 1992), black managers spoke of the everyday putdowns and humiliation they experienced but could not discuss for fear that their white colleagues would interpret them as exaggerations, as unsubstantiated claims of racism. From this perspective, diversity is "embraced" as long as members of lower status groups avoid bringing up issues and themes that are too far removed from the shared experiences of the majority in the organization or that might reflect poorly upon members of the dominant group (see also Dickens & Dickens, 1991).

Many members of lower status groups face a classic double bind rooted in identity conflict: If they fail to act with decisiveness and power, they are seen as not being aggressive enough to manage the challenges of executive roles; however, if they do act with decisiveness and power, they are seen as threatening or aggressive. As 59-year-old Peg Simpson states in relation to her chief executive officer's decision not to give her the presidency of a service industry corporation, even when she was the most qualified candidate, "There are glass ceilings for women because women won't fight in the same way that a man will fight. Women won't demand the same things. And the male hierarchy doesn't *expect* women to demand the same things" (Gallese, 1991, p. 134).

People deal with social identity conflicts in a variety of ways. For example, they deny that they experience them or rationalize them, depending upon to whom they have to justify their actions, for example, members of their profession, members of their ethnic or gender identity groups, and so on (Ashforth & Mael, 1989). For others, social identity conflict may lead to disillusionment and burnout under the stress of having to live with ongoing dissonance (Dickens & Dickens, 1991). Still others, in the interest of career advancement, attempt a social mobility strategy by emulating the behaviors and values of the dominant group. However, this strategy can backfire: As Navy pilot, Paula Coughlin, stated after being sexually assaulted in public by male Navy pilots at a convention to honor Gulf War veterans, "I've worked my arse off to be one of the guys, to prove that women can do whatever the job calls for. And what did I get? I was treated like trash. I wasn't one of them."

In the push to bring diversity to organizations, we suggest that individuals from lower status groups are faced with having to expend considerably more energy and effort managing the double binds and competing requirements of multiple group identities than, for example, members of higher status groups. We fear that any difficulties they face will be used as a basis for maintaining the status quo and manufacturing simplistic, ethnocentric explanations (e.g., "they" don't seem to care or "they're" not trying) for a complex problem. In this backlash scenario, the intended beneficiaries could easily become the scapegoats for "failed" diversity initiatives.

THE RISE OF ETHNOCENTRISM
AND INTERGROUP AGGRESSION
IN AN ERA OF DECLINING RESOURCES

Sociologist William Graham Sumner (1906) conceptualized ethnocentrism as a "universal syndrome" in which one's own group is the center of everything, and all others are scaled and rated with reference to it. . . . Each group nourishes its own pride and vanity, boasts itself superior, exalts its own divinities, and looks with contempt at outsiders. (pp. 12-13)

LeVine and Campbell (1972) use Sumner's definition as the starting point from which to investigate and compare a range of sociopsychological (e.g., frustration-aggression-displacement theory; psychoanalytic theory) and societal (e.g., realistic group conflict theory; reference group theory) theories of ethnocentrism. Although they find more areas of disagreement than agreement across these theories, the areas of agreement are pertinent to the concerns we have raised about efforts to manage diversity in the 1990s.

First, consistent with research discussed earlier in the chapter, LeVine and Campbell (1972) find agreement across the theories that real differences between in-groups and out-groups are often distorted in a "stereotype image of the out-group" (p. 222). For example, men often see women (and vice versa) or African Americans often see whites (and vice versa) in stereotypical ways, rather than as individuals with a range of differences and similarities *across* and even *within* their respective groups.

Second, they find convergence on the proposition that ethnocentrism is likely to occur in "more politically centralized, socially stratified, and economically differentiated societies of the modern world than among primitive tribes" (LeVine & Campbell, 1972, p. 223). Given the decline of the middle class and the growing income disparity between "haves" and "have nots" in the United States during the late 1980s and 1990s (Phillips, 1994; Strobel, 1993), ethnocentrism is likely to play an important role in how people from different economic and social categories relate to one another—both outside of and within the organizations in which they work.

Related to this point, LeVine and Campbell (1972) also find agreement on the proposition that ethnocentrism tends to increase as competition for scarce resources grows. Recently in the United States, meaningful, well-paying jobs have become a scarce resource. The emphasis on improving efficiency, lowering costs, and flattening organizational structures has led to the permanent elimination of many positions in middle management—a career level many women and minorities have only recently achieved. In addition, many high-paying jobs in U.S. manufacturing have disappeared and been replaced by lower paying jobs in the service sector (Heye, 1993).

As a result of these forces, competition for high-paying, high-status jobs in industry has grown substantially. White men, women, and people of color have been forced to compete for fewer good jobs in management and manufacturing.

We suggest that competition for fewer jobs has led to the increasing use of race and gender as a basis for explaining why members of some groups acquire or retain such positions and members of other groups do not. Each attributes the causes of its own economic uncertainty to the unjustifiably privileged status of the Other. There is every reason to believe that the trend toward downsizing, reengineering, and outsourcing that drives the competition for good jobs will continue into the next century; intergroup ethnocentrism, in our view, is an inevitable outcome of this process.

In the fourth and last area of agreement, LeVine and Campbell (1972) find support for the proposition that groups tend to return acts of aggression with aggression. We define intergroup aggression as individual behavior rooted in group identity that obstructs members of other groups from achieving their goals or enhancing their status within the social system. We interpret this proposition to mean that acts of aggression—acts that can be either physical (e.g., inflicting physical injury or pain) or symbolic (e.g., using derogatory language to describe or refer to members of another group)—are likely to be responded to in kind.

In organizations, because of the importance placed on minimizing overt conflict and maintaining instrumental control (Deetz, 1992), symbolic rather than physical forms of aggression are more common. In this form, aggression can be passive (e.g., forgetting important deadlines or failing to comply with requests for assistance) or active (withholding important information or telling derogatory stories and jokes to or about members of the out-group, often under a "just kidding" guise). It can occur even under circumstances where relationships are reciprocally interdependent and, in theory, should contain a high degree of trust, dialogue, and understanding (Connelley, 1994; Elmes & Wilemon, 1991). Acts of aggression can also lead to accusations of racism or sexism (as women might express about off-color jokes) and to counterclaims of "hypersensitivity" or "inappropriate hostility" (as whites might express about "black rage") (Kotlowitz & Alexander, 1992), thus reinforcing each group's belief in the superiority and righteousness of its point of view.

Caproni (1991) has suggested that because of the "cultural relativity of script knowledge," members of different groups "will to some degree have, and be expected to have, different scripts for understanding and enacting workplace aggression" (p. 6). From this perspective, the thresholds and rules for behaving aggressively toward members of other groups will reflect the norms and value systems of a particular social identity group. For example, Caproni (1991) found in her research that those at higher levels of the hierarchy were more likely to use coercive power (e.g., to give someone a "kick in the rear to get him going") than were managers at lower levels of the hierarchy.

Thus, intergroup aggression may occur not just as a response to some hostile act perpetrated by an out-group, but also as a result of factors within the group that influence what information they "discover" that confirms their biases about the Other (Chapman & Chapman, 1967; Hastorf & Cantril, 1954). For example, a man who assumes that women are "overly sensitive" to interpersonal conflict is likely to see and remember evidence in the workplace that confirms this bias. As a result, he may choose to provide only selected information to female colleagues under the belief that, if given the full story, they would become "overly emotional" and "ineffective." Of course, from their point of view, his withholding of information is patronizing and aggressive; it impedes their ability to work and to collaborate effectively on projects.

To conclude, LeVine and Campbell's (1972) work suggests that the predisposition for groups to "nourish" their "own pride and vanity" and to stereotype and engage in hostile acts against members of other groups is made worse when competition for scarce resources increases and issues of economic opportunity and class become salient. In this context, efforts to "manage" diversity in the 1990s by enhancing awareness of and appreciation for differences seem simplistic given current socioeconomic conditions that accentuate differences and raise tensions (Brewer, 1986).

IMPLICATIONS FOR RESEARCH

This chapter argues that issues of diversity management cannot be viewed independently of intergroup dynamics. Below are some important questions about diversity and intergroup relations worthy of further exploration.

We need to better understand how processes associated with social identification with demographic groups affect individual careers. For instance, what differentiates women and minorities who have moved up the hierarchy from those who have not? Contextual factors? Organizational demography? Interpersonal strategies? To what do women and minorities who have moved up the hierarchy attribute their success? To what do women and minorities who have not moved up attribute their own lack of progress, as well as the progress of those lower status individuals who have moved up the hierarchy? To what do senior managers attribute the progress (or lack of progress) of individuals from lower status groups who have (or have not) progressed up the hierarchy? How do these different interpretations of diversity and ascendancy reflect and shed light upon the socially constructed realities of various social groups by, for example, gender, hierarchy, ethnicity, or function?

What defines the dominant identity group in an organization? Is there any way to change the parameters for defining that group to make it more inclusive? What strengthens and raises the salience of demographically based identity group boundaries? Are there ways of decreasing the salience of these boundaries without denying a group's distinctiveness?

What are the various kinds of social identity conflicts that organization members experience? How do they deal with them? As members of subordinate groups ascend the hierarchy, do they experience more double binds and, if so, what are they and how do they manage them?

What are the most common methods that change agents and senior managers use to foster diversity in organizations? What are the theoretical sources of these initiatives? At whom are they targeted? How do people from both dominant and subordinate groups experience these initiatives before and after they are executed? In what ways are people frustrated by diversity initiatives? In what ways do these frustrations differ by social category?

What impact do economic decline and downsizing have on diversity initiatives? We have proposed that levels of social identity conflict, ethnocentrism, and intergroup aggression are likely to increase under declining organizational (or societal) conditions and performance. What data would support or not support this proposition? We would suggest that growing hostility toward affirmative action programs in recent years provides some support for this proposition.

IMPLICATIONS FOR PRACTICE

The intergroup perspective offers a variety of implications for change agents and managers who wish to foster diversity in organizations. First, change agents need to understand the impact that intergroup relations has on organizational processes. They must acknowledge that subordinate groups may not share the same normative and value systems that the organization embodies. Becoming aware of how their own social identities and group memberships affect what they see and what actions they take is important with regard to any diversity initiatives.

Second, change agents need to recognize that structural changes, that is, changes in workforce makeup, promotions of women and minorities into higher levels of the organization, represent just the beginning of an effective diversity initiative. Addressing the underlying emotions and group membership issues associated with diversity is a far more important, yet difficult and complex task.

Finally, change agents need to differentiate diversity programs that create an impression of embracing diversity from those that acknowledge the real complexities and barriers to diversity that are discussed in this chapter. Although management's espoused theory of diversity may appear sensitive and progressive, its theory-in-action (Argyris & Schon, 1978) may, in fact, only patronize differences and obfuscate underlying issues rooted in status maintenance, identity conflict, and ethnocentrism. These issues must be recognized and addressed if genuine diversity throughout all levels of the organization is to become a reality. Indeed, we argue that neglecting to recognize and deal with these more subtle and difficult aspects of diversity management dooms structural initiatives to failure.

CONCLUSION

The purpose of this chapter is not to dishearten or to dissuade managers and change agents from moving forward with more effective ways of promoting diversity. To the contrary, our purpose is to emphasize what a formidable task lies ahead if we are to intervene in ways that are truly effective and long-lasting. What concerns us more than ignoring or denying the need for management of diversity programs in organizations is the danger of developing an ideology of diversity that is faddish and superficial.

Embracing diversity raises fundamental questions about how individuals in organizations define themselves, how they feel good about themselves, and how they experience and relate to others. If organizations are to embrace diversity, then they must find creative approaches to helping people become fully aware of the impact that social identity has on sense making and behavior. How can social identity conflict and dissonance be managed with greater patience and courage? How can meaningful discussions around race, gender, and status in organizations be encouraged? In the face of internalized scripts and strong emotions, how can blaming and the threat of retaliation among members of social groups be reduced and dialogue sustained? In short, how can diverse groups within organizations create a narrative of diversity that embraces the uniqueness inherent in social differences yet finds common ground? In our view, these are the questions we face in dealing with diversity in organizations; they are difficult ones to answer. Yet, as West (1993) warns, if we fail to "hang together by combating the forces that divide us," we may very well "hang separately" (p. 159).

NOTES

1. For excellent reviews of the minimal group studies, see Turner and Giles (1981).

2. Kanter (1977) calls this homogeneity among managers "homosocial reproduction" (p. 63). However, she attributes the practice as a response to uncertainty rather than an attempt by the dominant group to preserve status.

REFERENCES

Alderfer, C. P., & Smith, K. K. (1982). Studying intergroup relations embedded in organizations. *Administrative Science Quarterly, 27*, 35-65.

Alex, N. (1969). *Black in blue: A study of the Negro policeman.* New York: Appleton-Century-Crofts.

Allport, G. W. (1954). *The nature of prejudice.* Cambridge, MA: Addison-Wesley.

Argyris, C., & Schon, D. (1978). *Organizational learning: A theory of action perspective.* Reading, MA: Addison-Wesley.

Ashforth, B. E., & Mael, F. (1989). Social identity theory and the organization. *Academy of Management Review, 14*(1), 20-39.

Block, J. H. (1983). Differentiation premises arising from differential socialization of the sexes: Some conjectures. *Child Development, 54*, 1335-1354.

Brewer, M. (1979). In-group bias in the minimal intergroup situation: A cognitive-motivational analysis. *Psychological Bulletin, 86*, 307-324.

Brewer, M. (1986). The role of ethnocentrism in intergroup conflict. In S. Worchel & W. Austin (Eds.), *Psychology of intergroup relations* (2nd ed., pp. 88-102). Chicago: Nelson-Hall.

Caproni, P. J. (1991). *Doing workplace aggression: Social cognition and the aggressive employee.* Paper presented at the Annual Meeting of the Academy of Management, Miami, FL.

Chapman, L. J., & Chapman, J. P. (1967). Genesis of popular but erroneous psychodiagnostic observations. *Journal of Abnormal Psychology, 72*, 193-204.

Chemers, M. A., Oskamp, S., & Costanzo, M. A. (Eds.). (1995). *Diversity in organizations.* Thousand Oaks, CA: Sage.

Connelley, D. L. (1993). *Toward an intergroup theory of diversity management: The role of social identity and relational models on intergroup conflict in a heterogeneous workforce.* Doctoral dissertation, Cornell University, Ithaca, NY.

Connelley, D. L. (1994). Social identity as a barrier to understanding: The role of gender and race. *Academy of Management Best Papers Proceedings 1994.* Madison, WI: Omnipress.

Cota, A. A., & Dion, K. L. (1986). Salience of gender and sex composition of ad hoc groups: An experimental test of distinctiveness theory. *Journal of Personality and Social Psychology, 50*, 770-776.

Cox, T. H., Jr. (1993). *Cultural diversity in organizations: Theory, research, and practices.* San Francisco: Berrett Koehler.

Deetz, S. (1992). *Democracy in an age of corporate colonization: Developments in communication and the politics of everyday life.* Albany: State University of New York Press.

Dickens, F. D., Jr., & Dickens, J. B. (1991). *The black manager: Making it in the corporate world.* New York: AMACOM.

Doise, W. (1978). *Groups and individuals: Explanations in social psychology.* Cambridge, UK: Cambridge University Press.

Dominguez, C. M. (1990, August 27). Crack the glass ceiling. *Information Week,* pp. 38-43.

Du Plessis, R. B. (1985). For the Etruscans: Sexual difference and artistic production—The debate over a female aesthetic. In H. Eisenstein & A. Jardine (Eds.), *The future of difference* (2nd ed., pp. 128-156). New Brunswick, NJ: Rutgers University Press.

Elmes, M., & Wilemon, D. (1991). A field study of intergroup integration in technology-based organizations. *Journal of Engineering and Technology Management, 7,* 229-250.

Elmes, M., & Wynkoop, C. (1990). Enlightened upheaval and large-scale transformation: The Polish Solidarity Trade Union Case. *Journal of Applied Behavioral Science, 26,* 245-258.

Fagenson, E. A. (1993). *Women in management: Trends, issues, and challenges in managerial diversity.* Newbury Park, CA: Sage.

Fiske, S. (1993). Social cognition and social perception. In *Annual Review of Psychology.* Palo Alto, CA: Annual Reviews, Inc.

Gallese, L. R. (1991). Why women aren't making it to the top. In *Annual Editions: Human Resources 92/93* (pp. 133-137). Guilford, CT: Dushkin.

Gecas, V. (1989). The social psychology of self-efficacy. *Annual Review of Sociology, 15,* 291-316.

Gery, G. J. (1977). Equal opportunity—Planning and managing the process of change. In M. Beer & B. Spector (Eds.), *Readings in human resource management* (pp. 361-375). New York: Free Press.

Gurin, P., Gurin, G., & Morrison, B. M. (1978). Personal and ideological aspects of internal and external control. *Social Psychology, 41,* 275-296.

Gudykunst, W. B. (1994). *Bridging differences: Effective intergroup communication.* Thousand Oaks, CA: Sage.

Haight, G. (1990). Managing diversity. In *Annual Editions: Human Resources 92/93* (pp. 39-42). Guilford, CT: Dushkin.

Hastorf, A. H., & Cantril, H. (1954). They saw a game: A case study. *Journal of Abnormal and Social Psychology, 49,* 129-134.

Hewstone, M., & Brown, R. (1986). Contact is not enough: An intergroup perspective on the "contact hypothesis." In *Contact and conflict in intergroup encounters.* Oxford: Basil Blackwell.

Hewstone, M., & Jaspers, J. (1984). Social dimensions of attributions. In H. Tajfel (Ed.), *The social dimension* (Vol. 2). Cambridge, UK: Cambridge University Press.

Heye, C. (1993). *Five years after: A preliminary assessment of the U.S. industrial performance since* Made in America. Cambridge: Industrial Performance Center, MIT.

Hogg, M. A., & Abrams, D. (1988). *Social identifications: A social psychology of intergroup relations and group processes.* London: Routledge.

Hyman, H. H. (1942). The psychology of status. *Archives of Psychology, 269.*

Jackson, S. E. (1992). *Diversity in the workplace: Human resources initiatives.* New York: Guilford.

Kanter, R. M. (1977). *Men and women of the corporation.* New York: Basic Books.

Kotlowitz, A., & Alexander, S. (1992, May 28). Tacit code of silence on matters of race perpetuates divisions. *Wall Street Journal,* pp. A1, A10.

LeVine, R. A., & Campbell, D. T. (1972). *Ethnocentrism: Theories of conflict, ethnic attitudes and group behavior.* New York: John Wiley.

Marques, J. M., Yzerbyt, V. Y., & Leyens, J. P. (1988). The black sheep effect: Extremity of judgments towards in-group members as a function of group identification. *European Journal of Social Psychology, 18,* 1-16.

McGuire, W. J. (1984). Search for the self: Going beyond self-esteem and the reactive self. In R. A. Zucker, J. Aronoff, & A. I. Rabin (Eds.), *Personal and the prediction of behavior.* New York: Academic Press.

Mirowsky, J., & Ross, C. E. (1983). Paranoia and the structure of powerlessness. *American Sociological Review, 60,* 393-404.

Morrison, A. M. (1992). *The new leaders: Guidelines on leadership diversity in America.* San Francisco: Jossey-Bass.

Mumby, D. K. (1987). The political function of narrative in organizations. *Communication Monographs, 54,* 113-127.

Nemeth, C. (1986). Intergroup relations between majority and minority. In S. Worchel & W. Austin (Eds.), *Psychology of intergroup relations* (2nd ed., pp. 220-243). Chicago: Nelson-Hall.

Nord, W. R. (1978). Dreams of humanization and the realities of power. *Academy of Management Review, 3*(3), 674-679.

Oakes, P. J., & Turner, J. C. (1986). Distinctiveness and the salience of social category membership: Is there an automatic perceptual bias towards novelty? *European Journal of Social Psychology, 16,* 325-344.

Oakes, P. (1987). The salience of social categories. In J. Turner et al. (Eds.), *Rediscovering the social group,* (pp. 117-141). Oxford: Basil Blackwell.

Pettigrew, T. F. (1979). The ultimate attribution error. *Personality and Social Psychology Bulletin, 5,* 461-476.

Phillips, K. P. (1994). *Boiling point: Democrats, Republicans, and the decline of middle class prosperity.* New York: Harper Perennial.

Powell, G. N. (1993). *Women and men in management.* Newbury Park, CA: Sage.

Simpson, P. (1991). How Lynn Martin's career will affect yours. *Business and Society Review, 16*(10), 84-92.

Strobel, F. R. (1993). *Upward dreams, downward mobility: The economic decline of the American middle class.* Savage, MD: Rowman & Littlefield.

Sumner, W. G. (1906). *Folkways.* New York: Ginn.

Tajfel, H., & Turner, J. C. (1979). An integrative theory of intergroup conflict. In W. G. Austin & S. Worchel (Eds.), *The social psychology of intergroup relations.* Monterey, CA: Brooks/Cole.

Turner, J. C. (1981). The experimental social psychology of intergroup behavior. In J. C. Turner & H. Giles (Eds.), *Intergroup behavior* (pp. 66-101). Oxford, UK: Basil Blackwell.

Turner, J. C. (1982). Toward a cognitive redefinition of the social group. In H. Tajfel (Ed.), *Social identity and intergroup relations* (pp. 15-40). Cambridge: Cambridge University Press.

Turner, J. C. (1987). *Rediscovering the social group.* Oxford, UK: Basil Blackwell.

Turner, J. C., & Giles, H. (1981). *Intergroup Behavior.* Oxford: Basil Blackwell.

West, C. (1993). *Race matters.* New York: Vintage Press.

DILEMMAS OF DIVERSITY
MANAGEMENT IN PRACTICE

8

Dueling Discourses

Desexualization Versus Eroticism in the Corporate Framing of Female Sexuality in the British Airline Industry, 1945-1960

ALBERT J. MILLS

This chapter examines the role of corporate image making and the social construction of gender in the British airline industry over the period 1945 to 1960. Using a feminist postmodernist analysis (Ferguson, 1984), the chapter traces the development of gendered imagery over time in two airlines, the British Overseas Airways Corporation (BOAC) and British European Airways (BEA), predecessors of British Airways (BA). In particular, the employment of women and their treatment in the airlines' company materials (i.e., newsletters, memo-

AUTHOR'S NOTE: This chapter is based on a paper presented at the British Sociological Association annual conference, March 28-31, 1994: *Sexualities in Social Context,* University of Central Lancashire, Preston, England. The research was supported by a general research grant (#92-0476) from the Social Sciences and Humanities Research Council of Canada.

randa, and annual reports) are traced through a period that began with a publicly heralded commitment to a form of employment equity (desexualization), which steadily gave way to the promotion of female bodily sexuality as a central aspect of company imagery and marketing (eroticization).

It is argued that the policy of desexualization ultimately failed due to the fact that (a) it was ultimately motivated by values of propriety rather than a genuine commitment to equity and (b) the top decision makers failed to address the values and practices that constituted the corporate culture—in particular, the processes associated with the development of corporate imagery. It is concluded that a genuine commitment to employment equity is only half the battle and will not succeed unless key organization decision makers are prepared to address the deep-rooted, mundane aspects of sexism.

INTRODUCTION

Since the late 1970s, a vast body of management literature has focused on the importance of organizational culture for organizational outcomes. Until recently, the concern with outcomes was largely focused on issues of organizational efficiency, growth, and success (Davies 1984; Deal & Kennedy, 1982; Ouchi, 1981; Peters & Waterman, 1982), but lately, a growing body of work has begun to investigate the relationship between an organization's culture and discriminatory practices (Abella, 1984; Benson, 1986; Collinson, 1992; Hearn, Sheppard, Tancred-Sheriff, & Burrell, 1989; Mills, 1988). An important aspect of the recent debate involves analysis of the role of corporate materials in the development of discriminatory images (Tinker & Neimark, 1987).

Corporate image is a particularly interesting aspect of an organizational culture, in that it helps us to understand something of what and who is valued in the organization. Broadly defined, corporate image refers to "the impression the culture makes on its environment" (Alvesson & Berg, 1992, p. 90); the mental picture that clients, employees, and others associate with a particular organization. That impression is usually the result of a combination of unconscious, unintended, conscious, and intended factors that arise out of the interactions of organization members and the decision making of organizational leaders. Company materials—including annual reports, advertisements, and in-house or external magazines—provide a rich source for viewing a company's image. These materials, each developed to serve specific purposes, provide literal images (textual, photographic, design) of the company. It is on this narrow aspect of image making that the chapter focuses.

Based on an extensive study of the airline industry in Britain (Mills, 1994a, 1994b, 1994c, 1995, 1996a, 1996b), this chapter examines the role of corporate image making in the everyday life of organizations and its contribution to the mundane reproduction of discrimination. In particular, the chapter is concerned with the role of the corporate image in the routine construction of female sexuality; it will show how organizational images can restrict diversity by identifying certain organizational roles and positions with specific demographic characteristics. It is suggested that (a) corporate images can sanction and encourage certain types of "male/female" behavior and implicitly prohibit other types of behavior, and (b) corporate images can encourage the exclusion of women from positions of power, authority, and prestige. Through a case study of two major airline companies—BOAC and BEA—it is argued that the management of diversity is not only ill-defined but will not succeed unless organizational leaders are prepared to deal with the deep-rooted, mundane aspects of sexism. The power of the mundane image is explored through a period (1945-1960) when the corporate policies of BOAC and BEA (desexualization) and their corporate imagery (eroticization) came into conflict. Through textual analysis, it is shown that a series of photographic, graphic, and text-based images of women as sex objects consistently overwhelmed a consciously devised, equal rights policy that sought to characterize women as co-professionals.

THEORETICAL DEBATES AND ISSUES

In 1974, an article by Joan Acker and Donald van Houten set the stage on what was to become a growing interest in the study of sexuality and the workplace. Using a sociological frame of analysis, Acker and van Houten set out to expose the existence of "sex segregation and differential sex power in organizations" (p. 153) and the impact of these factors on organizational behavior. In making their point, the authors use the terms *women* and *men* in an unquestioned form—as relatively fixed entities. Yet, implicitly throughout the article and more explicitly in the conclusion, the authors suggest that organizational structuring may have a powerful influence on a person's sexuality: the contention that males generally have more power in organizations than females carries the implicit, but undeveloped suggestion that maleness and organizational power are somehow associated. The role of organizations in associating certain characteristics with the notion of womanhood is a little more explicit in the concluding statement:

Sex differences in organizational participation are related to (1) differential
recruitment of women into jobs requiring dependence and passivity, (2) selective
recruitment of particularly compliant women into these jobs, and (3) control
mechanisms used in organizations for women, which reinforce control mechanisms to which they are subjected in other areas of the society. (p. 162)

Two key works in 1977 left unquestioned the concepts of women and men
but placed sharply contrasting emphasis on the relationship between organizations and sex discrimination. Wolff (1977) moved the debate away from organizational factors of explanation toward a focus on *extraorganizational influences.* Wolff argues that "women's position in any organization is inseparable
from women's position in society," and she concludes that "the very question of
women's role and position in organizations can only be answered by a macro-
sociology which situates the organization in the society which defines its
existence, goals, and values" (p. 20). Although it is important to remind ourselves that issues of discrimination and sexuality are rooted in a series of broadly
located social processes, Wolff's argument discourages analysis of the role of
organizations as part of those processes.

It was left to Kanter (1977) to move the debate back to the role of the
organization. Through analysis of numbers, power, and the *opportunity structure,* Kanter argues that the structures of organizations contribute to the way
that women (and men) come to view their worth within an organization. Again
the link between sexual identity and organizational factors is left implicit,
but Kanter contributed to a growing feeling that how we are viewed in
organizations influences our notions of femininity and of masculinity. Nonetheless, she achieves this end through a closed-system perspective that mini-
mizes the role of social attitudes and practices in the construction of organizational discrimination.

In the early 1980s, the work of Burrell (1992), Ferguson (1984), and Hearn
and Parkin (1983) strengthened the focus on sexuality at work, raised questions
about the interrelationships between organizations, society, and sexuality, and
questioned the notion of women and men as concrete categories.

Hearn and Parkin's (1983) work was one of the earliest within an organizational analysis framework to explicitly discuss the issue of sexuality at work and
to argue for analysis that attempts to understand the interrelationship between
organizational and social life in the construction of sexuality. The concept of
sexuality itself is largely undeveloped but is used to refer to such things as
"sexual attractiveness," sex roles, sexual preference, and notions of masculinity
and femininity:

> In effect, the structuring of sex roles, in terms of both work and authority, is reproduced both *between* organizations and *within* organizations . . . ; for example, Bland et al. (1978) argue for the connection between the organization of production and social definitions of masculinity and femininity. (p. 240)

Burrell (1992) and Ferguson (1984), drawing upon the work of Foucault, shaped the debate in a number of interesting ways. Both authors argue that organizational discourses play central roles in the way that we come to view and respond to women and to men. Ferguson (1984, p. xii) explores the organizational "production of individuals and relationships by the prevailing language and structures of power," which are re/produced through the discourse of bureaucracy: bureaucracy is viewed as a discursive practice which, in its utilization of notions of rationality, objectivity, and lack of emotion, contributes to the construction of particular forms of masculinity and femininity and serves to exclude women from the higher levels of bureaucratic power. Although using Foucault's notion of the construction of subjectivities, Ferguson retains the notion of human agency, without which "the promise of resistance that the submerged discourse of outsiders can offer is rendered mechanistic, flat and empty":

> Foucault neglects to explicate a crucial aspect of our experience as both social and temporal beings . . . [and his] "rejection of all recourse to the interiority of a conscious, individual, meaning-given subject" . . . renders much of our day-to-day experience incomprehensible. I see the creation of meaning both as unavoidable and as a potentially ennobling process, allowing us to order our collective lives in light of values we embrace and in a language we make our own. (p. xiv)

Burrell (1992) also focuses on bureaucracy but examines those features of the broader set of practices that contribute to a discourse of desexualization. Burrell views sexuality as a social construct that is understood differently over time—"an historical construct which needs to be understood historically"—but he goes on to argue that

> clearly, there is the possibility of conceptualizing a continuum of sexual relations in which full genital sexuality involving penetration is near one end of the scale while the other end is marked by a plurality of polymorphous pleasurable sensations and emotions. In this paper, most considerations will be directed toward the former end of the continuum because the acts found there are more "clearly" sexual in terms of contemporary definition. (pp. 72-73)

Despite the curiously heterosexist imagery conjured up by this framework, Burrell includes homosexual relations within his charting of organizational desexualization, which he defines as the purging of sexual relations and emotions from organizational life.

Hearn and Parkin (1987) and Pringle (1989) have challenged the extent to which sexuality can be said to be absent from organizational life. Pringle argues that secretaries stand apart from the bureaucratizing trend of modern organizations and are expected to exude emotionality, inhabiting an organizational discourse in which sexuality plays an important role. Hearn and Parkin contend that sexuality permeates organizational life and the very construction of organizations. Although it is true that Burrell may have oversimplified the extent to which the desexualization of organizations has actually occurred, the point remains that desexualization has been a powerful impulse within many organizations.

Since the mid-1980s, a growing body of work has examined the relationship between sexuality, work, and the broader society (Gutek, 1985; Hearn & Parkin, 1987; Hearn et al., 1989), including the question of masculinities (Collinson, 1988) and sexual preferences (Hall, 1989). In general, this research has remained focused on the organizational level of analysis, with reference to other social influences being made in broad and unspecified terms. More recent studies that use a Foucauldian frame of analysis have been useful in conceptualizing the organization-society interface as an interrelated series of discursive practices (Kerfoot & Knights, 1993; Morgan & Knights, 1991). However, within this framework, Ferguson's (1984) plea for human agency has been overwhelmed by an emphasis on *subjectivities* and a deep questioning of the stability and value of the concepts of woman and of man (Calas & Smircich, 1992). This questioning has, on the one hand, been valuable in helping "us to notice how the signs 'women' and 'feminine' function as general limits in our discourses and institutions" (Calas & Smircich, 1992, p. 232). On the other hand, it has made it more difficult to argue for counterdiscriminatory strategies based on the development of alternative voices or discourses. Comparing a *women's voices approach* with that of *poststructuralist feminism,* Calas and Smircich (1992) state that

> while the women's voices perspective still expects to effect a radical change in the world, which will come to value women's experiences, post-structuralist feminism is skeptical about these goals. The expectation of making a better world, which women's voices espouses, is questioned by post-structuralist feminism as another attempt to reinscribe a dominant sign in a world that is more complex than what women's voices often believes it to be. From a post-

structuralist feminist approach, the work is never done; you have to keep on questioning who you can be as you are today. (p. 232)

Ironically, this approach to post-structuralist feminism accords well with the established traditions of (malestream) social science with its emphases on objectivity and academic purity: the object being not to substitute meaning systems but to question them. The limitation of this approach is that it distances itself from the world of meaning that is central to the experiences of women and men. It does not address the issue of the *meaning-given subject* raised by Ferguson (1984) earlier.

The post-structuralist feminism of Flax (1990) and Acker (1992) attempts to bridge the divide between individual human agency and collective subjectivities through the notion of embodiment. Flax (1990) proposes that we locate "self and its experiences in concrete social relations":

A social self . . . come[s] to be partially in and through powerful, affective relationships with other persons. These relations with others and our feelings and fantasies about them, along with experiences of embodiedness also mediated by such relations, can come to constitute an "inner" self that is neither fictive or "natural." Such a self is simultaneously embodied, gendered, social, and unique. It is capable of telling stories and of conceiving and experiencing itself in all these ways. (p. 232)

Acker (1992, pp. 250-251) begins by questioning the established feminist distinction between *gender* as socially constructed and *sex* as biologically given. Today, that distinction is more and more problematic as we understand the social construction of the body and of sexual acts and relations. But, she continues, "that is not to deny the physical materiality of the body and of sexuality but to emphasize the importance of meaning in the use and comprehension of the body" (p. 251).

Within this framework, Acker (1992) attempts to walk a fine line between viewing gender and sexuality as processes of social construction, which none-theless have real consequences for "particular women and men" (p. 251). For Acker, "sexuality is part of the ongoing production of gender as patterned differences [which] usually involves the subordination of women, either con-cretely or symbolically" (p. 251). She attempts to capture the tension between concrete and symbolic experiences through a focus on *gendered processes,* which refer to the fact that advantage and disadvantage, exploitation and control, action and emotion, meaning and identity, are patterned through and in terms of a distinction between male and female, masculine and feminine.

Gendered processes are concrete activities, what people do and say and how they think about these activities, for thinking is also an activity. The daily construction, and sometimes deconstruction, of gender occurs within material and ideological constraints that set the limits of possibility. For example, the boundaries of sex segregation, themselves continually constructed and reconstructed, limit the actions of particular women and men at particular times (Acker, 1992, p. 251).

BOAC AND BEA:
LOCALIZED SITES OF SEXUALITY

The current study of BOAC and BEA attempts to incorporate some of the insights generated by the debate on sexuality over the last two decades.

First, it assumes that organizations play a key role in the processes of the social construction of gender: Organizations are cultural phenomena that play a central role in the landscape of the modern world (Denhardt, 1981).[1] When we talk about "broad social influences" on organizations, we are usually referring to other institutions (e.g., other companies, school, the church, government agencies, etc.). The main exception to this is the impact of family life, but even here, there is evidence that "the family" itself is a cultural phenomenon that is shaped in large part by the organizational contours and structure of society (Lewis, 1992; Mills & Murgatroyd, 1991).

Second, if individual organizations contribute to the social construction of sexuality and discrimination, then we need to understand not only an institution's contribution to the overall pattern but the unique aspects of that contribution which are played out and enacted in a local situation. This is a two-way process. On the one hand, we need to understand how any particular organization contributes to a general understanding of the character of men and women; how an organization generates and maintains certain images of male and female sexuality. On the other hand, we need to understand how understandings of men and women are enacted in a particular place; after all, when we talk of general understandings of men and women, we assume that those understandings are played out somewhere, that they are not just abstractions.[2]

Third, sexuality is viewed as "the social expression of or social relations to physical, bodily desires, real or imagined" (Hearn & Parkin, 1987, p. 15). How those expressions are understood and enacted, however, will depend on the "diverse social practices that give meaning to social activities, of social definitions and self-definitions" (Weeks, 1986, p. 25) and of resistance in a given place and period of time. In other words, we need to understand the construction of sexualities in BOAC and BEA in the context of the period in which they were in the process of construction.

Fourth, following Foucault (1979, 1980), it is argued that how a person comes to understand his or her self is framed by and through a series of discursive practices in which language and power play a vital and interrelated role. Thus, the study of BOAC and BEA seeks to identify significant sets of discursive practices through which people's sense and understanding of sexuality come to be understood. This chapter focuses on one aspect of sexual imagery that is directly linked to the issue of organizational power and language—the (textual and visual) images of men and women contained in the company materials (in-house journals, annual reports, and memoranda) of the time.

Fifth, as part of the process of identifying significant discursive practices, Burrell's (1992) theory of desexualization is critically examined in the light of developments within BOAC and BEA.

Sixth, the role of human agency is examined in the process of developing or resisting certain images of sexuality.

THE IN-HOUSE NEWSLETTER AND
THE RISE OF FEMALE EMPLOYMENT

The predecessor of BOAC and BEA, Imperial Airlines, employed a handful of women (less than 1% of employees) at its formation in 1924. By 1939, this number had grown to about 500 (9% of employees); airline growth had been accompanied by an increasing need for support staff (e.g., stenographers, telephonists, secretaries), and—following a growing employment trend—the company hired female office staff.

It was not until March 1939 that the company employed its first female manager, with strictly gendered duties: to "be responsible for the engagement, training, and administration of all women staff employed in the United Kingdom" (*Imperial Airways Staff News,* 7/9, 1939).

In 1926, the company introduced its first in-house newsletter designed to inform staff about timetables, fares, and route developments (Mills, 1996a). Beginning as a one-page, monthly news sheet (*Imperial Airways Monthly Bulletin*), the newsletter was developed into two weekly productions (a four-page *Imperial Airways Staff News* and a two-page *Imperial Airways Weekly News Bulletin*) by 1939.

Prior to 1930, with virtually no women in the company, the early newsletter images were of men and masculinities (Mills, 1996a)—referencing the activities of male staff. On the rare occasions when the newsletter did refer to women, it focused on the assumed characteristics of womanhood rather on the specific contribution of a female employee (Mills, 1996b).

As the number of female employees steadily grew during the 1930s, the newsletter did not seem to know how or whether to report their activities. By and large, the newsletter confined reports on female staff to appointments, departures, and marriage: In contrast, detailed reports were filed on individual male employees and of the contribution of men to the developing commercial air services (Mills, 1996b).

Images of Sexuality

In terms of images of sexuality, the company newsletter projected several masculinities: the hero, the sportsman, the serviceman, the leader, the business-man, the pioneer, the skilled craftsman, and so on. The narrow reportage of female employees, on the other hand, did not lend itself to sexual imagery, except in the broadest, and heterosexual, sense.[3]

The War Years

In line with a general policy across organizations, the airline, now renamed BOAC, recruited greater numbers of female employees, to "release men for war duties." By 1942, the company employed 2,000 (34% of employees) women (*BOAC Newsletter,* 32, 1942). The sheer number of (male) positions to be replaced ensured a place for women in several roles and levels of the organiza-tion that had been traditionally restricted to men.

The great influx of women employees, the war itself, and the novelty of women in certain positions provided the airline's newsletter editors with plenty of copy. Several detailed reports appeared of female "firsts" in certain jobs, but the overwhelming images of women (and men) employees were framed by wartime needs and concerns. A central male character was that of the wartime hero, braving danger in defense of his country. A central female character, on the other hand, was that of Mrs. Miniver,[4] the long-suffering wife who works in the background to support the menfolk at the front. Shades of the Mrs. Miniver imagery of womanhood appear throughout the airline's newsletters in the form of copy that "reminded" readers that most female employees were temporarily "filling-in" while the real—male—employees were at the front (Mills, 1996b).

Events during the progress of the Second World War were to influence the postwar airline companies in a number of ways. Major changes were occurring in regard to:

Technology (faster and more long-range airplanes were being developed)

Airline routes (the North Atlantic route, for example, had become a reality)

Passenger demographics (in Britain the business*man* [sic] had replaced the upper-class elite as the majority passenger, and in North America, a new generation of demobilized, air-minded soldiers had become an important part of the airline market) and numbers (passenger numbers grew rapidly)

Competition (international air travel, especially across the Atlantic, became more competitive)

Sociopolitical attitudes (calls for greater democracy and the establishment of a welfare society became a powerful political force)

Government policy (a 1945 White Paper on British Air Transport recommended that BOAC be split into two separate entities—with a reduced BOAC responsible for intercontinental routes and a new British European Airways that would operate all domestic and European services)

DESEXUALIZATION AS AN ORGANIZATIONAL DISCOURSE

Staffing

With the ending of the war in Europe, BOAC experienced a rapid upturn in its employee numbers. From a staff of under 6,000 in 1942, the airline was employing more than three times that number by July 1945. With the war's end, most of the prewar activities were resumed along with the development of new routes. Many of the company's former male employees returned to the fold and took up their old positions.

The new postwar situation affected the situation of the airline's female employees in a number of ways. On the one hand, the greatly expanded clerical and general administrative sectors helped to ensure that many women retained positions[5]—with the total number of female staff actually rising by 300. On the other hand, the rapid increase of male employee numbers meant that the percentage of BOAC staff who were women actually fell from 34.4% to 12.7%. Nonetheless, women were now a permanent part of the company landscape, and the airline's policy making, recruitment, advertising, and internal communication systems had to take account of that fact.

In 1945, there was still one area where the company had resisted the recruitment of female staff,[6] airline stewarding. However, the company was beginning to experience pressure on the new transatlantic routes, where passengers were becoming accustomed to being served by female flight attendants on competitor airlines.[7] In 1946, BOAC, yielding to market pressures, began hiring a limited number of female stewardesses on their North Atlantic routes but soon extended the practice to other routes. The newly formed BEA followed suit.

Uniformed Female Staff
and the Corporate Image

Despite the fact that BOAC and BEA employed a significant number of women, the editorial staff of the in-house newsletters and journals still did not seem to know what to make of them. The *BOAC News Letter* (and its successor, *Speedbird*), for example, continued to discuss the activities of male employees at length, while providing only brief factual reports on female employees, limited to references to engagements and marriages, to terminations of employment and announcements of new appointments. The increasing use and prominence of photographs in the postwar in-house newsletters seems to have posed less of a problem, and from 1946 onward, large numbers of photographs of both female and male employees appeared with regularity. However, against a background of limited and restricted editorial comment on women, photographs of female employees were used to serve a different function from the use of photographs of male employees. Whereas photographs of male employees were used to accompany a story of the activities of the individuals involved, those of female employees were used either to illustrate some aspect of company policy or, unconsciously,[8] to "glamorize" the page. For example, the first issue of *Speedbird* (April 1946) carried a front-page photograph of a uniformed female staff member, ostensibly to inform readers about the introduction of uniforms for female staff.

The hiring of female flight attendants in 1946 was done only after much soul searching among leading decision makers within the respective airline companies (Bray, 1974; Penrose, 1980), and it caused those in charge to define their attitudes to female employees. In particular, senior officials were concerned to distance their airline from any suggestion that they were hiring "glamour hostesses" as a strategy to sell seats. Undoubtedly, this attitude was influenced by events in the U.S. airline business, where female flight attendants had first been introduced. U.S. airline bosses had initially had a similar sense of sexual propriety and would only hire females with nursing qualifications, giving the impression that the new female attendants were airborne nurses (Hochschild, 1983). But this eventually gave way to an emphasis on glamour as airlines vied for business from a (largely male) public that seemed to like the idea of female attendants. Nursing uniforms gave way to "fashionable outfits," and the nomenclature changed from *steward(ess)* to *hostess.*

In the austere atmosphere of postwar Britain, the bosses at BOAC were concerned to deemphasize glamour. Instead, the emphasis was on professionalism and hard work. Initially, the image was controlled through such things as the design of the new air stewardesses uniform, which closely resembled that of the male steward, and through a careful monitoring of the women's uniform hem lengths to ensure that they were not too revealing. Blouses, for example, were designed with an extra long shirt tail that tucked into skirts to ensure that, as stewardesses bent across to the window passenger, they wouldn't expose "any enticing flesh" (Wright, 1985, pp. 7-8).

BEA adopted a similar policy and set of practices and, if anything, took a narrower approach to the question of glamour and female sexuality:

We Had To Kill the Stewardess

We launched the slogan "Glamour is Out"; we even de-sexed her by knocking the -ess of her title. Picture Post did us proud over the whole thing, showing the intelligence and hard work that goes into making a good stewardess: foreign languages and training in first aid and navigation, apart from the expected ability to serve hot coffee and administer air-sickness pills. We thought of substituting the steward, boy instead of girl, but somehow it hasn't worked out. The steward is another hard worker, with lots of training and experience, as well, usually, as an RAF background, but there's no doubt that his lady colleague has stolen the market for the time being. So we're keeping him in cold storage. (*BEA Magazine,* September 1947)

As with BOAC, BEA dressed their male and female flight attendants alike, in dark blue uniforms.

Conflicting Imagery

Nonetheless, within both airlines, each new reference to female flight attendants and other uniformed staff revealed evidence of conflicting trends in how female sexuality was to be imaged. By October 1946, BOAC had modified its approach. Seemingly about the announcement of new uniforms for female staff, the front cover of the October 1946 issue of *Speedbird* carried a photograph of a female staff member under the headline, "Miss BOAC steps out":

> A fanfare of trumpets introduced Miss BOAC in her new uniform at the Corporation's display of art and industrial design, held in the Orchid Room at the Dorchester Hotel, London. . . .
>
> Our front cover . . . show[s] how attractive the new uniform is. The aim of Mr. Maurice Helman, the designer, was to produce a uniform that would meet the practical requirements of airline personnel, including traffic staff, nursing sisters and transport drivers.
>
> The uniform is modern, streamlined, and typifies the spirit of the new air age. Nearly all existing women's uniforms are based on men's. But a woman's build being entirely different from a man's, the result can never be entirely satisfactory. Miss BOAC wears a uniform designed from the start for women.

Here a number of themes vie for attention. References to fashion frame the discussion and in conflicting ways. At one level, it cannot fail to conjure up images of glamour (e.g., steps out, fanfare, display, Orchid Room); yet, at another level, the statement tries hard to focus on organizational concerns of practicality and standardization and on the attractive nature of the uniform (rather than of the woman herself). Issues of sexuality are not far from the surface, as we are informed, albeit in an understated way, that the female body differs from that of the male.

To some extent, the themes of equality of the sexes and professionalism were also used to de-emphasize glamour and were used in the materials of both airlines to foster a particular image of the new female air stewards [sic]:

The Art of the Steward

> During a ten-weeks' course at the Aldermaston Training School, pupil steward and stewardesses learn the practice and theory of the catering art. They learn about cutlery, crockery, and glassware; about dish and plate appeal; about carving and serving, and how to compile balanced menus. But that's only the beginning. They are given elementary medical training. They study "catering documentation" and "voyage procedure." Most important of all, the catering instructors inculcate an ideal of "personal service" to passengers.
>
> During their course, stewards and stewardesses go on an overseas training flight to put what they have learned into practice. They serve meals in the air, watched by instructors, who point out later any errors in service or deportment. Then comes a period of "polishing" at Airways Terminal and finally, the steward or stewardess is posted to one of the divisional pools for service (*BOAC News Letter,* November 1947).

BEA's editorial staff also drew on the equity theme to promote its version of the desexualized image of the female flight attendant.

Selecting Stewards

We had twenty-eight vacancies this year and wanted a predominantly female recruitment. Our policy is "half male, half female" but the female element was below strength. . . . In the past we have carried only one steward on each aircraft. Our girls were the first of any airline . . . to earn as much as men—they did the same job, so they were paid the same money. Periodically, we ran polls to see which the public preferred. The last of these showed that 55 per cent were in favor of men and 45 per cent for girls.

Policy for the new aircraft—which will require two stewards—is therefore clear; one man and one girl—to please, we hope, everyone. (*BEA Magazine,* April 1950)

In terms of work practices, however, the reality was far from the projected ideal. Although she received the same training as male attendants, the BOAC air stewardess was not allowed in the galley or on the flight deck; she was seen as an assistant to the male steward, helping the sick and feeding babies. The situation was similar on BEA flights, where the stewardess

seemed more like a housekeeper in the air—tending to all the housekeeping arrangements for the journey, washing up, and ensuring that crockery is stowed away. During the flight she would change into a white mess jacket, prepare and serve a light meal. (Wright, 1985, pp. 6-7)

As early as 1950, there is evidence that the antiglamour policy was beginning to come into conflict with developing social practices and editorial conventions, as witnessed in the following item:

Miss Airways 1950

BEA has been invited to enter an international Airline Contest to find the Perfect Airline Girl.

It is stressed that this is NOT a beauty competition. The accent will be on charm, personality, poise, and professional competence. The contestants must be girls who normally work in the uniform of their airline. In the case of BEA, therefore, they must be stewardesses or traffic clerks. BEA is lucky in having so many attractive girls.(*BEA Magazine,* June 1950)

The statement reflects the writer's (and behind him,[9] the organizers') dilemma of supporting something that appears to be a beauty contest in a company that is vocally condemning the use of glamour. Thus, we find an unmistakable stress on personality and professional competence alongside clear references to attractiveness. The writing was, so to speak, on the wall, and within a few short years, desexualization would give way to its almost exact opposite, eroticization.

SOCIAL DISCOURSE AND DESEXUALIZATION

It is not too difficult to understand how a concern with desexualization took hold in one of Britain's leading state industries. The 1940s and early 1950s were characterized by a number of social factors, including austerity, bureaucratization, welfarism, changing family values, and the influence of popular culture, which discouraged public displays of certain forms of glamour.

Austerity: An emphasis on glamour would have been out of place in a postwar Britain marked by austerity, rationing, and shortages, including a serious labor shortage. BOAC and BEA hired female flight attendants in a situation where airline seats were in short supply, with priority passage given to those on business, and where a British government campaign was emphasizing national survival to encourage more women to return to the workforce.

Bureaucracy, Sexuality, and the Rise of the Welfare State: The conditions of the immediate postwar era—including austerity, the expansion of government ownership (nationalization), and the establishment of welfare agencies (Welfare State)—saw a strengthening of bureaucratic control of industrial and social life.

The airline industry was undergoing a period of restructuring and government regulation, and the discourse of bureaucratization (Ferguson, 1984) throughout the industry was stressing efficiency and professionalism. For example, in early 1947, Lord Knollys, BOAC's chairman, informed staff that "the keynote for the financial year is Economy through Efficiency":

> There will be few who cannot contribute in some way either to organize their work so that it can be done with greater efficiency by fewer personnel, or to review some extravagance which will head to economy without prejudice to the quality of the service given to the travelling public, or by suggesting now some new method into their work which will save time and money. (*BOAC News Letter,* 1947).

In the meantime the Welfare State, with its stress on family values, population growth, child care, and motherhood, was influencing how people thought about womanhood, contributing to new expectations of marriage as "a partnership of equals" (Pugh, 1992, p. 293), while retaining many of the traditional values of woman as housewife and mother.[10]

POPULAR CULTURE AND IMAGES OF SEXUALITY:
A NIGHT AT THE MOVIES

A focus on traditional themes of motherhood and domesticity was very much to the fore in the cinema of the 1940s. Popular films of the time tended to portray women as wholesome young women (*Courage of Lassie, Little Women*) or traditional wives and mothers who keep the family together (*Best Years of Our Lives, Life with Father*). Women who "stray" from their traditional roles were often portrayed as troublesome and doomed to failure—*Brief Encounter, Forever Amber, Samson and Delilah, The Woman in the Window, The Postman Always Rings Twice, Mildred Pierce.*[11]

ORGANIZATIONAL DISCOURSE
AND DESEXUALIZATION

Many of the social themes of the time can be found in some fashion or other within BOAC and BEA. In particular, the state- owned airlines found themselves under increased government control and pressures to become more efficient. Cost-cutting and restructuring were very much issues of the time within both airlines.

Restructuring and Bureaucratization: Prior to the war's end, the government had established a Select Committee to look into the future of civil aviation. That committee recommended the establishment of three separate public corporations to oversee airline operations internationally (BOAC), in the domestic and European markets (BEA), and in South America (British South-American Air Lines). The resulting Civil Aviation Act set in motion a major restructuring of the existing airline business and its separation into three separate entities, each with its own chairman and board of directors.

Within the burgeoning bureaucracies of these airlines, a series of formalized practices and committees was developed to deal with the growing staff numbers, including a system of industrial psychology for reincorporating former (male) employees, and for general recruitment. The primary focus of the new work methods was to achieve better ways of coordinating employees and making them more efficient.

The Metaphors of Leadership: Not unexpectedly, the metaphors that dominated the airline companies at the time were drawn from the themes of austerity, bureaucracy, and narrow images of the family.

An early version of the family metaphor was invoked to celebrate the inauguration of BEA in 1946. Under the headline, "Happy Landings," BOAC's newsletter described BOAC as "the mother company" and BEA as "the child" (*Speedbird,* No. 6, September 1946). The family metaphor was to reappear on numerous occasions, including the Christmas address to staff by the respective chairmen of BOAC and BEA:

Chairman's New Year Message

The essence of good teamwork is mutual confidence and understanding. Now let me say at once that we have found in BOAC a fine team and a fine team spirit. ... We have the finest human equipment of any airline in the world today.

We are a big family because our task is worldwide. (*BOAC News Letter,* No. 22, January 1948)

A Christmas Letter from Mr. Gerard d'Erlanger [Chairman of BEA]

The family of BEA, though still a very young one, has clearly developed to a marked degree a spirit of comradeship and pride in its achievements. (*BEA Magazine,* No. 5, Christmas edition, 1947)

Glamour and Moral Concern: In the United Kingdom of the 1940s, there was still a strong moral objection to the idea of young women being hired to travel to exotic places. This, in part, was why the airline chiefs resisted hiring women flight attendants. Thus, when the decision was made to hire female flight attendants, those in charge of the airlines wanted to make quite clear to one and all that they were hiring "proper" young women to do a professional job. The stress on professionalism fit nicely with the bureaucratization that was occurring throughout the industry, and the austere dress and moral code fit well with the cost-conscious, efficiency drive that marked the airlines at the time.

EROTICIZATION AS AN
ORGANIZATIONAL DISCOURSE

In less than two decades following the introduction of female flight attendants into British airlines, the image of the "desexualized professional" had given way to "the sexy air hostess." What had happened? The early professional look had accorded well with a number of strongly rooted features of the airline companies. To find the answer, we need to look at a number of social and organizational changes that were occurring over time.

Competition and Strategic Management: It is clear that as airlines moved into the jet age, they were under increasing pressure to sell airline seats: planes and competition had grown considerably over the period. Airlines had a greatly increased number of seats to fill and several competitors vying for available passengers. Airlines needed to find ways to attract passengers, and this led to limited price wars but also to a move to sell airline service through the sexuality of their female flight attendants. BOAC and BEA did not hold back from this contest (Mills, 1996b).

The "Permissive Society": Erotic images were not out of place in the Britain of the 1960s. Although the label of permissiveness glosses over a number of social contradictions (Weeks, 1989), there were several changes in the way that sex and sexuality were viewed, with women experiencing the most obvious sexualization: "Abortion and divorce reform, family-planning legislation, even reform of the obscenity law, had as their points of reference the changing social and sexual imagery and roles of women" (Weeks, 1989, p. 256).

A number of factors contributed to this changing image of female sexuality, including an increased role for women in the workforce as "a vital element in the expansion of the consumer economy," and the increasing utilization, stimulation, and reshaping of female sexuality to the demands of mass marketing (Weeks, 1989, pp. 257-258).

Some of the newer journals aimed at women (e.g., *Cosmopolitan*) were redefining female sexuality in terms of its possibilities for pleasure and enjoyment "unbounded by the old exigencies of compulsory childbirth or endless domestic chores": the female body was being constructed as "sensitive and sexual," capable of stimulation and excitation, and "therefore demanding care and attention if women were to be sexual and sexually desirable to men" (Weeks, 1989, p. 258). In short, "Women were asserting their own perceived sexual needs, though largely within a heterosexual framework and in the terms allowed by commercialism" (Weeks, 1989, p. 258).

At the movies, the "sex kitten" and the "sex bombshell" became new popular images of women and female desirability. Now audiences—especially male audiences—were lured by a new female icon: Marilyn Monroe in *The Seven Year Itch*, Ursula Andress in *Dr. No*, Jane Russell in *The Paleface*, Carroll Baker in *Baby Doll*, Brigitte Bardot in *And God Created Woman*.

Eroticism and Organizational Discourse

It would be tempting to suggest that much of the changing imagery of female sexuality within the British airlines was due to economic pressures and changing sexual attitudes. Indeed, it would be hard to divorce those external factors from actual events within the airlines. Nonetheless, there is considerable evidence to indicate that many of the pressures for change developed *within* the airlines themselves.

Desexualization as a Sexual Discourse: To begin with, it seems evident that the notion of desexualization within BEA and BOAC was inspired as much by moral panic and bureaucratic concerns as by a concern for equity. As a result, many of the expressions of desexualization contained contradictory references to sexuality.

Gender, Fashion, and Conformity: Several of the earliest feminizations of the female airline uniform came from the women themselves. The so-called neutral look had been premised on the male uniform, and many female staff, unhappy with the "unfeminine" look, pressed for changes. This accorded with the interests of senior airline staff, who wanted their women staff to have a professional but feminine image (Mills, 1996b).

From Personality to Body: Changing Corporate Images: In the prewar era, textual images of female employees in the airline newsletter were almost nonexistent, but in the late 1940s, this began to change with the expanded use of photographs. Initially, photographs of female staff were solely used to report trends in female recruitment, but soon such photographs were regularly used to add a "touch of glamour": rarely was a photograph used to highlight the work of a particular woman. That the glamour approach was not the outcome of an unconscious editorial policy is revealed in its earliest examples involving photographs of female staff alongside furry animals or children. For example, under the headline, "Beauty and the Beast," the front cover of the October 1948 issue of the *BEA Magazine* pictured a uniformed female staff member with an elephant. BOAC took up the pet theme in the February 1950 issue of the *News Letter,* picturing "Stewardess Faith Sisman" with a Siamese cat on her shoulder; it was a theme that continued over time: Only the animals changed, including raccoons (April 1950), a baby kangaroo (August 1950), an elephant and a lion cub (October 1950), a baby crocodile (May 1951), a turkey (January 1953), and a baby chimp (February 1953).[12]

Photographs of this type, and others, imaged women as caring and motherly. But by the end of the 1950s, this type of image gave way to more explicitly erotic images. This occurred through a series of images that increasingly focused on the body and away from personality and occupational task.

The advent of airline beauty contests was one avenue that contributed to an emerging focus on bodily beauty. Initially, organizers of such competitions were at pains to state that they were "*not* beauty contests" but were focused on personality; reporting on the subject was limited and matter-of-fact: "Miss Eileen Danten (of material records) was chosen from among twenty competitors as 'Miss Airways'!" (*BOAC News Letter,* February 1948).

It did not take long, however, before these competitions were being advertised as displays of attractiveness, with the newsletter editors making much of the "beauty" of the contest winners. As the years progressed, little effort was made to pretend that these events were not beauty contests:

BOAC's Choice

Stewardess Anne Price has been chosen by BOAC to represent the Corporation in a "Queen of the Air" contest. The competitors will be judged not only for beauty but for personality, charm, and deportment. (*BOAC Review and Newsletter,* April 1955)

By 1957, they were referring to "bathing beauty contests" (*BOAC Review and Newsletter,* August 1957).

In the meantime, references to physical beauty were becoming a standard part of company descriptions of female staff. A typical example is a 1949 story on BOAC's Chicago Office, which factually listed the work of male staff but could not resist comment on the physical attractiveness of a female staff member: "The baby of the party is 21-years-old Janice de Young, who has been with the office for only two months and graduated straight from business college.

She is as pretty as a picture on the cover of *Life*" (*BOAC News Letter,* No. 35, January 1949).

Even a rare story focused on the actual work of BOAC's "only woman engineer" referred to her as having been, at one time, "a slim girl with a head of dark curls" (*BOAC News Letter,* No. 12, March 1947).

By the late 1950s, references to bodily sexuality were becoming commonplace in the BOAC newsletters:

> If I were asked . . . who, among the Corporation's New York staff, has the most pleasing telephone voice, I should certainly nominate Miss Margaret Ann ("Peggy") Cohan of Reservations.
>
> "Peggy" . . . is blessed with a voice of bell-like resonance . . . [and to] compound her listener's pleasure, [she is] a slim blonde with dancing blue eyes. (*BOAC Review,* November 1957)

Whereas the changing focus from personality to body occurred slowly but surely in BOAC, it was a more rapid change in BEA. Three distinct trends are evident.

1. A number of items began to appear that extolled the virtues of female bodily beauty. The first explicit sign of this development is a cartoon in the June 1948 issue of the *BEA Magazine.* Using character drawings reminiscent of British seaside postcards, the cartoon shows a helicopter pilot flying over a voluptuous, naked woman swimmer. His co-pilot is shown as saying, "Come on Henry, Old Chap—concentrate on the mails—not the blinking females."

Four months later, the magazine carried its first picture of women in bathing suits, but the accompanying text is more revealing:

> Happy Island. Miss Una LeHuray of BEA . . . and her sister made the most of the summer sunshine.
>
> Note: The editor has had this picture on his desk for the last 2 months but now thinks that it is only fair that the rest of the staff should have a chance of seeing it. (*BEA Magazine,* No. 9, October 1948).

2. In an associated trend, a number of items appeared which denigrated physical features that fell short of a supposed ideal of female attractiveness. Examples of this trend can be seen in a September 1947 cartoon making fun of a woman who is depicted as "fat," or the mid-1950s series of cartoons which contrasted the sexy, large-breasted character Andya Ticketova with a number of plain, flat-chested, or overweight women. Andya's first cartoon appearance has her sexily bulging out of an airline uniform, surrounded by a group of unattractive women in ill-fitting uniforms. The caption reads, "And here, girls, is Miss Andya Ticketova to show us how we shall all look in our new uniforms" (*BEA Magazine,* No. 73, November 1954).

3. A third trend shifted attention from personality to body by associating female sexuality with stupidity. This trend can be seen in 1949 cartoon depicting a very shapely woman with her dress blowing up. The caption reads, "Dumb types— the girl who thought that 'prop wash' was something you did in the garden on Mondays" (*BEA Magazine,* No. 18, November 1949).

By the end of the 1950s the *BEA Magazine* began to feature "pin-ups" under the discreet title: "Picture of the Month," focused on the faces of young, attractive, female employees—male faces were never included in this series.

By the early 1960s, it was not unusual to find in the newsletters and other corporate materials of both airlines pictures of women in bathing suits, female nudity being displayed in cartoons, pin-up style photographs of female staff, and descriptions of the bodily dimensions, hair and eye coloring, and general appearance of female staff members.

Perhaps it is not surprising that airline recruitment and training practices also moved from an emphasis on personality and ability to an emphasis on physical and bodily attraction. BEA, for instance, had, by the late 1960s, dropped technical knowledge from its stewardess training program and replaced it with sessions on deportment, makeup application, and personal hygiene (*BEA Magazine,* No. 237, March 1969).

Signs of the changing practices can be glimpsed in BOAC's introduction of "a new uniform for Stewardesses" in 1953: "The new uniform is discreetly feminine, classical in style and cut and within the best traditions of English tailoring. The new model is quite the smartest and most feminine BOAC uniform yet designed" (*BOAC Newsletter,* January 1953). In an associated article, the glamorous role of the airline stewardess is described:

> One of the most sought-after jobs in BOAC at the moment is that of steward-ess—over fifteen hundred applications have been received this year.
> When I asked [Mr. L. C. Pace, the staff supervisor] what he thought of meeting so many attractive girls all anxious to create a good impression, he said: "Firstly, I enjoy meeting people. Secondly, I find that interviewing such charm-ing girls is a pleasant task."

BEA echoed the same sentiments in a 1952 cartoon that depicted a woman and her "attractive" daughter in the office of a psychoanalyst; the mother is saying, "I thought I had better bring my daughter along to you. . . . she doesn't want to be an air stewardess" (*BEA Magazine,* No. 43, February 1952).

A poem in the January 1955 issue of *BEA Magazine* evidences that the growing discourse of glamour had already overwhelmed the early concerns of desexualization:

Saga of a Stewardess

'Twas many, many moons ago
When I first felt aviation's glow.
A glamour queen of air I'd be
And everyone would envy me.

Exactly one year later, we can find the first direct association of bodily sexuality with the job of stewardess. A cartoon shows two male air crew members eyeing a vivacious female flight attendant. One says to the other, "Sure she's cute—but that's just what makes her such a menace to fly with; every time she comes up on the flight deck, even the compass needle spins around and points at her" (*BOAC Review and Newsletter,* January 1956).

CONCLUDING REMARKS

Eventually a discourse of eroticism took hold within BOAC and BEA, and the notion of desexualization was something in the airlines' distant and forgotten past. What could have potentially developed into a situation of greater equity turned rapidly into a set of practices that constrained female sexuality to narrow and often demeaning images. No doubt the process found an echo in the developing consumerist society of the 1960s, but it also seems reasonable to suggest that many aspects of the image making originated within the airlines themselves, due in large part to the gendered structures and processes of the airlines (Mills, 1996a).

That the policy of desexualization failed was due in part to its roots in moral panic rather than a firm commitment to employment equity, but primarily it was due to a failure to deal with the underlying processes and practices that contribute to an organization's culture (Abella, 1984).

Unlike the period prior to 1960, many companies today view corporate image as a vital aspect of their strategic planning and positioning. However, as several recent studies have indicated, gender is viewed more as an *issue* to be addressed separately from strategic concerns rather than as a *dynamic* that frames the very way strategies are developed and understood—with fundamental consequences for the way women and men are themselves understood and valued (Kerfoot & Knights, 1993; Mills, 1996a, 1996b; Morgan & Knights, 1991; Tinker & Neimark, 1987). To use the framework of Mintzberg, Brunet, and Waters (1986), gender dynamics can be viewed as forming part of an emergent strategy, which, unaddressed, can overwhelm an organization's intended (supposedly gender-neutral) strategy.

It is notoriously difficult to address gender dynamics across an organization's culture, but decision makers can take an important step by recognizing that gender dynamics are a central element of the makeup of their organization. Recognition of that fact may help organizational leaders to deal with the less difficult, more clearly defined area of corporate imagery. A clear understanding of the role of gender dynamics and its relationship to corporate imagery and discrimination may assist organizational leaders to avoid not only the blatant (e.g., the "bunny club" outfits used at one time by a major U.S. airline; Hochschild, 1984) but some of the more subtle forms of sexism (e.g., British Airways' current advertisement, which features a female flight attendant rocking a baby with the face of middle-aged male passenger) that we have witnessed in company marketing strategies.

NOTES

1. By 1945, BEA and BOAC, and their predecessors, were organizations that had played an important and visible role in British social life for 26 years; BOAC, for example, was for many years the flag bearer and "chosen instrument" of government foreign policy (Pudney, 1959). British Airways, formed from a merger of BOAC and BEA in 1974, is a large multinational company that employs nearly 37,000 people and is one of the world's top airlines.

2. In the period 1945 to 1960, there were significant changes in British society regarding sexuality (Lewis, 1992): moving from "a clear concern with the conditions of 'reproduction' " (Weeks, 1989, p. 232)—characterized by the metaphors of motherhood and marriage—to a period of interest in the potential joys of sex—captured (somewhat unfairly) by the metaphor of the permissive society. An examination of BOAC and BEA during the same period might be expected to reveal a similar change in perceptions and behaviors. But if so, what is cause and what is effect and how are general social trends shaped by internal processes? Examination of distinct elements within the culture of British Airways can indicate how different sexualities were being understood at a given time and how those understandings changed over time. It is far harder to unravel the complex nature of social interactions between individual organizations and social beliefs, and I will not attempt it in this chapter. What I am concerned with, however, is to throw doubt on the "normal" assumption that social life shapes the organization rather than the equally valid view that social life is shaped, in large part, by a myriad of organizational realities.

3. Women were always designated Miss or Mrs. and were only reported when they were appointed, when they married, and when they had children.

4. In 1942, one of the most popular films on both sides of the Atlantic was *Mrs. Miniver.* Produced in Hollywood, Mrs. Miniver starred Greer Garson as a wholesomely beautiful, middle-class English wife who does all that she can to support and minister to her husband (played by Walter Pidgeon) who is called to war duty: Sir Winston Churchill stated that the propaganda value of the film was worth many battleships (Eames, 1976, p. 176).

5. These sectors had been feminized in the period between 1911 and 1939, with the percentage of women in the clerical and related workforce rising from 21% to 44% (Pugh, 1992).

6. Even during the war years, the company had employed 14- to 16-year-old boys rather than women as air stewards—a policy they continued as late as 1946 (Mills, 1996b).

7. By 1945, air stewarding had become a largely female occupation throughout the airlines of the world. Boeing Air Transport (the forerunner of United) was the first to introduce female stewardesses in 1930. Eastern was the next U.S. carrier to introduce female flight attendants in 1931, followed by American (1933), TWA (1933), Western and National Airlines (1935), Braniff (1937), Delta (1940), Continental (1941), and Pan Am (1943). In Europe, Air France (1933), Swissair (1934), KLM (1935), and Lufthansa (1938) were all employing female flight attendants prior to the Second World War.

8. It is far from clear—especially in the face of a stated antiglamour policy—that the use of female imagery was consciously used for decorative purposes.

9. The author was a male journalist.

10. Despite the war years, the female share of the workforce only increased from 29% to 31% in the period 1931 to 1951 (Pugh, 1992). Nonetheless, the number of married and older (25 years old and above) women in the workforce increased, respectively, from 10% to 22% and from 50% to 67% over the same period (Pugh, 1992).

11. There was, of course, the odd film that received critical acclaim for portraying women as successful outside of the home—*A Letter to Three Wives, Adam's Rib.*

12. Interviews with former female employees of BEA who appeared in photographs of this type indicates that they were recruited for their photographic appeal. The normal work of the women photographed had no connection with the transportation (cargo) of animals.

REFERENCES

Abella, R. S. (1984). *Equity in employment: A Royal Commission report.* Ottawa: Ministry of Supply and Services Canada.

Acker, J. (1992). Gendering organizational theory. In A. J. Mills & P. Tancred (Eds.), *Gendering organizational analysis* (pp. 248-260). Newbury Park, CA: Sage.

Acker, J., & van Houten, D. R. (1974). Differential recruitment and control: The sex structuring of organizations. *Administrative Science Quarterly, 9*(2), 152-163.

Alvesson, M., & Berg, P. O. (1992). *Corporate culture and organizational symbolism.* Berlin: deGruyter.

Benson, S. P. (1986). *Countercultures: Saleswomen, managers, and customers in American department stores, 1890-1940.* Urbana: University of Illinois Press.

Bray, W. (1974). *The history of BOAC 1939-74.* Camberley, Surrey: BOAC/Wessex Press.

Burrell, G. (1992). Sex and organizational analysis. In A. J. Mills & P. Tancred (Eds.), *Gendering organizational analysis* (pp. 71-92). Newbury Park, CA: Sage.

Calas, M. B., & Smircich, L. (1992). Using the "F" word: Feminist theories and the social consequences of organizational research. In A. J. Mills & P. Tancred (Eds.), *Gendering organizational analysis* (pp. 222-234). Newbury Park, CA: Sage.

Collinson, D. L. (1988). Engineering humor: Masculinity, joking, and conflict in shopfloor relations. *Organization Studies, 9*(2), 181-199.

Collinson, D. L. (1992). *Managing the shopfloor: Subjectivity, masculinity, and workplace culture.* Berlin: deGruyter.

Davies, S. (1984). *Managing corporate culture.* Cambridge, MA: Ballinger.

Deal, T. E., & Kennedy, A. A. (1982). *Corporate culture.* Reading, MA: Addison-Wesley.

Denhardt, R. (1981). *In the shadow of organization.* Lawrence: Regents Press of Kansas.

Eames, J. D. (1976). *The MGM story.* New York: Crown.

Ferguson, K. E. (1984). *The feminist case against bureaucracy.* Philadelphia: Temple University Press.

Flax, J. (1990). *Thinking fragments: Psychoanalysis, feminism, and postmodernism in the contemporary West.* Berkeley: University of California Press.

Foucault, M. (1979). *Discipline and punishment.* New York: Vintage.

Foucault, M. (1980). *The history of sexuality: Vol. 1.* New York: Vintage.

Gutek, B. A. (1985). *Sex and the workplace.* San Francisco: Jossey-Bass.

Hall, M. (1989). Private experiences in the public domain: Lesbians in organizations. In J. Hearn, D. L. Sheppard, P. Tancred-Sheriff, & G. Burrell (Eds.), *The sexuality of organization* (pp. 125-138). London: Sage.

Hearn, J., & Parkin, P. W. (1983). Gender and organizations: A selective review and a critique of a neglected area. *Organization Studies, 4*(3), 219-242.

Hearn, J., & Parkin, P. W. (1987). *"Sex" at "work"—The power and paradox of organizational sexuality.* Brighton: Wheatsheaf.

Hearn, J., Sheppard, D. L., Tancred-Sheriff, P., & Burrell, G. (Eds.). (1989). *The sexuality of organization.* London: Sage.

Hochschild, A. R. (1983). *The managed heart.* Berkeley: University of California Press.

Kanter, R. M. (1977). *Men and women of the corporation.* New York: Basic Books.

Kerfoot, D., & Knights, D. (1993). Management, masculinity, and manipulation: From paternalism to corporate strategy in financial service in Britain. *Journal of Management Studies, 30*(4), 659-677.

Lewis, J. (1992). *Women in Britain since 1945.* Oxford: Blackwell.

Mills, A. J. (1988). Organization, gender, and culture. *Organization Studies, 9*(3), 351-369.

Mills, A. J. (1994a). The gendering of organizational culture: Social and organizational discourses in the making of British Airways. In M. DesRosiers (Ed.), *Proceedings of the Administrative Sciences Association of Canada, Women in Management Division* (Vol. 15, pp. 11-20). Halifax, Nova Scotia: ASAC.

Mills, A. J. (1994b, June). *Gendering organizational culture: From theory to analysis—identifying discriminatory discourses in the making of British Airways.* Paper presented at the Annual Conference, Administrative Sciences Association of Canada, Business History Section, Halifax, Nova Scotia.

Mills, A. J. (1994c, July). *No sex, please, we're British Airways: A model for uncovering the symbols of gender in British Airways' culture, 1919-1991.* Paper presented at the Annual Standing Conference on Organizational Symbolism, Calgary, Alberta.

Mills, A. J. (1996a). Corporate image, gendered subjects, and the company newsletter—The changing face of British Airways. In G. Palmer & S. Clegg (Eds.), *Constituting management: Markets, meanings, and identities.* Berlin: de Gruyter.

Mills, A. J. (1996b). Strategy, sexuality, and the stratosphere: Airlines and the gendering of organization. In E. S. Lyon & L. Morriss (Eds.), *Gender relations in public and private: Changing research perspectives*. London: Macmillan.

Mills, A. J. (1995). Man/aging subjectivity, silencing diversity: Organizational imagery in the airline industry—The case of British Airways. *Organization, 2*(2), 243-269.

Mills, A. J., & Murgatroyd, S. J. (1991). *Organizational rules.* Milton Keynes: Open University Press.

Mintzberg, H., Brunet, J. P., & Waters, J. A. (1986). Does planning impede strategic thinking? Tracking the strategies of Air Canada from 1937 to 1976. In R. Lamb & P. Shrivastava (Eds.), *Advances in strategic management* (Vol. 4, pp. 3-41). Greenwich, CT: JAI Press.

Morgan, G., & Knights, D. (1991). Gendering jobs: Corporate strategies, managerial control, and dynamics of job segregation. *Work, Employment, & Society, 5*(2), 181-200.

Ouchi, W. (1981). *Theory Z.* Reading, MA: Addison-Wesley.

Penrose, H. (1980). *British aviation: Ominous skies, 1935-1939.* London: HMSO.

Peters, T., & Waterman, R. (1982). *In search of excellence.* New York: Warner Communications.

Pringle, R. (1989). Bureaucracy, rationality, and sexuality: The case of secretaries. In J. Hearn, D. L. Sheppard, P. Tancred-Sheriff, & G. Burrell (Eds.), *The sexuality of organization.* London: Sage.

Pudney, J. (1959). *The seven skies.* London: Putnam.

Pugh, M. (1992). *Women and the women's movement in Britain 1914-1959.* London: Macmillan.

Tinker, T., & Neimark, M. (1987). The role of annual reports in gender and class contradictions at General Motors: 1917-1976. *Accounting, Organizations, and Society, 12*(1), 71-88.

Weeks, J. (1986). *Sexuality.* London: Tavistock.

Weeks, J. (1989). *Sex, politics, & society.* London: Longman.

Wolff, J. (1977). Women in organizations. In S. Clegg & D. Dunkerley (Eds.), *Critical issues in organizations* (pp. 7-20). London: Routledge & Kegan Paul.

Woods, W. (1992). Unfriendly skies. *Fortune International, 126,* 30-31.

Wright, C. (1985). *Tables in the sky: Recipes from British Arways and the great chefs.* London: W. H. Allen.

Women in the Academy

Cycles of Resistance and Compliance

PATRICIA BRADSHAW
DAVID WICKS

During the past few years, there have been an increasing number of studies and reports on the experiences of female academics. Many of these studies contain common themes about the challenges and problems facing women in universities, their desires to create a different organization, and their hope to speak with a different voice. At the same time, however, the prescriptions that these reports recommend will not lead to radical or deep structural change. They provide advice to women about how to play the game, and tend to be based on traditional male models of power and achievement. Unquestioningly following these strategies, we believe, has multiple costs for both the individual women and their institutions. In this chapter, we explore these costs. The chapter also provides alternative models for female academics in their efforts to resist the dynamics of compliance, co-optation, and control, which the existing systems of authority and our own unconscious internalizations of them tend to encourage.

I was so frustrated with the "chilly climate" at my university, which on the surface appeared to many as fair and equitable, that I felt I *had* to do something about it, to let everyone know what it is really like to work in a place like this. I went to the media with my story, so everyone would hear firsthand my story of isolation, discrimination, and harassment. This caused me a great deal of stress, but it did make me feel enormously empowered, and I had few doubts that change would result. (Julia, 1990)

Always, in any institution, I have been bugged by the things that you are required to be present at and "on the team," with no other purpose than making a show. Pre-tenure, there were certainly a few tense years where I really had to force myself to shape up and do what the institution expected of me in addition to the teaching, which was what I really enjoyed. But post-tenure . . . I mean there was still some pressure to publish, but really in my heart I knew that I could do what I liked for the rest of my life. I ended up leaving academe because my life circumstances changed in such a way that I had the freedom to now do full-time anything I wanted to do. When I quit I was head of my department, I was a full professor, I had a big teaching fellowship—people thought I was quite loony to walk out right at that precise moment. I seemed to have everything one could want. (Nuala)

When I was trying to decide on a topic for my dissertation, I figured that to do a Ph.D. in anything was going to be a bore unless it was something that I could relate to. But I was hesitant to talk about a lot of things to anyone, but at the same time, they were things I desperately wanted to do. One of the things I dreaded was coming out as a lesbian. I was afraid of being attacked, that I was going to be peripheral, and my work was always going to be peripheral. I even had to give my dissertation a noncommittal kind of title—it was dreadful! (Alberta)

I remember my first academic job—I learned a lot there, but I found it personally a really painful thing to go through. There were a lot of rules, and I found out I didn't know them. I learned that teaching doesn't count—I mean, I really didn't know that. And I took a maternity leave when I was there, and I don't think any of the men there would say that I broke the rules, but unconsciously they thought that. *Obviously* I wasn't serious. Shouldn't having your first child be a really special time in a person's life? I was really a marginal person there in many ways, but I just assumed that if I did a good job that would do it. I take way less shit now than I did then—well, I can't afford to if I am going to survive. (Frances)

These stories demonstrate a variety of institutional pressures, behavioral responses and associated feelings that characterize the work lives of many women in the academy. Taken from documents and interviews with women holding tenure-track positions in Ontario universities, these stories represent actual instances of compliance and resistance. Unfortunately, these stories are true and vividly depict the multitude of exogenous pressures to comply and the associated responses (of both compliance and resistance) of these professional women.

INTRODUCTION

This chapter is the result of a continuing dialogue[1] and is based on a combination of personal experiences, observations, and a series of in-depth interviews with female academics. These dialogues have been based on the topic of how different women define their experiences of holding tenure-track jobs within Canadian universities. Our questioning began with an exploration of the strategies available to women to enact feminist change agenda(s) and why some women became advocates for change whereas others appeared to go along and not "rock the boat" (see Bradshaw & Newell, 1992). It has evolved into a conceptual framing of the cycles of resistance and compliance. The grounded nature of this exploration now has a conceptual home in the growing research on the dynamics of resistance and power (e.g., Hodson, 1991; Jermier, Knights, & Nord, 1994). Within this body of literature is an understanding that resistance is best understood when examined within specific sites with definite sociohistorical conditions and can most fruitfully be explored through grounded studies (Jermier et al., 1994). It is the objective of this chapter to contribute to this literature and to articulate a framework for understanding academic women's strategies of feminist resistance and modes of compliance.[2] Women within universities provide a particularly interesting context in which to explore feminist resistance because of the relatively unstructured nature of the work and the amount of autonomy a university professor can create within the context of her or his work. Most previous studies of compliance have focused on laborers in manufacturing settings where the work is highly structured and the rules defining acceptable or expected behaviors are clearly defined (e.g., Burawoy, 1979).

We take as our starting point the assumption that universities, and the societies in which we live, are patriarchal and biased against women (Dodson-Gray, 1982; Lerner, 1986). We do not accept the assumption that universities represent a level playing field, and that if women work hard they will necessarily succeed. Although a number of individuals in potentially disadvantaged positions within the university system face their own challenges in terms of resisting hegemonic structures and practices, we do not attempt in this chapter to illustrate the ways in which sexism, racism, homophobia, and classism within universities operate to privilege certain individuals and disadvantage others (see, for example, Chuchryk & Greene, 1990; Martin, 1994). Those who do not agree with these fundamental assumptions may have difficulty understanding the way the chapter unfolds and the logic underlying it. We encourage readers to dialogue with us around these ideas and reflect on the extent to which the framework we propose makes sense, or resonates, given your own personal experiences. We start with a review of some of the organizational behavior literature on compliance and resistance, followed by a brief review of the feminist perspectives on change and resistance. We originally sought out this literature to help us understand the context in which women are working. Unsatisfied with the advice we found there, we have attempted to frame a model of compliance and resistance that helps us understand, in a different way, the choices women in universities face every day.

LITERATURE REVIEW

Theories of Resistance and Compliance

The construct of resistance has primarily been associated with class domination from a Marxist perspective (Marx, 1967) and with domination of labor in unionized manufacturing sectors (e.g., Edwards, 1990; Littler, 1990). In the former case, resistance, although present in many forms, is derived *only* from revolutionary class consciousness, the struggle against the exploitation of labor for the purpose of extracting surplus value. In the latter case, resistance results simply from employee objections to managerial control. In either case, little or no theory exists about how and when resistance occurs and the variety of forms it may take (Jermier et al., 1994).

Resistance has not largely been the domain of organizational research, as any theories of management control assume that either resistance does not occur at all or that it can be contained and/or managed in order to achieve organizational goals. Instead, there has been considerable attention paid to compliance, the polar opposite of resistance; apparently compliance is a more desirable outcome than resistance, and as such, organizational scholarship has examined a number of positive organizational outcomes that are correlated with the display of compliance behaviors. Barnard's (1938) foundational theorizing of managerial behavior recognizes the centrality of "willing" employees in achieving organizational goals. Barnard suggests that not only is spontaneous cooperation among employees possible, but also that individuals have a _zone of indifference_ within which managerial directives are viewed as "unquestioningly acceptable." These two observations call into question the objectivity and rigidity of authority systems, thus questioning the ubiquity of compliant subordinates. If compliance is never assured, then resistance is a phenomenon to which management theorists should pay attention. Since that time, however, little research has attempted to question or validate the basic tenets of Barnard's theory.

Etzioni (1961) presents a typology of compliance relations, attempting to link appropriate strategies of managerial control to organizational goals. In marked contrast to Barnard, Etzioni views compliance as universal, the quintessential relationship between those who have power and those who do not. Strikingly similar to labor process theorists that seek to better control "labor," Etzioni suggests three types of control (coercive, remunerative, and normative), each of which is ideally suited for individuals displaying three types of involvement (alienative, calculative, and moral) in three types of organizations (order, economic, and cultural). Implicit in this theory is the assumption that compliance is a tool to be used by management to effectively control subordinates, resulting in the survival of the organization. In this view, compliance is a necessity, and resistance is a deviant behavior to be extinguished.

A similar view is implicit in theories of organizational commitment, "the strength of an individual's identification with and involvement in a particular organization" (Porter, Steers, Mowday, & Boulian, 1974, p. 604). Research in this area is typically interested in the relationship between commitment and turnover (Porter et al., 1974), absenteeism (Pierce & Dunham, 1987), length of organizational membership (Meyer & Allen, 1984), and performance (DeCotiis & Summers, 1987); ostensibly the more committed an employee is, the more desirable he or she is for the organization. More recent theorizing (Meyer, Paunonen, Gellatly, Goffin, & Jackson, 1989), however, suggests that not all commitment is created equal; affective commitment (those who want to remain employed) is deemed to be more advantageous to the organization than continuance commitment (those who have to remain employed). From this perspective, efforts to coerce organizational members (by either strict regulation or lack of alternatives) into exhibiting certain behaviors, attitudes, or roles will not necessarily have the desirable organizational outcomes that Etzioni suggests. In this paradigm of managerial omniscience and subordinate docility, it is assumed that managerial control is both desirable and effective, with subordinates participating in the organization simply as reactive agents who willingly accept formal and normative expectations. More recently, however, it is being suggested that a workforce of "committed" employees might not represent a utopian state from the perspective of management because coercing individuals into appearing committed and having employees maintain membership in the organization only to, for example, earn a living and provide material benefits consumed outside the organization provides few of the benefits typically associated with a group of committed employees (Meyer et al., 1989). When organizational commitment is viewed in this manner, the compliant individuals necessary for high levels of commitment might not necessarily result in benefits to either the organization or the individual; only when certain varieties of commitment (i.e., affective) are present do organizations and their members benefit. If compliance with organizational expectations or directives is secured by coercion and domination, turnover, absenteeism, performance, and length of organizational membership will be less favorable than if individuals *choose* to be committed to their organization.

In response to that notion, Kelman's (1958) framework for attitude change has been adopted in order to explain psychological attachment to the organization, a fundamental component of organizational commitment (O'Reilly & Chatman, 1986). Kelman identifies three factors (compliance, identification, and internalization) by which accepting influence can be explained. Compliance here occurs when "attitudes and behaviors are adopted not because of shared beliefs, but simply to gain specific rewards;" it does not result from any sort of congruence between the attitudes and behaviors of individuals and the organization in which they function (O'Reilly & Chatman, 1986, p. 493). Here we again see a departure from the Marxist and labor process theorist perspectives, which suggest resistance is omnipresent in a capitalist society. Compliance will result when individuals feel it is "worth it," and otherwise they might resist.

Crucial to a more complete understanding of the dynamics of compliance and resistance are aspects of individual subjectivity that influence individual responses to the variety of pressures they face in the context of their work. Braverman (1974) began to question individual subjectivity, advocating the need to move beyond simple measures of job satisfaction or self-reports of class identification. As much as we feel this is a move in the right direction, many aspects of subjectivity remain unquestioned (Jermier et al., 1994). Although relating to only a narrow aspect of subjectivity, we focus in this chapter on feminist consciousness and feminist political agendas of women in the academy, each of which help to define the local conditions and power dynamics present in Canadian universities. By doing so, we contribute to the emerging debates on how resistance is shaped and how specific forms of compliance and resistance change over time and vary between individuals.

Feminist Theory

Feminist theorists increasingly understand that women construct their lives, but do so within determinant conditions that may disadvantage them. As described by Davis and Fisher (1993), there is a relationship between structured forms of constraint and women's agency, between the limits imposed by differential allocations of power and the ability to be active participants in the construction of our social lives, and between power and resistance. These tensions between conformity and creativity/agency (Mahoney & Yngvesson, 1992) inform much feminist theory and sociology in general (Giddens, 1984; Smith, 1987). To illustrate this tension, Davis and Fisher (1993) describe how Marxist and radical feminist perspectives focus on the ways in which power oppresses women and the structural determinants of women's subordination in terms of the structures of capitalism and/or patriarchy. These perspectives, however,

> run the risk of victimizing women by representing them as passive objects of monolithic systems of oppression. From this perspective, women are presented as the victims of economic domination, patriarchal oppression, or a combination of both. This perspective leaves little conceptual or political space for uncovering the subtle and ambivalent ways women may be negotiating at the margins of power, sometimes constrained by but also resisting and undermining asymmetrical power structures. (Davis & Fisher, 1993, p. 6)

These more structural perspectives may lead us to conclude that because women's subordination is the result of systemic forces, the only solution is massive collective action and a movement to totally change dominant systems and structures. The existing power relations are seen as hierarchical, with power moving *only* from top to bottom. The outcome is seeing certain systems as an "objective reality," containing universalistic categories of analysis in which women become essentialized and frequently marginalized.

Liberal feminist positions are similar in terms of their underlying assumptions of the rigidity and permanence of structures and processes, although they suggest a different change agenda. Rather than dislodging hegemonic institutions, structures, or processes, the liberal agenda focuses on operating within existing constraints to effect change. Caplan (1993), for example, is concerned with the status of women in Canadian universities and suggests that incorrect stereotypes and assumptions of women's traits and values are simply obstacles to overcome, and the best way to accomplish this is through persistence and presence. Similarly, Kanter (1977) views women's disadvantaged position as a result of lack of power, the "ability to *do*" (p. 166). Women's lack of ability to "get things done" results from a lack of the necessary tools for action, namely power. From a liberal perspective, women's lack of success in acquiring power has nothing to do with being women; women and men are essentially rational, self interest-seeking agents, and as such should be able to work within the same organizational systems with similar levels of success.

Postmodern feminist perspectives, many of which draw on the work of Foucault and Derrida, in contrast, lead to a reconceptualization of power as a process, oftentimes discursively constructed.

> Thus modern power operates continuously in a subtle but penetrating manner. It is a "capillary" circulating through the social body and exerting its authority through self surveillance and everyday, disciplinary micropractices—practices more fundamental than beliefs (ideology). These practices insinuate themselves within gestures, habits, bodies, and desires. Power exercised in this way seems to be everywhere and nowhere. . . . With power dispersed in this way, resistance cannot be reduced to a single locus of rebellion or revolt. (Davis & Fisher, 1993, p. 8)

For Foucault, when these disciplinary micropractices or determining factors become all-encompassing, there can be no relationship of power because some individuals or groups will have no agency. There must be a fine balance between determination and resistance; power can only be exercised over a "free" subject (Mahoney & Yngvesson, 1992), and the potential for exercising agency is available to any member of the intricate capillary system of power. From this perspective, instead of advocating or striving for systemic and/or quantum change, strategies for political action rest in the exploration of micropolitics, contests over meaning, counterdiscourses, and negotiations at the margins (e.g. Fisher, 1993; Gregg, 1993; hooks, 1994; Ross, 1993; Wilson, 1993). The goal, therefore, becomes opening up *multiple* sites of resistance.

Bridging the gap between structural and postmodern feminist positions and drawing on an understanding of both structural constraints and individual agency can help us explore a range of ways of resisting power and influence, as well as uses of strategies that can range from heroic to mundane (Davis & Fisher, 1993). In this chapter, however, we want not only to explore resistance but also to understand women's compliance with the status quo and institutionalized expectations, and their complicity with systems that are inherently racist, sexist, classist, and homophobic.

CYCLES OF COMPLIANCE AND RESISTANCE

We have observed that some women faculty appear to conform to the dominant rules and norms of the university whereas others articulate and advocate a feminist agenda; some play the game whereas others blow the whistle, quit, and protest the chilly climate; some exhibit behaviors that appear compliant whereas others resist. Martin (1994) concludes that women on faculty in universities tend not to admit that gender biases exist in evaluations of merit.

> Ironically, because universities have made such a concerted effort to create a fair and thorough evaluation process, it is particularly difficult to get universities to consider exploring the possibility that bias may exist. To complicate matters, women faculty may be particularly unlikely to push for such an investigation. Crosby (1982) has shown that although most women agree that sex discrimination is in general a problem, they tend to be unwilling to admit that they personally might be victims of discrimination, even when faced with clear evidence to the contrary. (Martin, 1994, p. 414)

Why does the myth of meritocracy still dominate and why do so many people believe that the playing field is level and unbiased in universities? In contrast, why do some female scholars undertake feminist work, take on affirmative action jobs, and advocate women's issues? The liberal beliefs in equality (with the corresponding suggestions that women's presence is "enough") and the belief that we need to advocate for change coexist *within* the context of universities. We believe, and our data illustrate, that female academics constantly live with the tension between compliance and resistance and that they cycle between the two at various times as their awareness of inequalities changes.

The context of these cycles is the university and larger social system in which women are embedded, with its social norms, cultural conventions, and socially constructed structures of power and authority. Many of the rules of these systems are explicit and obvious, whereas many others are taken for granted and implicit, remaining largely unconscious. These "rules" are usually assumed to be gender neutral when in fact, they are frequently gendered in ways that disadvantage women (Bradshaw & Wicks, 1995; Martin, 1994; Mills, 1988, 1994; Wicks & Bradshaw, 1995). For example, Frances recounts her experiences, in her first academic job, of identifying and deciphering the "rules of the game." Her experience was one of trial and error, where her mistakes along the way were communicated to her by her (mostly male) colleagues, usually in terms of her "inappropriate" behavior. She came to realize that "teaching didn't count" and that her maternity leave was viewed as evidence of her lack of commitment to the job. Similarly, Martin (1994) identifies how female academics are less likely than men to move up the organizational hierarchy and typically earn less than men of comparable skill and ability. Although academic environments espouse equal treatment of women and men, the fact remains that the nonwork lives of many women restrict their access to the organization and its members; the tenure clock discriminates against women who have children early in their careers. Although these are only two ways in which organizational rules disadvantage women, the potential harm they have on both women and men stems from the way in which these rules are presented and interpreted as gender neutral, taken for granted, and institutionalized, when in fact, they serve to maintain sex inequalities that disadvantage women. We all live in the context of similar systems of rules, and we constantly make both conscious and unconscious "choices" about how and when we comply and obey and/or resist and defy.

Psychological perspectives can help explain what motivates individuals to comply or resist. Mahoney and Yngvesson (1992), for example, explore the psychological perspective of women's agency and victimization and show how the struggle to create new forms of change or conformity are shaped by, and dependent upon, old meanings. The dependence-independence paradox faced by the young child, they suggest, gets resolved in the presence of the Other (primary care givers) and leads to a particular posture of the psyche with regards to the integration or splitting of this paradox. They suggest that if one side of the dependence-independence dialectic is devalued and the other idealized, then we may be able to understand the grip of gender domination in the unconscious. For example, a woman who splits off from feelings of dependence and who unconsciously overvalues independence may seek out situations where she can avoid feeling vulnerable and can achieve "success" according to gendered notions of that achievement. Likewise a women who splits off from her independent side may unconsciously seek out situations in which she can feel dependent and thus unconsciously replicate the stereotypical view of women as helpless, passive, or dependent. Thus, how each of us carries our own unconscious early experiences of obedience and creativity influences our relationship with others.

These unconscious dynamics may be one way to make sense of the silence about (and compliance with which women often greet) authority systems and

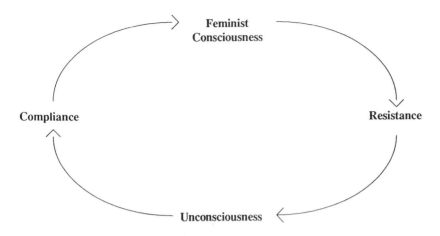

Figure 9.1: Cycle of Resistance and Compliance

external rules of universities. For example, if, in a patriarchal world, women unconsciously identify with the independent, authoritarian, and apparently powerful male figures who dominate in their world, they can become what has been called "daughters of the patriarchy" (Albert, 1992; Bolen, 1992; Woodman, 1993). Characteristic of this pattern is a need to be in control, to respond to inner voices of authority, and to stifle creativity and spontaneity. Thus, in accordance with Foucault's suggestion that we do not need external systems of punishment and control because we have internalized the micropractices of self-surveillance and discipline (Rabinow, 1984), women frequently internalize the "patriarchal father" and unconsciously comply with the existing rules.

We suggest that within the context of gendered rules and the unequal distributions of power and privilege, and given the individual's unconscious orientations, female academics cycle between the dialectic of compliance, obedience, conformity, and consent and resistance, agency, and empowered action. The movement between the two shifts with levels of awareness and feminist consciousness of the choices they have to resist and the consciousness that they even *have* choices in the first place (see Figure 9.1). In this model, women who have not brought their compliance to the level of consciousness are compliant because they know of no other way or are not even aware of their compliance in the first place. As feminist consciousness increases, women move to the other side of the dialectic, where resistance can be displayed in a variety of forms. Once a woman exercises her agency in this regard, she opens herself up for gradually bringing to conscious awareness new and different ways in which she complies, thereby perpetuating this cycle between compliance and resistance.

A central component of our model is feminist consciousness, without which women may remain unaware of the ways in which they comply (and consequently are unable to resist) indefinitely. Lerner (1993) traces the creation of what she calls *feminist consciousness* from the Middle Ages to 1870.

> It was under patriarchal hegemony in thought, values, institutions, and resources that women had to struggle to form their own feminist consciousness. I define feminist consciousness as the awareness of women that they belong to a subordinate group; that they have suffered wrong as a group; that their condition of subordination is not natural, but is socially determined; that they must join with other women to remedy these wrongs; and finally, that they must and can provide an alternative vision of societal organization in which women as well as men enjoy autonomy and self-determination. (Lerner, 1993, p. 14)

It is this type of consciousness that we see as the first step in women's resistance. We want to stress that this type of consciousness is not easy to create; it may be painful for women to see and acknowledge the extent of their oppression; individuals have *many* defense mechanisms that can work to keep them unaware of their own domination. Patriarchal consciousness is pervasive and difficult to name and reveal. We also believe that obedience can be "so deeply ingrained, compliance comes so naturally, that it sneaks up on us when we intend the opposite" (Starhawk, 1990, p. 79). Thus, in our model, female academics appear to cycle between unconscious compliance through the development of a feminist consciousness to a place where resistance in some form becomes possible. Feminist consciousness in itself is not necessarily enough to result in acts of resistance; individuals must also be *motivated* to act, and this requires that they move out of their "zone of indifference" (Barnard, 1938, p. 163) to begin to question the expectations they perceive and the formal directives or organizational members. The zone of indifference is the space in which the women acknowledge problems but are not inclined to attempt to solve them. Something, however, will make an issue salient (i.e., a movement outside the individual's zone of indifference) resulting in acts of resistance in subtle or obvious, planned or spontaneous fashions.

Although individual responses to influences and expectations vary along a continuum from complete compliance to active resistance, we restrict the focus in this chapter to individuals who have some level of feminist consciousness and operate outside their personal zone of indifference, thus engaging in acts of resistance. Of course, conditions might exist where individuals do have an amount of feminist consciousness but continue to behave in a compliant manner nonetheless. These individuals may, for example, feel that they have no choice but to comply, that the issues in question are not significant enough to warrant speaking out against the workplace majority, or that the personal costs of resistance are too high. There are *many* dynamics that can force women back into operating within their personal zones of indifference, including feelings of vulnerability, peer pressure, financial need, or inadequate perceived payoff or benefit to resistance (Wicks, 1996). Fear may be one of the greatest of these forces, and realistically so in many cases. When women root their awareness in the political realities of their cultures and truly recognize the extent to which patriarchal rules have limited their vision, then they may also more accurately understand the power structures in all their depth, insidiousness, and violence. The 1989 slaying of 14 women in a Montreal university because they were seen as feminists, and the collective memories of women of the witch hunts (Barstow, 1994), work both consciously and unconsciously to heighten the fear. As Starhawk (1992) suggests, the memory of events like the witch hunts "remain with us today as a wound in the collective psyche" (p. 17).

The cycle of compliance and resistance, as we conceptualize it, does not end in the zone of indifference or in acts of resistance because there is no possibility to be fully conscious of all sources of inequity or discrimination at once, and women remain unconsciously trapped in complicity within systems of inequality at some level. No sooner are women able to speak with a new voice or challenge the dominant construction of reality with an attitude of resistance than they find new areas of blind conformity, other aspects of unconscious privilege, and unexplored ways in which they have internalized the rules and been in complicity with the system. According to our model, even women who are resisting in some ways are simultaneously living within the confines of compliance in ways of which they may not be conscious; they cannot completely avoid compliance because none of us are, or can remain, fully aware. As a result, women remain silent, obey, and comply unknowingly with the relations of power, with the dynamics of sexism, racism, homophobia, and classism. Women's silence and lack of awareness prohibit them from resisting these dynamics even though they often get hurt, devaluing themselves, their colleagues, and their students. The pain of awareness can be too great, and more awareness can lead to more distress (Brown, 1994). How can women let in the extent of the problems? How can they understand the roots of the internalized dependence, perhaps originating in early childhood? How do they name the ways in which they reinforce and institutionalize bigotry, hatred, and violence? By gradually increasing feminist consciousness, women can begin to recognize the ways in which they have been compliant and understand the detrimental consequences to themselves and others around them. Only after consciousness has been raised to this level can effective resistance occur.

Dynamics of Compliance

We would first like to explore the dynamics of compliance as we have conceptualized them in this chapter. As stated earlier, we define compliance behaviors as unconscious acceptance of a wide range of influence and authority. Our model posits that once women move out of this state of unconscious acceptance, they will be led to resist those very structures and processes of which they were previously unaware. One could argue, however, that women could engage in resistance without a strong level of feminist consciousness, in essence effecting feminist change "by accident." We do not support the concept of an unconscious feminism in which women fulfill feminist change agendas unknowingly. For example, we do not think the cycle illustrated in Figure 9.1 can go backward from compliance through unconsciousness to resistance. Nor do we accept the belief that women's mere presence in the university is enough, or that women can make a difference by just "being there." When women are unaware that they are acting in terms of the rules of the system, when they are not reflective of how they are obeying the "authorities," then we define their behaviors as compliant, obedient, or consensual. This differs from playing the game in a consciously subversive way, such that women *appear* to be going along with the current systems of reality construction and the distributions of power and privilege but do so in a self-conscious fashion, fully aware of the choices they are making and the consequences of their actions. Compliance, in our definition, involves unquestioned and unconscious obedience, complicity, and consent. Thus, the same outward behaviors can be viewed as either compliance or resistance, depending on the level of feminist consciousness that informs them. Sometimes, however, compliant behaviors are perceived as resistance by others and are met with punishment and stigmatization, for example when women avoid teaching, research, and committee involvement concerning affirmative action; by remaining silent on this type of issue, or avoiding it entirely, women tacitly support the male-dominated structures and processes of their institution, in essence complying. When women's silence is met by backlash from feminists or other groups fighting for equity, the opportunity exists for awareness of the harmful effects of compliance to be demonstrated, thereby increasing feminist consciousness at the same time women are criticized by their peers. Punitive responses, in whatever form they take, to behaviors that are compliant are often met with surprise, and the pain of the process can actually lead to the creation of feminist consciousness.

Starhawk (1990) suggests that related to more passive acts of compliance such as playing the game or just doing the job are acts of rebellion, withdrawal, denial, and manipulation. Although these are all deliberate acts of defying authority, they are unlikely to result in the type of change needed to alter the deep-rooted inequalities faced by many female academics. None of these behaviors constitute resistance in our definition of the term, unless they are also informed by feminist consciousness. For example, rebellion alone may not challenge the dominant relations of power, and through acts of rebellion, women often remain trapped by the alternatives and realities provided by the system. Furthermore, rebellion provides the system with a rationale for applying more punishment when compliance is not forthcoming, which in turn sets an example for others, warning them not to rebel. The problem with this form of protest, in our opinion, is therefore the likelihood of increased organizational control in the future, which consequently makes resistance that much more difficult. As a form of counterdependence, rebellion frequently maintains the status quo and does not challenge its underlying assumptions. Women who, for example, refuse to play the game or to publish and then are denied tenure and promotion have neither explicitly nor consciously questioned or resisted the systems of tenure and promotion, the criteria for making these decisions, or the inherent sources of bias contained within the apparently gender-neutral rules.

Withdrawal is another form of compliance in which women pull back and disengage from the system. This can take the form of apathy on the part of women who feel that the rules are too entrenched to ever change. By unquestioningly deferring to these rules, by saying "I only work here," "this is only a job," or "there is nothing I can do about it," some women withdraw. If someone is not actively part of the system of domination, then it becomes easier to subsist within the system—to claim it is beyond their control. By working to rule, emphasizing one's own limitations, and/or remaining personally detached from controversial issues, a safe space is created within which women can pull away from the source of their own oppression and consequently remove those pressures from the salient influences and pressures that guide their individual judgment and choice.

Denial, which accompanies withdrawal, occurs when women refuse to see, hear, and/or acknowledge the inequalities, inequities, and injustices of the workplace and larger social system. Some women withdraw physically and work at home; others deny the existence of discrimination and live within the safety of the liberal worldview while claiming that everything is fine; the systems are fair and women all have to accept the consequences of choices they make within the status quo. Although denial may provide short-term psychological benefits to women choosing to live this way, over time, the costs become increasingly difficult to bear and make it more difficult to resist the system after ostensibly accepting it for so long.

Finally, manipulation occurs when individuals figure out the system and how to win within it. Using manipulation, women create the illusion that they are in control, they reap the rewards of success and never challenge the low value placed on women and/or feminist scholarship. As Starhawk (1990) says, "we are still accepting the system's terms, unspoken rules, and values, including the lack of value it accords to us" (p. 87). For example, women who think they can beat the men at their own game, who publish more, serve on more committees, and teach with the highest student evaluations, often perceive that they are outsmarting the system and thereby winning a male-defined game with male-defined rules. From another perspective, however, their behaviors can actually serve to reinforce the system and perpetuate values that work against women. If some women can be overachievers and succeed by conventional criteria, then questions about how the system works against women in general may never be raised.

Although these four acts are all ways that appear to challenge the dominant systems, they in fact perpetuate them by not challenging their efficacy or legitimacy in the first place; by focusing on how to beat the rules and subsist in a system that is largely discriminatory, women can tacitly enhance the perceived legitimacy of the systems themselves, making feminist change all the more difficult. In the worst case, this complicity with the system becomes what we call collusion. In this state, women actively work against other women and reject their claims to be suffering from discrimination or harassment. In some cases, they actually protect the status quo and belittle, stereotype, and discriminate against other women, tell sexist and racist jokes, and/or actively undervalue feminist scholarship.

Some forms of compliance can result in feelings of isolation and pain, whereas other forms can provide a sense of security, the promise of reward, a feeling of belonging, and the illusion of empowerment. Compliant women can often become a part of the "old boy networks," being rewarded with opportunities to sit on prestigious and high-powered committees, to earn extra income through teaching in executive development programs or consulting to industry. The rules of the game appear clear, and the rewards tangible and visible to all. These women are provided with a perceived sense of value and worth. The alternatives can appear to be a form of punishment; those who resist are often described as radical feminists and consequently are labeled, rejected, and punished in other ways. The quotations at the beginning of the chapter reflect women's fears of being marginalized, being peripheral, or being attacked. Often resistors are seen to "rock the boat," are described as not being "team players" or as only pursuing some "special interest." Resistors undermine the communities' sense of stability and security, and for this reason are feared by all members of the system. For whatever reason, the potential threat that resistors may pose to hegemonic systems is frequently not realized by individuals, and as a consequence, many women remain unconscious and unaware of their complicity (or their alternatives to it) in a system that both undervalues and discriminates against women.

Women do not typically remain in states of unconscious compliance and denial forever. In our model, this represents a move toward feminist consciousness and eventually resistance. Something happens to raise awareness (e.g., a new feminist colleague, the death of a friend, social movements that attract national press) and consciousness shifts; women see a pattern, practice, or behavior and consequently name it and move to a position of agency, resulting in the opportunity to resist.

Dynamics of Resistance

Starhawk (1990) describes resistance as a *discipline of awareness* similar to other forms of spiritual practice. Oftentimes, women find the awareness that precedes resistance to be painful and discomforting, yet once they gain some new insight, they cannot go back to denial and avoidance. The increased consciousness typically comes in pieces as women are ready to deal with it, as they are challenged by fieldwork, students, colleagues, and dreams (Bradshaw & Newell, 1994).

Our definition of resistance is agency and action, based on feminist consciousness, directed against the systems of power that work to undermine and disadvantage women. Examples of women's disobedience to the rules of the collective and other forms of resistance are beginning to be identified and named (e.g., Fisher & Davis, 1993; Gilligan, Rogers, & Tolman, 1991; Ross, 1993). A growing fascination with the story of Eve's disobedience and subsequent fall from the garden of Eden may be reflective of this trend (e.g. Polster, 1992). Gilligan et al. (1991) see resistance as the refusal of women to merge with the dominant cultural norms and instead to attend to their own voice and integrity. Feminist resistance encompasses a fundamental challenge to the way reality has been constructed and the ways in which existing meaning systems work to disadvantage women. As described by Abu-Lughod (1993), resistance gives women new ways to understand the power structures and also is a type of power itself. Acts of resistance within universities, however, can be small or large, subtle or extravagant, private or public (Bannerji, Carty, Delhi, Heald, & McKenna, 1991). Bradshaw and Newell (1992) describe a continuum of behaviors displayed by academic women, which starts with strategies of apparently fitting in while subverting the authority of the male-dominated systems and goes all the way to public defiance, whistle blowing, and quitting. These strategies differ from the compliance described earlier because they are informed by feminist consciousness and seek to question and change the very structures and processes that originally gave rise to the compliance. For example, withdrawal that we view as compliant does not question the existing power relations whereas withdrawal as a form of resistance involves an awareness of the oppression of women and has the goal of subverting the system. Although on the surface the behaviors may appear the same, to the women involved, the awareness that accompanies an act of resistance provides a sense of empowerment, agency, and liberation that the act of compliance does not. Awareness of self as embedded in systems of inequality and the ability to contain that awareness and find the courage to resist in the face of potential threat, violence, and harm distinguishes between these behaviors. Ironically, all women face threats and harms, even those who comply. Building on this continuum, in the rest of this chapter, we will describe some of the acts of resistance that we have seen within universities and that were described during in-depth interviews with nine women in three Ontario universities.

1. Subtle Subversion

Within this category we include acts of resistance that are subtle but that subvert the dominant meaning systems and call into question the taken-for-granted and conventional ways things have been done within the university. Although they appear to be playing the game, women's disobedience provides them with a way of redefining the rules and exerting their own meaning and power over their work lives. These are seen as small but repeated acts of liberation:

- Challenging the implicit dress code, whether by wearing jeans or modifying the "business look" with jewelry and comfortable, low-heeled shoes (similar to Gottfried's 1994 description of women changing their appearance)
- Undermining the public/private split by having pictures of children and family in the office, actually breast feeding a baby in a meeting, or admitting that one is

leaving early to pick up a child from day care or to take an elderly parent to the doctor

- Taking positions that are reflective of what Starhawk (1990) calls a "bad attitude" (p. 326), for example, challenging sexist and racist jokes, questioning procedures and policies, expressing minority positions, supporting critiques of the way things are or have always been
- Joining women's support groups, participating in women's studies activities and projects, establishing a women's group within the school, co-authoring papers with other women, and otherwise challenging excessive individualism (Robinson & Ward, 1991)
- Raising questions of gender and diversity in the classroom, problematizing the curriculum, and disrupting the gender-neutral assumptions that dominate the university

The vignette of Alberta[3] presented at the beginning of the chapter demonstrates this type of resistance. Although she pursues feminist research topics, Alberta also "sneaks" issues of homosexuality into her research, uses qualitative methods in a field dominated by empiricism, and positions administrative involvement in lieu of publications in her tenure file. Although not an overt nonconformist, Alberta in many ways typifies the use of subtle subversion. By gaining initial support from her well-known, influential dissertation supervisor, by making a name for herself in a narrow range of social science research, and by establishing a strong network of supporters through her extensive committee involvement, Alberta has been able to "do her own thing," while not operating in a radical or confrontational manner. Alberta, while feeling vulnerable, says that she has probably reached as far as she has because of her "nice" disposition.

> One of the things that allows me to do the kind of work I do, and be at the same time threatened but not threatening, is that I have a nice manner. I come from the upper class, and I think that has functioned well for me. I have an ability to negotiate with people on very difficult subjects—I know that from my classes. I am not always successful, but for the most part I am, and I think that if you ask my colleagues, they would first tell you that I am a very nice person to work with, that I have something to offer the faculty, and that what I am doing is interesting. What they *know* about what I am doing is not a whole lot.

2. Defiance and Use of Legitimacy

These are more openly disruptive and outrageous acts (Steinem, 1992) performed in the workplace, which are explicitly designed to resist the current hegemony of male domination and create empowered action within the organization. Behaviors we have seen under this category include

- Taking on legitimate roles within a faculty to represent marginalized interests; for example, being an affirmative action advocate on hiring and tenure committees, being a union steward, or representing the school as a member of a status of women or race relations committee. These positions provide a legitimate role and voice for many women, and when advocating, they can claim, in a Weberian sense, that they "are just doing our jobs." Such positions justify and empower the challenges women bring forth and make resistance less personal and more institutional.

- Heading a "women in management" session or interest group at a conference, encouraging other women to work in the area, generating women's electronic networks, trying to articulate subversive agendas in professional associations, getting into positions of authority such as department head, dean, division chair-person, and so on, and then raising "women's issues" and channeling resources to support changes

- Speaking out, protesting, championing, and disrupting the dominant discourses in the face of hostility and criticism from colleagues, standing their ground despite labeling, marginalization, and censorship

- Writing papers using feminist perspectives, deconstructing the dominant dis-courses of the field, teaching feminist and antiracist courses, using feminist pedagogy

The vignette of Frances demonstrates this type of resistance. Although at one time, Frances tried to conform to institutional pressures, she was not successful. After a rather "painful" experience at one Ontario university, Frances took a government job for a number of years, then followed her husband to another Ontario university to take another tenure-track position. Frances, however, can certainly not be viewed as an overt nonconformist because there are too many things with which she disagrees that she lets go by. For example, in situations where the stakes are too high, or the potential for effecting successful change is too small, she acquiesces completely as she continues to operate within her zone of indifference. She talks of the "teaching problem" within universities in terms of the commonly used pedagogical practices that in her opinion fail to provide students with the education they require. Because this problem is something too big for her to tackle, she remains quiet about it, stating how she is not so "stupid" as to say anything about the problem. A result, however, is that she feels "implicated" by the system, and thus complicitous by her silence. Frances, in many ways, typifies the use of defiance, using her tenured status and connections within the university to voice opinions regarding which she is not about to keep quiet.

> The department made the decision that they were going to hire somebody, and they interviewed a bunch of people, and the one they wanted to hire was a guy who had finished his B.A. degree here in the mid-1980s and had just started a Ph.D. program. He was *really* one of the boys. He drank with them at the pub, and I mean, I thought he was just a complete asshole. Anyway, personal feelings aside, he gave what I think was the worst academic paper I have *ever* heard, and they all voted to hire him. I couldn't believe it. And I thought, well, there is just no way I can survive—if they have him in the department, that's it for me. I'm finished. So I went to the dean, and I went to the vice president and said, "You cannot allow this appointment. This is a crummy department anyway, and you are just giving in to them. . . . if you let them hire this guy, there is just no way, there is no hope for this department . . . *ever*." So the dean wrote a letter to the department saying that they would not approve the appointment for a whole bunch of reasons, good reasons really. And one of my colleagues asked me if I had gone to the dean, and I said yes because I wasn't about to lie about it. I was not about to volunteer that I had also gone to the vice president. Well, I was not too popular after that. My crime? Not being "loyal" to my department.

3. Whistle Blowing and Public Censuring

We also know women who have gone further in their resistance and who have blown the whistle in a highly public and visible fashion and who have protested discrimination and injustice outside of academia. Such acts include:

- Going to the newspapers with stories about the "chilly climate"
- Taking complaints to human rights tribunals or launching complaints through legal channels; taking concerns outside the organization to increase awareness in other constituencies
- Going "over the heads" of those in power in the department, and/or faculty to expose discrimination and identify perpetrators

The experiences of Julia Bristor (1990) vividly illustrate this alternative. After attempting to deal with systemic discrimination and harassment within her own university system, Julia felt she had no other choice than to speak out publicly and go to the newspapers with her story. All her meetings with faculty committees, advisory boards, and senior administrators met with the same result, that it was somehow her problem and that she was going to have to change because the university could not. After working within a system that clearly was not going to take her concerns seriously, Julia spoke out.

My experiences over the past few years have left no doubt in my mind that this place is a largely hostile environment for women, and probably also for men, who expect equal treatment. I mean, nobody would believe what I said. I was continually asked for additional examples and anecdotes to substantiate my "claims," and people would believe idle third-party gossip over my own words. They always defended the perpetrators and reinterpreted my reality. I was told my career at the university was undoubtedly at risk because I spoke out, and that perhaps I should go away for a while. All that would have done is admit defeat, and I never did feel that it was uniquely my problem. Through all my meetings, memos, and phone calls, I had created a file of carefully documented descriptions of my experiences, including, on occasion, witnesses. And I was willing to be named. I figured that I had exhausted all sources within the university that might possibly take my claim seriously and do something about the problems. So I began to draft a human rights complaint, which attracted a lot of attention and put the mass media's spotlight on the school. My only hope is that continued public attention will change this situation. (Bristor, 1990)

4. Dropping Out and Distancing

As described in one of the opening vignettes, women can also quit their jobs as a form of resistance. This conscious strategy leaves remaining colleagues questioning and often rethinking the dynamics for women within the university (or perhaps secretly pleased that the woman is gone). Collinson (1994) describes "resistance through distance" as a way for subordinates to try to escape or avoid the demands of authority and to distance themselves either physically or symbolically from the prevailing power structure. In a similar way, women can resist by refusing to support and promote systems and dynamics that work to disadvantage other women or that are inherently gender biased. Examples of distancing include:

- Leaving the institution to pursue a career in another, more "warm" academic environment
- Quitting the academy completely, rejecting the status and authority of the university by becoming, for example, self-employed, or becoming a part of a commercial organization

The vignette of Nuala demonstrates this type of resistance. "Resistance with your feet" is perhaps the most strident form of resistance. Although it might appear on the surface that quitting merely reinforces hegemonic organizational structures and processes, quitting need not be viewed as such an act of compliance. If we look at Nuala's exit from the perspective of the organization, by making life so difficult for her, the organization has removed an individual who does not "fit in," and compliance with and/or acceptance of the "way things are done" appears to be successfully accomplished. But has the organization succeeded in forcing out the nonconformists like Nuala? In Nuala's situation, the controversy surrounding her departure from the university had long-lasting impact, well in excess of any ramifications that she had even conceived of; Nuala made the decision to quit entirely for her own reasons because the organization was incapable of providing her the type of environment she required in which to work.

> This university is a really corrupt organization, and you can quote me on that. There is something seriously wrong, basically wrong with the picture. The whole place plays little games and never deals with the real issues. That upsets me. There always seemed to me to be this wonderful potential in our faculty that wasn't happening, and even now as I think about it and what went wrong, I get passionate about it. But you couldn't exactly go to Faculty Council and talk about it. What I did was ignore these things as much as possible and show up to the meetings I *had* to go to, and not the ones I didn't. I didn't fight passionately about things I knew I couldn't get. I mean, there is all this stuff directed to faculty self-interest; getting as much free time as possible for professors to consult, enhancing public image because that helps your consulting image, executive teaching because that gets you a lot of money, and more recently world travel. It is a terribly cynical view, I know. I just knew that I didn't fit into all that. I didn't fit in because I wasn't a boy, I didn't fit in because of the kind of person I am. In some ways, when I got to the corridors of power, I got the feeling I didn't belong there, and I didn't really want to be there.

All these forms of resistance involve costs; time taken from research or away from family, risks in tenure and promotion evaluation, as well as being excluded, stigmatized, or marginalized within the university, being stereotyped, or even feeling a general sense of insecurity and lack of fit. Antifeminist backlash, growing rejection of political correctness, elimination of affirmative action programs, and white male anger are all signs that women's resistance is itself being resisted. Acts of resistance are difficult to sustain, and inevitably women find new insights into how they are unconsciously in complicity with other parts of the systems that create and sustain inequities. Resistance, however, is also an act of power and can be both distressing and liberating. Brown (1994) describes feminist therapy as a subversive dialogue in which resistance, as a form of truth telling, allows for personal and systemic change. The development of feminist consciousness, whether in a formal therapy process or more informally, creates the opportunity for the individual to liberate the collective and work toward a transformation of the dominant discourses.

It replaces the illusion of equality and power embedded in patriarchal discourse
with clear and more honest visions of self in a social context where power is
unevenly distributed and value is parcelled out according to arbitrary characteristics rather than effort and talent. [It] involves the process of finding, in the
face of such realities, the ability to engage in individual or collective acts of
courage, strength, and integrity in response to violence, threat of harm, wrongdoing, or untruth, as well as the ability to know when one is participating in such
an act, so that we can give ourselves credit for our courage. (Brown, 1994, p. 26)

CONCLUSIONS

As women with feminist agendas cycle between compliance and resistance,
the larger constraints of the structures in which they live constantly limit what
they can do and how they see and understand the socially constructed realities
in which they are trapped. The structures of capitalism and patriarchy cannot be
ignored, and the *illusion* of free, unconstrained choice must be contextualized
within these structures and systems of power (Probyn, 1993). Individual action
has its limits, and women must also look to collective action and the role and
influence of political movements. As Davis and Fisher (1993) point out, agency
is always constrained by power and structure. As a result, women are left holding
a number of paradoxes; the paradoxes of agency and structure, of powerless-
ness/dependence and power/independence, of consciousness and unconsciousness, and of compliance and resistance. Meyerson and Scully (1995) aptly point
out the feelings of ambivalence faced by many women in the academy, personally committed to causes, communities, interest groups, and/or ideologies that
are often different from, and in conflict with, the dominant cultural values of the
universities in which they work. The "tempered radical" exemplifies the movement between compliance and resistance illustrated in our model as she recon-
ciles the tension between personal and professional identities and seeks to
transform the organizations in which she works from *within* a structure that can
so often be systematically and systemically biased against her.

We believe that women are still struggling to learn about how to create social
change. Complexity and contradictions are inherent in the process, with change
resting on stability just as resistance rests on compliance. Women will keep
struggling to create new realities while trying to live within the current ones.
Recommendations to play the game and work within the liberal frameworks are
clearly not enough. We believe that many forms of resistance are important and
that women need to challenge the meaning systems that dominate in universities
and continue to search for awareness of women's disadvantage and compliance

in order to fuel strategies of resistance. First comes feminist consciousness and then comes empowered action and localized resistance.

NOTES

1. The authors want to recognize the contribution of Stephanie Newell to the earlier conceptualization of this chapter and the importance of her voice in the dialogue process.

2. We recognize that oppression does not only affect women as a group and that oppression on the basis of, for example, race, class, and sexuality is also problematic in our society. The discrimination against women presents an interesting case to study, however, because unlike other groups, women actually represent a majority (albeit a small one) in the Canadian workforce and society.

3. The names Alberta, Frances, and Nuala are pseudonyms created in order to protect the confidentiality of these informants.

REFERENCES

Abu-Lughod, L. (1993). Analyzing resistance: Bedouin women's discourses. In L. Ross (Ed.), *To speak or be silent: The paradox of disobedience in the lives of women.* Illinois: Chiron.

Albert, S. (1992). Work of her own. *Psychological Perspectives,* Issue 27, p. 7077.

Bannerji. H., Carty, L., Dehli, K., Heald, S., & McKenna, K. (1991). *Unsettling relations: The university as a site of feminist struggles.* Toronto: Women's Press.

Barnard, C. I. (1938). *The functions of the executive.* Cambridge, MA: Harvard University Press.

Barstow, A. L. (1994). *Witchcraze: A new history of the European witch hunts.* London: Pandora.

Bolen, J. (1992). *Ring of power: The abandoned child, the authoritarian father, and the disempowered feminine.* San Francisco: Harper Collins.

Bradshaw, P., & Newell, S. (1992, May). *The role of nontenured women in business schools.* Paper presented at a symposium, Women's choices: Stages of an academic career, Eastern Academy of Management, Baltimore.

Bradshaw, P., & Newell, S. (1994, October). *Exploring deep structures of power using Jungian dream analysis.* Paper presented at the International Conference on Jungian/Archetypal Approaches to Organizational Behavior, Omaha, NE.

Bradshaw, P., & Wicks, D. (1995). *Investigating the gendered nature of organizational culture* (Working paper). Toronto: Faculty of Administrative Studies, York University.

Braverman, H. (1974). *Labor and monopoly capital.* New York: Monthly Review Press.

Bristor, J. (1990). *The chilly climate at a Canadian business school: Personal experiences and reflections* (Working paper). Houston: College of Business Administration, University of Houston.

Brown, L. (1994). *Subversive dialogues: Theory in feminist therapy.* New York: Basic Books.

Burawoy, M. (1979). *Manufacturing consent.* Chicago: University of Chicago Press.

Caplan, P. J. (1993). *Lifting a ton of feathers: A woman's guide for surviving in the academic world.* Toronto: University of Toronto Press.

Chuchryk, P., & Greene, M. (1990, May 28). *Career paths of academic women: A discussion paper.* Paper presented at the Annual Meeting of the Canadian Association of Anthropology and Sociology, Victoria, BC.

Collinson, D. (1994). Strategies of resistance: Power, knowledge, and subjectivity in the workplace. In J. Jermier, D. Knights, & W. Nord (Eds.), *Resistance and power in organizations* (pp. 25-68). London: Routledge.

Crosby, F. (1982). *Relative deprivation and working women.* New York: Oxford University Press.

Davis, K., & Fisher, S. (1993). Power and the female subject: The gendered discourse of power and resistance. In S. Fisher & K. Davis (Eds.), *Negotiating at the margins.* New Brunswick, NJ: Rutgers University Press.

DeCotiis, T. A., & Summers, T. P. (1987). A path analysis of a model of the antecedents and consequences of organizational commitment. *Human Relations, 40,* 445-470.

Dodson-Gray, E. (1982). *Patriarchy as a conceptual trap.* Wellesley, MA: Roundtable Press.

Edwards, P. K. (1990). Understanding conflict in the labor process: The logic and autonomy of struggle. In D. Knights & H. Willmott (Eds.), *Labor process theory* (pp. 125-152). London: Macmillan.

Etzioni, A. (1961). *A comparative analysis of complex organizations.* New York: Free Press.

Fisher, S. (1993). Gender, power, resistance: Is care the remedy? In S. Fisher & K. Davis (Eds.), *Negotiating at the margins.* New Brunswick, NJ: Rutgers University Press.

Fisher, S., & Davis, K. (1993). *Negotiating at the margins.* New Jersey: Rutgers University Press.

Giddens, A. (1984). *The constitution of society: Outline of the theory of structuration.* Los Angeles: University of California Press.

Gilligan, C., Rogers, A., & Tolman, D. (Eds.). (1991). *Women girls and psychotherapy: Reframing resistance.* New York: Harrington Park Press.

Gottfried, H. (1994). Learning the score: The duality of control and everyday resistance in the temporary help service industry. In J. Jermier, D. Knights, & W. Nord (Eds.), *Resistance and power in organizations* (pp. 102-127). London: Routledge.

Gregg, N. (1993). Trying to put first things first: Negotiating subjectivities in a workplace organizing campaign. In S. Fisher & K. Davis (Eds.), *Negotiating at the margins.* New Brunswick, NJ: Rutgers University Press.

Hodson, R. (1991). The active worker: Compliance and autonomy at the workplace. *Journal of Contemporary Ethnography, 20,* 47-78.

hooks, b. (1994). *Teaching to transgress: Education as the practice of freedom.* New York: Routledge.

Jermier, J., Knights, D., & Nord, W. (1994). *Resistance and power in organizations.* London: Routledge.

Kanter, R. M. (1977). *Men and women of the corporation.* New York: Basic Books.

Kelman, H. C. (1958). Compliance, identification, and internalization: Three processes of attitude change. *Journal of Conflict Resolution, 2,* 51-60.

Kritzman, L. (Ed.) (1988). *Michel Foucault: Politics, philosophy, culture.* New York: Routledge.

Lerner, G. (1986). *The creation of patriarchy.* New York: Oxford University Press.

Lerner, G. (1993). *The creation of feminist consciousness.* New York: Oxford University Press.

Littler, C. R. (1990). The labor process debate: A theoretical review 1974-1988. In D. Knights & H. Willmott (Eds.), *Labor process theory* (pp. 46-94). London: Macmillan.

Mahoney, M., & Yngvesson, B. (1992). The construction of subjectivity: Reintegrating feminist anthropology and psychology. *Signs: Journal of Women in Culture and Society, 18*(1), 44-73.

Martin, J. (1994). The organization of exclusion: Institutionalization of sex inequality, gendered faculty jobs, and gendered knowledge in organization theory and research. *Organization, 1*(2), 401-432.

Marx, K. (1967). *Capital: A critique of political economy.* New York: Dutton.

Meyer, J. P., & Allen, N. J. (1984). Testing the "side-bet theory" of organizational commitment: Some methodological considerations. *Journal of Applied Psychology, 69,* 372-378.

Meyer, J. P., Paunonen, S. V., Gellatly, I. R., Goffin, R. D., & Jackson, D. N. (1989). Organizational commitment and job performance: It's the nature of the commitment that counts. *Journal of Applied Psychology, 74*(1), 152-156.

Meyerson, D. E., & Scully, M. A. (1995). Tempered radicalism and the politics of ambivalence and change. *Organization Science, 6*(5), 585-600.

Mills, A. J. (1988). Organization, gender, and culture. *Organization Studies, 9,* 351-369.

Mills, A. J. (1994). The gendering of organizational culture: Social and organizational discourses in the making of British Airways (Proceedings of the annual conference of the Administrative Sciences Association of Canada). *Women in Management, 15*(11), 11-20.

O'Reilly, C. A., & Chatman, J. A. (1986). Organizational commitment and psychological attachment: The effects of compliance, identification, and internalization on prosocial behavior. *Journal of Applied Psychology, 71*(3), 492-499.

Pierce, J. L., & Dunham, R. B. (1987). Organizational commitment: Preemployment propensity and initial work experiences. *Journal of Management, 13,* 163-178.

Polster, M. (1992). *Eve's daughters: The forbidden heroism of women.* San Francisco: Jossey-Bass.

Porter, L. W., Steers, R. M., Mowday, R. T., & Boulian, P. V. (1974). Organizational commitment, job satisfaction, and turnover among psychiatric technicians. *Journal of Applied Psychology, 59,* 603-609.

Probyn, E. (1993). Choosing choice: Images of sexuality and "Choiceoisie." In S. Fisher & K. Davis (Eds.), *Negotiating at the margins.* New Brunswick, NJ: Rutgers University Press.

Rabinow, P. (1984). *The Foucault reader.* New York: Pantheon.

Robinson, T., & Ward, J. (1991). "A belief in self far greater than anyone's disbelief: Cultivating resistance among African American female adolescents. In C. Gilligan, A. Rogers, & D. Tolman (Eds.), *Women, girls, and psychotherapy: Reframing resistance.* New York: Harrington Park Press.

Ross, L. (1993). *To speak or be silent: The paradox of disobedience in the lives of women.* Illinois: Chiron.

Smith, D. E. (1987). *The everyday world as problematic: A feminist sociology.* Toronto: University of Toronto Press.

Starhawk. (1990). *Truth or dare: Encounters with power, authority, and mystery.* San Francisco: Harper Collins.

Starhawk. (1992, July-August). The heritage of Salem. *Common Boundary,* pp. 17-20.

Steinem, G. (1992). *Revolution from within.* Boston: Little, Brown.

Wicks, D. (1996). *The dynamics of compliance: Influences on individual responses to institutional expections.* Unpublished doctoral dissertation, Faculty of Administrative Studies, York University.

Wicks, D., & Bradshaw, P. (1995). The oppression of women in Canada. In S. E. Nancoo & S. Ramcharan (Eds.), *Canadian Diversity 2000 and Beyond* (pp. 145-162). Toronto: Canadian Educators' Press.

Wilson, E. (1993). Deviance, dress, and desire. In S. Fisher & K. Davis (Eds.), *Negotiating at the margins.* New Brunswick, NJ: Rutgers University Press.

Woodman, M. (1993). *Conscious femininity.* Toronto: Inner City Books.

"We Have to Make a MANagement Decision"

Challenger and the Dysfunctions of Corporate Masculinity

MARK MAIER

Prologue. On January 28, 1986, the space shuttle Challenger lifted off on the 25th mission of NASA's shuttle program. Its voyage was tragically cut short by an explosion just 73 seconds into flight. Its seven crew members, including New Hampshire school teacher Christa McAuliffe, perished on impact as their crew cabin slammed into the Atlantic Ocean. The shock of the tragedy humbled a once-proud agency and was followed by months of investigations as a presidential commission searched for the cause. In its final report, the commission (Rogers, 1986) noted that the immediate, technical reason for the disaster was the inability of a pair of slim (one quarter inch) rubber O-rings in one of the

AUTHOR'S NOTE: This article builds on and extends earlier efforts to analyze the gendered origins of Challenger, which appeared in both my instructional module (1992, with Kathy Ferguson and Paul Shrivastava) and in the journal *masculinities* (1993a). I am especially indebted to Kathy Ferguson for her substantial contributions to the feminist analysis presented here. I am also grateful to Michael Kimmel and James Messerschmidt for their role in the evolution of this piece. Roger Boisjoly, Richard Cook, Larry Mulloy, and Allan McDonald generously cooperated with my research into the disaster, supported in part by a 1991 GTE Lectureship in Technology and Ethics.

shuttle's reusable solid rocket boosters (SRBs) to seal properly. Hopelessly hardened by frigid temperatures preceding liftoff, the twin O-rings between two of the interlocking rocket segments on Challenger's righthand SRB lacked the resiliency necessary to maintain an impermeable seal. Searing combustion gases penetrated the joint, causing the fuel tank to rupture and snap the orbiter into pieces. But the commission also singled out flaws in the decision-making process, noting that explicit warnings—some dating back years and others voiced just hours before the fateful launch—were repeatedly ignored.

" Is it a boy or a girl?"
This seemingly innocuous question carries within it the roots of the space shuttle Challenger disaster. For the question lays bare our society's preoccupation with gender as a master status, a preoccupation that indelibly shapes our lives from the moment of our birth. From that day forward, society goes to great lengths to ensure that males and females become gendered in significantly different ways. Gender, it is generally accepted, is socially constructed, and even though societal conceptions of masculinity (as well as femininity) are neither monolithic nor static, at any given point in time and place, there is clearly a dominant form of masculinity that may be described as *hegemonic* (Connell, 1989), and to which all other forms of masculinity will be subordinate. Of equal import is the oft-noted point that masculinity is generally "elevated" as the human standard, serving implicitly as the norm against which *both* genders are measured (Hare-Mustin, 1988). Hegemonic masculinity, then, assures that "man" becomes the generic, but hidden, referent in our culture (Gilligan, 1982). As Spender (1984) noted, "Women can only aspire to be as good as a man; there is no point in trying to be 'as good as a woman' " (p. 201).

As organizational scholars have similarly discovered, the values that undergird bureaucratic functioning and managerial styles in the United States are similarly "masculine" (Ferguson, 1984; Kanter, 1977; Maier, 1993b). Powell and Butterfield (1989) discovered in a review of the literature that "managerial identity remains as masculine as it ever was" (p. 230). Wilson-Schaef (1981) describes the cultural ethos of organization as following the norms of a "white male system." Because corporate masculinity has been unconsciously assumed and largely uncritically accepted as the organizational behavior standard, little attention has been devoted to exploring its implications for managerial dysfunction in the workplace.

The 1986 space shuttle Challenger disaster serves as a prominent focal point for this exploration. Not only is the selection of Challenger appropriate to this endeavor, as an occurrence that most readers have at least some familiarity (and perhaps even identification) with, but also—it turns out—because it resulted from practices and dynamics that are fairly common in hierarchical organizations (Maier, 1992, 1994). We assume here that because the Challenger debacle was not only widely experienced but had painful impact, if people recognize the connection between the causes of Challenger and the masculinist dynamics that undergird conventional organizational assumptions and managerial styles, they will be motivated to question those assumptions and challenge those styles. In essence, we will demonstrate that a primary factor in *not* "launching a Challenger" in one's own career or organization is a willingness to abandon the attachment to the standard (hierarchical) way of organizing and the conventional masculinist managerial approaches it promotes, in favor of alternatives. We aim—using the legacy of Challenger—to enhance awareness of and "unfreeze" attachment to that taken-for-granted system, with its underlying gender bias, thus providing further support to diversity initiatives aimed at transforming existing organizational cultures rather than blindly assimilating others into its dysfunctional ways.

Specifically, then, this chapter identifies the largely taken-for-granted features of conventional managerial practices and how they are inherently "gendered" (e.g., coincide with a *masculine ethos*) and demonstrates how these features were at work in the organizational dynamics and decision processes that led to the tragic space shuttle Challenger launch decision 10 years ago. Selected events from the year immediately preceding the disaster will be reviewed, along with an assessment of the final decision-making process itself, to demonstrate how the men who made the decisions that culminated in the ill-fated launch may have internalized (all too well) our culture's prescriptions for "manhood." The data from which the Challenger story has been reconstructed here come from a number of sources, assembled over a 6-year period (1988-1994). Principal among these are: original interviews with several of the key participants in the launch decision (including NASA and Morton Thiokol insiders); a review of the videotaped testimony by NASA and Morton Thiokol officials and employees before the presidential commission (obtained under the Freedom of Information Act); dozens of hours of historical video footage from the NASA archives; and the presidential commission report itself (Rogers, 1986).

A FEMINIST CRITIQUE OF MANAGEMENT: ON THE GENDERED FOUNDATIONS OF ORGANIZATION

Our review of the gendered foundations of organization begins with the Industrial Revolution, Frederick Taylor's ideal of *scientific management,* and the writings of the 19th-century sociologist, Max Weber. Taylor was captivated by the ascendancy of science, fascinated in particular with the potential organizational applications of the empirical method of knowledge and control. Like Taylor, Weber saw the rationalization of life under bureaucratic structures as essential to social progress, embracing rationality as the central ideal of organizational life; the culmination of organizational development was an institution devoid of emotion and passion. Paraphrasing Weber's classic title, Kanter (1977) has pointed out that "the evolving 'spirit of managerialism' was infused with a 'masculine ethic'l" (p. 20)—a legacy that persists to this day. This ethic, according to Kanter,

> elevates the traits assumed to belong to some men to necessities for effective management: a tough-minded approach to problems; analytic abilities to abstract and plan; a capacity to set aside personal, emotional considerations in the interests of task accomplishment; and a cognitive superiority in problem solving and decision making. (p. 22)

One lasting consequence of the industrialization of society (and the related sex segregation of human activity) was to create a bureaucratic social order grounded in norms conventionally—and increasingly—ascribed to men. Feminist responses to that order offer a valuable political and epistemological lens through which to view the events surrounding the launch of the Challenger.[1]

One central idea in much feminist theory addresses the relationship between gender and the shape of human experience in daily life. In other words, whether we proceed through the world in a male or female body makes all the difference in the world. These different life worlds, generally speaking, shape each sex in profoundly different ways and produce significant outcomes not only for individual behavior, but for how others interpret and react to that behavior. In a society that differentiates sharply between males and females from birth, and that accords greater status and worth to males, the dominant understandings of selfhood and society that are available to men and women (and the prevailing assumptions about social relations, measures of success, organizational structure, leadership, ways of communicating, reasoning, and decision making, practices of power, politics, and morality) tend to differ along gendered lines. Although such categories are not ironclad (men and women do partake of the life worlds of the other), they nonetheless form distinct arenas in which the experiences and perspectives of women as a group are distinguished from, and usually subordinated to, the experiences and perspectives of men as a group. These differences may be conceptualized along the *masculinist* and *feminist* dimensions delineated in Table 10.1.

TABLE 10.1 Contrasting Male System and Female System Archetypes

	Male System	*Female System*

Selected core values	Hierarchy-status
	Competitive/winning
	Maximizing—quantity
	    ("More/bigger is better")
	Action/agency
	Success (advancement)
	Dependence—responsibility/
	    "Leadership" at top
		Equality-intimacy
		Collaborative/sharing
		Optimizing—quality
		    ("Small is beautiful")
		Reflection/communion
		Balance (life/work)
		Interdependence—shared
		    responsibility/
		    leadership

Image of strength and power	Rigid, uncompromising;
	    "command & control"
	Authoritarian father
	Standing at the top; being at the
	    head
	Fighting; power over (win-lose)
	
	Leader as commander
		Adaptive, flexible; "inspire
		    and entrust"
		Nurturing mother
		Standing in the center; being
		    in the circle
		Engaging; power with
		    (win-win)
		Leader as servant

View of social relations	Exclusionary politics/ranking
	    (rivals/subordinates)
	Task-focused
	    ("get the job done!")
	Telling-demanding
	Dissent = Disloyalty
		Inclusionary politics/linking
		    (colleagues)
		Process-focused
		    ("how are we doing?")
		Hearing-responding
		Dissent = Loyal opposition

View of self	Autonomous, separate,
	    independent
		Relational, connected,
		    interdependent

Basis of reasoning	Sensing, thinking (mind)
	Distanced, objective,
	    logical/rational
		Intuitive, feeling (heart)
		Connected subjective,
		    emotional

Key influence strategies	Intimidating, "forcing,"
	    complying
		Supporting, "submitting,"
		    enabling

Decisional guide	Authority or majority rule	Participation and consensus

Principal ethic	Rights (consistency-
	    impartiality-universality)
		Caring (exceptions-empathic-
		    situational)

Organizational metaphors	Pyramids, channels, chains of command	Webs, networks, teams

Thus, we use the designations masculinist and feminist largely as potent metaphors for contrasting modes of apprehending and acting upon the world. To call upon such differentiation to understand organizations and to imagine alternatives is not to claim that such differences are biologically determined, or that they reflect some essence of male and/or female. Men can sometimes be put into situations in which they are perceived, and come to act, "like women," just as women can come to act "like men." The point is not that all individual women and men always act in predictably feminine or masculine ways, but that organizational structures and processes generally reinforce and legitimize a particular form of masculinity while dismissing that which appears feminine. The pyramidal structure ensures that management and masculinity will be virtually synonymous. Indeed, gender emerges as perhaps the dominant factor driving the Challenger launch decision, even though no women were present in decision-making roles.

Women's perspectives on self and society are, like everyone else's, shaped and sometimes distorted by their interactions with the dominant points of view. But because women's subjectivity and worldviews emerge within a context of subordination to men, feminine experiences and interpretations are not by themselves sufficient to generate an alternative perspective. But, interpreted in a way that is attentive to the consequences of the differences in power between women and men, female experience can offer a substantially different approach to the understandings of self, relations with others, strategies of power, and practices of organizations (as suggested in Table 10.1). From this perspective, gender becomes central to understanding organizational phenomena . . . even when women are absent. Thus, when we suggest that organizational practices are gendered, we do so here not to focus attention on male privilege (although that, too, does result), but to provide graphic evidence of how men's organizational experience is profoundly influenced by *men's* conformity to bureaucratic, that is, masculinist, prescriptions. In the case of Challenger, as shall be demonstrated, that influence should no longer be uncritically taken for granted but should be examined for the ways in which it can become dysfunctional.

Women's worlds typically require of their participants a particular kind of labor: maintaining relationships, attending to the needs of others, caring for bodies as well as minds and spirits. Women (generally) learn to see themselves and others as embedded in relations, as interdependent with others and responsible for their collective well-being (see Gilligan, 1982). In contrast, men's worlds (typically) entail a very different set of language and labors, one that conceives of individuals as separate, autonomous beings, that values independent achievement, and that eschews commitments that might hinder success in competitive endeavors. Success in the masculine worldview becomes defined as distancing oneself from those lower in the hierarchy, competing successfully with those positioned similarly, and emulating (and eventually joining) those placed "above." In a feminine framework, however, actions that allow the maintenance of relations (e.g., mentoring, vicarious achievement) are more highly valued than those that advance the individual but leave others behind.

Consequently, communication in the female life world—where individuals struggle to minimize differences and reach consensus—is used primarily to establish intimacy; in the male life world, as Tannen (1990) explains in her influential work, communication is a primary means for establishing and maintaining one's position; hence,

> independence is key because a primary means of establishing status is to tell others what to do, and taking orders is a marker of low status. Though all humans need both intimacy and independence, women tend to focus on the first and men on the second. (p. 26)

As a result, men (generally) find hierarchical relations comfortable and look to such arrangements to legitimate the process of ranking and exclusion, as well as to mediate the conflicting rights of autonomous selves. Conflicts are resolved by relying on an *ethic of rights* (Gilligan, 1982), which emphasizes consistency and impartial and objective evaluations of competing claims, as well as due process and equal treatment for all individuals, regardless of their place in the social order. Women, on the other hand, tend to find greater comfort in inclusive relations, to value their links to others more than their ranking over them (Eisler, 1987). The feminine worldview is thus more likely to be grounded in an *ethic of care* (Gilligan, 1982), in which rules are regarded as inherently context dependent (and exceptions legitimized by attention to circumstance).

Power, in a feminine framework, is used to give "voice" to the conventionally disenfranchised; it is a basis for empowering others. Feminine notions of justice call for the avoidance of harm to others, for an active response to others' needs, and for an appreciation of the particularities of time and place. Where masculine politics is grim and instrumental, suppressing dissent frequently to the point of violence (even physical), feminine politics aims for cooperation, compromise, and allowance for—even encouragement of—difference (Chodorow, 1978; Di Stefano, 1991; Gilligan, 1982; Hartsock, 1983; Ruddick, 1989). Where masculine leadership often relies on force (expressed or implied) to get the job done, feminine leadership is responsive and focused on the process by which common objectives are defined and pursued.

In symbolic terms, the masculine manager stands at the top of an exclusionary pyramid, the feminine manager in the center of a web of inclusion. Where organizational subordinates in a masculine system are expected to know their place, focusing narrowly on compartmentalized duties in the horizontal division of labor and ingratiating themselves to "higher-ups" in the vertical chain of command, in a feminine system, they are expected and encouraged to share responsibility for reaching the common vision —even if it means that superiors' authority (and colleagues'—or one's own—"turf") will be challenged.

As one can surmise, the worldviews that men typically bring to organizational life in many ways mesh neatly with the requirements of bureaucracies, whereas those that women bring tend to clash with that social order. The managerial viewpoint stresses instrumental rationality, orderliness, conformity to the requirements of authority, and respect for the chain of command. Objectivity is defined as lifting oneself above the particulars of one's situation and applying universal standards in an impartial and consistent fashion, to embrace a "separate" way of knowing, in which one distances oneself from the object of inquiry and truth emerges from impersonal procedures (Belenky, Clinchy, Goldberger, & Tarule, 1986; Harding, 1986; Kanter, 1977) Reason and logic are construed rather narrowly, referring mainly to quantifiable factors that count as evidence in a linear process of sensing, thinking, and deduction. "Disinterested reason," unblinded by passion (i.e., objectivity), is the ultimate value in a discourse built on challenge, argument, suspicion, and critical judgment. The resulting "doubting game" constitutes "a rational form of masculine ceremonial combat" (Ong, quoted in Belenky et al., 1986, p. 110), in which the listener is perceived as a potentially hostile judge, not as a potential ally in conversation. As Belenky et al. note, the objectivity demanded by this perspective expects participants to

> exclude your own concerns and to adopt a perspective that your adversaries may respect, as in their own self-interest. It means to exclude all feelings, including those of the adversary, examining the issue from a strictly pragmatic, strategic point of view. (p. 109)

In contrast, women's worldviews tend to employ a more *situated* objectivity, to value those kinds of insights that are difficult to quantify but that come from the heart, from feeling and from intuition. From a feminine perspective, truth is discovered not through separation but through connection and direct personal experience, through an essential subjectivity (Belenky et al., 1986). Where doubting and judgment occupy center stage in masculinist discourse, trust and understanding predominate in its feminist counterpart; where masculinist discourse derives its moral legitimacy from impersonal procedures, feminist discourse stakes its moral claim in caring; where masculinist discourse aims for generalities, feminist discourse focuses on particularities; and where masculinist discourse stresses agency and action (separation and control), feminist discourse strives for community (acceptance and fusion) (Belenky et al., 1986).

Which discourse one employs, and with what consequences, is not only a function of one's prior socialization but of one's current context; one's organizational structure, in particular. Although it exceeds the scope of this chapter to elaborate, readers should assume the sociological maxim that individual behaviors are structure-bound (if not determined): Masculine managerial styles flow inexorably from hierarchical, pyramidal organizational structures.

Men and women recruited into positions of dominance within organizations tend to internalize the requirements of their position, becoming "like men"—valuing competition over cooperation, focusing more on rights than on needs, internalizing the requirements of a narrow technical rationality, and so on. Women and men recruited into subordinate positions or relations, tend, correspondingly, to become the kind of people their organization requires them to be; they become "like women" in their attention to the requirements of others, need to please their superiors, reluctance to assert themselves, and so on. In complex ways, therefore, masculine dominance and feminine subordination are reproduced and reinforced, and gender becomes a potent metaphor for power (Ferguson, 1984).

Schaef's (1981) classic elaboration contrasting the *White Male System* with the *Female System* offers similar distinctions. In Schaef's view, the White Male System (or WMS), is characterized by the following:

1. "One-up; one-down" relations (vs. egalitarian/peer relations typical of the Female System)
2. Self and work ("doing") as one's center of focus (as opposed to self-awareness or relations with others)
3. A "zero-sum/scarcity" model of power (in contrast to a synergistic orientation, which assumes that power, life, love, or knowledge is not diminished by sharing it, but in fact is enhanced)
4. A vision of "leading" anchored in commanding or directing others (vs. facilitating or enabling)
5. Differences seen as competitive threats that must be reduced, assimilated, or eliminated, instead of (in what Schaef describes as the Female System) being seen as collaborative opportunities to learn, grow, and change.

Using a feminist lens to focus on the consequences of the White Male System allows us to shift our attention away from the traits of the individual men making decisions about Challenger (were they intelligent or foolish? Cautious or rash?)

and toward the characteristics of the structures and processes within which men and women are required to operate. These structures and processes tend to be gendered in predictable ways; ways that elevate typically male experiences to the level of unquestioned norm, while dismissing that which appears "feminine" as irrational, illogical, unsubstantiated, or irrelevant. When managers—male and female alike—are acting "normally" as bureaucracy defines it, they are acting masculine. We shall argue that decision-making processes such as those producing the ill-fated launch of the Challenger are not aberrations or "flaws" in the standard operating procedure of organizations—they are its logical and inexorable consequences. As my colleague Kathy Ferguson (personal communication, August 4, 1992) put it to me, "Masculinity run amok is not bad bureaucracy; it is bureaucracy as usual." Drawing on previous work (Maier, 1993a), we shall demonstrate how these gendered power factors literally managed, as Messerschmidt (1995) has asserted, to kill the crew of Challenger.

We turn now to the Challenger chronology, keeping these gendered foundations of MANagement and the White Male System in mind.

CHALLENGER: A MANAGEMENT CHRONICLE

The Historical Context of Challenger

Although most of us were stunned by the news of Challenger, the presidential commission observed that, in fact, this had been a disaster waiting to happen, an "Accident Rooted in History." Concerns with the rocket boosters dated back to 1977, when engineers at NASA's Marshall Space Flight Center (MSFC, the unit responsible for monitoring the development and performance of the shuttle's components) first warned of deficiencies in the contractor's (Morton Thiokol's) design of the reusable rockets. Those early fears were confirmed when the shuttle actually began flying in 1981. Although President Reagan declared the system to be "fully operational" after just four test flights, recovery and inspection of the boosters revealed that, in fact, hot gases from inside the rockets were somehow impinging on the fragile quarter-inch thick, 12-foot diameter twin rubber O-rings intended to seal the rocket segments, causing them to be partially eaten away. In the years that followed, flights continued unabated, despite increasing incidents of erosion. Because the missions were "successful" (i.e., the integrity of the joints had never been *fully* compromised to the point of a total burn-through), NASA officials concluded the damage constituted "an acceptable flight risk." Each incidence of erosion reinforced a "can't-fail" decision-making philosophy that Commissioner Richard Feynman described as "a kind of Russian Roulette. . . . We can lower our standards a little bit because we got away with it last time." (Rogers, 1986, p. 2469)

Two near disasters in early 1985 put that complacency to the test. During a particularly cold (53 degrees Fahrenheit) launch in January 1985, hot gases for the first time actually *burned through* the primary O-ring in one of the SRB joints, charring (but not eroding) the critical secondary seal, the booster's thin last line of defense. Alarmingly, two missions later, a primary seal in a nozzle joint failed completely, allowing its secondary O-ring to be partially eaten away. The seal failures sent shock waves through Morton Thiokol, Inc. (MTI) and NASA. AT MTI, Roger Boisjoly, the rocket engineer who had inspected the disassembled rockets from both missions, sent a blistering memo to Vice President of Engineering Robert Lund, warning that "the mistakenly accepted position on the joint problem was to fly without fear of failure." Boisjoly stressed that failure to address the problem head-on could result in "a catastrophe of the highest order: Loss of human life." A task force was established at MTI to rectify the problem.

At NASA, meanwhile, Richard Cook, a newly hired budget analyst, had just interviewed headquarters engineers at the Office of Space Flight about the potential budgetary implications of the O-ring dilemma. Told by the engineers that they "held their breath" at each liftoff because "this thing could blow up" (Maier, 1994), Cook sent a detailed memo to his superior, warning that "there is little question that flight safety has been and is still being compromised by potential failure of the seals, and it is acknowledged that failure during launch would certainly be catastrophic." The worst case scenario, he noted, would require halting shuttle flights while the boosters were redesigned and existing rockets were scrapped. The potential budgetary impact was "immense."

In August 1985, NASA's top shuttle official, Associate Administrator for Space Flight Jesse Moore, convened a meeting with senior MTI and MSFC personnel for a comprehensive review of the O-ring problems. Although MTI stressed that "the lack of a good secondary seal in the joint is most critical" and urged that "efforts need to continue at an accelerated pace to eliminate SRM [Solid Rocket Motor] erosion," NASA decided against a flight ban, electing instead to continue flying the shuttle "as is," searching for the solution as they went along. The commission would later conclude that the briefing was suffi-ciently detailed to require corrective action before the next flight. No action was taken because meeting flight schedules and cutting costs were given a higher priority than flight safety (Maier, 1994).

By the fall of 1985, complacency had sunk in again at NASA and MTI. The Seal Task Force at MTI, which had been established in response to Boisjoly's memo, was turning out to be a paper tiger, stymied in its efforts by bureaucratic inertia. Bob Ebeling, the task force leader, wrote an unusually blunt appeal to MTI's SRM Project Director, Allan McDonald, which began simply: "HELP! The seal task force is constantly being delayed by every possible means." It ended, "We wish we could action by verbal request, but such is not the case. This is a red flag." The Vice President of the Space Boosters Program at MTI, Joseph Kilminster, met with the task force to appease them. He insisted they continue to follow established policies and routines, working through existing channels to do "whatever was necessary" to "nurse each task" through to completion.

On January 21, 1986—just one week prior to the eventual Challenger launch date—NASA, responding to pressure from Congress, announced that it was seeking bids from four competitors to supply additional rocket boosters for the shuttle. MTI's exclusive contract with the agency—a contract worth over $1 billion—was up for grabs.

Challenger's Final Hours:
"We Have to Make a Management Decision"

On January 27, 1986, following its third postponement in 6 days (and right on the heels of the most delayed flight in shuttle history), Challenger appeared destined for yet another delay: A cold front was approaching and the temperature forecast for launch time the next morning was 29 degrees F—well below the record coldest launch of January 1985 (53 degrees). An afternoon telephone conference call (telecon) took place between MTI in Utah and MSFC personnel in Alabama and Florida.

MTI was resolute: Based on their engineering judgment, they would oppose the launch as long as the temperature fell below their previous experience base (53 degrees). NASA asked the contractor to fax its data to MSFC and the Kennedy Space Center for a fuller deliberation and final determination during a subsequent telecon beginning at 8:45 p.m. Figure 10.1 summarizes the names and locations of the participants in the deliberations.

Unwilling to vouch for the safety of the seals in the rocket motor joints at such a low temperature, MTI, as anticipated, entered the final telecon recommending against the launch. But their stance was challenged with unprecedented vigor. Larry Mulloy, the SRB Program Manager for NASA, aggressively attacked the MTI position, pressing the engineers for quantitative proof that the

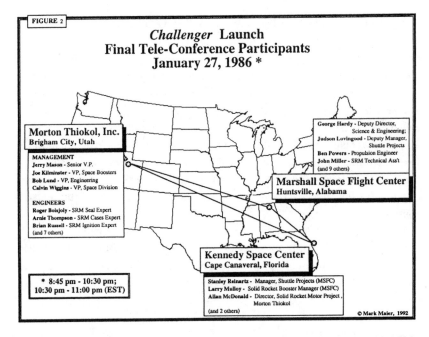

Figure 10.1: Challenger Launch, Final Teleconference Participants, January 27, 1986

joint would fail. Exasperated by MTI's intransigence, and stressing that no official launch criterion for joint temperature existed, Mulloy bristled, "My God, Thiokol. When do you want us to launch? Next April? The eve of a launch is a hell of a time to be generating new Launch Commit Criteria!" Because NASA had "successfully flown with the existing LCC 24 previous times," Mulloy questioned whether it was "logical—*truly logical*—that we really have to have a system that has to be 53 in order to fly?" (Rogers, 1986, p. 1541) George Hardy, the Deputy Director of Science and Engineering for NASA's Marshall Center, was asked for his reaction to the MTI recommendation. Hardy responded that he was "appalled" by their no-go decision but added that he "would not recommend launching over the contractor's objection" (Maier, 1992).

Accustomed to defending the wisdom of recommendations *to* launch, the company now found itself on the defensive for a conservative stance. It was the first time in the entire history of space flight that a contractor's recommendation not to launch had been challenged. When Mulloy summed up the deliberations with the statement that the MTI data were inconclusive (i.e., they had not established with certainty that the joint *would* fail . . . not work), Stanley Reinartz asked MTI's Joe Kilminster for a final recommendation. Pressed to establish with absolute certainty that the joint would not work, MTI management instead called for a short "time-out" from the telecon in order to caucus and, ostensibly, "re-evaluate their data." As soon as the mute button was pushed, Jerry Mason, the Senior Vice President at MTI, turned to the vice presidents clustered around him and softly announced, "We have to make a management decision."

Correctly anticipating that Mason's comment was a signal the managers would reverse the no-launch recommendation, the company's two top engineering experts on the O-ring seals—Arnie Thompson and Roger Boisjoly—vigorously urged their superiors to stand by their original decision. Thompson rose from his position at the end of the table and sketched the problems with the joint on a note pad in front of the managers. He abandoned his effort and returned to his seat after Mason disciplined him with an unfriendly look, as if to say, as Boisjoly described it, "Go away and don't bother us with the facts."

Infuriated by the brushoff given his colleague, Boisjoly (1991) stood up from his seat across from the managers, slammed his photographic evidence from previous postflight inspections down in front of them, and, "literally screaming at them, admonished them to look at what the data are telling us: Namely that cold temperature indeed increases the risk of hot gas blowing by the joint." But he, too, backed down when Mason glared at him icily with "the kind of look you get just prior to being fired." Although Thompson and Boisjoly both knew the launch would be unsafe, they were unable to get their managers to listen to them. Instead, as Boisjoly observed, "The managers were having their own little meeting right in front of us, to the total exclusion of myself and my engineering colleagues." About midway through the caucus, Mason threw down the gauntlet before his executive subordinates, asking pointedly, "Am I the only one who wants to launch?" (Maier, 1992)

"What followed made me both sad and angry," Boisjoly explained. "They were taking our data, which supported a position *not* to launch, and trying to turn it around to support a launch decision. It was really disgusting" (Boisjoly, 1991). The lone holdout among the senior managers, Bob Lund, the Vice President of Engineering, finally capitulated 25 minutes into the caucus when Mason turned to him and instructed, "Take off your engineering hat and put on your management hat." A poll was taken of only the four senior managers, who voted unanimously to launch. As the General Manager explained to the Rogers commission, "We only polled the management people, because we had already established that we were *not* going to be unanimous" (Rogers, 1986, p. 1362).

At 11 p.m., MTI went "back on the line," and Joe Kilminster announced their reversal to Reinartz, who promptly accepted the new recommendation. MTI had provided NASA with the perfunctory "green light" to proceed with the fatal count-down. Challenger would be launched just a few hours later, at 11:38 a.m. (EST).

On the basis of the available evidence, it is clear that the ensuing disaster could—and should—have been prevented. The string of warnings unheeded, of recommendations ignored—from the early developmental stages all the way through to the "flawed decision-making process" (Rogers, 1986) of Chal-lenger's final hours—culminated in the disaster that has become part of our collective consciousness.

As has been noted elsewhere, those horrific twisted-Y plumes etched into our memories represent an inevitable outcome of fairly typical organizational proc-esses (Maier, 1992; Starbuck & Milliken, 1988; Vaughan, 1996). Less obvious, however, is how these processes reflect the tragic triumph of a decidedly masculinist managerial system. This connection is made explicit below, in an analysis of how the events in the Challenger chronology mesh neatly with several key dimensions of our culture's prevailing blueprint for masculinity; it raises serious questions about the extent to which any organizational partici-pant—female or male—should be expected to conform to such a standard.

THE CHALLENGER LAUNCH DECISION:
"BOYS WILL BE BOYS?"

Perhaps the most well-known framework that articulates the core dimen-sions of masculinity is the one developed by David and Brannon (1976). According to David and Brannon, the central dimensions of masculinity include

1. "No Sissy Stuff": The Stigma of Anything Vaguely Feminine
2. "The Big Wheel": Success, Status, and the Need to Be Looked Up To
3. "The Sturdy Oak": A Manly Air of Toughness, Confidence, and Self-Reliance
4. "Give 'Em Hell": The Aura of Aggression, Violence, and Daring

Played out in organizational roles, this gives rise to the White Male System summarized above (Schaef, 1981). Although this enumeration is not all-encompassing, it provides a useful and appropriate starting point for analysis.[2]

Theme No. 1: "No Sissy Stuff": The Stigma of Anything Vaguely Feminine

One of the earliest messages males in this culture receive is to distance themselves from girls and anything vaguely feminine. Leaving aside for a moment the obvious fact that NASA and its contractor were virtually (white) male-only clubs, the men whose actions ultimately cost the seven Challenger astronauts their lives show ample evidence of such conditioning. This correspondence is most vividly reflected in the events surrounding the evening telephone conference call between NASA officials and MTI on January 27, 1986.

Shortly before the final telecon took place, the NASA officials who would lead it (Stanley Reinartz and Larry Mulloy) caucused with their institutional superior, MSFC Director William Lucas to apprise him of the impending "no-launch" recommendation from MTI. Lucas had an autocratic reputation among MSFC employees, creating, according to one source, "an atmosphere of rigid, often fearful, conformity among Marshall managers. . . . Like many demanding task-masters, he demanded absolute personal loyalty" (McConnell, 1987, p.108). According to Mulloy (personal communication, May 15, 1991), the Solid Rocket Booster Program Manager for NASA, when Lucas was told of MTI's position, he responded, "This sure is interesting: We get a little cold nip, and they want us to shut the Shuttle System down? I sure would like to see their reasons for that." Lucas's reaction harkens back to the old mental tape, "What-a-bunch-of-wussies!" It also not incidentally encapsulates the masculine worldview that presupposes scientific dominion over nature (as in "man's conquest of space").

Reflecting on his meeting with Lucas, Mulloy explained,

If they [MTI] were going to come in and say, "We can't launch tomorrow 'cause we can't operate an SRM [Solid Rocket Motor] at 30," we were going to demand to know *why* and *not accept it on the basis of some hand-wringing emotion.* [italics added] (personal communication, May 15, 1991)

Although he couched it in more articulate language, Mulloy was essentially admonishing the MTI engineers for being "cry-babies."

During the teleconference itself, Mulloy rejected Boisjoly's data as qualitative, insisting the rocket engineer "quantify" his concerns. His invocation of
logic, rationality, and data (i.e., masculine-gendered values) to claim legitimacy
for himself while simultaneously framing (and thus disqualifying) the engineers'
data as based on "hand-wringing emotion" and "gut feelings" (i.e., feminine
qualities) is summed up in his assertion that the 53-degree lower limit advocated
by MTI was not "truly logical." As he elaborated in his testimony,

> If somebody is giving me a recommendation and a conclusion, I *probe* the data
> to assure that it is sound and it is logical. I think that has been interpreted [that]
> when one challenges someone [i.e., Boisjoly] who says, "I don't have anything
> too quantitative, but I'm worried," that that is pressure, and I don't see it that
> way. (Rogers, 1986, p. 1532)

Even 4 years after Challenger, Mulloy (1990) clung stubbornly to this mas-
culinist-anchored defense:

> You could not reach that conclusion [not to launch] on a quantitative basis alone.
> I kept examining what we had done, and I concluded then—and I'm confident
> now—that we made, based on the information available to us, a logical decision
> that had a disastrous result. (pp. 23-24)

After MTI called for the time out on the telecon and the managers began
caucusing on how to deal with the rebuke from their major customer, Boisjoly
and Thompson vigorously attempted to persuade their managers to stand firm.
Shaken by NASA's unprecedented refusal to accept a conservative "don't-fly"
recommendation, however, Jerry Mason, the Senior MTI official, dismissed his
engineers' vociferous warnings on the basis that, "Although they were outspoken . . . we listened to their *reasons* more than their *intensity*, and the reasons
boiled down to the fact that we found ourselves in a position of uncertainty that
we were unable to quantify" (Rogers, 1986, p. 1365). Coding Boisjoly's confrontational outburst as intensity, he in essence feminized the rocket engineer
and therefore discounted him. Note also the specious reasoning that the launch
could proceed on the basis of uncertain and inconclusive data, suggestive of the
"Go for it; No-guts, No-glory" theme of masculinity we will take up below ("The
aura of daring"). The irony, of course, is that although the managers requested
the caucus ostensibly to "reevaluate their data" and determine a quantifiable
justification for their position, they ended up, by Mason's own admission,
relying "on a judgment, rather than a precise engineering calculation, in order
to conclude what we needed to conclude" (Maier, 1992).

Theme No. 2: "The Big Wheel": Success, Status, and the Need to Be Looked Up To

This theme actually subsumes several powerful subdimensions of hegemonic masculinity: (a) a near-compulsive orientation to task accomplishment and competitive advancement (sometimes euphemistically referred to as ambition or dedication); (b) a corresponding ingrained respect for hierarchy, exclusionary politics, and established procedure (wanting to be "on top," which requires the presence of others who can be "looked down upon"); and (c) a willingness to subordinate all other life obligations to one's employment/economic role and a focus on self as the metaphorical "center of the universe."

"Just Do It:" The Masculine Premium on Action and Being "Number One"

The masculinist focus on *activity, action,* and *achievement,* on "giving 150%" and the obsession with "being Number One," played themselves out on Challenger in a number of ways, relected in the following examples.

Although NASA had normalized the anomalous O-ring erosion as acceptable, two near disasters in 1985 called that judgment into question. Yet, fearful of bursting NASA's "Can-Do" bubble, no one was willing to do what it took to correct the problem. The Seal Task Force at MTI is an excellent illustration of this. When engineers informed management that standard operating procedures were obstructing the task force in its efforts to find a solution, management was unwilling to authorize exceptions to those procedures. Joe Kilminster, the Vice President of Space Boosters, met with the rocket engineers, but gladly told them that they would just have to make do with the resources at their disposal. As Boisjoly made clear in an Activity Report dated October 4, 1985, "He plain doesn't understand that there are not enough people to do that kind of nursing of each task, but he doesn't seem to mind directing that the task nevertheless gets done." Clearly, the task force efforts were *not,* as Boisjoly correctly surmised, a top priority to management. ("The basic problem boils down to the fact that *all* MTI problems have No. 1 priority and that upper management apparently feels that the SRM project is ours for sure and the customer be damned!") Rather than acknowledge the flaws in its design, MTI management elected to project a "strong front" by continuing to support NASA's flight program.

The excessive devotion to task (meeting flight projections) is similarly reflected in the fact that despite warnings raised at the NASA headquarters briefing in August 1985, top shuttle officials decided not to ground the fleet, believing the problem posed "an acceptable flight risk." Although the Rogers commission noted that the briefing was "sufficiently detailed to require corrective action prior to the next flight" (Rogers, 1986, p. 148), no corrective action was taken, according to a congressional investigation of the tragedy, because meeting flight schedules and cutting costs were given a higher priority than flight safety ("Investigation," 1986).

William Lucas, the autocratic Director of the MSFC, had consistently made it known to his subordinates that "under no circumstances is the Marshall Center to be the cause for delaying a launch" (cited in McConnell, 1987, p. 109).

Pyramidal Politics:
Team Players and Kings of the Mountain

To grow up masculinized is to learn to value hierarchies. We are taught that it is a positive thing to "move up" (this overlaps with the achievement theme discussed previously). Emulate, imitate, *join*, if possible, those "above" you (the "higher ups"); distance and disassociate yourself from the people on your level or "below." In this manner, the values of stratification, exclusion, and an ethic of rights (Gilligan, 1982) occupy center stage in the lives of boys, at the expense of the more feminine values of egalitarianism, inclusion, and an ethic of care enumerated previously. These tendencies to emphasize ranking (one-up/one-down relations) over linking (peer relations), dominance over empowerment, winning over sharing, authority over participation, are central themes not only in masculinity (see Belenky et al., 1986; Eisler, 1987; Tannen, 1990) but in bureaucratic life (Ferguson, 1984). Here is how they were painfully well-represented in the events of the evening telecon proceeding the Challenger launch.

"Going by the Book": The Primacy of Procedure. The lives that were at stake were rarely, if ever, mentioned during the entire 2-hour telecon; that fact is a telling reflection on the masculine preoccupation with bureaucratic/procedural matters; a blind devotion to task that can render all other factors invisible and/or irrelevant. Mulloy was distressed not only by the *content* of MTI's message (i.e., "don't launch") but also by its *timing*. His bellicose reaction ("My God, Thiokol! When do you want me to launch? Next April? The *eve of a launch is a hell of a time* [italics added] to be generating new Launch Commit Criteria!") is nonsensical from a feminine perspective attuned to safety and caution,

regardless of what "proper protocol" dictated. As MTI's Director of the SRM Project, Al McDonald (who was seated next to Mulloy at the Kennedy Space Center for the telecon) opined in an interview (July 1, 1992), "He was believing more in the system than in the people inputting into that system." As such, Mulloy's approach *does* mesh with the respect for organizationally sanctioned rules (and for one's institutional superiors) typical of masculinist systems anchored in rank and hierarchy.

MTI, by advocating a 53-degree threshold for *this* particular launch, was—in Mulloy's view—essentially proposing the establishment of a new Launch Commit Criteria "after we have successfully flown with the existing LCC 24 previous times." Mulloy was incensed partly because his (masculine) reasoning did not allow him to accept that MTI's recommendation was restricted to this particular launch. He saw a conflict between the MTI position and *existing* policy ("no LCCs existed for joint temperature;" higher-ups had committed to accepting erosion anyway). Whereas MTI was following a (feminine) logic of being attuned to this specific context, Mulloy was also concerned about the *future* policy implications of accepting the MTI recommendation ("How are we going to live with this in the future?"). According to Mulloy, "The logic for [MTI's] recommendation did *not* specifically address, "Don't launch 51-L [Challenger]." What it said was, "Within our experience base, we should not operate *any* Solid Rocket Motor at any temperature colder than 53" (Rogers, 1986, p. 1529).

Defending one's actions with reference to the masculinist ethic of procedure occurred with predictable regularity during presidential commission testimony. When middle-level NASA managers Larry Mulloy (the fourth-ranking launch official) and Stanley Reinartz (the third-ranking shuttle official) were asked why they reportedly did not pass the MTI concerns (including their original "no" vote on launch) up their chain of command, they retreated into a classic I-was-going-by-the-book stance, insisting that "no launch commit criteria were violated" (Rogers, 1986, p. 1680) and that "it was clearly a Level III issue that had been resolved" (p. 1557).

In a similar vein, MSFC director William Lucas, who *was* informed by Reinartz and Mulloy of the Thiokol concerns but did not mention those reservations to higher level launch officials even though he sat side-by-side with them throughout the morning of the launch, explained, "That would not be my reporting channel" (Rogers, 1986, p. 1877).

Exclusionary Politics: The Significance of Rank. In masculinist interactions, confrontation and intimidation are implicit. In feminine-gendered interactions, intimacy and connection predominate. As Tannen (1990) notes, both styles can be effective influence strategies, but men tend to use communication primarily as a means of establishing status and telling others what to do, whereas taking orders (or compromising) is perceived as a marker of low status. An approach more attuned to a feminine worldview (which is possible for both men and women, but more common of the latter), instead of focusing on jockeying for position, focuses on making connections, deliberately minimizing status differences while striving for consensus and mutual understanding. How was masculinist discourse in evidence during the Challenger launch decision process?

When Jerry Mason, the Senior Vice President of MTI, softly announced at the onset of the MTI caucus, "We have to make a management decision," it was for the benefit of the other senior officials seated close to him in the Management Information Center; a signal about who would be included and who would be excluded from the discussion. As Boisjoly (1991) explained, "He wasn't talking to me. He was talking to his three vice presidential colleagues." By emphasizing that a management decision was necessary, Mason was effectively defining both the *type* of decision that would be made and *who* would be entitled to make it: It would be based on *managerial* criteria (a point punctuated by Mason's eventual command to Bob Lund, the Vice President Engineering, to "take off your engineering hat and put on your management hat!") And it would also be a decision made by the *managers* (and only the managers). To *belong* to this team, you had to prove your loyalty by voting to launch; to continue to resist (as Lund at first did), resulted in ostracism and conformity pressure. Only "real men" (i.e., men willing to launch!) could belong to this team; "No Girls Allowed" (i.e., anyone who was fearful or subordinate).

The masculinist attachment to rank is also reflected in the engineers' acquiescence to management. As Boisjoly emphasized, "I had my say, and I never take away any management right to take the input of an engineer and then make a decision based on that input. . . . There was no point in me doing anything any further." The stratification between managers and engineers was also alluded to by Brian Russell, another telecon participant, who noted, "We were not asked as the *engineering people* [italics added]. It was a management decision at the vice presidents' level" (Rogers, 1986, p. 1486). Engineering people were a disempowered class in the Management Information Center. Of the 14 men in the room, evidently the only ones entitled to speak were the four vice presidents.

The masculinist tendency to deny voice to the less powerful, and to respect the voices of the powerful, is further captured in Mason's incredulous explanation for why he did not even ask the engineers to participate in the final vote: "We only polled the management people because we had already established that we were not going to be unanimous" (Rogers, 1986, p. 1362). This non sequitur is meaningful only in a context in which dissent, especially from below, is unwelcome. In this case, the managers had every reason not to listen to the (hysterical) warnings of the engineers, because, after all, they were subordinate (inferior). Note that because Mulloy's emotionally charged challenge ("My God . . . When do you want me to launch? Next April?") originates from a "one-up" position (MSFC vis-à-vis MTI), it is not labeled (nor denigrated) as emotional but is simply evidence of his entitlement to demand what he regards as a logical argument. This contradiction was lost on the participants that night.

Lurking in the background through all of the deliberations about "getting Challenger up" by January 28 was the pressure (however direct or indirect, however real or implied) to please the ultimate authority: President Reagan himself. He was the one who prematurely had declared the system "operational" in 1982; that declaration had provided the basis for his "Civilian-in-Space" program (announced during a 1984 election campaign stop); and he had personally insisted that the first such civilian would be a schoolteacher, picking out New Hampshire's Christa McAuliffe for the mission from among 142 applicants. Everyone at NASA knew how important this particular mission was to Reagan. Having Challenger aloft in time for the State of the Union Address on January 28 was clearly a priority for the White House, as evidenced by a flurry of telephone calls between the President's scheduling office and the Kennedy Space Center in the days leading up to the launch. The wishes of the "King of the Mountain" were known to all.

Work and Male Identity

One of the central themes of the male system in organizations is the expectation that one should subordinate all other life interests to one's work. If the earlier theme on "action" defines men by what they do, then this theme reminds us that a cornerstone of masculinity is one's paid employment status. There were numerous examples where this primacy of economics and the "male model of work" ultimately factored in to doom the Challenger and its crew.

Boisjoly's description of Mason's disciplinary gazes (during the MTI caucus) as "the kind of looks you get just prior to being fired" reminds us that one of the most powerful means of controlling men in organizations is to threaten this cultural centerpiece of adult manhood, gainful employment. Not incidentally, both Boisjoly and Richard Cook noted elsewhere that this may have been a crucial factor in why no one with sufficient authority stepped forward sooner to insist on a flight moratorium. As Cook pointed out, "You aren't going to find an engineer with 20 years experience *and a livelihood to protect* stand up and say, 'Excuse me, but we might have an explosion on the next flight because the O-rings might break'!" (Maier, 1992). Or, as Boisjoly (1991) explained, "It would have been tantamount to terminating one's career in the Space Program."

Economic considerations almost certainly affected MTI's submission to NASA's pressure ("Say Uncle!"). When it was clear that their major customer was displeased with their no-launch recommendation (as evidenced by their outright refusal to accept it), MTI asked for a time-out from the telecon to "re-evaluate the data." In hierarchical terms, MTI was being "bullied" into submission. As the less powerful of the two units (MTI depended more on NASA's good graces than vice versa, especially in the midst of ongoing contract negotiations), MTI (inferior = feminized) understood it had to be responsive to NASA (superior = masculinized) or suffer potentially drastic consequences. With a substantial continuing contract at risk, it is no wonder the Rogers commission concluded that, "Thiokol Management reversed its position and recommended the launch . . . in order to accommodate a major customer" (Rogers, 1986, p. 104).

When the Seal Task Force at MTI ran up against the bureaucratic brick wall, Kilminster's lack of responsiveness to members' plight meant overtime working hours for them. Roger Boisjoly noted in his October 4 Activity Report that "I for one resent working at full capacity all week long and then being required to support activity on the weekend that could have been accomplished during the week." Employers can make such demands only on employees they assume are unfettered by domestic concerns (i.e., men) . . . or whom they assume to be married to people (i.e., "wives") who will accommodate to the spillover effects of work on family life.

Excessive work involvement was directly implicated as a contributor to the Challenger disaster by the Rogers commission:

> One factor which may have contributed significantly to the atmosphere of the teleconference at Marshall is the effect on managers of several days of irregular working hours and insufficient sleep. . . . The willingness of NASA employees to work excessive hours, while admirable, raises serious questions when it jeopardizes job performance, particularly when critical management decisions are at stake. (Rogers, 1986, p. G-5)

As long as work and success are presumed to reign supreme in men's lives (and therefore be more highly valued than familial obligations which are— still—presumed to be "women's work"), then organizations can and will make demands on *men qua men* to "be there." This same rationale applied to why the MTI and MSFC representatives who flew to Florida for the launch, leaving their families behind, "happened" to be male.

Theme No. 3: "The Sturdy Oak": A Manly Air of Toughness, Confidence, and Self-Reliance

Appearing tough and in control, whatever the reality, is another hallmark of American hegemonic masculinity that plays out in organizations. This theme also implies that "real men stand tall;" they do not allow themselves to be put down, nor do they back down. Here is a sampling of how this theme permeates the events around Challenger.

From its inception, space flight was an arena where our self-image as a nation was placed on the line, the gauntlet having been thrown down by the Soviet launch of Sputnik. It was Cold War posturing that led John F. Kennedy to commit the United States, "to achieving the goal, before this decade is out, of landing a man on the moon and returning him safely to the earth." The unstated subtext, of course, was that we would get there *before* the Soviets; that we would "beat" them in this "space race."

Our successful moon landings, which rank undeniably among the top technological achievements of our time, sowed the seeds, however, of an arrogant hubris within the space agency. As Richard Cook pointed out, when the early evidence of O-ring damage began to emerge, NASA management failed to interpret the developments with alarm. According to Cook (1991), "NASA, with its history of spectacular successes, tended to view itself as a uniquely all-knowing and perfected entity." The agency boldly promised to accelerate the flight schedule from 9 missions in 1985, to 15 in 1986, up to 24 a year by 1990 (unrealistically ambitious, yet still well below the original 60 missions a year projected by the agency when it sold the program to Congress in the 1970s).

Hardy, the Deputy Director of Science and Engineering at MSFC, who during the telecon indicated he was "appalled" by MTI's data, offered a sublimely circular rationale for why his challenge was justified, one that encapsulates the masculinist fascination with toughness: "I have found in most cases [that] engineers, managers, or whatever else who have a true conviction in the data that they are presenting to you will 'hang tough' and not resent someone probing and penetrating that data" (Rogers, 1986, p. 1632). In other words, he was correct to challenge them because, after all, they backed down in the end. Obviously, MTI's initial tenacious defense of the 53-degree threshold for launch did not constitute "hanging tough" (a masculine virtue), but was pure "resentment" at being "probed and penetrated" (i.e., analogous to feminine irrationality).

Theme No. 4: "Give 'Em Hell": The Aura of Aggression, Violence, and Daring

The dominant themes of masculinity overlap and intersect to reinforce one another. As alluded to above, the toughness and confidence evidenced by NASA in its race to the moon and its willingness to press ahead with an accelerated flight schedule despite increasing incidents of erosion can also be construed as evidence of a near reckless bravado. The clearest example of this is the virtual absence, in thousands of pages of testimony, of any hint that the decision makers on Challenger considered the *possibility* of being wrong. In all of the debate about whether procedures were followed or not, about who communicated what to whom and when, about who was responsible, with rare exception did the lives of the astronauts themselves emerge as an issue. There are many other instances where the masculine aura of aggression shone through to ultimately take the lives of the Challenger crew.

Richard Cook revealed that safety concerns got submerged at the space agency because "the whole culture of the place calls for a can-do attitude that NASA can do whatever it tries to do, can solve any problem that comes up as it roars ahead toward 24 shuttle flights a year" (Boffey, 1986, p. B4).

The media, for all of their grandstanding *after* the disaster, chimed in to compound NASA's problems prior to it. When the launch was delayed, rather than welcoming the news as evidence of respect for the safety of the astronauts, the TV networks ridiculed the agency, referring to the postponement as "another red-faces-all-around space shuttle launch delay" (CBS), or quipping, "a flawless lift-off proved too much of a challenge for Challenger" (ABC). From a masculine-gendered perspective, such ridicule constitutes an implicit dare for the target to "deliver" (translated, "Nyah-nyah-nyah-nyah-nyah! NASA can't get it up! Betcha-can't-launch-on-time!").

The dare would be made more explicit during the pivotal telecon, with Mulloy setting the tone by lambasting MTI with "When do you want us to launch? Next April?" In other words, "What's wrong with you? *We're* ready!" The aura was embellished with profanity (*"My God,* Thiokol . . . " and "[This] is a *hell of a time* to be generating new Launch Commit Criteria!"). Mulloy's institutional superior, William Lucas, had signaled his view to the SRB Manager before the telecon had begun: "We get a little cold nip, and they want to shut the Shuttle System down? I sure would like to see their reasons for that!"

During the MTI caucus, while the managers were midway through their private discussion, the General Manager, Jerry Mason, rhetorically asked his vice presidential subordinates, "Am I the only one who wants to launch?" (translated, "What'samatter? You *chicken*?")

Mason's outright rejection of Boisjoly's and Thompson's input to the discussion (in effect, "Sit down and shut up. We didn't ask you!") and his willingness to exclude the engineers from the final vote ("because we had already established that we were not going to be unanimous") is a form of aggression and psychological violence common in (and to) hierarchical systems. To silence the voices of those who dissent, on the grounds of their disagreement and/or on the basis of their "inferior status," is a deliberate act of intimidation in order to get one's own way. The same can be said for his virtual dictation to Bob Lund, "Take off your engineering hat and put on your management hat."

CONCLUSIONS

As the foregoing elaboration attests, the pressures and dynamics, the organizational processes that allowed Challenger to happen reflect the tragic triumph of a decidedly masculinist (and *unfortunately* pervasive) managerial mind-set. We have seen how the processes and actions that contributed to what the presidential commission referred to as "the flawed decision" are strikingly linked to the four cornerstones of masculinity identified by David and Brannon (1976): No Sissy Stuff, The Big Wheel, The Sturdy Oak, and Give 'Em Hell, which parallel the elements of the White Male System presented by Schaef (1981). As such, it raises a question that strikes at a central dilemma in the diversity debate: By focusing on white males' relative ease of *success* in the White Male System, attention has been diverted away from the more fundamental issue of whether we should be encouraging anyone—including white males—to assimilate to (and hence replicate, maintain, and perpetuate) that system. Indeed, the foregoing analysis suggests that our organizations, and white males in particular, stand to benefit tremendously from questioning the normative foundations upon which organizational and individual success has been predicated. In diversity terms, this means grappling with the central issue of changing the culture of corporate masculinity; or moving beyond MANagement.

As hierarchical systems, NASA and MTI empowered superiors and denied voice to subordinates. Views that challenged managerial prerogatives or that violated NASA's "can-do operational shuttle" ideology were suppressed or submerged. In effect, the managers in this chain of events were men, the engineers women (metaphorically speaking). NASA management's invocation of logic to invalidate the "qualitative, gut feelings" and "hand-wringing emotion" of the MTI engineers allowed NASA to insist that "no data showed conclusively that cold temperature increased the risk" (Mulloy, personal communication, May 15, 1991). Following the rule of reason, NASA managers felt insulated from blame for having made a "logical decision that had a disastrous result." Those who were opposed to the launch essentially were branded as "sissies" and pressured to change their stance ("Real men take risks. Real men are always ready to fly.")

In acting out adult equivalents of "King of the Mountain" and "Chicken," NASA and MTI were, by the time the telecon took place on the evening of January 27, already at the edge of the precipice. The "Russian Roulette" that allowed top NASA officials to keep the shuttles flying (at an ever-accelerating pace, no less) all but guaranteed the tragic outcome that resulted on January 28, 1986. The willingness to take ever greater (institutional) risks while denying one's weaknesses and neglecting to even consider the consequences of being wrong (Give 'Em Hell), the blind devotion to and projection of the image of an operational shuttle that never was (The Sturdy Oak) were fueled in part by these men's fears that ferreting out and speaking the truth might have threatened their personal livelihood or the viability of their organizations (The Big Wheel).

I find it impossible to reflect back to Challenger without experiencing deep regret and pain, feelings that are probably shared by many readers recalling the event, exacerbated by the knowledge that it was entirely preventable. My research into the disaster, as explored herein, has convinced me that we would not have experienced that loss or pain if the key decision makers and the organizations themselves had been guided by a different set of managerial principles and organizational priorities than the masculine ones that so indelibly shaped their actions. This analysis does not assume that men are inherently "bad," but that the norms by which they are expected to pattern their lives can be dysfunctional to the point of disaster. Gender is central to our understanding of organizational phenomena, even when (as illustrated here) all of the participants are male. Masculinity, as currently conceived, is both inherent to organizations and problematic. By making corporate masculinity (the implicit and unquestioned norm of organizational life) both visible and problematic, it is hoped that organizations and the people (i.e., men) who run them will commit to adopting alternatives (e.g., empowerment over dominance; participation and linking over authority and ranking; connection over confrontation; intimacy over intimidation; egalitarianism and inclusion over stratification and exclusion), alternatives I explore in greater depth elsewhere (Maier, 1996). Absent such a commitment, countless Challengers, metaphorically speaking, will be launched every day. Exposing this factor as one of the root causes, if not the ultimate source, of the tragedy can serve as a catalyst to inspire managers and organizations to reexamine their basic assumptions not only about masculinity (i.e., about what it means to "be a man" in this society), but also about *management* and the masculine underpinnings of organization.

Thus, we are left with a final dilemma: To adopt such alternative managerial approaches requires more than just the "will," as the saying goes. It also requires a "way," an altogether different form of organizational culture . . . and structure, than those which predominate today.

From a diversity perspective, one need look no further than Challenger for the compelling case to embrace a multicultural approach to organizational development, rather than blindly assimilating more numbers of diverse people *and* white males themselves into the existing (and dysfunctional) white male system.

NOTES

1. Kathy Ferguson collaborated extensively on the analysis in this section.
2. The analysis in this section draws from my previous research in masculinities (1993a).

REFERENCES

Belenky, J., Clinchy, B., Goldberger, N., & Tarule, T. (1986). *Women's ways of knowing*. New York: Basic.
Boffey, P. (1986, February 14). Analyst who gave shuttle warning faults "gung-ho, can-do" attitude. *New York Times,* p. B-4.
Boisjoly, R. M. (1991, April 18). *Ethical decision-making in organizations: Morton Thiokol and the space shuttle Challenger disaster.* Paper presented at the GTE Lectureship on Technology and Ethics, Binghamton, NY.
Chodorow, N. (1978). *The reproduction of mothering*. Berkeley: University of California Press.
Connell, B. (1989). Masculinity, violence, and war. In M. Kimmel & M. Messner (Eds.), *Men's lives* (pp. 176-183). New York: Macmillan.
Cook, R. C. (1991, April 18). *The NASA space shuttle Challenger disaster: The view from within.* Paper presented at the GTE Lectureship on Technology and Ethics, Binghamton, NY.
David, D. S., & Brannon, R. (1976). *The forty-nine percent majority: The male sex role*. Reading, MA: Addison-Wesley.
Di Stefano, C. (1991). *Configurations of masculinity: A feminist perspective on modern political theory*. Ithaca, NY: Cornell University Press.
Eisler, R. (1987). *The chalice and the blade*. New York: Harper-Collins.

Ferguson, K. (1984). *The feminist case against bureaucracy.* Philadelphia: Temple University Press.

Gilligan, C. (1982). *In a different voice.* Cambridge, MA: Harvard University Press.

Harding, S. (1986). *The science question in feminism.* Ithaca, NY: Cornell University Press.

Hare-Mustin, R. T. (1988). Family change and gender differences: Implications for theory and practice. *Family Relations, 37,* 36-41.

Hartsock, N. (1983). *Money, sex, and power: Toward a feminist historical materialism.* New York: Longman.

Investigation of the Challenger accident (House Report #99-1016). (1986, October 29.) Washington, DC: Government Printing Office.

Kanter, R. M. (1977). *Men and women of the corporation.* New York: Basic.

Kimmel, M., & Messner, M. (1992). *Men's lives* (2nd ed.). New York: Macmillan.

Maier, M. (Writer/Director). (1992). *"A major malfunction . . ." The story behind the space shuttle Challenger disaster. A pedagogical documentary about organizational politics, ethics, and decision making* (Videotape and Instructional Materials). Albany: The Research Foundation of the State University of New York.

Maier, M. (1993a). "Am I the only one who wants to launch?" Corporate masculinity and the space shuttle Challenger disaster. *masculinities, 1*(1-2), pp. 34-45.

Maier, M. (1993b). Revisiting (and resolving?) the androgyny/masculinity debate in management. *Journal of Men's Studies, 2*(2), 157-171.

Maier, M. (1994). Challenger: The path to disaster. *Case Research Journal, 14*(1), 1-49; 150-155.

Maier, M. (1996, August). *Confronting the (f)laws of the pyramid: The enduring legacy of the space shuttle Challenger disaster?* Paper presented at the Academy of Management Annual Meetings, Cincinnati, OH.

McConnell, M. (1987). *Challenger: A major malfunction.* New York: Doubleday.

Messerschmidt, J. (1995). Managing to kill: Masculinities and the space shuttle Challenger explosion. *masculinities, 3*(4):1-22.

Mulloy, L. (1990). Interview transcript, Cosgrove-Meurer Productions (*The story behind the story).* Courtesy of Larry Mulloy.

Powell, G. N., & Butterfield, D. A. (1989). The "good manager:" Did androgyny fare better in the 1980s? *Group and Organization Studies, 14,* 216-233.

Rogers, W. (1986). *Report on the space shuttle Challenger accident.* Washington, DC: Government Printing Office.

Ruddick, S. (1989). *Maternal thinking.* New York: Doubleday.

Schaef, A. W. (1981). *Women's reality.* New York: Harper-Collophon.

Spender, D. (1984). Defining reality: A powerful tool. In C. Kramarae, M. Schulz, & W. O'Barr (Eds.), *Language and power* (pp. 194-205). Beverly Hills, CA: Sage.

Starbuck, W., & Milliken, F. (1988). Challenger: Fine-tuning the odds until something breaks. *Journal of Management Studies, 25*(4), 319-340.

Tannen, D. (1990). *You just don't understand.* New York: Ballantine.

Vaughan, D. (1990). Autonomy, interdependence, and social control: NASA and the space shuttle Challenger. *Administrative Science Quarterly, 35*(2), 225-257.

Vaughan, D. (1996). *The Challenger launch decision.* Chicago: University of Chicago Press.

11

When Organizations Do Harm

Two Cautionary Tales

PAULA CAPRONI

JOCELYN A. FINLEY

This chapter explores two troubling events that occurred in the United States in 1991. The first is the incident in which over 80 naval officers and civilians, mostly women were assaulted, many sexually, as they were forced down a gauntlet of male naval aviators and others attending the annual Tailhook convention. The second is the incident in which black motorist Rodney King was clubbed and kicked over 53 times in 81 seconds by four white police officers after a high-speed car chase. The beating, videotaped by an onlooker, was viewed by stunned television viewers worldwide.

By any definition, the Tailhook and King events can be characterized as organizational crises. Organizational crises are typically brief, extraordinary events in an organization's life that are followed by significant long-term human, organizational, and societal consequences. They involve real or potential harm to organizational members or to those who come in contact with the organization. Such crises cause feelings of danger and anxiety among organizational members, threaten valued organizational goals, and lead to significant organizational setbacks. They are threatening and dangerous because the demands of the situation typically exceed the organization's capability to understand and respond quickly and appropriately.

Notably, for the U.S. Navy and Los Angeles Police Department, the events that set the crises in motion were not the abuse of the women and King, respectively. Abuses such as these were not extraordinary organizational events nor were they considered why and how such harmdoing could occur.

Based on a cross-case analysis of these two events, the chapter identifies five organizational characteristics and processes that helped create conditions that fostered the violence that occurred:

1. The existence of organizational ideologies that promoted the moral exclusion of out-group members
2. The enactment of taken-for-granted rites and routines that reflected those ideologies
3. The use of language that reinforced the exclusion and abuse of out-group members
4. The use of rationalizations that prevented those who participated in the Tailhook gauntlet and the King beating from understanding those they violated as victims and themselves as victimizers
5. The use of codes of silence that were designed to protect those who participated in the abuses

The chapter also considers how the lessons from the Tailhook and King cases can be applied to all organizations.

METHOD:
CROSS-CASE ANALYSIS

The cross-case analysis involved three phases: case development, within-case analysis and cross-case analysis. We constructed the two cases by drawing on a variety of archival resources. We developed the Tailhook case by integrating data from the U.S. Office of the Inspector General's Investigative Report of Tailhook 1991. The report, based on interviews with over 2,900 conference attendees, represents the Pentagon's official analysis of the many improprieties that occurred at Tailhook, including the infamous gauntlet. We developed the

King case by integrating data from verbatim transcripts of the Simi Valley criminal trial in which the four officers were accused and later acquitted of excessive use of force. We also drew on a special 1994 issue of the *UCLA Law Review* that focused on the lessons learned from the federal trial in which the four officers were charged with violating King's civil rights and in which two officers were found guilty and sentenced to prison terms. Levenson, the author of the special issue, based her analysis on her attendance at the federal trial, as well as her review of the Christopher Commission report, which details the results of an independent investigation of the Los Angeles Police Department with specific attention to the King incident.

For both the Tailhook and King cases, we also integrated information from media accounts. These accounts included articles from widely read popular press magazines such as *Time* and *Newsweek,* as well as from major metropolitan newspapers such as the *Los Angeles Times* and the *Washington Globe.* We identified relevant media sources by conducting a comprehensive library search of four databases—Wilson Indexes to Journal Articles, American Psychological Association, the National Newspaper Index, and Lexis/Nexis Index—for the time period from September 1991 to February 1993.

Before we present the cases and analyses, we want to address two concerns. First, we recognize that the cases that follow are graphic and may be disturbing to readers. However violence, by its nature, is disconcerting. We chose not to temper the descriptions of the violence that occurred during the Tailhook gauntlet and the King beating because doing so would misrepresent the extent of the abuses that occurred and minimize the seriousness of these events. We believe that many important lessons can be learned from exploring incidences of violence at work, not the least of which is that organizational members acting as representatives of their organizations can do horrific things. Furthermore, although most organizational scholars have tended to shy away from research on workplace violence (Hearn, 1994), we believe the topic is increasingly relevant in North America as people who work in and are served by organizations become more diverse and as hostility toward cultural groups that have traditionally been excluded from or devalued by organizations becomes a more visible and troubling characteristic of organizational life.

Second, we recognize that these cases are controversial and that there are multiple interpretations of the events that occurred. Shrivastava (1987) points out that such controversy is unavoidable and predictable because various constituencies in crisis situations have different stakes in how the events are portrayed and thus construct versions of reality that support their own interests.

Given that many of the facts in the Tailhook and King cases are elusive and interpretations remain many-sided, our goal in this chapter is to present meaningful, although unavoidably partial, accounts of these events so that the knowledge gained provides useful lessons for all organizations.

THE CASES

The Tailhook Convention

The Tailhook Association is a private organization composed of active duty and retired naval and Marine Corps aviators and defense contractors. The convention had been held annually since 1958. About 4,500 people attended the 1991 convention held September 8 to 12. Professional seminars were held on subjects such as aviation safety, technology, and Operations Desert Storm and Desert Shield. The convention was well-known for its official and unofficial social activities. In 1991, the Navy

> supported and encouraged the attendance of as many as 4,000 naval officers despite the fact that at most only 2,100 people . . . actually registered for the professional aspects of the conference, and even fewer actually attended the professional events. Navy support included the use of naval aircraft and other vehicles, as well the use of various administrative personnel to facilitate attendance by naval officers. (Office of the Inspector General, 1993, p. 1)

The estimated cost was $400,000 (p. viii).

According to the Naval Investigative Service (NIS) report released in April, 1992, the social events at the conference included,

> scantily clad female bartenders; the hiring of strippers, who generally ended up nude and participated in simulated sexual acts with the audience; the showing of pornographic films; the practice of shaving women's legs and other body parts; women encouraged to expose their breasts in exchange for squadron T-shirts, and obscene drink dispensers. (*Washington Post*, May 1992)

A variety of other sexual and assaultive behaviors also occurred. Although both men and women were involved in many forms of misconduct at the Tailhook convention, the most serious abuses—those that involved the physical, often sexual, assault of unwilling women—were committed predominantly by men. Despite the widespread abuses cited in the NIS report, the inquiry identified about 26 women, both officers and civilians, as victims and 18 male naval officers as suspects.

In June 1992, the Pentagon's Inspector General, Derek J. Vander Schaaf, questioned the integrity of the initial NIS inquiry. The Pentagon charged that the investigations were deficient and suggested that "the deficiencies in the investigations were the result of an attempt to limit the exposure of the Navy and senior Navy officials to criticism regarding Tailhook '91" (Office of the Inspector General, 1993). The Pentagon investigators discovered that 55 pages of interviews were omitted from the NIS report, including one that implicated Navy Secretary Garrett as being present at many of the indecent activities and assaults. Although some argue that "the decision to delete this particular block of information apparently was entirely discretionary and made in good faith" (Proceedings, 1994, p. 96), Vander Schaaf ordered the Navy to suspend further questioning or disciplinary proceedings against the officers implicated in the Tailhook scandal, and the Pentagon's Inspector General took over the investigation.

The Pentagon's investigation concluded that at least 83 women and 7 men, naval officers and civilians, had been sexually and otherwise assaulted at the 1991 Tailhook convention. In total, the Pentagon's investigation implicated 117 officers "in one or more incidences of indecent assault, indecent exposure, conduct unbecoming to an officer, or failure to act in a proper leadership capacity" (Office of the Inspector General, 1993, p. 2). The Inspector General's report also concluded that "the number of individuals involved in all types of misconduct or other inappropriate behavior was more widespread than these figures would suggest" (p. 2). Many of these assaults occurred while victims were being forced to traverse a gauntlet of drunken military aviators on the third floor of the Las Vegas Hilton, where the convention was held.

The Gauntlet: The gauntlet had been an informal convention activity since 1986 and was well-known among naval aviators as a Tailhook tradition. The Inspector General's (1993) report noted that the gauntlet had "evolved over the years from somewhat innocuous nonassaultive behavior to the assaultive acts that occurred in recent years" (p. 38). The report described the gauntlet as follows:

> A male Marine Corps captain told us that the gauntlet was operated in an organized manner. He said that on Saturday night between 10:00 and 11:00 p.m., he observed the gauntlet. . . . He saw a group of about 30 men, whom he believed to be military personnel, milling around in the hallway. As he watched, women approached and someone yelled "wave off," at which time the women walked

through without being molested. On separate occasions, he saw two women walk into the group of men and, once inside, the men turned on the women and began jostling and pushing them along the hallway. When a woman entered the group, both ends of the gauntlet closed with men blocking any avenue of retreat. Once a woman escaped from the gauntlet, someone yelled, "mill about," which would be repeated over and over in low voices by the men all along the gauntlet. In response, the men slowly shuffled their feet and faced at odd angles until the next woman approached, giving the appearance they were just standing along the hall socializing with each other. (p. 44)

The Inspector General's (1993) report described the gauntlet as being composed of "two to three hundred young people—young men. . . . [The gauntlet was] probably as long as maybe 30 yards or so" (p. 41). The report described gauntlet victims being "groped, pinched, and fondled on their breasts, buttocks, and genitals. Some victims were bitten by their assailants, others were knocked to the ground, and some had their clothing ripped or removed" (p. 55). A male aviator noted to investigators that "the more the women fought the men [in the gauntlet] who were attacking them, the more the males attacked" (p. 45). Furthermore, the assaults escalated from Friday to Saturday night. Eleven assaults took place on Thursday night, 15 on Friday night, and 68 on Saturday night (p. 45). Among those molested was Lieutenant Paula Coughlin, an admiral's aide and helicopter pilot. Coughlin was the first to go public and blow the whistle on the gauntlet. On the second night of the convention, Coughlin headed over to the Hilton from her nearby hotel to meet friends on the third floor. She stepped off the elevator and into the gauntlet. Although she was wearing civilian clothing, a man she did not recognize shouted out "admiral's aide." Coughlin described her ordeal, which began when one of the gauntlet participants deliberately bumped her:

[He] then grabbed me by the buttocks with such force that it lifted me off the ground and ahead a step. . . . I wiggled from his grip, turned around, and asked the man. "What the [expletive] do you think you are doing?" As I did this, I was grabbed by the buttocks again by someone behind me. Each time I turned to face a new assault. . . . I would receive several others. . . . [The first attacker] then put both his hands down the front of my tank top and inside my bra. . . . I turned my head to the left and sank my teeth into the fleshy part of the man's left forearm, biting hard. . . . As I was attempting to regain my balance, someone in front of me . . . reached under my skirt and grabbed the crotch of my panties . . . at this point I felt as though the group was trying to rape me. I was terrified. (*Washington Post,* May 1992).

In an interview, Coughlin said,

This was such a terrible issue to deal with. It would have been different if I had walked into a low-life biker bar in San Diego and gotten mugged . . . but these were my peers. They knew who I was and abandoned the idea that I was one of them. (*Washington Post,* May 1992)

When Coughlin complained about the episode to her boss, Rear Admiral John W. Snyder, Jr., has been widely quoted as responding, "That's what you get when you go to a hotel party with a bunch of drunk aviators" (*Washington Post,* May 17, 1992, p. C1), although he has denied responding as such (*Newsweek,* August 10, 1992, p. 3). Coughlin said she went public in frustration over the Navy's apparent lack of concern for her and others who were victims of similar incidents that took place at Tailhook 1991.

As discussed in the Marine Corps captain's description of the gauntlet, the gauntlet was a planned, highly controlled event, and the men involved were not out of control, as is often assumed. Additional evidence from the Inspector General's investigation supports this view. Code words such as *clear deck, foul deck,* and *wave off* were used to describe approaching "attractive" and "unattractive" women, and *bolter* was used to announce approaching senior officer and security personnel. When there were not enough women coming through the area to satisfy the gauntlet participants, some of the men left the gauntlet area to recruit more women. Although some of the women they recruited willingly entered the gauntlet having some knowledge of what they would endure, others were tricked into naively walking toward the gauntlet, and others were physically carried to the gauntlet area. The recruitment efforts and assaults were selective, and men typically proceeded unmolested through the gauntlet.

That the men who participated in the gauntlet were not out of control is further reflected in the following incident described in the Inspector General's (1993) report:

Two female victims told us that, after they were pushed and shoved through the gauntlet where they were grabbed on the breasts and buttocks, one of them realized that she had lost a pager. According to one of the victims, the . . . "whole crowd stopped and began to look for the pager." The pager was located and returned to the woman without further incident. (pp. 52-53)

The blatancy with which the officers engaged in the gauntlet and other misconduct at the Tailhook convention was striking. Squadron members placed their squadron's stickers on the bodies of women as the women were passed through the gauntlet, a process known as "zapping" at the Tailhook convention. Some Tailhook attendees wore T-shirts that read "women are property" and "he-man women haters club." In addition, over 800 photographs, three quarters of which were taken by civilian women and many of which documented a variety of Tailhook improprieties, were collected by the Office of the Inspector General. Many officers willingly posed for the photographs that later provided evidence against these officers. The blatant attitudes and behaviors that characterized the improprieties that occurred during the three convention days are further reflected in the Inspector General's (1993) finding that "a few officers recorded over combat footage in a video camcorder to memorialize their mooning activities. They left the videotape in the camcorder to the later surprise of the squadron [commanding officer] who owned the equipment" (p. 61).

The Aftermath: Although the public displays of misconduct during the convention were blatant, the Inspector General's investigation found evidence of systematic attempts to deny knowledge of the widespread misconduct through the use of a Lieutenant's Protective Association and Junior Officers' Protective Association, once the misconduct was publicly challenged and investigations began. These informal associations were "described as being an allegiance among officers" (p. 22).

The Tailhook accusations also resulted in backlash against those who criticized the Tailhook activities. One senior officer was quoted that Coughlin was the kind of woman "who would welcome this kind of activity" and cited her use of profanity in her NIS statement as evidence (*Newsweek,* 1992, October 5, p. 58). One naval officer expressed his opinion that

> There's women out there who are looking for real men. [Tailhook] is one of those places you can find them. Are these women going to be warriors or not? He suggested that women soldiers should deal with unwelcome sexual advances by hitting back on the spot—or return with enough friends to even the score. That's how a warrior would handle it, he said, "they don't go crying to daddy. . . . If women want to get respect, that's how they earn it" (*Los Angeles Times,* July 1992).

Furthermore, "those who deflect sexual advances risk being labeled by some men as lesbians, a threat that can cost a woman her military career. Those who dare to complain are often branded as too soft" (*Time,* July 1992).

After the publicity surrounding the Tailhook scandal, the Navy's annual Tomcat Follies, a show designed to honor the Navy's top gun pilots, included a caricature of representative Patricia Schroeder, who had criticized the Navy's handling of the harassment charge, in a sexually compromising position. Disciplinary action was taken against 5 high-ranking naval aviators who were relieved of duty and 16 other aviators who received warnings and counseling, none of which appeared on the officers' records. After her criticism of Tailhook misconduct, Schroeder's office also received an obscene fax message that originated from the Marine Corps Air Station at New Rier, North Carolina.

Rationales: In the aftermath of the public exposure of the Tailhook events, various rationales were given for the gauntlet behavior. The Inspector General's (1993) report concluded that

> the most common rationale was that such behavior was "expected" of junior officers and that Tailhook was comprised of "traditions" built on various lore. Another reason given by many attendees was that their behavior was somehow justified or at least excusable, because they were "returning heroes" from Desert Storm. . . . Furthermore, at the time when the thing started, they were the elite, they thought they could do anything they wanted in naval aviation and not have to answer the questions they were answering today about it. Many officers told us they believed they could act free of normal constraints because Tailhook was an accepted part of a culture in some ways separate from the mainstream of the Armed Forces. . . . [There was a] live for today because you may die tomorrow attitude. (pp. 82-84)

The Inspector General's (1993) report also suggested that "animosity toward women" contributed to the misconduct, citing the T-shirts and stating that "not in my squadron" lapel pins worn by many male attendees "signified contempt for women in naval aviation and specifically the desire to maintain the combat exclusion with respect to women" (p. 85). Several sources contended that a heated discussion at a symposium during the 1991 Tailhook conference may have contributed to the animosity toward women. The Flag Panel, a seminar that encouraged dialogue between senior and junior officers in naval aviation, was the most highly attended event during the 1991 conference. It was also the most widely discussed session, in part because of controversial statements made regarding the potential future of women in combat. In an article published by the Navy's Proceedings, Colonel Parks (1994) described the events as follows:

> Tension at the Flag Panel increased when a female aviator asked the panel when women would be allowed to fly aircraft in combat. Vice Admiral Dunleavy initially responded with a "Hoo-boy!" in acknowledgment of the sensitivity of the question. He quickly continued, saying, "If Congress directs [the Secretary of the Navy] to allow women to fly combat aircraft, we will comply. . . . At the same time, the question generated audience comments described by one officer as "downright ugly." (p. 91)

Although many have suggested that this exchange in particular fueled some of the later abuse toward women at the conference, the Inspector General's report concluded that "the Flag Panel was conducted in a responsible and professional manner." Nonetheless, Colonel Parks (1994) suggests in the Navy's Proceedings that, while naval officers' comments regarding women in combat did not necessarily contribute to widespread animosity toward women at the conference, naval leaders were remiss in not intervening in the junior officers' inappropriate responses to the comments and that leaders "cannot be ambiguous in their response to blatantly unprofessional conduct" (p. 91). This sentiment was clearly reflected in the Inspector General's (1993) report, which concluded that a "failure in leadership" significantly contributed to the attitudes and behaviors exhibited at Tailhook: "Tailhook '91 is the culmination of a long-term failure of leadership in naval aviation. . . . Senior aviation leadership seemed to ignore the deteriorating standards of behavior and failed to deal with the increasingly disorderly, improper, and promiscuous behavior" (p. 86).

The Inspector General's (1993) report suggested that the gauntlet activities were known to many higher level officers and were overlooked by some of these officers because they themselves had participated in similar improprieties when they were junior officers. Other high-level officials stated that "they saw no reason to stop anything that hadn't been stopped before" (p. 87).

Notably, the Inspector General's (1993) report found evidence that the "rowdy and improper behavior" culminated at Tailhook in 1985 (p. 27) and that Tailhook 1991 was "mild" compared to previous years.

> After receiving a number of complaints after the 1985 convention, the association held two special board meetings. Although a number of solutions were suggested during these meetings, these solutions were rejected by the board. Instead, the board recommended that the parties and other events in the suites be "low key" and monitored by "adult supervision" (p. 27).

Although some senior officers took actions that effectively curbed misbehavior in the suites for which they were responsible, many improprieties continued to occur with few or any restrictions imposed or enforced by senior officers in subsequent years.

Leadership's failure to effectively curtail Tailhook misconduct led to a number of high-level naval leaders being demoted, losing anticipated promotions, and being forced to resign or take early retirements. The press cited several examples, Snyder, the commanding officer who failed to respond appropriately and promptly to Coughlin's complaint, was demoted. In response to the inadequacies of the initial NIS investigation, Admiral Williams, the Commander of NIS, and Admiral Gorden, the Judge Advocate General, took early retirement. Rear Admiral Davis, the Naval Inspector General, was relieved of his duties and reassigned. Vice Admiral Richard M. Dunleavy, Assistant Chief of Naval Operations at the time of Tailhook 1991, was given a reduced rank for having observed the gauntlet without making efforts to intervene. Navy Secretary Garret resigned at the request of the White House, in part for being present at some of the activities and assaults and making no efforts to intervene.

The officers who directly participated in the gauntlet and other Tailhook misconduct were also penalized. The Navy's Proceedings (Parks, 1994) noted that

> 39 Navy officers received nonjudicial punishment for indecent exposure, conduct unbecoming an officer, or making false statements; another dozen received less severe administrative rebukes; all other cases were dismissed. No one was convicted by court-martial for criminal conduct at Tailhook '91. (p. 101)

The gauntlet and other Tailhook improprieties were characterized as having "plunged the Navy into a moral and morale crisis over its treatment of women in the service" (*Los Angeles Times,* September 1992). A year following the Tailhook scandal, O'Keefe noted, "I need to emphasize a very, very important message. We get it. We know that the larger issue is a cultural problem which has allowed demeaning behavior and attitudes toward women in uniform to exist with the Navy" (*Washington Post,* September 1992).

Rodney King and the Los Angeles Police

On March 3, 1991, George Holliday videotaped Timothy Briseno, Lawrence Powell (field training officer), and Timothy Wind (trainee in Powell's patrol car), all white officers in the Los Angeles Police Department (LAPD), as they clubbed and kicked Rodney King, an unemployed black construction worker, over 53 times in 81 seconds, with many of the blows occurring after he was on the ground. Sergeant Stacey Koon, the officer in charge, supervised the incident. "Approximately twenty other officers watched the beating from a few feet away," some saying that they "just went to the scene to see what was happening" (Levenson, 1994, p. 520).

The day after the beating, Holliday offered the videotape to the desk officer at the Foothill police station, the locale in which the beating occurred. The desk officer would not confirm that the station's officers had been involved in the incident, so Holliday instead chose to give the videotape to a local television station. Within 24 hours, the videotape of the beating was shown throughout the world (Levenson, 1994, p. 524). The videotape provoked public outrage and controversy, inspiring investigations both internal and external to the LAPD. These investigations included the widely publicized 1992 Simi Valley trial in which the four officers were tried and acquitted of charges of assault and the use of excessive force. The superior court judge decided to retry Lawrence Powell, the only officer not fully acquitted of wrongdoing.

The verdict sparked the Los Angeles riots, called by various media sources a "bloody wake up call," the "fireball in the night," "a city at war," a "tectonic jolt in the nation's soul," and the "most expensive riots in U.S. history." The riots, primarily located in a 45-square-mile area of South Central Los Angeles, resulted in over 40 deaths (all but 15 victims were African American), over 2,000 wounded, 17,000 arrests, more than 3,700 fires, the destruction of over 5,000 buildings, $775 million to $1 billion in destruction of property (mostly commercial), and more than 6,000 insurance claims. Related riots on a smaller scale emerged in San Francisco, Atlanta, Seattle, Pittsburgh, and other cities. The riots are believed to have inspired the federal civil rights trial in which the four officers were charged with "willfully violating the constitutional rights" of Rodney King (Levenson, 1994). In response to the riots, then-president George Bush was quoted by *Time* magazine ("A shocked nation," 1992) as stating that

> "the [Simi Valley] verdict was not the end" . . . and [Bush] ordered federal authorities to speed an investigation with a view toward starting a federal prosecution of the four cops for violating King's civil rights, utilizing a law enacted specifically to apply in cases where state courts and juries could or would not convict. (p. 25)

The Chronology of Events. At 12:40 a.m. on March 3, 1991, officers Melanie and Tim Singer began to pursue King because he was speeding. After a high-speed chase that lasted about 10 minutes, King stopped. He and his passengers, Bryant Allen and Freddie Helms, were ordered out of King's Hyundai. Allen and Helms immediately submitted to handcuffs and were unharmed by the police. However, King's interactions with the police officers were more complex. Levenson (1994, pp. 518-521), in a special issue of the *UCLA Law Review* that focused on the "lessons of the Rodney King trial," described these interactions*:

---

* Originally published in 41 UCLA L. Rev. 509. Copyright 1994, The Regents of the University of California. All rights reserved.

Once King was out of the car, the officers ordered him to put his hands up and "come down to his knees." Confused, King instead put his hands on top of the car, spread-eagle position, as if he were waiting to be searched. In response, the officers continued to order King to get on the ground. King did not comply immediately.

Instead, he started to do a little dance, and got down on his hands and knees and shook his rear end. . . . officer Singer approached King with her gun drawn, but Sgt. [sic] Koon ordered her away. Sgt. Koon later characterized this incident involving Singer and King as a "Mandingo Sexual Encounter." Koon, who arrived while King was getting out of the car, ordered Singer to holster her weapon and threatened to electrocute King with a taser if King did not lie down in a prone position.

King eventually lay down on the ground. Once he did, Koon ordered LAPD officers to handcuff and arrest him. Defendants Powell, Wind, Briseno, and Officer Solano, defendant Briseno's partner, approached King to handcuff him. When the officer bent back King's wrist in a pain-compliance maneuver, King resisted and the officers fell off him. At that point, Koon ordered the officers back and decided to use the taser. Sgt. Koon fired two darts. . . . The taser then sent an electrical impulse into King, incapacitating him. King fell to the ground.

King then [rose] quickly to his feet and [took] a couple of steps. Defendant Powell, who [was] in a batter stance with his pr-24 side handle baton, [swung] at King's head while he [rose]. Powell struck King in the face, knocking him to the ground. According to King, he rose in an effort to escape from the officers who were taunting him with shouts of "oh, we're going to kill you, nigger. Run." Defendants argued at the trial that they believed King was charging defendant Powell or trying to escape into the nearby wooded Hanson Dam area.

Defendant Powell hit Rodney King in the head with his baton at least once and perhaps more. Two prosecution medical experts testified that blows fractured King's face in 15 places. The injuries were so severe that fluid and tissue from King's eye socket and brain dropped down into his crushed sinus cavities. King's face was split open and suffered multiple lacerations and bruising. While defendants argued that a fall to the ground (precipitated by a coincidental second shock from the taser) caused King's facial injuries, King suffered no injury to those portions of his face that protrude farther than his fractured cheeks.

About thirty-two seconds into the beating, as King lay on the ground, defendants Powell and Wind continued to strike him in the legs, torso, and ankles with their batons. As the defense admitted at the trial, the officers were trying to break King's bones. King rolled over two times to avoid the blows. As he lay on his back, defendant Powell hit King in the chest with his baton.

After approximately one minute, King lay motionless. Officer Powell, Koon, Wind, and Briseno surrounded him. Approximately twenty other officers watched the beating from a few feet away. Many watched the beating with their arms folded. At sixty-five seconds into the videotape, after King had been lying motionless for approximately ten seconds, defendant Briseno stomped on King's neck and King moved in response. Reacting to King's movement, defendant

Powell struck King again. Defendant Powell continued the beating for the next twenty seconds, hitting King five or six times with his baton. During the same period, defendant Wind kicked King and struck him with his baton.

The beating ended eighty-one seconds after it began. Defendant Briseno hand-cuffed King, and several officers dragged him across the asphalt to the side of the board, leaving him face down, hog-tied, and moaning in his own blood and saliva.

While King was handcuffed, defendant Powell called for an ambulance on his hand-held police radio. Powell laughed as he requested a rescue ambulance. An ambulance transported King to Pacific Hospital for medical treatment.

While at Pacifica Hospital, as King lay on the hospital gurney, defendant Powell joked that, "We played a little hardball" and "we hit a few home runs." He also told King that the police had won and King had lost. The hospital emergency room doctor treated King and released him for transport to County-USC Medical Center, which has a hospital jail ward. Defendant Powell and his partner defendant Wind, however, did not transport King directly to County-USC but instead detoured to the Foothill police station. There, as the injured King sat in the back seat of the police car with defendant Wind who was completing reports, defendant Powell went into the Foothill station and told war stories about beating King. Two hours after the beating, the officers finally delivered King to the USC Medical Center. There King was diagnosed as having suffered multiple [15] facial fractures and a broken leg.

Although required by regulations to do so, defendants Powell and Koon did not include in their use-of-force reports the fact that the officers had kicked King, struck him in the face, or caused severe injures. Moreover, neither of their reports noted that King was on the ground during the use of force.

Transcripts of taped conversations that took place after the beating revealed that Koon told a fellow officer that he had just been involved in "a big time use of force." Powell commented to fellow officers that "I haven't beaten anyone this bad in a long time."

The Legal Debate. That these events transpired was not in question in either the state or federal trial. Evidence showed that "King was speeding, that he did not stop, that he acted silly, that he didn't cooperate initially" (People of the State, 1991, pp. 5267-5268), that the officers' behaviors were "violent" and "brutal" (p. 7861), and that the officers were "entitled to use some force to get him to cooperate" (p. 5270). The controversies revolved around whether the officers used excessive force during their attempts to handcuff King and, in the federal case, whether the force used constituted a violation of King's civil rights.

The defense contended that the officers behaved appropriately under the circumstances, that "each of the 56 baton blows to King was justified" (Levenson, 1994, p. 526), that the beating reflected a "managed, controlled use of force"

(People of the State, 1991, p. 7859), and that the officers followed the policies and procedures of the LAPD. The defense also attempted to show that King was controlling the situation and that the officers were responding to his "aggressive" and "combative" behaviors with "pain compliance maneuvers" (e.g. kicks, blows with batons, the use of the taser) that were reasonable and necessary under the circumstances. Indeed, a juror in the Simi Valley trial that resulted in the acquittal of the four officers commented that she believed it was King, not the police, who was "directing the action" during the beating ("Special Report," 1992).

The defense characterized King as an ex-convict who "constituted a serious threat to police" ("A Shocked Nation," 1992) and presented the police officers as men who were putting their lives on the line to defend private citizens from harm. The defense also tried to show that fear, fatigue, and inexperience influenced the officer's behavior. The defense claimed that the officers were threatened by King's large size, suspected that King was on the drug PCP (which was believed among officers to give suspects extraordinary strength), and were concerned that King might have had a concealed weapon. The defense also argued that the officers did not have the training or the tools to deal more appropriately with the situation. As one jury member in the Simi Valley trial commented, "the officers simply did what they are trained for, using the tools they were given" ("Special Report," May 1992).

Briseno, the officer who stepped on King's neck after King lay "motionless" for about 10 seconds, argued that he believed at the time that the other officers' behavior was "wrong." He stated that he "stomped" on King's neck to stop King from making any further movements, and in doing so was trying to protect King from additional blows from the other officers. The defense further argued that King was not as badly beaten as the prosecution contended.

The prosecution tried to show that the officers knowingly used force beyond what was reasonable and necessary and that they had several opportunities to safely handcuff King during the 81 seconds in which the beating occurred. They argued that although King resisted the officers early in the incident, he soon complied with the officers' orders to get on the ground and put his hands behind his back. The prosecution also claimed that many of King's movements were natural bodily responses to protect himself from the officers' painful blows rather than attempts to resist or threaten the officers and that these movements were beyond King's control. They also argued that King was frightened of the police, was trying to protect himself from the officers' assault, and at one point, asked officers to "please stop."

The prosecution also tried to show that the officers' claims that they suspected King of using PCP and carrying a gun were unsubstantiated because the officers never requested an official drug test for King, nor did they ever search him for a weapon. The prosecution also noted that the officers were not aware of King's criminal record at the time of the beating. Laboratory tests after the incident found that King was not on PCP at the time of the incident, although he was legally drunk, which the prosecution argued would make King a less, rather than more, threatening subject. The prosecution further suggested that the officers falsified reports because they knew their actions were inappropriate. The prosecution noted that although Briseno stated at the trial that he felt the other officers' conduct was inappropriate, he did not report the perceived misconduct to anyone. Finally, the prosecution implied that the officers' behavior was motivated by racist tendencies. They cited a taped radio conversation among officers in which Powell "described an African American couple's domestic dispute as "right out of *Gorillas in the Mist*" (Levenson, 1994, p. 517). This conversation occurred less than an hour before the King incident.

The Consequences: Although the jury in the state trial acquitted all four officers of excessive use of force, the jury in the federal trial found Sergeant Koon and Officer Powell guilty of

> violating King's civil rights under color of authority. . . . Powell's conviction was based upon a Fourth Amendment violation of King' s right to be free from unreasonable search and seizure, while defendant Koon's conviction was based on his willful failure to prevent unlawful assault on King that deprived King of his liberty without due process of law. (Levenson, 1994, p. 532)

Koon and Powell were sentenced to 30 months in jail and served their sentences in "an institution generally reserved for white-collar nonviolent criminals" (Levenson, 1994, p. 553). Officers Wind and Briseno were acquitted. Notably, the LAPD was placed on "full city tactical alert" while the federal jury deliberated (Levenson, 1994, p. 532).

LESSONS FROM THE TAILHOOK AND KING CASES

In our analysis of these cases, we sought answers to two questions:

1. Did the U.S. Navy and LAPD share particular organizational characteristics and processes that may have created conditions that promoted the abuses that occurred?
2. If so, can these cases provide lessons that are relevant to all organizations?

We found several similarities in the characteristics and processes of the two organizations that we believe contributed to the abuses that occurred, and we discuss these similarities in this section. We will save our discussion of the general lessons that these cases provide for all organizations for the last section of this chapter.

The U.S. Navy and the LAPD share four characteristics that are particularly ironic and disturbing given the types of abuses that occurred. First, they are public service organizations charged with *protecting* citizens from harm. As one woman who attended Tailhook 1991 explained, "These people protect our country. . . . I assumed I was OK" (*Newsweek,* August 1992). Yet officers in both organizations were charged with and found guilty of unduly harming the citizens they were entrusted to protect. Second, these organizations depend on the legitimate use of physical violence for their existence. Although such violence is intended to be used judiciously to protect the moral and social order, officers of the Navy and LAPD used gratuitous violence against citizens while many other officers, similarly entrusted with the safety of citizens, stood by and watched the harmdoing.

Third, at the time of the Tailhook and King incidents, there were long-standing policies prohibiting sexual harassment and excessive use of force in the Navy and LAPD, respectively. However, both organizations had a recent history of abuses suggesting that there was considerable leniency in enforcing these policies and that these policies often went unheeded. Fourth, the organizational leadership at the time these events occurred was aware that such events occurred in their organization yet did not take sufficient action to help the victims or penalize those who participated in a way that acknowledged the severity of the abuses or would deter similar abuses in the future. Notably, although more women and racial minorities have joined the U.S. Navy and LAPD in the past few decades, the leaders of these organizations historically have been primarily white males, as they were at the time that these events occurred.

The assaults also were similar in many ways. Both assaults involved the use of violence by majority group members in the organization against minority group members. In both cases, the victims pleaded with the officers to stop the abuse. In both cases, the assaults, as well as the victims' appeals to stop the abuse, occurred in full view of the public and other organizational members. Both incidences were recorded, the King beating on videotape and the gauntlet and other Tailhook improprieties in photographs. Both events captured the attention of the media and inspired public outrage. In both cases, officers directly involved in the abuses, as well as organizational leaders, were subjected to official investigations. And in both cases, some of the officers directly involved in the abuses, as well as organizational leaders, were penalized.

The U.S. Navy and the LAPD also shared cultures of exclusion that created the conditions that made the violence that occurred not only possible but probable. Based on our cross-case analysis, we identified the following five cultural characteristics that, taken together, made the assaults, as well as the organizational members' reluctance to see the assaults as *unreasonable* assaults, practically inevitable:

1. Ideologies that promoted the moral exclusion of out-group members
2. Rites and routines that targeted out-group members for systematic abuse, coordinated the action of the victimizers, and numbed those who participated in the rituals from seeing and understanding the consequences of their actions
3. Language that promoted harmdoing by demeaning and dehumanizing out-group members and by obscuring the abusive behaviors through the use of terminology that made the abuse appear legitimate
4. Rationalizations that prevented those who participated in the moral exclusion and the associated harmdoing from understanding those they violated as victims and themselves as victimizers
5. Codes of silence that were intended to protect the victimizers from being exposed and punished.

The Role of Ideology in Moral Exclusion

All organizations have explicit and implicit ideologies. Organizational ideologies are "relatively coherent set[s] of beliefs that bind people together and explain their world in terms of cause and effect relations" (Beyer, 1981, p. 166). Notably, these beliefs are not necessarily rational or based on fact. Rather, ideologies are typically based on emotionally laden, taken-for-granted, unquestioned beliefs, values, and norms that tell organizational members "what is, how it got that way, and what ought to be" (Trice & Beyer, 1993, p. 2). Organizational ideologies are critical to organizational survival because they help organizational members feel secure in an otherwise overwhelming and uncertain world. In addition, ideologies bind organizational members together, help them identify common goals, assist them in coordinating their efforts toward particular ends, and enable them to feel and express a sense of personal and organizational legitimacy. But organizational ideologies also "identify enemies who supposedly interfere, by their action or by their very existence, with fulfilling the ideology and thus with improving the nation or humanity" (Staub, 1990, p. 54). Embedded within organizational ideologies are strongly held assumptions about what people and beliefs are good and evil, right and wrong, and worthy and unworthy. Although these assumptions may not be explicitly pronounced in written mission, value, or vision statements, they are reflected and reinforced in the organizationally sanctioned day-to-day practices of the organization's members. Not surprisingly, when organizational ideologies identify enemies to the organization's mission, these enemies often face moral exclusion by organizational members. As a consequence of this exclusion, such enemies become devalued, demeaned, and targeted for systematic abuse. Opotow (1990) explains,

> Moral exclusion occurs when individuals or groups are perceived as outside the boundary in which moral values, rules, and considerations of fairness apply. Those who are morally excluded are perceived as nonentities, expendable, or undeserving; consequently, harming them appears acceptable, appropriate, or just. (p. 1)

Although the U.S. Navy and the LAPD are charged with protecting citizens from harm, the Tailhook and King cases provide considerable evidence that women and African American males have been partially excluded from these missions. Indeed, these cases suggest that women and African American men have been targeted for abuse at the hands of people entrusted with their safety because of the cultural groups to which they belong. Supporting this view is the conclusion of the Inspector General's investigation that long-term "animosity toward women" contributed to the Tailhook misconduct and assaults. Media reports, as well as the state and federal trials of the four police officers accused of beating Rodney King, provide ample evidence that the LAPD may have had a history of racism.

Certainly, not all members of the U.S. Navy and LAPD actively participate in or condone ideologies that promote the moral exclusion and abuse of women and African Americans, respectively. Some organizational members do intervene to stop morally exclusive attitudes and abusive behaviors. However, the Tailhook and King cases suggest that the dominant moral logic in the Navy and the LAPD—that is, the set of beliefs, values, and norms that significantly guides many day-to-day attitudes and behaviors regarding acceptable and unacceptable treatment of others and that prevents alternative ways of thinking and acting—is remarkably powerful. After all, the abuses described in the Tailhook and King cases could not have occurred without the active support and tacit collusion of most organizational members.

Such widespread collusion is made possible through the day-to-day enactment of cultural practices that "express, affirm, and communicate" (Trice &
Beyer, 1993, p. 2) an organization's ideology. The cultural practices that were
particularly salient in the Tailhook and King cases include rites and routines,
language, rationalizations, and codes of silence.

The Role of Rites and Routines

Both rites and routines socialize organizational members into understanding
and supporting organizational ideologies. Rites, such as the Tailhook gauntlet,
are "public performances" that are "enacted over and over, on similar occasions
... with well-defined roles for people to perform; they are sufficiently elaborate
and detailed to require preplanning; and they are invariably collective activities
that have audiences" (Trice & Beyer, 1993, p. 110). The Tailhook gauntlet had
been a well-known annual event at the conference for at least 4 years. It was an
orchestrated public spectacle, held in the third-floor hallway of the Las Vegas
Hilton. The men involved adhered to an organized, coordinated set of rules and
procedures, including guidelines for who could and could not be assaulted,
techniques for enticing and forcing women into the gauntlet, methods for
creating and disbanding the gauntlet, and well-known code words for passing
on information relevant to gauntlet participants. As the Tailhook gauntlet illustrates, organizational rites have ceremonial overtones and occur at predictable
times and places.

Routines, on the other hand, are "habituated action patterns" (Weick, 1993,
p. 632) that appear mundane to organizational members and may occur ser-
endipitously. However, once they are initiated, typically in response to a familiar
stimulus, a predictable pattern of behaviors unfold. Based on this criteria, the
King beating is an example of an organizational routine. Because the beating
was so severe, and because the chase that preceded it was an unplanned event,
it may be difficult to think of the beating as the enactment of an organizational
routine. However, the chase and the subsequent beating of a suspect were
familiar scenarios to the officers involved. The LAPD had a history of excessive
use of force by police officers, suggesting that police assaults on suspects were
not uncommon events in the LAPD. Notably, three of the four officers involved
in the King beating previously had been disciplined by the LAPD either for
excessive use of force toward suspects or for falsifying reports after incidents
involving the use of force.

The Tailhook and King cases illustrate the similarities between rites and
routines. Both are taken-for-granted organizational practices that require coor-

dination and interdependence among organizational members. Both are cultural phenomena; that is, the practices persist in the organization even though the individuals involved may change over time (Feldman, 1995; Trice & Beyer, 1993; Weick, 1993). Because rites and routines serve to uphold organizational ideologies that are well-understood by members of the organization, the appropriateness of organizational rites and routines is rarely officially challenged within the organization (Trice & Beyer, 1993, p. 128).

The unquestioned nature of rites and routines is powerfully illustrated in the Tailhook and King cases. In both cases, the abuses that occurred were observed without significant, if any, intervention by many other organizational members. For example, the Inspector General's investigation of the Tailhook abuses and improprieties reported that "several hundred officers were aware of the misconduct and chose to ignore it" (p. 81). Many of the officers noted that they "saw no reason to stop anything that hadn't been stopped before" (p. 87). The report also concluded that hotel security staff "failed to act in the absence of a specific complaint by the victims," were "laughing while watching the assaults," and joined the naval officers "in the hospitality suites [to watch] strip shows and pornographic movies." Only one victim—an intoxicated, underage college student who was stripped naked to the waist as she was passed over the gauntlet and then left dazed and alone at the end of the gauntlet—was helped by security after her assault (p. 78).

Similarly, the videotape of the King beating showed at least 20 other officers watching the beating, many of whom had their arms folded. When King's brother and George Holliday, the bystander who videotaped the beating, reported the beating to the police the next day, both claimed they were met with hostility, denial, and indifference (Levenson, 1994, p. 524).

The Tailhook and King cases illustrate how rites and routines can be problematic, even dangerous. Although they can be a source of meaning making, bonding, and security for some organizational members, they also can be a source of confusion, disenfranchisement, and fear for others. When rites and routines are expressions of ideologies of moral exclusion, organizational members who enact them may become blind to the ways in which they may victimize those targeted for exclusion. This blindness occurs because the habitual enactment of rites and routines encourages organizational members to focus on the "quality of the performance" (Benford & Kurtz, 1987, p. 477) and efficient methods while ignoring consequences, routinizes harmdoing by transforming it into mechanical steps, and diffuses responsibility by fragmenting the implementation of harmful tasks through collective action (Bandura, 1990; Opotow, 1990).

The Role of Language

Organizational language is also central to perpetuating moral exclusion and associated abuses because it is a "key instrument in socialization" (Kress & Hodge, 1979, p. 1). One way it socializes organizational members is to help them "differentiate and structure a social system" (Evered, 1983, pp. 125-127). It does so by enabling organizational members to separate people into distinct groups such as male or female, white or black, insider or outsider, one of us or one of them. Organizational language also enables organizational members to arrange these distinct groups into moral hierarchies in which more valued characteristics—such as competence, trustworthiness, and goodness—are attributed to members of some groups, typically those who dominate upper levels of the organizational hierarchy, than to other groups. Consequently, members of nondominant groups may come to be viewed not only as expendable, but also as deserving of exclusion and punishment. The Tailhook and King cases illustrate how organizational language can fuel violence against out-group members. Investigations of the gauntlet and King beating found that naval and police officers systematically used language that degraded and dehumanized the women and King, respectively. The Inspector General's (1993) report (p. 85) stated that

> one disturbing aspect of the attitudes exhibited at Tailhook 91 was the blatant sexism displayed by some officers toward women. That attitude is best exemplified in a T-shirt worn by several male officers. The back of the shirt read "women are property," while the front read "he man women haters club." . . . The shirts as well as demeaning posters and lapel pins expressed an attitude held by some male attendees that women were at Tailhook to "serve" the male attendees and that women were not welcome within naval aviation. . . . [The] "not in my squadron" [lapel pins were a] parody of the Navy's "not in my Navy" slogan, which is intended to express the Navy's prohibition of sexual harassment against women. Some officers told us that the pins signified contempt for women in naval aviation, and specifically the desire to maintain combat exclusion with respect to women.

Both the state and federal trials found that Los Angeles police officers used demeaning and dehumanizing language toward King, as well as toward suspects and African Americans in general. Officers involved in the beating said that King growled, acted like a "wounded animal," and gave out a "bearlike yell" during the beating. After the incident, when Koon sent his message to the station that he had just had a "big time use of force," the computer operator at the Foothill Division responded, "Oh, well. . . . I'm sure the lizard didn't deserve it. . . . Ha ha." Dehumanizing language toward suspects was not uncommon and appeared to be an officially acceptable organizational practice in the LAPD. During the Simi Valley trial, the prosecution exhibited an LAPD training document that characterized "suspects" as "street lizards." The reference to an African American couple' s domestic dispute as being "something right out of *Gorillas in the Mist*" also suggests that dehumanizing language toward African Americans was within the bounds of normal organizational behavior.

Using language that demeans and dehumanizes out-group members has several consequences. It may make victims seem more deserving of abuse; it may make the abuse itself seem less violent than it actually is; and it may make the victimizers and their actions seem praiseworthy because they are viewed as protecting the organization from the potential harm that out-group members are perceived to inflict on the organization.

The Tailhook and King cases illustrate another way in which language promotes violence against out-group members. Whereas demeaning and dehumanizing language may target individuals for abuse, euphemisms may be used to mask the brutality of organizational sanctioned actions and thus may make violent organizational acts seem less harmful and more legitimate than they really are. The Tailhook aviators, for example, used traditional naval code language during the gauntlet—clear deck, foul deck, wave off—to notify gauntlet participants that attractive or unattractive women were approaching and to prepare for action. The LAPD described the baton strikes, kicks, stomps, and the use of the taser during the beating as "pain compliance maneuvers."

The Role of Rationalizations

Not surprisingly, organizational members involved in taken-for-granted, organizationally sanctioned harmdoing engage in a variety of "elaborate rationales" (Trice & Beyer, 1993, p. 6) that are designed to deny, minimize, and legitimate harmful behaviors (Bandura, 1990; Opotow, 1990). Rationalizations contribute to moral exclusion and the associated abuses toward out-group members because they defend those engaged in the harmdoing from understanding a *problematic reality* (Kress & Hodge, 1979) and their role in creating it. The Tailhook and King cases illustrate several types of rationalizations: blaming the victim; trivializing, distorting, and discrediting any evidence of the harmdoing toward victims (Bandura, 1990); emphasizing the positive characteristics of the victimizers; framing the harmdoing as necessary; and stretching a partial truth.

Blaming the Victim: In both the Tailhook and King cases, the victims of the abuse were characterized as inviting and earning the abuses that they endured. Coughlin, for example, was characterized as a woman who used foul language, as voluntarily having had her legs shaved by male officers at the Tailhook convention (although she denied that she did so), and as being the kind of woman who would welcome the sexual fondling and groping she endured as she was forced through the gauntlet. One aviator who attended Tailhook 1991 said that the women at the conference "weren't women off the church bus for a Sunday picnic" (*Newsweek,* 1992). Richard M. Dunleavy, then the Assistant Chief of Naval Operations, stated that it was his impression at the time that no one was upset, and he believed that the women "would not have gone down the hall if they did not like it" (Office of the Inspector General, 1993, p. 92). Rationalizing that going through the gauntlet was a matter of the women's free choice persisted despite evidence that many women walked naively into the gauntlet or were tricked or forcibly carried into the gauntlet and that many women's appeals to officers to stop went unheeded.

In both the civil and federal trial, King was characterized as a very large, threatening ex-convict who may have been on PCP and was suspected of carrying a weapon during the attack. These characterizations of King persisted despite the fact that officers did not know at the time of the beating that he was an ex-convict, nor did they check to see if he was indeed carrying a weapon or ask that he be tested for PCP after the beating.

Trivialization and Distortion of Consequences to Victims: In both cases, the victims' distress and injuries were minimized. For example, one officer involved in the Tailhook gauntlet was quoted as saying during the Inspector General's investigation, "If I thought that going around and goosing a few girls on the breast was going to cause a national incident, do you think I would have done that?" (Inspector General's Report, p. 88). The defense at the LAPD officers' Simi Valley trial tried to show that King's injuries were less serious than those described in the medical examiner's report and further claimed that King's facial injuries were a result of a fall on the pavement rather than a consequence of direct blows from Powell's baton. Also during the Simi Valley trial, one officer claimed that he believed that King had been on PCP at the time of the beating and thus was "impervious to pain." In response to this comment, the prosecutor asked the officer, "Would you consider him oblivious to pain in view of the fact that he appears [in the video] to be moving away from the person who is delivering the blows?" The officer replied, "Yes, sir" (People of the State, 1991, p. 7941).

Emphasizing Positive Characteristics of the Victimizers: Tolerance of violence toward out-group members depends not only on demeaning and blaming the victims, but also on elevating the status of the victimizers so that their status appears incongruous with abusive and illegal acts. The naval officers were characterized as "returning heroes" from Desert Storm. The police officers were characterized as men who were putting their lives on the line while protecting citizens from harm.

When victimizers who are attributed elevated status are found actually to have engaged in harmdoing, their actions are often seen as understandable or forgivable, if not altogether appropriate. For example, the Inspector General's investigation suggested that the recent victory in Desert Storm may have contributed to the naval officers' rowdy behavior at the convention and may have made their behaviors appear more forgivable in light of their status as returning heroes as well as the pressures they recently had endured in combat. In the King case, the defense claimed that any excessive force used during the King beating was a consequence of understandable fear rather than any pleasure the officers may have taken in harming King. The defense also characterized the behavior of Briseno, the officer who stepped on King's neck after he lay motionless for approximately 10 seconds, as compassionate, arguing that he stepped on King's neck only to prevent King from making moves that might trigger more abuse from the other officers.

Stretching a Partial Truth: Certainly some of the explanations offered by the naval and police officers were partially true. Some of the women who went through the gauntlet, in fact, did participate willingly and with full knowledge of the gauntlet activities. Indeed, some women were said to have gone through the gauntlet twice. However, the Tailhook aviators projected the enjoyment of the women who willingly participated in the gauntlet as reflective of all women—including those who were forced down the gauntlet against their will, who protested, who screamed for help, and who were visibly shaken by the experience—and thus did not stop the fondling and groping even when the women pleaded them to stop. Similarly, it is true that officers in the King case regularly put their lives on the line and are undoubtedly fearful when they face new and potentially dangerous situations. Yet, the jury in the federal case concluded that at least two of the officers engaged in abusive behaviors that could not be reasonably justified by the nature of their job or by the particular characteristics of their confrontation with King.

Framing the Harmdoing as Necessary: Another form of rationalization expressed was that the attitudes that led to the abuses are necessary for fulfilling the Navy's and LAPD's mission. This logic implies that if these demeaning attitudes and abusive behaviors did not exist, naval and police officers would be less able to protect citizens from harm. For example, some Pentagon officials were quoted in the press as saying that "curbing Navy pilots' sexual feistiness [would] remove the edge [naval aviators] need for combat" (*Time,* July 1992). A police officer speaking in support of the LAPD was quoted as stating, "You can take the aggression out of a stud and see what happens. . . . We were a bull. We feel we've been castrated" ("Special Report," *Newsweek,* May 1992).

Consequences of Rationalizations: Rationalizations used by organizational members have several problematic consequences. Rationalizations such as those described above represent a form of "systematic distortion" (Kress & Hodge, 1979) that shape the perceptions and actions of organizational members. Trivialization and distortion prevent organizational members from seeing the gravity of the harmdoing that has occurred and consequently prevent organizational members from taking actions to prevent similar harmdoing in the future. Blaming the victim and elevating victimizers to heroic status makes it difficult for those who engage in harmdoing to see the abused as victims and the abusers as victimizers. Viewing harmdoing as unavoidable, necessary, or compassionate makes it unlikely that organizational members will seek out alternative, less harmful, courses of action. And stretching a partial truth makes it difficult for organizational members to see where reason ends and malevolence begins.

The Role of Codes of Silence

Trivino and Victor (1992, p. 39) argue that many organizations have "powerful norms against tattling," so it is not surprising that officers invoked codes of silence during the Tailhook and King investigations. The Inspector General's (1993) Tailhook report concluded that officers engaged in "collective stonewalling" (p. 22) during the investigation. This stonewalling included "limit[ing] responses so as to reveal only minimal information" (p. 21), and "deliberately lying. . . . to mislead our investigators in an effort to protect themselves or their fellow officers" (p. 81). The LAPD has had a code of silence since the 1950s (People of the State, 1991, p. 11032). During the investigation of the King beating, many officers responded to questions about the beating with statements such as "I didn't see it" and "I was looking the other way when it happened."

Such codes of silence serve several useful purposes. They bond members together by testing the loyalty and trustworthiness of colleagues. As one military employee commented to the press, "the reputation that's been created is that Navy pilots may be liars and sex offenders, but at least they don't squeal on each other" (*Washington Post,* May 1992). Codes of silence give those who engage in mistakes and misconduct time to rectify their errors on their own, without the stigma and potential penalties associated with organizational interventions. Yet, as the Tailhook and King cases illustrate, codes of silence also deter fact finding, increase the possibility that victims' accounts will be unsubstantiated, protect victimizers from punishment, and prevent organizational members from learning valuable lessons from the experience. Most important, codes of silence often ensure that similar assaults will continue to occur in the future.

Cultures of Exclusion

The above analysis frames the abuses that occurred in the Tailhook and King cases as a predictable outcome of organizational cultures that rigorously promote ideologies of moral exclusion through a variety of cultural practices. It is tempting to take a simpler view that assumes that the victimizers were a few bad apples among otherwise upstanding organizational citizens. But such a perspective does not help us understand why the acts of abuse blatantly were conducted in full view of the public, why so many organizational members stood by without intervening, why organizational leaders promoted the abuse through active support or lack of intervention, and why so many organizational members were surprised at the strong reaction the violence against the women and King evoked when exposed by the media.

A cultural perspective suggests that the attitudes and behaviors displayed by the officers in the Tailhook and King cases may have been acceptable characteristics of upstanding organizational citizens in the Navy and LAPD. A cultural perspective also suggests that the socialization processes involved in becoming an upstanding organizational citizen may have provided the naval and police officers with the inspiration and institutional support (e.g., lack of peer or leadership intervention) to engage in the harmdoing.

The five cultural characteristics that we focused on in this chapter—ideologies of moral exclusion, rites and routines, language, rationalizations, and codes of silence—were particularly powerful in the Tailhook and King cases because, taken together, they simultaneously promoted and concealed the harmdoing that occurred. Notably, the harmdoing was concealed not in the sense that it was done in private, but in the sense that the harmdoing was not seen by organizational members as excessively abusive, inappropriate, or illegal.

LESSONS FOR ALL ORGANIZATIONS

Some might argue that the Tailhook and King cases are extreme cases of sexism and racism in organizations. However, we agree with Starbuck, Greve, and Hedberg (1978), who point out that "organizations that encounter crises may be marginally extreme. . . . however these organizations are marginally extreme at most. Many organizations exhibit these characteristics, most organizations possess some disadvantageous characteristics, and all organizations make mistakes" (p. 16). Therefore, we believe that the Tailhook and King cases provide cautionary tales for all organizations.

These cases provide two important generalizable lessons. First, managing the multicultural organization means stopping systematic harmdoing toward outgroup members. This harmdoing takes a variety of forms, from the physical abuse that occurred in the Tailhook and King cases to less striking forms of mistreatment. For example, bank employees may limit the amount of money they loan to women or people of color, restaurant workers such as those at the Denny's restaurant chain may chose to provide poor service to African Americans, and academics may teach and conduct their research as though multiculturalism in our society is insignificant. Certainly, these practices do not represent the same kind or degree of abuse as that which occurred in the Tailhook and King incidences. However, these practices are similar to the extent that they are based on ideologies of moral exclusion that deem some members of society more deserving and noteworthy than others, serve to marginalize members of nondominant groups, teach members of nondominant groups to "know their place" as organizational outsiders, and subtly yet powerfully remind members of dominant groups that it is their role to help keep members of nondominant groups in their place as outsiders.

One of the most troubling aspects of the Tailhook and King cases is that organizational members and leaders were unable to see the abuse *as* abuse. Thus, our second lesson for all organizations is that managing the multicultural organization means paying attention to how taken-for-granted organizational ideologies and cultural practices promote the moral exclusion and harmdoing toward members of particular cultural groups in ways that make such exclusion and harmdoing imperceptible to organizational members.

To this end, organizational leaders and members can ask themselves a number of questions, including: Who are the "enemies" explicitly stated or implied in the organization's ideology? How can the core technology of the organization (e.g., financial services, food services, teaching and research) be misused in ways that are harmful to out-group members? What values and belief systems are expressed in organizational rites, rituals, and routines? Who is and who is not included in important organizational rites, rituals, and routines, and what roles do various organizational members play in these cultural practices? Does language used in the organization degrade or dehumanize members of out-groups? Does language used in the organization obscure the negative impact behaviors may have on out-group members? Are rationalizations used that may prevent organizational members from seeing or taking responsibility for the negative consequences of their actions? Are there codes of silence within the organization and, if so, why do they exist and with what consequences? What do organizational leaders do to promote attitudes of moral exclusion and associated abuses? For example, do organizational leaders draw attention to morally exclusive language and discourage its use? Do organizational leaders interpret acts of harmdoing as idiosyncratic to individuals (e.g., the "bad apple" interpretation) rather than as potentially symptomatic of cultural problems? Finally, organizational leaders could ask themselves what organizational attitudes and behaviors might cause embarrassment and harm to the reputation of the organization if exposed by the media for the public to scrutinize.

Organizational leaders and members who engage in the soul searching required to answer these questions would reap at least two rewards. First, they would identify the ways in which their organizations promote moral exclusion and associated abuses and thus be able to stop such attitudes and behaviors. Second, and equally important, they would find in their answers to these questions opportunities to build organizational cultures that foster cohesion and support rather than animosity and harmdoing.

REFERENCES

Bandura, A. (1990). Selective activation and disengagement of moral control. *Journal of Social Issues, 46*(1), 27-46.

Benford, R. D., & Kurtz, L. R. (1987). Performing the nuclear ceremony: The arms race as ritual. *Journal of Applied Behavioral Science, 23*(4), 463-482.

Beyer, J. (1981). Ideologies, values, and decision making in organizations. In the *Handbook of organizational design: Vol. 2. Remodeling organizations and their environments* (pp. 166-202). London: Oxford University Press.

Efron, S. (1992, July 19). Tailhook scandal rocks El Toro: Military sexual harassment investigation divides Marine base. *Los Angeles Times,* p. 3.

Evered, R. (1983). The language of organizations: The case of the Navy. In S. B. Bacharach (Ed.), *Monographs in organizational behavior and industrial relations* (Vol. 1, pp. 125-143). Greenwich, CT: JAI Press.

Feldman, M. (1995). *Organizational routines as practice.* Unpublished manuscript.

Healy, M. (1992, September 16). Pentagon's Tailhook report expected to detail obstruction, cover-up scandal. *Los Angeles Times,* p. 14.

Hearn, J. (1994). The organization(s) of violence: Men, gender relations, organizations, and violence. *Human Relations, 47*(6), 731-754.

Kress, G., & Hodge, R. (1979). *Language as ideology.* London: Routledge & Kegan Paul.

Lancaster, J. (1992a, May 1). Navy harassment probe stymied: Aviators refuse to help identify culprits at Tailhook party. *Washington Post,* p. A1.

Lancaster, J. (1992b, September 25). Pentagon blasts Tailhook inquiry: Navy leadership faulted in scandal. *Washington Post,* p. A1.

Lancaster, J. (1992c, May 17). The sex life of the Navy: After the Tailhook scandal, an attempt to reform. *Washington Post,* p. C1.

Levenson, L. (1994). The future of state and federal civil rights prosecutions: The lessons of the Rodney King trial. *UCLA Law Review, 509,* 516-523.

The Navy at its brassiest. (1992, October 1). *New York Times,* p. A24.

Office of the Inspector General (Department of Defense). (1993). *The Tailhook report.* New York: St. Martin's.

Opotow, S. (1990). Moral exclusion and injustice: An introduction. *Journal of Social Issues, 46*(1), 1-20.

Parks, W. H. (1994). Tailhook: What happened, why, and what's to be learned. Proceedings. September: 89-103.

The People of the State of California, Plaintiff, vs. Laurence Powell, Timothy E. Wind, Theodore Brisino, and Stacey Koon, Defendants. (1991). Superior Court of the State of California for the County of Ventura. Reporter's Daily Transcript of Proceedings of the Simi Valley Trial.

Reza, H. G. (1992, July 28). Tailhook workshop sets tone, officers say. *Los Angeles Times,* p. 1.

Ricks, T. (1992, September 25). Pentagon's report on Tailhook affair terms Navy unable to investigate itself. *Wall Street Journal,* p. A12.

Salholz, E. (1992, August 10). Deepending shame. *Newsweek,* pp. 30-36.

Schmitt, E. (1992, July 18). Harassment questions kill two admirals' promotions. *New York Times,* p. 1.

A shocked nation wonders what went wrong and how to mend it. (1992, May 11). *Time,* pp. 18-41.

Shrivastava, P. (1987). *Bhopal: Anatomy of a crisis.* Cambridge, MA: Ballinger.

Smolowe, J. (1992, July 13). An officer, not a gentleman. *Time,* p. 36.

Special Report. America on Trial: Fire and fury. (1992, May 11). *Newsweek,* pp. 26-54.

Starbuck, W. H., Greve, A., & Hedberg, B. (1978). Responding to crises: Theory and the experience of European business. In C. F. Smart & W. T. Stanbury (Eds.), *Studies in crisis management* (pp. 111-137). Toronto: Butterworth.

Staub, E. (1990). Moral exclusion, personal goal theory, and extreme destructiveness. *Journal of Social Issues, 46*(1), 46-64.

Tailhook: Throwing down the gauntlet. (1992, October 5). *Newsweek,* p. 58.

Trice, H., & Beyer, J. (1993). *The cultures of work organizations.* Englewood Cliffs, NJ: Prentice Hall.

Trivino, L., & Victor, B. (1992). Peer reporting of unethical behavior: A social context perspective. *Academy of Management Journal, 35*(1), 38-64.

Weick, K. (1994). The collapse of sensemaking in organizations: The Man Gulch disaster. *Administrative Science Quarterly, 38,* 628-652.

12

The Colonizing Consciousness and Representations of the Other

A Postcolonial Critique of the Discourse of Oil

ANSHUMAN PRASAD

The conquest of the earth, which mostly means the taking it away from those who have a different complexion or slightly flatter noses than ourselves, is not a pretty thing when you look into it too much. What redeems it is the idea only. An idea at the back of it; not a sentimental pretence but an idea; and an unselfish belief in the idea—something you can set up, and bow down before, and offer a sacrifice to. . . .

Joseph Conrad, Heart of Darkness

Language is the perfect instrument of empire.

Bishop of Avila to Queen Isabella of Castille, 1492, quoted in Peter Hulme,
Colonial Encounters

AUTHOR'S NOTE: An earlier version of this chapter was presented at the 13th International Meetings of the Standing Conference on Organizational Symbolism (SCOS), Turku, Finland, June-July, 1995.

As successive chapters in this book have continually noted, recent years in North America have witnessed the emergence and explosive growth of a large and significant diversity *industry,* comprising management practitioners, consultants, training professionals, workshop facilitators, business educators and researchers, and so on (Allen, 1991; Copeland, 1988a, 1988b; Cox, 1991, 1993; Cox & Blake, 1991; Fernandez, 1991; Jackson, 1992; Rossett & Bickham, 1994; Thomas, 1990, 1991). For the most part, this industry brims with optimistic homilies and prognostications about the implications, the consequences, and the future of workplace diversity, offering a wide array of tools, techniques, and methods (ranging from videos, manuals, and workshops to diversity audits and sensitivity seminars) for the successful management of diversity.[1]

Notwithstanding the feeling of euphoria that seems to saturate the diversity industry, however, as several of the contributions appearing in this volume suggest, critical analysts of the field remain concerned that the imposing edifice of this industry may well be based upon somewhat inadequate conceptual foundations. The present chapter represents an attempt to strengthen the theoretical bases of diversity research and practice—and, in the process, to enhance our own understanding of the dilemmas of workplace diversity—by means of drawing upon some of the insights emerging from postcolonial theory (or postcolonialism),[2] a new and increasingly important scholarly approach for analyzing the cultural dynamics of control and resistance in the period of colonialism and its aftermath (Ashcroft, Griffiths, & Tiffin, 1995; Barker, Hulme, Iversen, & Loxley, 1985; Bhabha, 1994; Guha & Spivak, 1988; Nandy, 1983, 1987; Prakash, 1995; Said, 1979, 1993; Spivak, 1990; Williams & Chrisman, 1994b).

As this chapter's reliance upon postcolonialism may suggest, the chapter seeks to theorize workplace diversity within the wider context of the (continuing?) history and experience of Euro-American imperialism and colonialism.[3] The use of colonialism/imperialism as a broad conceptual matrix for understanding workplace diversity is somewhat new and unusual in management research and practice. Even a brief look at the diversity literature is sufficient to suggest that, for the most part, diversity scholars and practitioners have tended to ignore colonialism as a sense-making framework. This chapter, however, submits that the colonial experience can provide a useful window for analyzing diversity and for developing a more complete understanding of the multiplicity of issues that seem to surround this complex phenomenon.

There are at least three reasons that render postcolonial theory a worthwhile perspective for developing a deeper understanding of workplace diversity. First, immigrants and people of color happen to provide one of the principal dimensions of the diversity phenomenon. In historical terms, however, it is important to remember that the ancestors and forebears of the same groups (who have now come to be identified in North America and parts of Europe as "immigrants" or as "people of color") also served as the objects or targets of Euro-American conquest, expansion, and colonization. The colonial encounter of the past several centuries, hence, was one of the most decisive and meaningful historical processes that influenced and shaped the West's perceptions of the non-West, that is, of the West's Others (Said, 1979, 1993). Moreover, as Edward Said's meticulous scholarship suggests, even today, the West[4] continues to view immigrants, people of color, and similar other members of the non-West through an imperial lens that was originally crafted during the colonial era. Postcolonial theory, therefore, can be a valuable perspective for understanding some of the complexities attending cultural and racial dynamics in contemporary Western organizations.

Second, for the West, the colonial experience holds some significant implications for gender relations and sexuality. As postcolonial scholars such as Nandy (1983) have noted, one of the most unfortunate by-products of colonialism was the production, reification, and privileging of a culture of aggressive hypermasculinity in the West—a culture that, among other things, devalued the role and importance of women and denigrated femininity. Postcolonial theory, therefore, can be helpful in shedding some extra light on the contentious diversity-related issues that surround sexuality and gender relations at the workplace. Finally, the postcolonial perspective is valuable also for its important insights into the dynamics of social and cultural marginality. As postcolonial theorists have frequently noted, at the paradigmatic level, the discourse[5] of colonization is structured around the exchanges taking place between the metropolitan "center" and the provincial "periphery." Postcolonial inquiry, accordingly, has devoted considerable scholarly effort toward understanding the center-periphery discourse. As a result, postcolonial theory can be a valuable aid for analyzing dominant group-marginal group dynamics. The next section of the chapter provides a brief overview of postcolonial theory.

POSTCOLONIAL THEORY: A BRIEF OVERVIEW

The twin processes of colonial conquest and decolonization represent a massive upheaval of truly global proportions, which touched and profoundly affected most of the world. To provide just one index of the scope of colonialism, by the early decades of the present century—when the infamous "Age of Empires" was at its zenith—Europe's colonies covered almost 85% of the Earth's surface (Headrick, 1981; Said, 1979). Given this magnitude of the colonial encounter, it is not surprising that colonialism has long served as a major object of scholarly research and inquiry. Such being the case, it may be useful and worthwhile to point out that postcolonial theory differs from earlier theorizations of imperialism and colonialism in some important respects.

Briefly stated, whereas early research on colonialism mostly concentrated upon "brute" aspects and sought to analyze the political, economic, and military impact of Western colonization, the primary focus of postcolonial theory is upon the more subtle dimensions of imperialism spanning culture, ideology, and discourse (Dirks, 1992; Nandy, 1983; Niranjana, 1992; Prakash, 1995; Said, 1979, 1993; Tiffin & Lawson, 1994). One of the major objectives of such focus upon the subtle aspects of colonialism is to understand the complex web of processes by means of which the colonial encounter worked to produce the subjectivities[6] of the colonizers and the colonized. In this process of focusing upon the subtle dimensions of colonialism, it is not as if postcolonial theory completely disregards or overlooks the political, the economic, and the military. Rather, instead of totally neglecting to consider the brute features of colonialism, postcolonial theory textualizes those features and aims to understand the role and effect of such features in the constitution of colonizer/colonized subjectivities. Postcolonialism, hence, may be seen as providing a more sophisticated, nuanced, and complex reading of imperialism, and as attempting to analyze those cultural and ideological aspects of colonialism that are sometimes said to have survived the formal end of the colonial era itself (Nandy, 1983; Tiffin & Lawson, 1994).[7]

Postcolonial theory came into prominence with Said's (1979) authoritative study, *Orientalism.* In this highly influential work, Said (1979) proffers an analysis[8] of the structures of the Western discourse (both scholarly as well as popular) on the Middle East and Islam, a discourse that he labels *Orientalism.* In brief, according to Said (1979), the discourse of Orientalism posited that the Occident and the Orient represented ontologically distinct and opposite entities and that the "essence" of the Orient consisted of such elements as "despotism, ... splendor, cruelty, sensuality" (p. 4), untruthfulness, lack of logic, absence of energy and initiative, intrigue, cunning, unkindness, lethargy, and suspicion (p. 38-39), as well as eccentricity, backwardness, indifference, feminine penetrability, supine malleability, and so on (p. 206). Thus, with the assistance of these and similar other tropes, the discourse of Orientalism constructed an image of the Orient around the themes of "decline, degradation, and decadence" (Dirks,

1992, p. 9), portraying the Orient as being fit *(in an ontological sense)* only for conquest, subjugation, and colonization.

Following the lead given by Said (1979), postcolonialism has gone through a period of intense and explosive growth, and any comprehensive overview of postcolonial research and inquiry is clearly beyond the scope of the present chapter. Nevertheless, it may still be useful to provide a brief catalog of some of the major tendencies exhibited by postcolonial theoretic scholarship. One important direction taken by postcolonial inquiry, for instance, broadly emulates Said's (1979) approach, seeking to provide in-depth analyses of the language and rhetoric of imperialism (e.g., Brantlinger, 1988; Spurr, 1993; Suleri, 1992). Another subfield of postcolonial scholarship (represented by Subaltern Group, the influential collective of South Asian historians) regards the old, colonialist accounts of history as instruments of domination and seeks to reinterpret the past with a view to recovering an insurrectionary history of the dominated groups (e.g., Guha, 1983; Guha & Spivak, 1988). On the other hand, the proponents of the *hybridization* thesis (e.g., Bhabha, 1985, 1994) work toward unveiling the record of the hybrid construction of *both* the West and the non-West, and another important group of scholars (e.g., Cesaire, 1972; Nandy, 1983, 1987) seeks to analyze the negative psychological and cultural consequences of colonialism *not only* for the non-West, but for the West as well. Simultaneously, other groups of postcolonial theorists can be seen to be occupied in such overlapping scholarly programs as (a) investigating the complicity of past and present Western scholarship with imperialism and the imperial mind-set (e.g., Asad, 1973; Bishop, 1990; Chakrabarty, 1992), (b) critiquing and problematizing the idea of the nation-state (Chatterjee, 1986, 1993; Nandy, 1992), and (c) deconstructing the mythic notion of (economic) development (Sachs, 1992).

Taken as a whole, the combined analytics of the various streams of postcolonial theory provide some important insights into the overall nature of the discourse of colonization. To begin with, according to postcolonial scholars, the discourse of colonization may be said to be fundamentally premised upon the constructed availability of an ontological Other, an Other that serves as the focal point for distilling and concentrating the *opposites* of all those privileged moral, ethical, and aesthetic attributes that have gradually accreted to constitute the very core of the colonizer's own self-image. Such being the case, the discourse of colonization needs to be seen as having worked simultaneously to produce (and naturalize) the subjectivities of both the colonizer and the colonized. Hence, for instance, Said's (1979) important observation that the discourse of "the Orient has helped to *define* [italics added] Europe (or the West) as . . . [the Orient's] contrasting image, idea, personality, experience" (pp. 1-2).

The discourse of colonialism conceived of the West's non-Western Other as the epistemological and ontological opposite of the West and saw the West as "superior" and the non-West as "inferior." The construction of the West/non-West dichotomy was fleshed out and completed by means of the production and institutionalization of an elaborate series of hierarchical binary polarities (Dirks, 1992; Nandy, 1983; Prakash, 1995). Table 12.1 provides a brief list of such binaries.

Along with the above, however, colonial discourse also evinced a great deal of ambivalence toward the "inferior" non-West, which gradually came to serve as the object of Western colonization. For instance, even though it was clearly the goal of this discourse to define the non-West as inferior and undesirable, the non-West was also regarded by this discourse as a highly desirable object for Western possession. Similarly, although the non-West was seen as "weak and effeminate," it was also viewed as a grave threat that represented "the unpleasant likelihood of a sudden eruption that would destroy . . . [the Western] world" (Said, 1979, p. 251). Thus, the discourse of colonization saw the non-West as simultaneously being undesirable and desirable, weak and potentially lethally explosive, something to be possessed and something to be feared, something needing to be controlled and something that never would (or could) be completely controlled (Said, 1979, 1993; Spurr, 1993). Against this backdrop of colonialism and postcolonial theory, the next section of the chapter will venture into the world of the American and Western European petroleum industry with a view to exploring, unraveling, unveiling, documenting, and theorizing the persistent imprint of the colonizing consciousness in the petroleum sector's representations of the Other.

THE COLONIZING CONSCIOUSNESS
AND THE DISCOURSE OF OIL

This chapter's interest in the oil industry (and in the discourse of oil)[9] springs from the privileged position occupied by oil in contemporary Western civilization. Oil, as the title of Tugendhat and Hamilton's (1975) remarkable book declares, is "the world's biggest business" (see also, Yergin, 1991, p. 13). Quite apart from sheer size, moreover, oil (as the preeminent source of energy and as an important raw material for such diverse products as adhesives, animal feeds, dyestuffs, explosives, fertilizers, paints, pesticides, plastics, synthetic fibers, etc.) so thoroughly saturates people's everyday lives in the West that, following Yergin (1991, p. 14), contemporary Western society may well be best understood as a Hydrocarbon Society. According to Yergin (p. 15) and several others, for

TABLE 12.1 The Hierarchical System of Colonialist Binaries

West	*Non-West*
Active	Passive
Center	Margin/periphery
Civilized	Primitive/savage
Colonizer	Colonized
Developed	Backward/undeveloped/ underdeveloped/developing
Fullness/plenitude/completeness	Lack/inadequacy/incompleteness
Historical (people with history)	Ahistorical (people without history)
The liberated	The savable
Masculine	Feminine/effeminate
Modern	Archaic
Nation	Tribe
Occidental	Oriental
Scientific	Superstitious
Secular	Nonsecular
Subject	Object
Superior	Inferior
The vanguard	The led
White	Black/brown/yellow

the West, the 20th century is truly "the century of oil." Furthermore, for the United States in particular, oil is part and parcel of the myths and dreams that make up "the life of the mind in America," being inextricably linked with the legends and the sagas of the frontier, the wildcatter, and the pioneer and with rags to riches tales. Symbolically and materially, therefore, petroleum occupies a position of great eminence in the Western life world, with the result that the discourse of oil is rightfully deserving of serious scholarly attention. Before turning toward the discourse of oil, however, some basic familiarity with the broad contours of the history of the Western oil industry may be useful.

The history of the present-day Western oil industry begins roughly around the middle of the last century (Al-Chalabi, 1980; Blair, 1976; Hamilton, 1986; Karlsson, 1986; Prasad, 1994; Roncaglia, 1985; Sampson, 1975; Terzian, 1985; Tugwell, 1988; Turner, 1978; Vallenilla, 1975; Yergin, 1991). In the United States, the fledgling industry soon came under the control of John D. Rockefeller's Standard Oil Company, which controlled as much as 90% of the industry by the 1880s (Prasad, 1994). During the early years of the present century, however, Standard Oil witnessed the rise of some important domestic competition in the shape of Gulf Oil Company[10] and the Texas Company (today's Texaco). At the global level, after an initial period characterized by both competition and collusion, control over the petroleum sector came to be wielded first by the "Big Three" (namely, Standard Oil of New Jersey,[11] Royal Dutch/Shell, and British Petroleum), and later by the Seven Sisters, the well-organized international cartel of seven Euro-American oil companies.[12] To give just a brief hint of the extent of the Seven Sisters' domination of the international petroleum system, in 1950, these seven companies controlled virtually the entire crude oil production of the Middle East, Venezuela, and Indonesia (the three major oil producing regions outside the United States and the then-U.S.S.R.) and accounted for about 85% of the total crude oil production outside North America and the Socialist countries. Similar levels of global control were wielded by the Sisters in other oil industry segments (e.g., refining, transportation etc.) as well.

Even a brief look at the history of oil is sufficient to reveal that the international dominance of the Seven Sisters was simply one of the plum fruits of colonialism. That is to say, the work involved in creating a Euro-American hegemony in the international petroleum system had gone hand in hand with the projection, establishment, and consolidation of European and American political and military power over the rest of the world during the colonial era. It was inevitable, therefore, that the political end of Western colonialism would be followed by an intense struggle (waged by those who had been colonized) aimed at changing the asymmetries of power that had so far characterized the political economy of international oil. In a nutshell, this is exactly what took place by means of the OPEC offensive of the 1960s and the 1970s.[13]

With the preceding introduction to the historical context, we now turn our attention toward examining the representation of Otherness in the discourse of oil. For this purpose, the present chapter isolates two key discursive events from the recent history of the Western petroleum sector and attempts to analyze and understand the two events from the perspective of postcolonial theory. In view of the fact that the Middle East has been at the very heart of Western oil imperialism for close to a century, we begin, appropriately enough, with the labeling (by the Seven Sisters) of the Saudi Arabian sheikh, Abdullah Tariki, as the *Red* Sheikh.

The Red Sheikh

Sheikh Abdullah Tariki of Saudi Arabia, who left an indelible imprint on the international political economy of oil and who is commonly regarded as one of the two cofounders of the Organization of the Petroleum Exporting Countries (OPEC),[14] was a pan-Arab nationalist and an ardent admirer of Egypt's charismatic leader, Gamal Abdel Nasser (Terzian, 1985; Yergin, 1991). Tariki's importance in the history of oil stems from the decisive role that he played in opposing oil imperialism.

A trained geologist, Tariki first rose to prominence in 1948, when he became the Director of the Oil Affairs Supervisory Bureau in the Ministry of Finance in Saudi Arabia. He came to head the Saudi Directorate of Oil and Mining Affairs in 1955 and was appointed the Oil Minister of Saudi Arabia in 1960, the same year in which OPEC was founded. An outspoken critic of (oil) imperialism, Tariki strongly denounced the activities and policies of the Seven Sisters on more than one occasion. He also insisted on invoking the Saudi rights to two directorships (which had never been used by Saudi Arabia in the past) on Aramco[15] and was himself appointed an Aramco director in 1959. As a result of his activism, he was promptly dubbed by the Seven Sisters as the Red Sheikh. From the perspective of postcolonial theory, this representation of Sheikh Tariki needs to be viewed as an important discursive event in the history and the "text" of imperial oil. The remainder of this section of the chapter will aim to briefly understand what such an act of naming or labeling may reveal about the colonizing consciousness itself.

To begin with, in a post-World War II hermeneutic context overwhelmingly defined by frenzied anti-communism in America and (parts of) Western Europe, the Seven Sisters' use of the Red (i.e., communist/socialist) label for pigeonholing and categorizing Sheikh Tariki offers a revealing glimpse into Western colonialism's frequently commented-upon tendency to quickly and hastily define the Other as embodying a grave danger that supposedly imperils the very existence of Western civilization (see, e.g., Said, 1979, 1993; Spurr, 1993). In addition, however, the use of the specific descriptor Red seems to tell us something more about the colonizing consciousness as it manifested itself through the Seven Sisters.

It can be rightfully argued, for instance, that the use of this particular label (Red) may be viewed as an index of the Seven Sisters' need to see Sheikh Tariki as an element (or a component) of a larger, anti-Western conspiracy—that is, as something much more sinister and diabolical than an isolated, stand-alone danger, howsoever menacing or threatening. In other words, by using the Red label, the Seven Sisters may have been attempting to impute far greater potential danger to Sheikh Tariki (because now he was represented as being a part of a large, powerful, and well-organized, communist conspiracy) than would have been the case if he were to be considered just another (non-Red) threat, enemy, or opposition. This, however, may not be all. Given the highly negative under-standing that people generally have of words such as conspiracy, conspirators, and so forth (which carry not-so-subtle hints of intrigue, deviousness, betrayal, back stabbing, and double crossing), in calling the sheikh Red, the Seven Sisters may also be seen as suggesting that the sheikh was dishonorable and treacherous enough to be a part of something as evil and immoral as a conspiracy. Hence, in labeling the sheikh Red, colonizing oil may be said to be claiming not only that the sheikh was an enemy of the West, but also that the sheikh was an evil and ethically debased enemy, undeserving of the courtesies and considerations that one normally extended to those enemies or opponents who were honorable and morally upright.[16]

However, the use of the Red label for the Saudi sheikh also points to a crucial paradox, tension, or ambivalence that invests colonialism's engagement with its Others. For, if on the one hand, the Red label is suggestive of colonialism's tendency to represent the colonized as ominous and threatening, and/or to demonize and vilify the Other, on the other hand, the same label is also indicative of colonialism's intense desire to seek to reduce the menace of the *difference* of Otherness by means of constituting the colonized (i.e., the Other) in the form of images that are already familiar to the colonizing consciousness. By the middle of this century, we need to recall, the discourse of revolutionary communism (the Red menace) had been a prominent part of Western history and imagination for more than 100 years,[17] with the result that communism, while undoubtedly being regarded as a grave generalized threat, nevertheless represented (for the West) something familiar and manageable, something which the West was capable of successfully containing and dealing with. Somewhat paradoxically, therefore, even as the label of the Red Sheikh underscored the material and moral graveness of the threat embodied in the Other, simultaneously, by means of gesturing toward the familiar and the already known, the selfsame label also made an attempt to redefine the different as not-so-different, and the new as not-so-new, and thus, to contain and reduce the Otherness of the colonized to more manageable proportions.

Thus, in part, the act of labeling Sheikh Abdullah Tariki as the Red Sheikh may be seen as a somewhat desperate effort on colonialism's part to seek to preserve and maintain an earlier, simpler, and more familiar, (Western) so-ciocultural schema for sense making, which was being subjected to increas-ing pressure and distortion as it confronted other, rival, cultural schemata that were unavoidably brought to the colonizers' consciousness during the course of colonialism's extended encounter with its Others. However, in labeling the sheikh Red, the colonizing consciousness can also be said to be attempting to achieve more than a simple containment of differences embodied in, and exhibited by, the colonized.

Specifically, one may argue that, buried in the act of naming Sheikh Tariki the Red Sheikh, was an implicit claim that it was *only* the 'red devil' that opposed the West's imperial project, and that, actively or passively, the rest of the world supported, valued, and cherished the colonialist enterprise of "bringing light and civilization" to the dark corners of the Earth.[18] In other words, we could say that in declaring the Saudi sheikh to be Red, (oil) imperialism may also be said to have been making the claim that the whole world, *except* the evil communists, was deeply appreciative (or welcomingly accepting) of the West's colonial rule and domination as a beacon of Hope, Prosperity, and Progress.

Carefully analyzed, the claim (which is implicitly embedded in the Red Sheikh label) that only reds oppose the West, offers us an important insight into the colonizing consciousness. We need to begin by noting that, in the West, communism has long been regarded as the devil's own handmaiden and as a symbol of all that is evil and immoral in this world. In such a context (where communism is synonymous with evil), the claim that it is *only* the Red devil that opposes the imperial West has the effect of reflexively creating an image of colonialism in the form of a contrasting figure to the evil that is communism. That is to say, the claim that only evil communism opposes Western imperialism works to produce a self-representation of Western colonialism as the repository of universal good. As noted by countless postcolonial scholars, such a self-representation of colonialism is crucial for the success of the colonialist enterprise.

Finally, in labeling Sheikh Tariki the Red Sheikh, colonialism also allows us a glimpse into its own conceptualization of global history. As postcolonial scholarship has frequently noted (see, e.g., Chakrabarty, 1992), the Hegelian notion of teleological history (e.g., Hegel, 1900)—which came to be reified and naturalized in the Western consciousness during the period of modernity— conceives of the West as the vanguard of human history and imagines the rest of the world to be by fate ordained to follow into the West's footsteps.[19] Concomitantly, this view of human history believes also in the universal applicability and validity of Western historiographical categories such as capital, feudal, bourgeois, liberal, and so on. Indeed, it may even be declared with due merit that the modernistic view of history considers these and other Western categories to be of universal *ontological* significance. Hence, the act of labeling Sheikh Abdullah Tariki a Red communist—which has the effect of interpretively situating the (Saudi) Arabian resistance to oil imperialism within a Eurocentric story of the conflict between bourgeois liberalism and communism—may be seen as an elisionary discursive maneuver that denies the uniqueness and the particularities of Arab history and that seeks to absorb Arab history in a globalizing and totalizing Western narrative with a view to reiterating/reinforcing the West's claim to its own universality.

Admittedly, the preceding is a fairly condensed reading of what may be called the Red Sheikh episode in the discourse of imperial oil. Even such a brief reading, however, does not fail to offer a number of important and interesting insights into the colonizers' consciousness. We will now turn our attention toward yet another discursive event in the history of the Western oil industry with a view to illuminating some other facets and aspects of the colonizing consciousness.

Oil, Camels, Sheikhs, and Bananas

In his immensely readable and highly impressive analysis of the politics, economics, and deadly intrigue surrounding international oil and oil imperialism, Terzian (1985) documents an incredible colonialist moment (in which extreme imperial hauteur seems to have freely and lavishly commingled with pique, exasperation, bitterness, contempt, derision, dismissal, rage, dread, and several other conflicting and not-so-conflicting passions) when he narrates how an American newspaper, the *Washington Post*—a newspaper that incidentally is frequently seen in the United States as one of the leading symbols of liberal America—once snappishly referred to OPEC as "a quarrelling collection of camel sheikhdoms and banana republics" (p. 163). For the postcolonial reader, such a representation of OPEC seems simply to overflow with rich meaning. The purpose of this section of the chapter, accordingly, is to provide a reading of this angry and tense *Washington Post* outburst with a view to affording some further insights into the colonizer's consciousness.

Founded in 1960, OPEC came into existence as a united front of a group of large oil-exporting countries[20] deeply desirous of overthrowing oil imperialism, with its legacy of exploitative petroleum concessions, colonial spheres of influence, and untrammelled Western control and domination of the political and economic lives of the oil-producing countries. That the founders of OPEC clearly envisioned this body as a coalition for opposing Western imperialism seems obvious when we consider the secrecy that shrouded the negotiations leading to the creation of OPEC (Terzian, 1985; Yergin, 1991).[21] Nor was such secrecy unwarranted. The founding of OPEC took place against the backdrop of the 1953 coup in Iran (following Iran's nationalization of its oil industry), which had been orchestrated by the secret intelligence agencies of Britain and the United States,[22] and the invasion of Egypt in 1956 by Britain, France, and

Israel, after the Egyptian government of Gamal Abdel Nasser had nationalized the Suez Canal.

In the colonialist discourse of oil, OPEC appears as something of an enigma. Looking at the Western discourse of oil and imperialism, it would seem that, although this discourse recognizes the clear nature of the challenge posed by OPEC to the enterprise of colonization and empire, it never quite succeeds in making up its mind about whether to treat OPEC seriously or not. Here an example or two may be useful in clarifying what is being suggested above. For instance, right from the moment of its inception, OPEC forced the Western oil cartel to give up the latter's unilateral control of the pricing of oil (Ghanem, 1986), and, as a result of such radical dilution of colonialist control, the activities and practices of international oil were fundamentally transformed. Notwithstanding such transformation effected by OPEC in the "text" of oil, however, somewhat surprisingly, the Western discourse of oil continued also to represent OPEC as incapable of posing a serious challenge to Western imperialism, and as something that could simply be brushed aside in a brief, dismissive gesture. As evidence, one may consider the in-depth report on Middle East oil prepared by the U.S. Central Intelligence Agency (CIA) in November 1960—that is, 2 full months after OPEC came into existence—which dismissed OPEC in "a mere four lines" (Yergin, 1991, p. 523).[23]

Similarly, a report in the *New York Times* on the occasion of OPEC's founding stated that the "'cartel' [i.e., OPEC] . . . would only last a year or two . . . following which everything would go back to normal" (Terzian, 1985, p. vii). This report is interesting on account of the deep ambivalence that it exhibits toward OPEC. On the one hand, the report's nostalgia for the pre-OPEC "good, old days" (as suggested by the report's prophecy that things would "go back to normal" after OPEC's hoped-for demise) indicates a clear acknowledgment of OPEC's *power* to affect the course of history and to make the state of oil affairs not-so-normal (from the Western perspective). Thereby, the report undoubtedly recognizes OPEC as a serious threat to oil imperialism. On the other hand, however, by stating that OPEC "would only last a year or two," the report also seems to suggest that OPEC may not be powerful enough to survive for long and, therefore, may not really be a serious threat to the imperial project. Hence, as a result of the highly uncertain position accorded to OPEC in the discourse of oil, this discourse would appear to be deeply ruptured and fissured. And it is from within such an ambivalent and fractured discourse that the *Washington Post* quip about camels, sheikhs, and bananas may be seen as emerging.

Recall that the *Washington Post*'s representation of OPEC reads: "a quarrelling collection of camel sheikhdoms and banana republics." The important question that we face here is how does one read this representation of OPEC. In short, are there meanings, allusions, and nuances buried deep in this representation that are in need of being excavated? In what follows, it will be argued that, from a postcolonial perspective, it is possible to read the preceding representation of OPEC as a complex and ambivalent outcome of the conflict and commingling among a number of discordant Western discourses including those of the Orient, the Savage, and the Nation-State.

To begin with, note that OPEC is not being referred to as, say, a collection of quarrelling nations (or, states, countries, peoples etc.). Why not, for example, call OPEC a collection (quarrelling or otherwise) of republics and monarchies spread over Asia, Africa, and South America? Why, in sum, the hesitation and reluctance on part of the *Washington Post* (in its references to OPEC) to employ signifiers that are commonly understood to suggest the nation and/or the nation-state? In part, the answer to this question may be found in the hierarchy of colonialist binaries referred to above (see Table 12.1). In brief, as Table 12.1 indicates, the ideas of the nation and the nation-state are such an intimate component of the "civilized, superior" West's own self-representation (and self-constitution) that any suggestion of the possible existence of nation-states in the non-West would seem to have the effect of denying the very Otherness of that non-West and, consequently, of radically disturbing the ontology of colonialism.[24] In other words, the reluctance to refer to the OPEC countries as modern nations may well be a reflection of the danger that such a mode of referring to OPEC poses for the West's own (sense of) reality.

However, if the discourse of oil must evince a reluctance toward addressing the OPEC countries as full-fledged, civilized, nations, are there any valid reasons that may offer some likely explanation as to why this discourse must be equally shy of referring to OPEC as a group of barbarians? Why not, for instance, designate OPEC as a quarrelling collection of primitives? What are the constraints, in other words, that inhibit the discourse of oil from calling OPEC, say, a horde of wild savages? In order to understand such constraints, we need to take a brief look at the historical trajectory followed by the Western discourse of the Savage (see, e.g., Hulme, 1986).

According to Hulme (1986), schematically, the discourse of the Savage is traceable to Herodotus of Classical Greece.[25] Constructed around notions of purely Other creatures, such as Amazons, Anthropophagi and Cynocephali,[26] the discourse of the Savage exhibited an amazing degree of continuity and changelessness in the European imagination as this discourse wound its way down through the millennia. During the centuries following the European voyages of discovery, however, the discourse of the Savage became exclusively tied to specific parts and sections of certain unique geographical locales, such as Africa, the Caribbean[27] and the Americas, the Andaman Islands, and the Malay Archipelago. As a result, by the 20th century, the discourse of the Savage was no longer available to be employed freely for representing Europe's Others. Even more specifically, that discourse was not unrestrictedly available for purposes of representing Iranians, Iraqis, Saudi Arabians, and so on, who formed a significant majority of OPEC's membership. Hence, working inevitably within the boundaries decreed by the preexisting Western discourses of Savagery and the Nation-State, the discourse of oil was placed in the unenviable position of being able to call OPEC neither savage nor civilized, neither modern nor primeval, neither the same nor a pure Other.

The discourses of the Savage and the Nation-State were, of course, not the only preexisting discourses operating to prescribe enunciatory limits to what could be articulated by the discourse of oil. A third such earlier discourse was that of the Orient. Similar to the discourse of the Savage, the origins of the discourse of the Orient may also be found in European antiquity (Said, 1979, p. 68). By all accounts, however, it would appear that the discourse of the Orient achieved a new intensity and salience following Marco Polo, the 13th-century Venetian traveler to the East, who is said to have visited the opulent and radiantly magnificent court of the Great Mongol Khan himself (Hulme, 1986). Briefly stated, this discourse saw the Orient as a land of gold, of immense riches, of mighty empires,[28] and of hoary, splendorous civilizations, as well as of mystery, novelty, danger, and terror. Through various twists and turns, the discourse of the Orient eventually came to take the form of, what Said (1979) calls Orientalism, with its distinctly pejorative construction of the Orient.[29]

One may well suppose that in Said's Orientalism the discourse of oil would have found precisely what it could be said to have been looking for, namely, the vocabulary, imagery, idioms, and styles of representation for addressing those of the non-West who could not have been rendered (in light of the already discussed enunciatory limits imposed by the discourses of the Savage and the Nation-State) as either pure savages or as fully civilized. However, for at least two reasons the discourse of oil seems to have been denied such an easy resolution of the dilemma that it faced. First of all, there was the issue of (what the discourse of oil understood as) the banana republics. As is generally known, OPEC began as an alliance between two of the richest oil-producing areas of the world, namely the Middle East and South America. And to a large extent, the perception of OPEC as being a group of Middle Eastern and South American countries (a perception that was formed at the moment of OPEC's origin) continues to persist. Orientalist vocabulary, however, as the discourse of oil could not fail to realize, was capable of being appropriately employed only in the case of the Middle East (or by extension, that of the East as such), but not for purposes of representing Latin America. Hence, as far as the discourse of oil was concerned, Orientalism could only offer a partial solution to its problems.

Second, there was the all-too-important matter of oil—the black gold. As suggested by our previous discussions, the transformation and evolution of the discourse of the Orient into its latest incarnation (namely, Orientalism) can be seen as involving the substantive displacement of an earlier chain of key tropes (in outline form, "gold," "immense wealth," "mighty empire," "the Great Khan," "powerful armies," "grand civilization," and so on) by another chain (to wit, "moribund society," "backward populace," "decadent sheikhs," "puny principalities," "weak armies," "degraded civilization," and so forth). One of the most significant shifts involved in this transformation seems to have been the gradual eclipse and disappearance of gold as a leading metaphor employed in conjunction with the Orient. Indeed, one may well argue that the successful discursive transformation of the Orient from the domicile of "the magnificently civilized" to that of "the not-fully civilized" was most crucially dependent upon this very effacement of gold from the sequence of key metaphors used in connection with the Orient. With the arrival of the *black* gold on the Middle Eastern scene, however, Orientalism's masterful elimination of gold (from the series of major Oriental metaphors) becomes questionable, with the result that (as far as the discourse of oil was concerned) Orientalist tropes alone may not have been considered sufficient for successfully representing the essence of the not-savage-yet-not-fully-civilized Others of the Western world.

Said (1979) has pointed out that, during the last couple of centuries or so, the pejorative discourse of Orientalism took such a powerful hold of the Western imagination that the very designation of someone or something as Oriental was sufficient to create a strongly negative impression of the object or the person so characterized. That is to say, as a result of the sedimentation and naturalization of the discourse of Orientalism, *Orient* (and the panoply of terms used for describing the Orient) had become a shorthand term for quickly and accurately telegraphing a dense constellation of overwhelmingly negative images to the Western mind. Thus, for instance, referring to a country as a *sheikhdom* was usually enough to clearly indicate to the average Western person that the country in question was backward, apathetic, squalid, nonmodern, despotic, and so on.

As suggested earlier, however, with oil becoming a symbol of richness and wealth, and the consequent reemergence of the trope of gold in the chain of key metaphors used for referring to the Orient, the (so far unambiguous) pejorative connotations of Orientalist vocabulary seem to have come under new pressures and strains. One possible result of this could be a degree of uncertainty (exhibited within the discourse of oil) regarding the stability and unambiguity of the senses, meanings, and images connoted by the old Orientalist terminology. Could it have been the case that it was this very uncertainty that found expression in the *Washington Post*'s compelling need to refer not simply to sheikhdoms, but to *camel* sheikhdoms, in its own representation of OPEC?

In a nutshell, what is being suggested above is that, with the arrival of oil (and the reemergence of the trope of Oriental riches), the term sheikhdom alone may no longer have appeared sufficient for communicating what was one of the long-established dogmas of Orientalism, namely, the pejorative essence of the Orient. Hence the need, apparently, to further calibrate and finetune the precise connotation of the term sheikhdom by means of adding the adjectival qualifier, camel. The sheikhs may be as wealthy as the richest in the capitalist West, this adjective seems to aver, but the sheikhs' wealth is not the dynamic, sleek, jet-setting, modern wealth that "we" have; the sheikhs' wealth is the discredited and compromised wealth of those who are organically linked to something as slow, bizarre, awkward, and premodern as the camel. And lest there be any doubts about the precise connotation of the phrase, camel sheikhdoms, the *Washington Post* thoughtfully provides its readers with a symmetrical phrase, *banana republics*. OPEC, as this newspaper's quote under scrutiny is careful to point out, is "a quarrelling collection of camel sheikhdoms *and* banana republics."

The *Washington Post*'s juxtaposition of camel sheikhdoms and banana republics would seem to be significant. The term banana republics has long been used in the West for derisively referring to a group of small Caribbean and Latin American countries that traditionally derived an overwhelming proportion of their foreign exchange earnings through the export of tropical fruits such as bananas (see, e.g., Enloe, 1989). The fruit plantations in these countries tend to be controlled by large foreign conglomerates such as the United Brands Corporation (formerly, United Fruit Company) of the United States, and the banana republics themselves are seen as being ruled by corrupt tinhorn dictators said to be in the pay of overseas governments and corporations. In sum, the expression, banana republics, conveys contempt rather than respect. And it is this contempt that is seemingly sought to be evoked by means of mentioning, in the same breath, the two expressions, camel sheikhdoms and banana republics. In addition, however, the reference to banana republics may be seen as also serving to make explicit OPEC's contiguity and imbrication with "that [wild and] primordial part of America, the Caribbean" (Hulme, 1986, p. xiii), and thus attempting to reintroduce (through the back door, as it were) the Savage into the discourse of oil.

Finally, of course, one cannot ignore the use of the epithet, *quarrelling*. After all, according to the *Washington Post,* OPEC is not any simple collection of camel sheikhdoms and banana republics, OPEC is a *quarrelling* collection of camel sheikhdoms and banana republics. Nations, according to one of the inviolable dogmas of the Western liberal doctrine of international relations, have no permanent friends, they only have permanent interests. Hence, nations (even Western ones) frequently quarrel among themselves. Indeed, nations (or, at least, their presidents, kings, and ruling elites) have fought and warred with one another since time immemorial. Such being the case, one may rightfully ask, what is so new or different about the OPEC member nations quarrelling among themselves? In other words, why this insistence by the *Washington Post* on this particular label (quarrelling) over the plethora of other labels that might have been available for characterizing OPEC? It is possible, at least to some extent, that the use of this label expresses a desire and a hope for OPEC's disintegration: If OPEC as a group is not cohesive—if its members are always at loggerheads with one another—the West may justifiably hope that OPEC will soon collapse, and, for the West, things may quickly go back to "normal." But there may be more to the use of the word quarrelling than a simple expression of the hope for OPEC's decline and fall.

In his impressive book, *The Rhetoric of Empire,* Spurr (1993) draws the reader's attention to an article in the *Harper's Magazine* that quotes a senior representative of the Iranian Revolution of 1978-1979 as saying: "You western-ers . . . why do you always talk about us as having power struggles while you yourselves merely have politics?" (p. 190) In his analysis following this quota-tion, Spurr perspicaciously points to the important rhetorical distinction between the "barbarism of 'power struggles' " and "the relative civility of 'politics' " (p. 191). In a similar vein, we need to note that the use of the word quarrelling may have the crucial rhetorical function of denigrating the politics and the internal differ-ences that inevitably attend the coming together of a number of sovereign states. Indeed, the word quarrelling almost has the effect of conjuring the image of a pack of ill-bred children who are in need of firm, adult supervision. And given that the ideology of colonialism often pictures the colonizer in the role of a mature adult who is duty-bound to be a trustee, guardian, and protector of the immature child that is the colonized (see, e.g., Nandy, 1983, 1987), could we not claim with sufficient reason that the *Washington Post*'s use of the word quarrelling may be seen as working to represent the OPEC as an underdeveloped child needing firm Western control, guidance, and discipline?

In sum, the preceding postcolonial analysis of two significant discursive events from the recent history of oil and imperialism offers some important insights into the colonizer's consciousness. It will be our endeavor in the rest of this chapter to use this understanding of the colonizing consciousness for purposes of developing a deeper appreciation of the dilemmas of workplace diversity in the West.

THE COLONIZING CONSCIOUSNESS AND
THE DILEMMAS OF WORKPLACE DIVERSITY

As we have already noted, the discourse of colonization is fundamentally dependent upon the construction of an ontological Other. Our foregoing analysis of the discourse of oil was intended to (a) develop a more sophisticated understanding of the topography of the discursive terrain that seems to condition and regulate the nature of the material and symbolic exchanges taking place between the colonizing Self and the colonized Other, and, in the process, (b) to adumbrate the persistent imprint of colonial discourse on the mundane and quotidian activities of one of the foremost spheres of Western political economy, namely, the petroleum sector.

To recapitulate briefly, our analysis suggests that the colonizing consciousness mostly tends to conceptualize the Other in a highly pejorative vein—to wit, as morally debased, as immature and not fully developed, as something that menaces the safety and well-being of the Western society, and so on. Moreover, employing simple contrast, the colonizing consciousness seems to view the colonial West itself as the storehouse of universal good, as developed and mature, and as morally obliged to serve in the capacity of a guardian and trustee for the non-West. At the same time, the colonial discourse is also the site where a number of somewhat discrepant discourses may be said to intersect and collide, with the result that the colonizing consciousness exhibits some deep ambivalence in its reception of the colonized Other. All in all, therefore, the colonizing consciousness sees the colonized as being, at the same time, a grave threat and as something too weak to pose a credible threat, as something needing to be contained that never can be fully contained, and as beings representing pure difference who can, nonetheless, be assimilated in the totalizing narratives of Western history. Not surprisingly, therefore, the colonizer's approach toward the colonized seems to be characterized by a sense of deep schizophrenia. It is this very schizophrenic attitude, this chapter submits, which the contemporary West brings in its encounters with workplace diversity, and it is only by grasping the implications of such schizophrenia that we may hope to develop a better understanding of the dilemmas of diversity faced by contemporary Western organizations.

The introductory parts of this chapter have already drawn our attention to the importance of postcolonial theory for understanding the dilemmas of workplace diversity. Nevertheless, at this point, the skeptical reader may be somewhat justified in posing the question: Is this chapter's analysis of colonial discourse of any continued relevance *today?* After all, isn't colonialism supposed to be dead now? In order to address this question, we do not necessarily need to enter into the contentious debate as to whether we inhabit a *neo*-colonial or a *post*-colonial world. What may be more important to point out is that discourses saturate us; they provide us with the everyday language, the idioms, and the vocabulary for speaking and thinking about "things" of interest to us. As a result, in the West, it may be virtually impossible to think and speak about the non-West without employing a colonialist vocabulary, the political demise of colonialism notwithstanding. Such vocabulary, furthermore, does not become impartial and nonpartisan simply because colonialism may have come to a political end. "Beneath the idioms," as Said (1979) observes in the context of Orientalism, there is always "a layer of [partisan] doctrine" (p. 203).[30] For instance, the imprint of such partisan, colonialist doctrine is visible whenever the various apparatuses of the Western world (and that includes Western individuals, governments, academics, scholarly journals, media, cultural agencies, corporations, and all the rest) assert their right (or obligation) to "guide" the rest of the world, be it for intellectual, economic, social, or political "development." Discourses, therefore, have enormous staying power. It is this chapter's claim, accordingly, that in order to develop a deeper appreciation of the dilemmas of diversity in Western organizations, we need to unveil the imprint of colonial discourse upon the handling of workplace diversity in the West.

As far as workplace diversity is concerned, given the continued persistence of colonial discourse, the white male power structure is likely to approach differences of race, culture, ethnicity, gender, sexuality, and so on within contemporary Western organizations with an incongruous combination of contempt and schizophrenia that may closely resemble the manner of the erstwhile colonizers in their engagement with the colonized Others. To varying degrees, the power structure is likely to see such differences as representing inferiority, irrationality, backwardness, immaturity, immorality, corruption, "a menace to society," a grave threat to meritocracy, an evil conspiracy designed to destroy the Christian West, and so forth. In addition, although they experience a sense of being threatened by such differences, the dominant groups are also likely to believe, at the same time, that different races, cultures, genders, and so on are too weak, contemptible, and so on to pose a strong threat to their own power, privilege, and hegemony. In other words, the dominant are likely to sense deep ambivalence as they are simultaneously buffeted by a host of often-conflicting feelings, ideas, and beliefs.

This brief list of ideas and emotions that seemingly constitute the worldview of the dominant gives us some indication of the problems faced by organizations seeking to "manage" workplace diversity. But this is not all. Although the preceding catalog is a good enough pointer to the formidable nature of the problems surrounding diversity, the real dilemma of managing diversity would seem to be that, with varying degrees of intensity, these same ideas, beliefs, passions, and emotions are likely to have a hold of the life worlds of even those who want to value diversity and to promote the interests of the marginal. Indeed, given that the discourse of colonialism saturates us (so that our very vocabulary for addressing difference is highly colonialist in nature), it could not be otherwise. In sum, what is being suggested here is that the discourse of workplace diversity is inextricably (and fatally) linked with the discourse of colonialism. In which case, are we caught in a labyrinth, and there is simply no way out? The question that we are ultimately brought to confront, therefore, is how do we deconstruct that discourse of colonialism that (by means of crucially configuring and conditioning the discourse of workplace diversity) permeates the very fabric of the practices that constitute management of diversity in Western organizations?

"The first step toward an alternative to colonial discourse, for Western readers at least," says Spurr (1993), "has to be a critical understanding of its structures" (p. 185). Analogously, a search for alternatives to the contemporary discourse of workplace diversity must begin with a critique of all those practices (engaged in by managers, researchers, consultants, workshop facilitators, etc.) that constitute the corpus of the diversity management industry. One of the basic purposes of such critique would be to understand how, at the fundamental level, the diversity industry may primarily be occupied in echoing and enacting the central propositions of colonialist discourse, and consequently, in being complicit with the continual production, reproduction, and perpetuation of a hegemonic system that is the source of immense material and symbolic violence directed against those cultural and demographic groups that mostly inhabit the margins of contemporary Western organizations.

Along with the above, the practical project of deconstructing the discourse of workplace diversity needs to proceed along a "double gesture" or a "double movement" (Derrida, 1981). The first movement (although not necessarily in a strictly chronological sense) is what may be referred to as inversion, or the "phase of overturning" (Derrida, 1981, p. 40). In this phase, the system of hierarchical binaries (see Table 12.1) that, as colonialism's legacy, continues to cast its shadow upon the diversity industry needs to be overturned and inverted. As Derrida (1981) put it, this is the phase "which brings low what was high" (p. 42). The enormous practical difficulties of this phase alone cannot be overemphasized. For this deconstruction to succeed, however, merely inverting the system of hierarchical binaries is not enough, because the phase of overturning continues "to operate on the terrain of and from within the deconstructed system" (Derrida, 1981, p. 42). Hence, the necessity of the second phase of deconstruction, which results in "the irruptive emergence of a new 'concept,' a concept that can no longer be, and never could be, included in the previous regime" (Derrida, 1981, p. 42). Only when we have engaged in both these phases of deconstruction would it be possible for us to contemplate organizations "in which the play of difference could range free of the structures of inequality" (Spurr, 1993, p. 201).

NOTES

1. See Nemetz & Christensen (1996) for a brief mention of some doubting voices that seem to question the desirability and usefulness of promoting diversity in organizations.

2. Despite sharing a somewhat similar label, postcolonialism, it is important to note, differs from other "posts," such as postmodernism, post-structuralism, and so on in many important respects. Any discussion of those differences, however, will clearly take us far afield from the principal concerns of this chapter. The reader interested in exploring the tensions among the various posts is referred to such sources as Adam and Tiffin (1990), Bhabha (1994), and Prasad (1997).

3. Although in a strictly technical sense, colonialism, that is, the direct control and administration of other people's territories, is only one form of imperialism (see, e.g., Lichtheim, 1974; Williams & Chrisman, 1994a), the distinction is not particularly important for our purposes. This chapter, accordingly, uses the two terms, colonialism and imperialism, somewhat interchangeably.

4. Sooner or later, all (postcolonial) theorists must wrestle with the wider implications of employing such sweeping terms as America, Europe, the West, non-West and so forth. Needless to mention, postcolonial theory is fully aware of the epistemological sins of essentialism, homogenization, and so on associated with the use of these and similar other terms. In his seminal article, "Postcoloniality and the Artifice of History: Who Speaks for 'Indian' Pasts?" Chakrabarty (1992, p. 1), for instance, emphasizes that such expressions need to be viewed as hyperreal terms, or "as figures of the imaginary." Along with such awareness, however, numerous postcolonial scholars (including Chakrabarty, 1992) continue to insist on the *value* of employing such terminology in their writings. In brief, this insistence may be said to be rooted in a concrete reality in which expressions such as Europe, the West, and so on, although undoubtedly fictive, are fictions of enormous material consequence. See, for example, Chakrabarty (1992), Nandy (1983, especially pp. xiii-xiv), Prasad (1997).

5. The recent discursive turn in the social sciences (including organization studies) has led to a far-reaching reconceptualization of such terms as *discourse, text, reading, writing, representation,* and so on. In brief, texts now refer not only to linguistic artifacts, but to extra-linguistic artifacts (e.g., culture, rituals, music, painting, architecture, social practices and institutions, history, etc.) as well, with the result that "textuality has become a metaphor for reality in general"

(Dirks, Eley, & Ortner, 1994, p. 25). This chapter, accordingly, often uses words such as text and discourse in their expanded sense.

6. Following the turn to discourse in social theory, human subjectivities are no longer conceptualized as occurring "naturally" but are seen as effects or products of specific texts or discourses. For a brief and lucid analysis of the implications of the discursive turn, see Dirks et al. (1994). For a discussion (in organization studies) of the discursive constitution of human subjectivities, see, for example, Jermier, Knights, and Nord (1994).

7. Nandy (1983) refers to such continuation of colonialism by ideological means as the "second colonization" (p. xi). For a subtle critique of the second colonization thesis, see Prakash (1992).

8. Said (1979) bases his analysis upon the works of some of the leading 19th- and 20th-century Orientalist scholars in Britain, France, and America—"the three great empires" (p. 15).

9. In the interest of clarity, it may be important to note here that the phrase, *discourse of oil,* employs the expression discourse in this term's expanded sense mentioned earlier.

10. Gulf Oil was acquired by Chevron Corp. (one of the descendants of Standard Oil) in 1984 for a sum of $13.2 billion, at that time the largest corporate takeover in U.S. history.

11. Incorporated in 1882 for purposes of skirting some legal problems, Standard Oil of New Jersey (often called Jersey Standard) eventually became the holding company that owned the shares of the various Standard Oil subsidiaries. The subsidiaries were given independent legal existence in 1911 following the U.S. Supreme Court-directed dissolution of Standard. Despite the so-called dissolution, the various Standard offshoots continued to act as a unified company for many years (Roncaglia, 1985; Sampson, 1975; Tugwell, 1988). In 1972, Jersey Standard was renamed Exxon Corporation.

12. The cartel of the Seven Sisters consisted of: Exxon Corp., Mobil Corp., Chevron Corp., Gulf Oil Corp., Texaco Inc., Royal Dutch/Shell, and British Petroleum. Exxon, Mobil, and Chevron are direct descendants of the original Standard Oil Company. Except for Gulf (which was taken over by Chevron in 1984), all the other Sisters continue to be very large and successful petroleum companies. However, as a result of (a) the OPEC revolution of the early 1970s and (b) the rise of large and powerful National Oil Companies (NOCs) all over the world, the global role and importance of the Sisters has considerably diminished. Nevertheless, the Sisters continue to be politically and economically influential organizations, especially in their home countries.

13. OPEC is the well-known acronym for the Organization of the Petroleum Exporting Countries.

14. The honor of being the other cofounder of OPEC belongs to Juan Pablo Perez Alfonzo of Venezuela.

15. Aramco, the Arabian American Oil Company, was the joint-production consortium of Exxon, Mobil, Texaco, and Chevron, which controlled crude oil production in Saudi Arabia.

16. The theme of being opposed by evil conspiracies has long been an integral part of the self-representation of the colonialist project. For example, traces of this theme may be discerned even in the myth of "a City upon a Hill," one of the important enabling myths of colonialism attending a significant moment in the history of Western imperialism, namely the colonization of North America. The origins of this myth are traceable to an oration given by John Winthrop to a group of Puritan colonizers he was leading from England to America in what became known as the Great Migration of 1630 (Miller, 1956). Emphasizing the momentous nature of this "errand into wilderness," Winthrop said to his fellow travelers: "wee must Consider that wee shall be as a City upon a Hill, the eies of all people are uppon us" (Miller, 1956, p. 11). If the colonizing pilgrims failed in this enterprise, warned Winthrop, God would make them "a story and a by-word through the world, wee shall open the mouthes of enemies to speak evill of the wayes of god and all professours for God's sake" (Miller, 1956, p. 11). In the pilgrims' consciousness, thus, while on the one hand, the project of America was endowed with sacredness and divine grace, on the

other hand, the project was also threatened by a conspiracy of its numerous, powerful enemies. In that event, one may offer that just as John Winthrop saw the Puritans' project of American colonization as imperiled by the existence of a conspiracy of that project's enemies, the Seven Sisters also saw the existence of a major conspiracy as threatening the global enterprise of oil and imperialism. For Winthrop, the conspiracy was of people who spoke "evill of the wayes of god" (Miller, 1956, p. 11); for the Seven Sisters, the conspiracy was that of international communism (of which, according to the Western oil cartel, Sheikh Tariki happened to be an important part).

17. Karl Marx and Frederick Engels' famous *Communist Manifesto,* for instance, first appeared in 1848 (see, e.g., Marx & Engels, 1948).

18. In order to clarify the point being made here, we need only to look at an illustrative argument of the following form: (a) only Reds oppose the West, (b) Sheikh Tariki opposes the West, (c) hence, the sheikh is Red. On the basis of the structure of the preceding syllogism, one can rightfully contend that the act of labeling the sheikh a Red may be said to contain an implicit claim that only Reds oppose the West.

19. It should come as no surprise that "the emergence of [this view of] history in European thought is coterminous with the rise of modern colonialism" (Ashcroft et al., 1995, p. 355).

20. In 1960, OPEC began with five founding members, namely, Iran, Iraq, Kuwait, Saudi Arabia, and Venezuela. During subsequent years, OPEC was joined by the following countries: Algeria, Ecuador, Gabon, Indonesia, Libya, Nigeria, Qatar, and the United Arab Emirates. Recently, Ecuador ceased to be a member.

21. Yergin (1991) quotes the Iranian participant in these negotiations as saying: "We met in a James Bond atmosphere" (p. 518).

22. Sampson (1975, p. 135) notes that for several years after the Iranian coup, Western oil companies would frequently warn Third World nationalist leaders by, in effect, saying, look what happened to Mossadeq. Dr. Mossadeq was the Iranian prime minister overthrown in the Anglo-American coup.

23. Yergin (1991) also points to the Seven Sisters' dismissive view of OPEC when he quotes Howard Page, one of the top Jersey Standard executives, as saying: "We attached little importance to . . . [OPEC], because we believed it would not work" (p. 523).

24. According to the linear "conveyer belt" view of history, only the countries of the West have so far succeeded in "reaching" nationhood; an overwhelming majority of the non-Western countries are still "on their way" to full nationhood. Achieving nationhood, in this view, also implies "arriving" in the modern era of universal history.

25. Right from the days of European antiquity, the discourse of the Savage displayed a basic dualism that eventually came to express itself along two dimensions, that of "fierce cannibal" on the one hand, and of the "noble savage" on the other. The following brief discussion, however, confines itself to the first dimension alone. See, in this connection, Hulme (1986, especially p. 45 ff.).

26. In standard European teratology, Cynocephali refer to men who have the head (or face) of a dog.

27. By way of understanding the special association (between the Caribbean and the discourse of the Savage) that developed in the European imagination following the voyages of discovery, it may be interesting to note that the word *cannibal* comes from *Canibalis,* the name used by Christopher Columbus for referring to the Carib people of the Antilles. Columbus ultimately came to claim that these people were man-eaters. For an erudite and fascinating analysis of how the discourse of the Savage uncertainly emerges to a position of dominance in Columbus's *Journal* (with the result that the Carib people eventually come to be labeled as anthropophagi), see Hulme (1986). On the basis of an in-depth analysis of extensive historical sources, Hulme (1986) arrives at the conclusion that "the entry of the word 'cannibal' into European discourse with the meaning

'man-eating savage' was, despite appearances, unsupported by what would legally be accepted as 'evidence' " (p. 47).

28. For several centuries right up to the 17th and the 18th, Europe's trade with the East (including with China and India) ran huge deficits and involved the eastward flow of large quantities of gold and silver (Abu-Lughod, 1989a, 1989b; Hulme, 1986). This fact may partly account for the prominent place accorded to Oriental wealth and power in the discourse of the Orient preceding Orientalism.

29. Because this part of the present chapter draws upon the scholarship of Said (1979) and Hulme (1986) in order to sketch the outlines of the discourse of the Orient, it is important to point out that whereas Said's primary analytical focus is the Western discourse with respect to the Middle East and Islam, that of Hulme focuses upon the civilization of China (see Hulme, 1986, p. 270, n.8). In addition, Hulme's historical period of reference precedes that of Said. Both of these variants of the discourse of the Orient, however, share common origins in European antiquity, and despite considerable differences, do contain important parallels and overlaps. In many respects, the discourse of the Orient (including its latest version, Said's Orientalism) can be said to represent Europe's portrayal of the entire East.

30. Derrida (1981) makes a similar point when he notes that "'everyday language' is not innocent or neutral" (p. 19). As a result, however, what Said (1979) observes in the context of analyzing Orientalism assumes crucial significance. Says Said (1979): "Orientalism was . . . a [partisan] system of truths. . . . It is therefore correct that *every* . . . [Westerner], in what he could say about the Orient, was consequently a *racist,* an imperialist, and almost totally ethnocentric" (p. 204; italics added). The stamp of such Orientalist racism and imperialism is visible, for instance, even in the writings of Karl Marx, the leading Western prophet of revolutionary emancipation (see, e.g., Said, 1979, pp. 153 ff.; Spurr, 1993, pp. 99-100). And this despite the fact that Marx (and several other Westerners like him) may not have consciously desired to be racists, imperialists, and so on.

REFERENCES

Abu-Lughod, J. (1989a). *Before Europe's hegemony.* New York: Oxford University Press.
Abu-Lughod, J. (1989b). On the remaking of history. In B. Kruger & P. Mariani (Eds.), *Remaking history* (pp. 111-129). Seattle: Bay Press.
Adam, I., & Tiffin, H. (Eds.). (1990). *Past the last post: Theorizing post-colonialism and post-modernism.* Calgary: University of Calgary Press.
Al-Chalabi, F. J. (1980). *OPEC and the international oil industry.* Oxford: Oxford University Press.
Allen, G. (1991). Valuing cultural diversity: Industry woos a new workforce. *Communication World, 8,* 14-17.
Asad, T. (Ed.). (1973). *Anthropology and the colonial encounter.* New York: Humanities Press.
Ashcroft, B., Griffiths, G., & Tiffin, H. (Eds.). (1995). *The post-colonial studies reader.* London: Routledge.
Barker, F., Hulme, P., Iversen, M., & Loxley, D. (Eds.). 1985. *Europe and its others* (2 vols.). Colchester, UK: University of Essex.
Bhabha, H. K. (1985). Signs taken for wonders: Questions of ambivalence and authority under a tree outside Delhi, May 1817. In F. Barker, P. Hulme, M. Iversen, & D. Loxley (Eds.), *Europe and its others* (Vol. 1, pp. 89-106). Colchester, UK: University of Essex.
Bhabha, H. K. (1994). *The location of culture.* London: Routledge.

Bishop, A. (1990). Western mathematics: The secret weapon of cultural imperialism. *Race and Class, 32*(2), 51-65.

Blair, J. M. (1976). *The control of oil.* New York: Pantheon.

Brantlinger, P. (1988). *Rule of darkness: British literature and imperialism, 1830-1914.* Ithaca, NY: Cornell University Press.

Cesaire, A. (1972). *Discourse on colonialism.* New York: Monthly Review Press.

Chakrabarty, D. (1992). Postcoloniality and the artifice of history: Who speaks for "Indian" pasts? *Representations, 37*(Winter), 1-26.

Chatterjee, P. (1986). *Nationalist thought and the colonial world.* Minneapolis: University of Minnesota Press.

Chatterjee, P. (1993). *The nation and its fragments: Colonial and postcolonial histories.* Princeton, NJ: Princeton University Press.

Conrad, J. (1983). *Heart of darkness* (P. O'Prey, ed.). Harmondsworth, UK: Penguin.

Copeland, L. (1988a, May). Learning to manage a multicultural work force. *Training,* pp. 49-56.

Copeland, L. (1988b, November). Valuing workplace diversity. *Personnel Administrator,* pp. 65-88.

Cox, T. (1991). The multicultural organization. *Academy of Management Executive, 5*(2), 34-47.

Cox, T. (1993). *Cultural diversity in organizations: Theory, research, and practice.* San Francisco: Berrett-Koehler.

Cox, T., & Blake, S. (1991). Managing cultural diversity. *Academy of Management Executive, 5*(3), 45-56.

Derrida, J. (1981). *Positions* (A. Bass, trans.). Chicago: University of Chicago Press.

Dirks, N. (1992). Introduction: Colonialism and culture. In N. Dirks (Ed.), *Colonialism and culture* (pp. 1-25). Ann Arbor: University of Michigan Press.

Dirks, N., Eley, G., & Ortner, S. (1994). Introduction. In N. Dirks, G. Eley, & S. Ortner (Eds.), *Culture/power/history* (pp. 3-45). Princeton, NJ: Princeton University Press.

Enloe, C. (1989). *Bananas, beaches, and bases.* Berkeley: University of California Press.

Fernandez, J. P. (1991). *Managing a diverse work force: Regaining the competitive edge.* Lexington, MA: Lexington Books.

Ghanem, S. (1986). *OPEC: Rise and fall of an exclusive club.* London: KPI.

Guha, R. (1983). *Elementary aspects of peasant insurgency in colonial India.* Delhi: Oxford University Press.

Guha, R., & Spivak, G. C. (Eds.). (1988). *Selected subaltern studies.* New York: Oxford University Press.

Hamilton, A. (1986). *Oil: The price of power.* London: Michael Joseph/Rainbird.

Headrick, D. (1981). *The tools of the empire.* New York: Oxford University Press.

Hegel, G. W. F. (1900). *Philosophy of history* (J. Sibree, trans.). New York: P. F. Collier.

Hulme, P. (1986). *Colonial encounters.* London: Routledge.

Jackson, S. E. (Ed.). (1992). *Diversity in the workplace: Human resources initiatives.* New York: Guilford.

Jermier, J., Knights, D., & Nord, W. (Eds.). (1994). *Resistance and power in organizations.* London: Routledge.

Karlsson, S. (1986). *Oil and the world order.* Leamington Spa, UK: Berg.

Lichtheim, G. (1974). *Imperialism.* Harmondsworth, UK: Penguin.

Marx, K., & Engels, F. (1948). *The communist manifesto.* New York: International Publishers.

Miller, P. (1956). *Errands into wilderness.* Cambridge, MA: Harvard University Press.

Nandy, A. (1983). *The intimate enemy: Loss and recovery of self under colonialism.* Delhi: Oxford University Press.

Nandy, A. (1987). *Traditions, tyranny, and utopias.* Delhi: Oxford University Press.

Nandy, A. (1992). State. In W. Sachs (Ed.), *The development dictionary* (pp. 264-274). London: Zed Books.

Nemetz, P., & Christensen, S. (1996). The challenge of cultural diversity. *Academy of Management Review, 21*(2), 434-462.

Niranjana, T. (1992). *Siting translation: History, post-structuralism, and the colonial context.* Berkeley: University of California Press.

Prakash, G. (1992). Science "gone native" in colonial India. *Representations, 40*(Fall), 153-178.

Prakash, G. (1995). *After colonialism: Imperial histories and postcolonial displacements.* Princeton, NJ: Princeton University Press.

Prasad, A. (1994). *Institutional ideology and industry-level action: A macro analysis of corporate legitimation in the United States petroleum industry.* Unpublished doctoral dissertation, University of Massachusetts at Amherst.

Prasad, A. (1997). Provincializing Europe: Towards a post-colonial reconstruction. *Studies in Cultures, Organizations, and Societies,* Vol. 3.

Roncaglia, A. (1985). *The international oil market.* Armonk, NY: M. E. Sharpe.

Rossett, A., & Bickham, T. (1994, January). Diversity training. *Training,* pp. 41-46.

Sachs, W. (Ed.). (1992). *The development dictionary: A guide to knowledge as power.* London: Zed Books.

Said, E. W. (1979). *Orientalism.* New York: Vintage.

Said, E. W. (1993). *Culture and imperialism.* New York: Knopf.

Sampson, A. (1975). *The seven sisters.* New York: Viking.

Spivak, G. C. (1990). *The post-colonial critic.* New York: Routledge.

Spurr, D. (1993). *The rhetoric of empire.* Durham, NC: Duke University Press.

Suleri, S. (1992). *The rhetoric of English India.* Chicago: University of Chicago Press.

Terzian, P. (1985). *OPEC: The inside story.* London: Zed Books.

Thomas, R. R. (1990). From affirmative action to affirming diversity. *Harvard Business Review, 68*(2), 107-117.

Thomas, R. R. (1991). *Beyond race and gender: Unleashing the power of your total work force by managing diversity.* New York: American Management Association.

Tiffin, C., & Lawson, A. (Eds.). (1994). *De-scribing empire: Post-colonialism and textuality.* London: Routledge.

Tugendhat, C., & Hamilton, A. (1975). *Oil: The biggest business.* London: Eyre Methuen.

Tugwell, F. (1988). *The energy crisis and the American political economy.* Stanford: Stanford University Press.

Turner, L. (1978). *Oil companies in the international system.* London: George Allen & Unwin.

Vallenilla, L. (1975). *Oil: The making of a new economic order: Venezuelan oil and OPEC.* New York: McGraw-Hill.

Williams, P., & Chrisman, L. (1994a). Colonial discourse and post-colonial theory: An introduction. In P. Williams & L. Chrisman (Eds.), *Colonial discourse and post-colonial theory: A reader* (pp. 1-26). New York: Columbia University Press.

Williams, P., & Chrisman, L. (Eds.). (1994b). *Colonial discourse and post-colonial theory: A reader.* New York: Columbia University Press.

Yergin, D. (1991). *The prize.* New York: Simon & Schuster.

Triple Jeopardy

Immigrant Women of Color in the Labor Force

E. JOY MIGHTY

This chapter describes the complex reality of workplace diversity from the perspective of minorities with three distinct cultural identities based on race, gender, and ethnicity. The chapter explores how these three dimensions of diversity operate in combination to create a "triple jeopardy" in organizations for such individuals. By describing the workplace experiences of a small sample of immigrant women of color, the chapter demonstrates the combined impact of these three cultural identities on individual career outcomes, including job satisfaction, organizational commitment, compensation, and promotion rates. The chapter provides important insights into diversity as a multidimensional phenomenon with the potential for adverse individual and organizational consequences. It concludes with practical recommendations for increasing organi-

AUTHOR'S NOTE: An earlier version of this chapter was presented at the Annual Conference of the Administrative Sciences Association of Canada at Niagara Falls, Ontario, in 1991.

zations' capacity for effectively meeting the challenges posed by the dynamics of diversity.

INTRODUCTION

Theories of organization have traditionally been derived from an ontological perspective with underlying assumptions of the universality and homogeneity of organizational actors. Such assumptions have used white males as the defining group for generalizing about organizational behavior. More recently, as the implications of the demographic, social, political, and economic trends driving the increase in workforce diversity have begun to be understood, scholars of organizational theory and behavior have begun to explore the experiences of women as a valid subject of study in developing knowledge about organizations. However, such studies have focused primarily on white women. Rarely have the experiences of men and women of other races been studied, except in the context of issues related to employment discrimination or government-sanctioned strategies for dealing with such discrimination, for example, affirmative action in the United States or employment equity in Canada. Typically, results from such studies are perceived as interesting but hardly useful in increasing knowledge and understanding about organizations or in developing organization theory (Nkomo, 1992). In North America, race, ethnicity, and gender have been profound determinants of place in society, particularly in the labor market. Yet, organizational analyses have for the most part failed to explore how these elements of identity and determinants of place affect organizational life. In the context of increasing workforce diversity and the growing need to manage that diversity effectively in order to maximize its potential benefits, there must be increased efforts to give voice to and understand the perspectives and organizational experiences of all social groups.

This chapter describes the complex reality of workplace diversity from the perspectives of individuals with three distinct social identities based on race, gender, and ethnicity. It explores how these three dimensions of diversity operate in combination to create unique organizational experiences for members who are immigrant women of color. The social positions accorded to each of these labels are closely interwoven, and each appears to have multiplicative, reinforcing effects on the others, resulting in what may best be described as a triple jeopardy for such women. The chapter begins with the exposition of a theoretical perspective, based on social identity theory and the theory of place; this is later used to demonstrate how the three elements of their social identity have placed immigrant women of color in marginal positions. A description follows of the workplace experiences of 14 immigrant women of color. Finally, the chapter discusses implications for managing diversity derived from an application of the theoretical perspective to the experiences of immigrant women of color.

THEORETICAL PERSPECTIVE

Together, social identity theory and the theory of place form a useful framework for understanding the experiences and place of immigrant women of color in the North American labor force. Social identity theory allows us to understand how individuals' membership in various groups may shape their perspectives and experiences in the workplace. The theory of place focuses on the structure of society and its numerous institutions on the basis of certain criteria.

Social Identity Theory

According to social identity theory, individuals define themselves in terms of their classification in different groups (Tajfel, 1978, 1982). This classification enables individuals to understand who they are based on personal characteristics as well as on their perception of belonging to social groups. Self-definition is relational and comparative because each definition is relative to individuals in other classifications (Tajfel & Turner, 1986). Thus, individuals' definitions of themselves involve accentuating similarities of people belonging to the same group and differences of people belonging to a different social group (Tajfel, 1981). For example, people's self-identification as belonging to the classification *old* becomes meaningful only in relation to their definition of others as belonging to the category *young* (Ashforth & Mael, 1989).

People identify with and attach different values to each group to which they belong so that positive, negative, or ambivalent feelings are aroused by their knowledge of each group membership (Tajfel, 1978). Acceptance of their identification in terms of social categories does not necessarily mean that people accept and incorporate the stereotypical values, attitudes, goals, and other attributes associated with those social groups. Rather, social identification means only that a person perceives him- or herself as "psychologically intertwined with the fate of the group" (Ashforth & Mael, 1989, p. 21). Thus, predictions of behavior on the basis of people's social identification may be inaccurate and unreliable.

Social identity is not only important in self-definition and understanding of the self-concept. It also influences how others view us. Even if an individual does not place much value or emotional significance on her membership in a particular group, others will still attribute what they perceive as typical characteristics of that group to her and interact with her on that basis. For example, membership in the female social group may be the primary basis on which colleagues interact with a female executive, even if she perceives her identity as an executive as a more salient social identity than her gender. Thus, interpersonal relations are influenced by the social identities of each of the people interacting (Cox, 1993).

Theory of Place

The following exposition of the theory of place is based on Miller's (1990) study, which seeks to describe the social, political, and economic factors that have affected the educational system in Jamaica for over 250 years. Miller (1990) develops the theory of place to explain the relationship between high schooling and the social stratification of Jamaican society. He argues against the widely accepted view that Third World or developing societies are special cases justifying study of their specific characteristics but without hope of yielding universal principles and proposes that his theory of place is useful in understanding societies and their institutions generally. Little known in the management literature, his theory states that a society "is structured, shaped and develops purpose on the basis of place—the relative position of the individuals of that society to each other and the relative position of that particular society to other societies" with respect to their power, resources, status, belief system, and culture (Miller, 1990, p. 26). Although they are interdependent and interrelated, each of these dimensions contributes a unique aspect to place. The places occupied by individuals may vary in centrality and marginality. The most central place has power, resources, and status and is justified and legitimized by the belief system and culture. The most marginal place has little or no power, resources, and status and either practices a culture at variance with that of the mainstream or is ascribed to a subordinate position by the mainstream culture. This position is then justified and legitimized by the belief system and culture.

Places in society are unevenly scattered in various patterns from the center to the margin, with clusters and cleavages occurring at different points. Ideally, in an egalitarian society, individuals would be located at the same position on each dimension. That is, they would occupy the same place relative to each other. However, several factors interfere with the attainment of equality of place, among them being the size of society and individual differences. These factors encourage variation, which creates conflict between individuals in central and marginal places not only because their interests and benefits differ, but primarily because the assignment of place cannot be permanently justified. Although people's place in society is determined on the basis of their relative location to others, paradoxically, there is no absolute basis on which that relativity can be justified. In the absence of an absolute basis for assigning place, society creates its own *operational absolutes* based on individual differences, which it uses to justify inequality (Miller, 1990). Operational absolutes are temporary and are only used to determine place over several generations before they are challenged by people on the margin and are replaced, sometimes violently but more often through cycles of negotiation, challenge, and renegotiation, by a new set of operational absolutes. A wide range of operational absolutes are used, including age and seniority, gender, race, color and ethnicity, ideology and religion, and merit and achievement.

The place structure of any society is pervasive. It is usually reflected in all the institutions of society including the state, government, education system, laws, and labor force. At the same time, the inequalities of place are also reflected among the societies of the world. Each society in the global community is in a relative relationship with all other societies with respect to all the dimensions of place. Central societies command considerable resources, enjoy high status, and often influence other societies to adopt their belief systems and culture. Central societies also have the power to determine outcomes favorable to their members, even against opposition from other societies. On the other hand, marginal societies cannot influence decisions that are favorable to their members, are often perceived as inferior to central societies, and have little or no status in the global community.

As is the case within a society, much variation exists among societies, and movement from margin to center and center to margin is possible. Many of the societies in the New World, including Canada and the United States, were marginal societies 200 years ago. Over time these societies have moved from marginal to central. Currently, central societies are considered developed, whereas marginal societies are perceived as either undeveloped or developing. A basic motivation of individuals and societies is to move to a more central place or, if already occupying a central place, to maintain it and resist any movement toward a more marginal place. The relative positions of societies also promote individual movement of place between societies. This occurs when people leave their place in one society and assume a place in another. Thus, it is possible for someone in a marginal position in a central society to move to a central position in a marginal society. A person can also move from a central place in a marginal society to occupy a marginal place in a central society. Several other permutations are possible.

Organizations in Canada reflect a convergence of the effects of social identity and place structure as described above. Organizational members who identify themselves as immigrant women of color are found mostly in marginal positions within the organizational structure. It appears that ethnicity, gender, and race act as operational absolutes that determine the marginality of such women. How does this occur and how do these individuals perceive and understand themselves and their marginal positions? Before examining how immigrant, gender, and color identities function as operational absolutes, let us explore some definitional problems related to the social identity of immigrant women of color.

DEFINITIONAL PROBLEMS

Immigrant

Multiple imprecise definitions of the term *immigrant* exist. In Canada, immigrant technically refers to people who have a certain legal status, people who are *permanent residents* or *landed immigrants,* rather than visitors, refugee claimants, temporary workers, or citizens (Arnopoulos, 1979). This is the definition commonly used in government programs designed to provide settlement and adaptation services to newcomers. Such services cease after newcomers have been "landed" for 3 years, by which time they are assumed to be fully settled and no longer in need of assistance. Indeed, after the third year immigrants may apply for Canadian citizenship. The word is also frequently used interchangeably with *foreign-born* and includes all people born outside of Canada, regardless of current citizenship status (Estable & Meyer, 1989). Thus, naturalized citizens may no longer be newcomers, but they are still often perceived as immigrants.

The most common usage of the term immigrant refers to a person of color, someone from a Third World or developing country, a person who does not speak English well and who holds a position low in the occupational hierarchy (Estable

& Meyer, 1989). In this sense, the term is frequently used interchangeably with *ethnic.* In other words race, country of origin, language, and class seem to be intricately related in popular conceptions of an immigrant. Thus, the immigration status or ethnicity of white Anglo-Saxons is unquestioned. For example, a white English-speaking university professor from the United States would not be commonly perceived as an immigrant, even if her legal status was permanent resident (Ng & Estable, 1987).

The significance of these various definitions of the term is that they all identify immigrants in ways that symbolize their exclusion from the mainstream. For the purpose of this discussion, the term immigrant refers to women who are legal immigrants as well as women who are legal citizens but are considered immigrant because of such factors as race and language competence.

People of Color

In Canada, people of color have been described as *visible minorities,* a term defined in the Employment Equity Act of 1986 as "persons, other than aboriginal peoples, who are non-Caucasian in race or nonwhite in color." However, this definition has been criticized as both offensive and misleading. Many people object to being described as visible minorities or people of color, claiming that such terms describe how they appear to others (whites) and what they are not (nonwhite), thereby identifying them by irrelevant characteristics that reinforce existing discriminatory concepts and structures and perpetuate their exclusion from Canadian society (Finlayson, 1990). Moreover, the definition implies that Caucasian and white are the norm, an implication that contradicts the reality in world population terms: People of color constitute the vast majority of the world's population. Instead, people of color prefer to be identified by what they are, that is by their countries or regions of birth, for example, African, Chinese, Indian, Jamaican, Latin American, South Asian, or West Indian (Das Gupta, 1986; Finlayson, 1990).

In reality, the term visible minority is commonly used to describe anyone who is identifiable as different from the white Canadian mainstream because of color or mode of dress (Daudlin, 1984). Foreign names and accents are also used to identify some racial groups as visible minorities (Henry & Ginzberg, 1985). For the purpose of this discussion, the term *people of color* will be used, although it fails to capture the great diversity among people of color and, more important, the reality that different racial groups have different experiences in the Canadian workforce (Finlayson, 1990).

IMMIGRANT, GENDER, AND COLOR
IDENTITIES AS OPERATIONAL ABSOLUTES

Women have historically experienced the injustice of systemic discrimination in all aspects of employment, including hiring, compensation, promotion, and career advancement. Occupational segregation along gender lines exists (Abella, 1984). For example, of all clerical and service positions in Canada, women occupy 79.3% and 62.7% respectively (Statistics Canada, 1991a; Status of Women, 1993). In contrast, clerical and service positions are held by only 20.7% and 37.3% males. Not only are these the lowest-paying jobs, but they are also the jobs with the least potential for promotion. Only 7.8% of all employed women in Canada occupy managerial positions (Statistics Canada, 1991a). Even where women occupy the same jobs as men, or jobs of equal value to organizations as those traditionally occupied by men, there is a 30% wage gap in favor of men (Statistics Canada, 1991b). These and other problems facing women in the workplace are increasingly being documented.

Less well-documented, however, are the experiences of women who face discrimination on three counts: their gender, their race, and their immigrant status. Until recently, most of the research on women at work has been based on the assumption that women constitute a homogeneous social group (Ontario Women's Directorate, 1987). Yet, organizations serving the needs of immigrant women of color assert that the experiences and needs of their clients differ significantly from those of white Canadian women (Coalition of Visible Minority Women, 1988; Ontario Immigrant and Visible Minority Women's Organization, 1988).

Immigrant Identity

In addition to those barriers to equal employment faced by women everywhere, immigrant women face barriers that are closely related to their social identity as immigrants. This is reflected in sociodemographic statistics indicating that despite participating in the labor force at a greater rate than Canadian-born women, disproportionate numbers of immigrant women are concentrated in the underpaid and underprotected sectors where they outnumber nonimmigrant women by three to one (Arnopoulos, 1979; Ontario Women's Directorate, 1987; Statistics Canada, 1991c). They experience extremely poor working conditions, have no job security, and have few prospects of upward mobility compared to male immigrants and nonimmigrant female employees, due mainly to the segregation of the labor market to which they have access (Dumon, 1981). For example, in Ontario, the home of 54% of the immigrant women in Canada, immigrant women make up 15% of the total workforce in processing and manufacturing occupations, whereas their nonimmigrant counterparts represent 6% (Estable & Meyer, 1989). Immigrant women are underrepresented even in the clerical positions to which females have traditionally been relegated. They occupy few managerial and supervisory positions and are rarely found in the higher paid traditionally "male" jobs (Urban Alliance on Race Relations & Ontario Women's Directorate, 1990). There is evidence that occupational segregation also exists among immigrant women, with women from different geographical regions being found in different occupations (Coté, 1991; Estable & Meyer, 1989). For example, whereas 36.5% of the women from the United States are employed in managerial, administrative, professional, and scientific categories, such positions are occupied by only 13.7% of the women from South America (Estable & Meyer, 1989). In short, immigrant women occupy marginal positions in the labor force. How does having the social identity of an immigrant act as an operational absolute on the basis of which place in the labor force is determined?

Nonacceptance of Credentials: Immigrant women's concentration at the bottom of the labor market is frequently assumed to be the result of low levels of education, which make them fit for only the least skilled jobs. Yet, since 1961, immigrant women have typically been better educated than either Canadian-born women or Canadian-born men (Coté, 1991; Employment and Immigration Canada, 1981). In particular, female immigrants are more likely to have university education than Canadian-born women (Abella, 1984; Coté, 1991). Despite evidence of comparable or higher levels of education, however, immigrant women are much less likely to be employed in professional jobs than their nonimmigrant counterparts (24% in comparison with 33%) (Estable & Meyer, 1989). What accounts for this disparity?

A major barrier to access into trades and professions faced by both male and female immigrants is the undervaluing and nonacceptance of their abilities, experience, and educational qualifications by Canadian employers, professional associations, and educational institutions. Typically, immigrants' previous training and credentials are considered below Canadian standards, and their previous work experience is ignored. Professional associations in particular are known for routinely failing to credit or grant equivalency to credentials obtained outside Canada (Cumming, 1989). Lacking expertise in comparative education and familiarity with international educational systems, such associations fail to make appropriate assessments of immigrants' prior learning. Thus, they usually advise immigrant accountants, engineers, lawyers, teachers, doctors, nurses, and other professionals to register for "upgrading" courses or to retrain altogether, often requiring them to undergo from 2 to 6 years of additional "professional" training before they can be granted licenses to practice in Canada (Cumming, 1989). Similarly, employers reject applications from immigrants who lack Canadian work experience, despite the fact that under the Human Rights Act, it is discriminatory for employers to use Canadian experience as a selection criterion. Thus, for most immigrants, the situation is a catch-22: they cannot obtain Canadian experience unless they receive employment, but they cannot obtain employment without having Canadian experience. Ironically, under the current Immigration Act, high levels of education and skills relevant to the Canadian labor market are two of the criteria necessary for gaining entry into Canada in the first place. Although their education and skills are evaluated as important to Canada by immigration counselors in the Canadian consulates and embassies of their homelands, immigrants experience severe discrimination in their efforts to gain access to employment when they arrive in Canada. In terms of the theory of place, their societies and institutions of origin are regarded as inferior and marginal relative to those of their new home.

Language Barriers. Lack of knowledge of either of Canada's two official languages is another barrier to employment and career advancement faced by many immigrants. About 42% of all immigrants to Canada know neither English nor French, and women are less likely to speak an official language than men (Statistics Canada, 1988). Although free language training is offered to those immigrants who can establish the need for an official language to obtain jobs, as in most other programs designed to help immigrants adapt to their new home, such training is regularly denied immigrant women because they are legal "dependents" of their husbands or because they obtain employment in factories, homes, and other places where knowledge of an official language is not considered essential (Arnopoulos, 1979). It is assumed that most of these women will acquire an official language on the job or take language courses after work. However, because of the occupational segregation and ghettoization of immigrant women, most never have an opportunity to speak any other language but their own on the job. They work among people who speak their language and, if necessary, communicate with their supervisors through interpreters. Also, after an extended workday at low wages, there is no time, energy, or money to attend night classes for language development.

Those women professionals who sit examinations to gain Canadian professional credentials must first pass standardized English as Second Language tests,
for example, the Ontario Test of English as a Second Language (OTESL), the
Test of Spoken English (TSE), Test of English as a Foreign Language (TOEFL),
and the Michigan Test Battery (MTB). Although some form of official language
assessment is essential in order to determine whether a person is sufficiently
proficient to carry out occupational duties effectively, few professional bodies
have been able to demonstrate that the required level of proficiency is appropriate and that the tests used are statistically valid and reliable (Cumming, 1989).
Moreover, there is evidence of a North American cultural bias in these tests, and
major deficiencies in their administration and application create significant
barriers to immigrants' entry into the Canadian workforce and professional
associations (Cumming, 1989). Thus, in general, the social identity of an
immigrant, especially one from a developing country, is associated with little in
the way of power, resources, or status relative to the social identity of a
nonimmigrant; this results in immigrants being ascribed to a marginal position
in the labor force.

Gender Identity

For immigrant women, the barrier created by the rejection of their credentials
is heightened by sexist attitudes that further devalue their abilities. Immigrant
women who are highly trained professionals with years of experience in their
respective fields have reported being advised to retrain as sewing machine
operators, cleaners, or caterers, jobs that are all perceived as "appropriate"
entry-level jobs for immigrant women (Estable & Meyer, 1989). When financial
necessity forces them to accept low-paying, unskilled jobs simply to survive,
they suffer from a process of *de-skilling* or *de-professionalizing* (Coalition of
Visible Minority Women, 1988). Among a group of 30 immigrant registered
nurses enrolled in a special Job Development Program run by the Coalition of
Visible Minority Women, 74% had more than 5 years nursing experience (27%
had more than 10 years) in their countries of origin, but all were employed as
factory workers, store clerks, pastry cooks, nurses' aides, counter helpers, or
receptionists (Coalition of Visible Minority Women, 1989). In general, such
ghettoization and underutilization of female immigrant professionals represent
not only a serious loss to their professions, but also an unnecessary and costly
setback to Canada's development. By denying qualified immigrant women
access to employment at professional levels, employers fail to benefit from
available trained human resources as intended by immigration policies. They

also create additional burdens for the economy, which ends up supporting such women through welfare and other social services.

The attitudes encountered by female immigrants reflect not only a sexually segregated society that discriminates against women, but also an ethnocentric society in which female immigrants have historically been ascribed to marginal positions, that is, to the lowest social class or to specific "female immigrant" roles. In the 19th century, Canada actively recruited Eastern European farm families because immigrant policymakers felt that the reproductive capacities of the women would provide the farm labor necessary to settle the prairies (Passaris, 1987). Later, women from impoverished areas in the British Isles were recruited expressly for the purpose of working as domestics in private Canadian homes so that Canadian-born women would be free to work outside their homes. At times, female immigrants were simply not accepted. Female Chinese immigrants were banned when male Chinese were being recruited to build the Canadian Pacific Railroad. It was felt that such a ban would prevent the permanent settlement of the Chinese (Coalition of Visible Minority Women, 1988). Thus, although immigration policies have always been designed to meet particular labor and economic needs in different periods of Canadian history, immigrant men have been targeted as the main suppliers of labor, and the women have been perceived as either support for the men or nonessential (Arnopoulos, 1979).

The sexism implicit in immigration policies is also reflected in the institutionalization of certain structures that exclude women. For example, the Immigration Act categorizes immigrants into several classes, the largest of which is the family class in which one member of the family is the formal applicant and the other members are identified as legal dependents who accompany the applicant. About 60% of all female immigrants belong to the family class and are classified as dependents, usually of their husbands (Estable & Meyer, 1989). This means that their husbands are financially responsible for them for 3 to 10 years (depending on the judgment of the immigration officer). Even if women are the main income earners in their countries of origin and have higher levels of education than their husbands, they are advised by Canadian consular and embassy officials (who have been socialized into sexist conceptions of breadwinners) that their husbands must be the principal applicants and the wives and children their dependents (Coalition of Visible Minority Women, 1988). Classification as a dependent is a major barrier to many immigrant women's economic advancement in Canada because it limits their access to programs designed to assist immigrants in settling. Such programs are frequently not intended for members of the family class but, when they are, they are officially

communicated to the legal head of the household, the male, not to his dependents. Only the male is usually allowed to participate in orientation sessions for
newcomers held by the Canadian Employment and Immigration Commission
and to receive benefits such as free language training and allowances for
transportation to job searches. Without such assistance, immigrant women are
implicitly assigned the task of homemaking because the costs of job hunting and
its related costs of child care and transportation then become prohibitive.

Not only does this system deny immigrant women equal opportunity to obtain
employment but, more important, it denigrates and dehumanizes them. Their
social identity denies immigrant women's rights as independent persons. It defines
women as extensions of men and is both discriminatory and sexist (Dumon, 1981).
Thus, lacking power, resources, and status and originating from societies that
also lack these determinants of central place, immigrant women face negative
stereotypical attitudes and systemic discrimination that make them severely
marginalized and disadvantaged in their efforts to achieve employment equity.

Color Identity

When the immigrant woman is also a person of color, the situation is even
more complex. In addition to the many disadvantages they face as immigrants
and as women, immigrant women of color also experience racism. There is
pervasive evidence that race is an operational absolute used to establish and
maintain people of color in marginal positions in the labor force. Studies have
demonstrated that people of color encounter exclusionary barriers at the job-
entry stage, where employers use negative group stereotyping of races rather
than direct assessments of individuals in their selection processes (Finlayson,
1990; Henry & Ginzberg, 1985; Muszynski & Reitz, 1982). Yet, people of color
have attained a higher educational level than the general population, with 60%
having some postsecondary education compared to 50% for the general population, and 20% having university degrees compared to 12% of other members
of the labor force (Coté, 1991). Even when they are allowed access into
organizations, people of color experience invalid differential treatment based on
their race compared to the treatment given to their white counterparts. It has
been reported (Billingsley & Muszynski, 1985; Finlayson, 1990; Zureik &
Hiscott, 1983) that they experience a lack of timely and accurate feedback on
job performance, biased performance evaluations, low expectations on the part
of supervisors, slower rates of promotion, smaller or less frequent raises, and
limited access to training and developmental activities.

Many organizations are unaware of how their practices unintentionally create discriminatory barriers that keep people of color on the margins. For example, people of color are frequently deprived of opportunities to apply for internal openings, which are only communicated to members of informal social networks that are inaccessible to them. They are also discriminated against in termination decisions, especially during a recession, because termination criteria affect primarily those employee categories in which people of color are most concentrated (Finlayson, 1990; Jones & Huff, 1989; Seward, 1990). These are also the very categories occupied by the majority of Canada's immigrant women of color. These women are especially vulnerable to employment discrimination. They are perceived as less valuable than other employees (Naidoo, 1990). Depending on the occupational category, the full-time salary of people of color is from 10% to 25% less than that of other Canadians in the labor force, but for *immigrant* people of color, it is even lower (Coté, 1991). On average, the employment income of people of color born in Canada is 10% higher than that of immigrant people of color. This is the reverse of the situation for other Canadians, among whom immigrants earn 8% more than nonimmigrants (Coté, 1991). Among people of color, females' salaries tend to be lower than those of their male peers (Brown & Ford, 1977; Coalition of Visible Minority Women, 1988; Coté, 1991). These facts emphasize the complexity of the problems related to being an immigrant woman of color in a labor force where immigrant, gender, and color identities operate as operational absolutes for determining place.

WORKPLACE EXPERIENCES OF
IMMIGRANT WOMEN OF COLOR

In order to gain a better understanding of how immigrant status, gender, and color serve as operational absolutes that are used to keep people in marginal places in the workforce, 14 immigrant women of color were interviewed about their workplace experiences. The main criteria for selecting the women were their color, gender, and immigrant social identities because it was assumed that only people selected on these bases would possess the relevant knowledge and be able to provide the information sought. The selection was done through a snowballing referral process, with each woman who agreed to participate being asked to suggest the name of another woman with the same selection criteria. The limitation inherent in this process is reflected in the fact that most of the women interviewed were educated professionals. Their experiences may therefore be positively skewed and are not described here as representative of all immigrant women of color.

The women range in age from 31 to 49 and immigrated to North America from Guyana, Jamaica, Pakistan, and Zaire. A range of 5 to 19 years have passed since their immigration and 11 have become legal citizens. Twelve of the women speak English as their native language. The other two acquired English as a second language at a very early age, because English is the official language of their country of birth and is the language of education. Most of the women immigrated as adults, with at least a bachelor's degree from their country of origin. Only one immigrated as a homemaker. Three others, a nurse's aide and two executive assistants, did not have degrees but were qualified and experienced in their respective fields. One woman had a master's degree and another was a medical doctor. After immigrating, several of the women returned to school, including the medical doctor. Collectively, the women now have eight master's degrees (one held by the medical doctor) and four bachelor's degrees. They occupy positions as engineers (3), early childhood educator (1), computer analysts (2), physiotherapist (1), high school guidance counselor (1), public service managers (2), French interpreter (1), executive assistants (2) and nurse's aide (1). None occupies a senior-level position. Despite their apparent career success, however, they expressed frustration at still having to struggle against prejudice and discrimination in their mostly white, male-dominated organizations. They reported on their experiences with gaining employment, relationships with different groups in their organizations, compensation and promotion rates, job satisfaction, organizational commitment, and strategies for coping with their marginalization.

Gaining Employment

One of the most common experiences was the difficulty in gaining employment. Only four of the women reported not experiencing any difficulty in obtaining employment. The others perceived that the difficulties they experienced related to one or more characteristics of their social identity rather than to their lack of ability, experience, or qualification. As the physiotherapist explained,

> My credentials had to be evaluated before I could even seek employment, and they were not accepted as being equal to [North American] standards nor were my years of experience in a foreign country validated. I had to go back to school and acquire additional credits.

This woman perceived that her immigrant status adversely affected her ability to obtain employment. Another, a public service manager with a master's degree in industrial relations, felt that she could not separate her race and immigrant status as social identity factors that operated against her.

> My race determined in advance the reaction showed to me even before I could speak. Then when I spoke, my foreign accent was used as an excuse not to hire me. Many times I was told that clients would not be able to understand my foreign accent.

Most of the women felt that gender had the least impact on their ability to obtain employment. As one of the public service managers explained, "They don't have to bother about my gender because there is enough overlap between my race and immigrant status to disqualify me. Gender is the least of their concerns."

Another common experience among the women was being forced to work in unskilled positions totally unrelated to their training and expertise while waiting to gain either North American accreditation or acceptance into their chosen profession. The physiotherapist reported having to work as a clerk in the mail room of a bank, and the medical doctor did volunteer work in various not-for-profit organizations just to keep herself busy and "maintain [her] sanity." She still works outside of her chosen profession and has in effect undergone a process of de-skilling and de-professionalizing, a common problem among professional immigrant women (Coalition of Visible Minority Women, 1988).

Relationships With Others

The women were asked to describe their relationship with other groups in their workplace, including other immigrant women of color, white nonimmigrant women, and males. Most of them were the only immigrant woman of color in their department and sometimes in their entire organization. When there were others, the women interviewed related well with them, seeking support in their common identity.

> We interact quite well on a professional and social level. We also look out for each other and often compare our past experiences before immigrating.

> We relate to each other well because we have common experiences of trying to fit into the workforce.

> You feel a bond of closeness with other immigrant women of color. . . . There is a greater openness, willingness and ease in discussing certain issues like personal and cultural problems.

Those who had no other immigrant women of color as coworkers experienced isolation, which was often a source of stress:

> I sometimes feel lonely and tense because nonimmigrant workers tend to forget that I am an immigrant and make negative comments about immigrants. I feel I have to defend immigrants or sometimes I feel I have to represent them.

> I try to make the best of the situation and make friends with the nonimmigrant women, but it isn't always easy because there are some things that you just cannot discuss with people who do not have the same background and experience.

In spite of the perceived difficulty, most of the women had good relationships with the white nonimmigrant women in their department or organization. However, these were mostly working relationships. Many commented on the fact that they have never been invited to their coworkers' homes or that they only interact socially in a work-related context such as a farewell lunch for a coworker, the organization's awards banquet, or a conference of a professional association.

> Professional rapport is satisfactory but there is no interaction in a social way outside the workplace. We often disagree on methods of dealing with students, but it is not confrontational.

> Our relationship is friendly but superficial and guarded.

> We are mostly passive or indifferent to each other.

When asked what they thought was the general attitude of white nonimmigrant female coworkers toward them, the women all commented on their coworkers' surprise at their experience, expertise, qualifications, and other accomplishments.

> Sometimes it's almost like they feel threatened and are often very surprised by your past and present achievements academically and socially. On the job most seem to accept you as an equal, but they still make no effort to socialize outside the workplace. It's almost as if they don't perceive you as their equal socially.

They respect me. They are often surprised at the extent of my experiences and knowledge because they stereotype me. But in general, they forget that I'm not white, which is both good and bad. It's good because it makes me feel accepted, but it's bad because when they make insensitive comments on something negative that is reported in the media about my race, I feel as if they are speaking about me. My race is partly what makes me who I am and if you don't like my race how can you like me?

Although none of the women perceived themselves as employment equity recruits, they believed that many of their nonimmigrant white coworkers perceived them in this way, even in cases where the organization did not have explicit employment equity policies and practices. This angered the women because they believed that such attitudes devalued their qualifications and put pressure on them to excel in order to prove their worth: "It suggests that I am inferior or less of a person, especially when such attitudes are coming from whites who lack qualifications and experience."

The women felt that their male coworkers had positive attitudes toward them. Men treated them with respect and did not seem to resent their presence in the workplace. This finding contrasts sharply with the predictions of the theory of place, which suggests that gender would be a strong basis for marginalization, given women's low organizational power, resources, and status relative to men. It may be explained by a gender difference in expressing emotions, with the men being less open and expressive than the women, or by recent heightened awareness of and sensitivity toward women's workplace issues.

Compensation and Promotion

The women's perceptions of their compensation levels relative to those of other groups of coworkers varied. Whereas a few felt that their compensation was the same as that of others, others felt that it was lower. However, the majority were unable to comment because they had no idea of their coworkers' salaries. This is not surprising because most people treat their income as a private matter and either do not reveal it or state it inaccurately. Although they were unable to compare their compensation levels with those of their coworkers, most of the women indicated that they were satisfied with their salary, the average range of which was between $46,000 and $60,000.

The women were less satisfied with their rate of promotion. Most felt that their rate of promotion was the same as other male employees and other female immigrant employees of color. The major difference appeared to be a slower promotion rate relative to their white nonimmigrant female coworkers. Once again, race and immigrant status were perceived to have more significant impacts on workplace experience than gender.

Because mentoring is an informal process that increases visibility and has a significant effect on career advancement (Fagenson, 1988; McKeen & Burke, 1989), the women were asked about their experiences with mentors. Few reported having mentors or other forms of organizational support that might be useful in advancing their careers. One woman's experience with mentors was positive. However, this was not a common experience.

[Mentors] have been open, available, and willing to share their ideas and experiences and to answer questions and give explanations. I found this very useful because it has helped me advance my career and become better integrated into the organization; maybe not totally integrated but enough to feel a part of the organization.

Job Satisfaction

On the whole, the women interviewed expressed high levels of job satisfaction. They were most satisfied with the content of their work, which they described as challenging, interesting, consuming, and fulfilling. They were least satisfied with opportunities for advancement. Some felt that in spite of their outstanding performance, they were always ignored when opportunities arose for more challenging roles with greater responsibilities. They perceived that the same people were favored for advancement over and over again, regardless of the quality of their performance. Most perceived that they had to work harder than their white counterparts and that they constantly had to prove themselves. They felt that doing good work was not enough; they had to excel to compensate for their immigrant, race, and gender identities. A few felt that they received the most difficult projects or those of greatest importance to their department because their bosses knew they had the necessary skills and work habits to do them well. Yet, they received little recognition for performing what one perceived as "the role of the workhorse" and were not rewarded with advancement. One claimed a lack of interest in seeking further advancement because of her negative experience with subordinates who resented having to report to an immigrant woman of color: "They went as far as hiding important information that I needed to accomplish my job and refused to answer to me as their boss."

Another major source of dissatisfaction was the relationship the women had with their coworkers. Although most described this relationship as cordial, they felt that it was very different from the relationships they had with coworkers in workplaces in their country of origin. They described those relationships as much more warm, relaxed, spontaneous, personal, and intimate. By contrast, the relationships with their coworkers remained professional. Most of the women interviewed were saddened by the fact that they felt isolated in their organization and described a marked distinction between their relationships inside and outside the organization. This finding is consistent with Bell's (1990) study of the bicultural life experience of black career-oriented women. The women in Bell's study perceived themselves as having membership in two distinct cultural contexts, one black, the other white. Although membership in one group was not considered more exclusive than membership in the other, nonetheless, the women experienced a cultural pull that stems from needing "to gain emotional wholeness with a sense of cultural integration among the groups in which one has membership" (Bell, 1990, p. 464).

Organizational Commitment

Although the women interviewed perceived themselves as loyal employees, few identified closely with their organization. Even when they perceived their organizational involvement to be high, several cited lack of mutual trust and social bonding as factors that prevented them from being totally committed to their organizations. They often attributed the absence of trust and social bonding to their social identity as immigrant women of color.

> I can never be sure of the reason for being denied the promotion. They all tell you what excellent work you're doing, and then when crunch time comes, they overlook it. You never know where you stand or why. You can't help feeling that if you were white or if you were a man things would be different.

> It's hard to feel committed when you are always reminded that you are different and don't belong. I mean, I am the only minority on staff. They find my accent interesting, sometimes amusing. They even see me as different from people of color who are born here. . . . I would feel better if I had more people like myself to whom I could relate on a different level.

The women did not believe that lack of complete commitment prevented them from performing well. They all took great pride in their work and said that they would do nothing to jeopardize their performance or their hard-earned reputations. Most were not considering leaving their jobs but said that they would leave "if the circumstances were right," or "for a different environment and different experience." For example, the high school guidance counselor was interested in transferring into the college level or specializing in another area, such as vocational counseling. In short, these women were professionals whose commitment was to their work rather than to a particular organization.

Coping Strategies

The women interviewed had all devised strategies for coping with the marginalization and discrimination they experienced on account of individual coworkers' attitudes and prejudices as well as organizational policies and practices. Despite working in a predominantly white organization, each woman rejected assimilation as an appropriate coping strategy. Assimilation is an approach to managing diversity that ignores differences and requires minority individuals to conform to the traditions, values, and norms of the majority (Bell, 1990; Cox & Nickelson, 1991). Instead of abandoning their culture and attempting to fit into the white, nonimmigrant culture, the women found themselves compartmentalizing their bicultural contexts. Compartmentalization is the establishment of rigid boundaries between "two distinct cultural spheres so the dynamics of one do not spill over into the other" (Bell, 1990, p. 472). This process meant that apart from the stress created by having to balance work and family life, a stress common among most women in the labor force, these women had the additional burden of having to balance the two very different cultural contexts in which they operate. However, this additional burden was perceived as much less stressful than the stress of becoming so assimilated at work that they would lose their social identity and their affiliation with others of the same race or ethnicity outside the workplace.

> It's probably a good thing that we don't socialize much because I don't think I could bear all that pressure. When I am with my friends and family, I can be myself. I am much more relaxed than when I am at work.

> That's why I go back home for my vacation almost every year. It gives me an opportunity to be with my own people, who don't treat me as different or inferior. I always tell them jokingly that I have to keep going home to regain my culture and to get enough inspiration to help me survive until my next visit.

The women were able to resist assimilation primarily because of another coping strategy, that is, the development of a strong social support system through close friendships and extended families. These bonding relationships (Denton, 1990) gave them the strength and self-confidence to face their marginalization and discrimination every day. These relationships enable them to discuss their experiences and share their feelings with loved ones who empathize and understand. The supportiveness of family and friends further allows them to compartmentalize their two worlds, the white world at work and their nonwork world shared by people of the same social identity: "I sought advice from friends who had immigrated before. They showed me the ropes and helped me to learn the system. Their willingness to listen gave me an outlet for my frustration and anger."

One woman explained that one of her best coping strategies was to withdraw. Withdrawal was manifested in frequent absences and limited involvement in the activities of her organization.

> When it becomes too much for me to handle, I simply take a day off. It doesn't happen often, but when it does, I can't tell anyone at work why I was absent. They would never understand that I just want to be myself for a change.

It is clear that although these women experience a great deal of stress on account of their experiences in the workplace, most of them are able to cope, some more effectively than others.

IMPLICATIONS AND CONCLUSIONS

Although governments at all levels have enacted legislation aimed at achieving employment equity for social groups that have historically suffered employment discrimination, recent studies indicate that the present legislation has been largely ineffective in removing barriers to employment equity (Finlayson, 1990; Minister of Supply and Services Canada, 1990). Organizations that comply with the legislative requirements have demonstrated increased diversity in their workforces (Leck & Saunders, 1992), but the quality of organizational life for groups targeted by such legislation has not always benefited. One reason for this ineffectiveness lies in the inadequate attention to the unique problems faced by each of these groups. By identifying and describing some of the problems encountered by immigrant women of color, this chapter has emphasized that women are not a homogeneous social group. The gains many white women have made in the labor force have not translated into improvements for women overall.

The interviews summarized above suggest that immigrant women of color face a triple jeopardy because of their social identity. Despite their achieved status as educated professionals, they are ascribed to marginal positions in the labor force. This is evidenced by their self-reported experience of difficulty in gaining employment; cordial but guarded relationships with their nonimmigrant white coworkers; and slower promotion rates than their white non-immigrant female counterparts. Although they are generally satisfied with certain aspects of their jobs, namely the work itself and the pay, they are less satisfied with the supervision they get, their limited opportunities for advancement, and their relationships with coworkers. A recurring theme among these women is the limited amount of socializing with other members of their workplace and the stress experienced from being the only person (or one of a few people) of color in their department or organization. They feel isolated and get little support from social networks within the organization. For many, one of the greatest stressors lies in their co-workers' perception that they are tokens, representatives of the racial or ethnic group with which they identify and occupying their positions only because of their social identity rather than because they are qualified. As perceived tokens, they are not fully integrated into the organization and feel the burden of constantly proving that they deserve their positions. Thus, contrary to popular belief, being an immigrant woman of color does not gain any extra advantage from employment equity policies and regulations. Rather, it is associated with occupying a marginal position in the workplace, even for educated, experienced women in professional occupational categories.

One implication arising from the experiences of the women interviewed is the need for organizations to increase the representation of such women in the workplace. Feelings of isolation and the accompanying stress can be considerably reduced if there are more coworkers with a similar social identity. The psychosocial support that these women feel when they can identify with others would help them to feel a greater sense of belonging and might increase their attitudinal commitment to their organization. Organizations seeking to increase the diversity of their workforce should therefore avoid engaging in tokenism, which is isolating and stressful and reduces the token's ability to become fully integrated into the culture of the organization or to feel committed to an organization with which she does not identify.

Increasing representation would also allow white employees to have more authentic contacts with other social identities. Increased contact would provide them with other frameworks on which to base their perceptions of their immigrant female coworkers of color instead of the negative stereotypes that they currently use. This would enable them to focus on their colleagues' qualifications, expertise, performance, and individual personality differences and not exclusively on their social identities. In turn, immigrant women of color might experience less pressure to excel or to represent others like themselves. The experiences of the women interviewed suggest that their biggest problems lie with the insensitivity of their coworkers. This suggests that organizations need to pay greater attention to educating and sensitizing all employees about valuing diversity. Organizations are increasingly sensitizing and educating management about diversity issues, but failure to sensitize other employees can have adverse effects on an organization's diversity climate. A study of the class of 1994 (Wynter, 1994) showed that black, Asian, and Hispanic students who were successful at gaining job offers used strategies that included developing extensive grapevines among their ethnic group with internship or employment experiences. These students' estimation of an organization's diversity climate far outweighed its name or industry position. They know that although many organizations claim to have diversity as a priority, this is not always true. Hence, they discount what the organizations say and turn to each other for credible information. Thus, a poor diversity climate can damage an organization's reputation among many racial and ethnic groups.

Another implication for managing diversity is the need to develop an action plan for the structural and informal integration of organizational members with social identities different from those of the mainstream. Given the tendency of people to interact with others having social identities similar to theirs, even the greater representation of people with different social identities will not be enough to guarantee their integration into the organization. Such integration, which is different from assimilation, must be planned. Structural integration refers to the proportion of various groups in the total workforce, as well as their participation in the power structure of the organization (Cox, 1993). Thus, the action plan for structural integration should not be limited to specifying goals and timetables for hiring and promoting underrepresented social groups, as is currently required by employment equity legislation. It also involves organizing work by multidisciplinary or multiskilled teams composed of culturally different employees from various sections or stages of the work process and reducing power imbalances among social groups. Organizing work into heterogeneous teams is not only more efficient but also more inclusive. It makes team members of people with different social identities from those of the mainstream rather than singling them out for their differences. In addition, their differences become positive rather than negative forces. Reducing power imbalances can be achieved by ensuring that different social groups are represented on significant decision-making bodies, including selection and promotion committees. This increases their opportunity to participate and to gain legitimacy, which can ultimately gain them greater centrality in the organizational structure.

Informal integration refers to access to informal networks such as mentoring programs, company-sponsored social events, and identity-based support groups (Cox, 1993). Objectives of the action plan for informal integration include increasing the levels of inclusion and participation of various social groups in the organization's social activities such as sports events, lunch or dinner meetings, and membership in social clubs frequented by organizational leaders. Such objectives are based on the assumption that important work-related contacts are often made outside of the normal working hours and in various social activities. Most mentoring, for example, occurs through informal communication networks, and because immigrant women of color have little participation in such networks, their opportunities for benefiting from mentoring are considerably reduced. Moreover, stereotypes of immigrant women of color as less capable may make potential mentors at higher organizational levels less likely to select such women as protégés. The low representation of immigrant women of color at senior levels also decreases the likelihood of women with a similar social identity at lower levels being selected by mentors. This implies that organizations seeking to manage diversity effectively need to create formal mentoring programs targeted for marginalized employees such as immigrant women of color who are disadvantaged in normal informal mentoring activities. This can be done by ensuring that such employees are included in career-relevant informal social activities, providing incentives for being a mentor, and training both mentors and protégés. Providing resources for the establishment and maintenance of identity-based support groups may also facilitate peer mentoring, which can at least provide useful psychosocial support if not support for career advancement. Thus, planning for the structural and informal integration of groups different from the mainstream not only reduces the isolation they experience, but also increases their opportunities for advancement. It provides access to the power, resources, and status that are necessary for moving from marginal to central positions.

The special employment problems confronting immigrant women of color are often overlooked in favor of an emphasis on commonalities with either white women or immigrant men of color. This chapter sought to increase awareness of the additional problems faced by such women due to the confluence in their social identity of race, gender, and ethnicity that differ from the mainstream. The experiences described here depict those of only a small number of women, all of whom are educated professionals. They are therefore not representative of immigrant women of color in general. However, they raise issues that need to be thoroughly investigated in the future using multiple data sources comprising immigrant women of color from a wide range of occupational categories. For example, how widespread are experiences of biculturalism and how prevalent are perceptions of isolation or lack of organizational commitment when there is a large number of immigrant women of color in one organization in contrast to only one or a few? In such cases what are the patterns of their relationships with white coworkers? How do the experiences of immigrant women of color affect their performance, especially in nonprofessional occupational categories? By researching these and other clearly underinvestigated issues, we may gain a fuller understanding of the complex reality of workplace diversity, develop new ways of managing that take into account the unique experiences of employees with different social identities, and diminish the triple jeopardy of organizational members who occupy marginal places as women, immigrants, and people of color.

REFERENCES

Abella, J. R. S. (1984). *Equality in employment: A royal commission report.* Toronto: Commission on Equality in Employment.

Arnopoulos, S. M. (1979). *Problems of immigrant women in the Canadian labor force.* Ottawa: Canadian Advisory Council on the Status of Women.

Ashforth, B. E., & Mael, F. (1989). Social identity theory and the organization. *Academy of Management Review, 14*(1), 20-39.

Bell, E. L. (1990). The bicultural life experience of career-oriented black women. *Journal of Organizational Behavior, 11,* 459-477.

Billingsley, B., & Muszynski, L. (1985). *No discrimination here? Toronto employers and the multiracial workforce.* Toronto: Social Planning Council of Metropolitan Toronto and the Urban Alliance on Race Relations.

Brown, H. A., & Ford, D. L. (1977). An exploratory analysis of discrimination in the employment of black MBA graduates. *Journal of Applied Psychology, 62*(1), 50-56.

Coalition of Visible Minority Women. (1988). *Employment equity: A social policy to address systemic racism.* Toronto: Author.

Coalition of Visible Minority Women. (1989). *Coalition of Visible Minority Women NEWS, 1*(1). Toronto: Author.

Coté, M. G. (1991, Summer). Visible minorities in the Canadian labor force. *Perspectives on Labor and Income,* pp. 17-26.

Cox, T., Jr. (1993). *Cultural diversity in organizations: Theory, research, and practice.* San Francisco, CA: Berrett-Koehler.

Cox, T., Jr., & Nickelson, J. (1991). Models of acculturation for intraorganizational cultural diversity. *Canadian Journal of Administrative Sciences, 8*(2), 90-100.

Cumming, P. (1989). *Access! Report of the task force on access to professions and trades in Ontario.* Toronto: Ontario Ministry of Citizenship.

Das Gupta, T. (1986). *Learning from our history: Community development by immigrant women in Ontario 1958-1986. A tool for action.* Toronto: Cross Cultural Communication Centre.

Daudlin, B. (1984). *Equality now! Report of the special committee on visible minorities in Canadian society.* Ottawa: Supply and Services.

Denton, T. C. (1990). Bonding and supportive relationships among black professional women: Rituals of restoration. *Journal of Organizational Behavior, 11,* 447-457.

Dumon, W. A. (1981). The situation of migrant women workers. *International Migration, 19*(1-2), 190-205.

Employment and Immigration Canada. (1981). *Integration of immigrant/migrant women into the Canadian labor market.* National Report of Canada to the Working Party on Migration and the Working Party on the Role of Women in the Economy. Ottawa: Organization for Economic Co-operation and Development.

Estable, A., & Meyer, M. (1989). *A discussion paper on settlement needs of immigrant women in Ontario.* Unpublished research sponsored by Canada Employment and Immigration Commission.

Fagenson, E. A. (1988). The power of a mentor. *Group and Organisation Studies, 13,* 182-194.

Finlayson, J. (Ed.). (1990). *A time for change: Moving beyond racial discrimination in employment.* Toronto: Social Planning Council of Metropolitan Toronto and Urban Alliance on Race Relations.

Henry, F., & Ginzberg, E. (1985). *Who gets the work? A test of racial discrimination in employment.* Toronto: The Urban Alliance on Race Relations and the Social Planning Council of Metropolitan Toronto.

Jones, K., & Huff, V. (1989). Plant closure: Its effect on immigrant and women workers. *Our Times, 8*(1), 22-25.

Leck, J. D., & Saunders, D. M. (1992). Employment equity programs in Canada's federal jurisdiction: Effects on selection and promotion of designated group members. In M. Belcourt & M. Tremblay (Eds.), *Proceedings of the annual conference of the Administrative Sciences Association of Canada, Human Resources Division* (pp. 65-73). Toronto: Administrative Sciences Association of Canada.

McKeen, C. A., & Burke, R. J. (1989). Mentor relationship in organizations: Issues, strategies, and prospects for women. *Journal of Management Development, 8,* 33-42.

Miller, E. (1990). *Jamaican society and high schooling.* Kingston, Jamaica: Institute of Social and Economic Research.

Minister of Supply and Services Canada. (1990). *Discussion paper on the employment equity act.* Ottawa: Author.

Muszynski, L., & Reitz, J. (1982). *Racial and ethnic discrimination in employment.* Toronto: Social Planning Council of Metropolitan Toronto.

Naidoo, J. C. (1990). Immigrant women in Canada: Toward a new decade. *Currents, 6*(2), 18-21.

Ng, R., & Estable, A. (1987). Immigrant women in the labor force: An overview of present knowledge and research gaps. *Resources for Feminist Research* [Special Issue on Immigrant Women], 16(1), 29-34.

Nkomo, S. (1992). The emperor has no clothes: Rewriting race in organizations. *Academy of Management Review, 17*(3), 487-513.

Ontario Immigrant and Visible Minority Women's Organization. (1988). *Is employment equity for all women?* Paper presented to the Human Resources Secretariat, Ontario Ministry of Labor.

Ontario Women's Directorate. (1987, Summer). Immigrant and Visible Minority Women in Ontario: Barriers to employment. *Currents, pp. 16-21.*

Passaris, C. (1987). The economics of Canadian multiculturalism. In K. A. McLeod (Ed.), *Multicultural education: A partnership* (pp. 27-43). Toronto: Canadian Council for Multicultural and Intercultural Education.

Seward, S. B. (1990). Immigrants and labor adjustment. *Currents, 6*(2), 15-17.

Statistics Canada. (1988). *Profile of the immigrant population: Canada, provinces, and territories.* Ottawa: Ministry of Supply and Services.

Statistics Canada. (1991a). *1991 census of Canada, labor force activity* (Vol. 1). Ottawa: Ministry of Supply and Services.

Statistics Canada. (1991b). *Earnings of men and women 1991.* Ottawa: Ministry of Supply and Services.

Statistics Canada. (1991c). *Profile of the immigrant population: Canada, provinces, and territories.* Ottawa: Ministry of Supply and Services.

Status of Women. (1993). Women in Canada: a statistical profile. Ottawa: Ministry of Supply and Services.

Tajfel, H. (1978). The achievement of group differentiation. In H. Tajfel (Ed.), *Differentiation between social groups: Studies in the social psychology of intergroup relations* (pp. 77-98). London: Academic Press.

Tajfel, H. (1981). *Human groups and social categories.* Cambridge: Cambridge University Press.

Tajfel, H. (1982). Instrumentality, identity, and social comparisons. In H. Tajfel (Ed.), *Social identity and intergroup relations* (pp. 483-507). Cambridge: Cambridge University Press.

Tajfel, H., & Turner, J. C. (1986). The social identity theory of intergroup behavior. In S. Worchel & W. G. Austin (Eds.), *Psychology of intergroup relations* (pp. 7-24). Chicago: Nelson-Hall.

Urban Alliance on Race Relations & Ontario Women's Directorate. (1990). *Employment equity for invisible minority women: A guide for employers.* Toronto: Author.

Wynter, L. E. (1994, September 7). Minority hires mapped their own paths to jobs. *Wall Street Journal,*

Zureik, E., & Hiscott, R. (1983). *The experience of visible minorities in the work world: The case of MBA graduates.* Report submitted to the Race Relations Subdivision of the Ontario Human Rights Commission. Ottawa: Ministry of Labor.

14

How International Is International Management?

Provincialism, Parochialism, and the Problematic of Global Diversity

DIANA WONG-MINGJI

ALI H. MIR

That the academic discipline of international management (IM),[1] as seen from the vantage point of U.S. scholars, demonstrates an overwhelmingly skewed interest in the industrialized (or "developed" or "Western") world[2] ought to come as no startling revelation to most observers of this field. After all, most of the management institutions of the world are located in the West, most management scholars are products of a Western environment, and most management journals are edited, composed, and distributed in the West.

The self-evidence of these contentions notwithstanding, a critique of the prevailing situation not only bears repetition but also offers opportunities for self-reflexivity to a field that is rapidly assuming center stage in an era of increasing globalization. This chapter has a simple agenda. By asking the question—How diverse is the field of IM?—it seeks to reiterate that IM is a field that is constrained by its relatively limited discourse, selective in offering voice to its constituencies, and in need of representational and nonexclusionary scholarship in order to face the challenges of newer global realities.

It would be easy to make a case for a greater amount of diversity in the study of IM. The forces of globalization are acting on a hitherto unimaginable scale. Corporate and national interests leak across increasingly permeable national boundaries. The complex interplay of a diversity of people, cultures, governments, and agendas demands a more nuanced understanding of the terrains of operation. The unilinear nature of the IM discourse tends to simplify and reduce the multiplicity of perspectives that are potentially available to organizational inquiry. The spirit of our argument, however, goes beyond this contention. Our chapter is neither a plea for the inclusion of alternate epistemologies into the discourse of IM nor a demand for the representation of excluded subjectivities. It is an attempt to demonstrate that the "parochial dinosaur" (Boyacigiller & Adler, 1991) is far from extinct and that even inherently diverse domains such as IM can be reduced by modern(ist) modes of inquiry into a relatively homogenous discourse that surrenders itself to the demands of the structures within which it operates.

In order to support these contentions, this chapter offers evidence from a thorough examination of the field. Based on a scrutiny of all 3,649 articles on issues related to IM that appeared in 16 selected journals during the period 1954 to 1994, it tries to answer the following questions: Who is doing IM research? Who are the subjects of this research? Who has the privilege of theorizing? Who is being theorized about? Who is being cited in these articles? Whose authority is valorized? Who is absent from this conversation? What are the issues of voice, representation, and power in this discourse?

DEVELOPMENT OF THE IM DISCOURSE

During the last few years, the study and practice of IM has become an integral part of the increasing globalization momentum (Adler, 1983a; Doktor, Tung, & von Glinow, 1991; Dunning, 1989). The driving forces underlying the global process stem from major changes in technological developments, economic infrastructures, political ideologies, social relationships, and environmental issues. Each one of these presents a host of complex issues within itself, and taken together they present a turbulent and chaotic operating environment for contemporary organizations. Thus, the study of IM is faced with some extraordinary challenges in its effort to develop a coherent body of knowledge.

One of the more important of these challenges is posed by the issue of diversity. Any discussion of workplace diversity, even when conducted on North American soil, cannot take place without an awareness of changing global realities. North American workplaces are encountering the pressures of diversity in more ways than one. Not only are their employee profiles within Canada and the United States becoming more diverse, but geopolitical and technological changes are forcing even those organizations situated in North America to constantly interact with culturally diverse populations from around the world whether they be customers, employees, contractors, or financiers. Increasingly, therefore, for most organizations, the terms *diversity* and *international* are becoming increasingly synonymous with one another. However, although IM has always recognized that, as a discipline, it needs to deal with cultures, traditions, policies, and people of several different kinds, its approach to diversity has been simplistic and unproblematic. Led to assume that Western modes of management are universally applicable, IM has treated culture as a variable to be manipulated in ways that would allow for the entry and sustenance of management paradigms generated in the postindustrial revolution West. The developments of late 20th century capitalism have forced IM to reevaluate this position, and IM scholars are increasingly being forced into reconsidering their approach. As IM comes into its own as a discipline, issues of diversity are pushing themselves to the forefront of the research agenda.

Recent trends indicate that international management will continue to grow as an important area of investigation. Individual efforts and energies by international management researchers have resulted in the establishment of institutional agendas and structures such as the 1974 mandate by the American Assembly of Collegiate Schools of Business to internationalize business school curricula (Kwok, Arpan, & Folks, 1994), the continuing growth of the Academy of International Business (Hawkins, 1984), the explicit inclusion of internationalization as one of the four major challenges of the Academy of Management, the subsequent symbolic convening of regional meetings of the Academy of Management at sites outside the United States, and the creation of the International Federation of Scholarly Associations of Management (Boyacigiller & Adler, 1991).

This growth of international management has been accompanied by a spate of articles in academic journals that have attempted to define the field, identify and operationalize its variables, and extend its boundaries in meaningful directions. The maturation of the field has been accompanied by the inevitable critique of its limitations and biases. Redding's (1994) harsh conclusion that IM suffers "from the excessive repetition of sterile reporting, from theoretical poverty, and from a lack of clear direction" (p. 32) echoes the voices of many works that precede his. Researchers have struggled with issues concerning the difficulties of generalizability (Sekaran, 1983), the parochialism of the field (Boyacigiller & Adler, 1991), the problems with research design and methodologies (Roberts, 1970; Schollhammer, 1973, 1975), and the obstacles posed by research logistics (Sekaran, 1983). Other concerns have included the quick obsolescence of research findings (Daniels, 1991); the lack of a unifying paradigm that guides research development (Roberts, 1970; Roberts & Boyacigiller, 1984); the importance accorded to something as nebulous as (national) culture (Roberts & Boyacigiller, 1983); the lack of analytical rigor in the research process (Schollhammer, 1973, 1975); the problems arising from the approaches of empirical positivism (Redding, 1994); the opportunistic and arbitrary selection of issues, countries, and samples; and the superficiality of cross-cultural management understanding (see also Adler, 1983a; Davidson, Jaccard, Triandis, Morales, & Diaz-Guerrero, 1976; Doktor, Tung, & von Glinow, 1991; Dunning, 1989; Dymsza, 1984; Hui & Triandis, 1985; Macharzina & Engelhard, 1991; Nasif, Al-Daeaj, Ebrahimi, & Thibodeaux, 1991; Negandhi, 1974; Peng, Peterson, & Shyi, 1991; Rieger & Wong-Rieger, 1988; Ronen & Shenkar, 1985; Tayeb, 1994; for a variety of critiques of the field along the dimensions mentioned above).

In addition to these works of critique, IM has engaged in a curiously substantial amount of navel gazing with over 50 review articles of the field being published between 1965 and 1994 (see Adler, 1983b; Redding, 1994). Given this unusual soul searching and given the contention that IM is "the study of the behavior of people in organizations located in cultures and nations around the world," which focuses "perhaps most importantly, on the interaction of peoples from different countries working within the same organization or within the same work environment" (Adler, 1983a, p. 226), one might reasonably expect to find a diversity of voices and ideas in the field. However, previous reviews have repeatedly discovered this not to be the case. Criticisms by scholars have found fault with the field's add-on approach to (old) Western management research agendas, the domination of U.S. researchers, and the selective attention focused on a few countries (Adler, 1983a; Boyacigiller & Adler, 1991; Dymsza, 1984; Godkin, Braye, & Caunch, 1989; Peng, Peterson, & Shyi, 1991; Roberts & Boyacigiller, 1984).

Our work is a part of this ongoing critique of IM. Through our effort, we hope to point out the trend of scholarship in this field and render visible its propensities and biases in order to help persuade the community of IM scholars of the need to expand their research agendas. The following sections present the nature of our data collection, describe the results of this effort, and make a tentative attempt to draw certain conclusions.

METHOD

Past reviews of the field have examined different facets of IM over different periods of time, such as 1962 to 1969 (Roberts, 1970), 1971 to 1980 (Adler, 1983a), and 1981 to 1987 (Peng et al., 1991). The following review is more extensive. It involves a scrutiny of 3,649 articles on IM published during a 41-year period, 1954 to 1994, in 16 prestigious management journals.[3]

Journal Selection

The decision process involved in ranking journals is rather complicated. Different scholars apply different criteria for evaluating journals, and although well-reasoned rationales are often given, a significant part of the process is arbitrary and subjective. Our own "arbitrariness" came from the use of the following method. In order to make a decision on the journals to be reviewed for this work, we examined nine review articles that rated journals of management (Coe & Weinstock, 1984; Sharplin & Mabry, 1985), organizational behavior (Blackburn, 1990; Extejt & Smith, 1990), strategic management (Franke, Edlund, & Oster, 1990; Macmillan, 1991), and IM (Adler, 1983a; Ebrahimi, Ganesh, & Chandy, 1991; Peng et al., 1991) according to their quality and degree of influence in the field. Using the feedback of these works,[4] we selected 16 journals for our investigation based largely on the following criteria: the selected journals should publish work of a high quality, have a significant influence in the community of management scholars, publish articles that have been refereed, and have a strong scholarly and research-oriented focus.

The following is a list of the journals we settled upon for the purposes of this research[5] (the year of the first issue is in the parentheses).

1. *Academy of Management Journal* (1958)
2. *Academy of Management Review* (1976)
3. *Administrative Science Quarterly* (1956)
4. *California Management Review* (1958)
5. *International Studies of Management and Organization* (1971)

6. *Journal of International Business Studies* (1969)
7. *Journal of Business Studies* (1980)
8. *Journal of General Management* (1974)
9. *Journal of Management* (1965)
10. *Journal of Management Studies* (1961)
11. *Long Range Planning* (1968)
12. *Management International Review* (1961)
13. *Management Science* (1954)
14. *Organization Studies* (1980)
15. *Sloan Management Review* (1960)
16. *Strategic Management Journal* (1980)

Having identified the journals for our study, we went through every single issue of each of these journals in order to identify articles on IM. Here we were faced with a quandary: What criteria determine the classification of an article as belonging to the field of IM? Given our location as researchers in the United States, does an article on the decision-making processes of a South African corporation (written by a South African) or an article on motivating British workers count as belonging to IM? Following Adler's (1983a) advice, we decided to use the following criteria to include articles in our domain of inquiry:

- All articles dealing specifically with the issue of IM (for example, an article on the cross-cultural management of research)
- All articles dealing with a nation-state or region other than that of the institutional affiliation of the authors (for example, an article on Korea written by a scholar from the California Polytechnic University)
- All articles published in a journal by authors whose institutional affiliation was with a nation-state other than the origin of the publication (for example, an article by a scholar from the Tel Aviv University published in the Academy of Management Review)

While the reasoning behind the first two criteria is obvious, we included the third category in our analysis under the assumption that research originating from different parts of the world (and published locally) is an integral part of our understanding of the current wisdom and the prevailing managerial paradigms of that region and thus forms part of the IM terrain.

Our careful perusal of our chosen journals yielded 3,649 articles for our examination. We coded the results of our search into a number of collectively exhaustive and mutually exclusive categories. For the purpose of this chapter, the following are the relevant questions we wanted the data to answer:

1. Who is doing IM research?

In order to answer this question, each article was coded according to the institutional affiliation of the scholar. If, for example, an article was written by a researcher from the University of Massachusetts, the origin of the study was deemed to be the United States. In the event of multiple authorship, where the authors were based in different nations, the article was coded in its own relevant category. The integrity of the order of authorship was maintained. For example, articles co-authored by one scholar from the United States and one from Canada were coded as either U.S./Canada (if the first author was from the United States) or as Canada/U.S (if the first author was from Canada).

2. Who is the subject of IM research?

Each article was examined to determine the nation-state or region of study. The category *region* included commonly used groupings such as Pacific Rim countries, Latin America, European Community, and so on. If the article examined more than one nation-state or region, it was coded in its own relevant category. For example, articles categorized under U.S. (area of study: exclusively United States) are different from those categorized under U.S./Japan (area of study: United States and Japan). Because our categorization of an article as belonging to the field of IM included those works on any management issue that were published by an international author, we came across a significant number of articles that dealt with issues of management but did not refer to any nation-state. In the coding process, these articles were categorized under the heading No Specified Nation.

We also came across a large number of studies that dealt with broad issues of IM either without identifying the region of study or by dealing with a large number of nations (eight or more) in the same piece of research. These articles were classified as Global.

3. What is the source of the knowledge upon which the research is based?

Here we were interested in knowing the sources of the information that were used to theorize, justify, and legitimize the research of each article. Again, given our focus, we were concerned with the affiliation of the journals that were being read and used (and therefore were serving as influencing and legitimizing mechanisms) in the research process of each article.

In order to answer this question, we examined every citation in the bibliography of each article. These citations were then coded according to the national affiliation of the journal it was published in. For example, a citation from the Academy of Management Journal was coded under U.S. A total of 75,752 citations were thus examined and coded in this process.[6] We came across a number of articles that did not cite any references. These were coded under the category No bibliography.

RESULTS AND DISCUSSION

The results of our work, summarized in Tables 14.1 through 14.7, offer clear answers to the questions raised above. This section revisits each of these questions, outlines the main findings of our research, and offers a discussion of our findings.

Who Is Doing IM Research?

Table 14.1 gives a summary of the countries of origin of the 3,649 articles we reviewed. A single country in the first column indicates that the articles in that row were authored solely by researchers from that nation. Dual country authorships are listed separately. Table 14.2 is a consolidation of some of the data from Table 14.1. Here, multiple country authorships are collapsed to indicate how many articles were written by at least one researcher from each of the listed countries.

The results of this tally are fairly unambiguous. The United States leads the pack easily with 1,365 of the 3,649 articles (37.41%) having at least one author from this country. Out of these, 923 articles (25.29%) were authored exclusively by researchers from the United States. The United Kingdom comes a distant (but significant) second contributing at least one author to 572 articles (15.68%) and all authors to 501 articles (13.72%).

Researchers from these two regions represent over half of all the articles written in the journals surveyed, with Canada offering another major segment to this medley (398 exclusive authorships, or 10.91%; 572 with at least one Canadian, or 15.68%). Other significant contributors include Germany (218 articles with German participation, 5.97%), Israel (181, 4.96%), France (177, 4.85%), the Netherlands (144, 3.95%), Japan (94, 2.58%), Australia (86, 2.36%), India (82, 2.25%), Switzerland (68, 1.86%), Sweden (63, 1.73%), Belgium (58, 1.59%), and Italy (52, 1.43%). The most common multinational teams com-

TABLE 14.1 Origins of International Management Research by Countries and
Country Combinations, 1954-1994

Country/ Country Combination	Number of Articles	Percentage of Articles
United States	923	25.29
United Kingdom	501	13.72
Canada	398	10.91
Germany	191	5.23
the Netherlands	124	3.40
France	116	3.18
Israel	109	2.99
India	71	1.95
Australia	67	1.84
Japan	63	1.73
United States/Canada	61	1.67
Canada/United States	60	1.64
Switzerland	56	1.53
Italy	49	1.34
Sweden	48	1.31
Belgium	35	0.96
United States/Israel	35	0.96
South Africa	30	0.82
Norway	28	0.77
France/United States	25	0.68
Hong Kong	20	0.55
Austria	18	0.49
Ireland	18	0.49
Scotland	18	0.49
Poland	17	0.47
Finland	16	0.44
United States/France	16	0.44
New Zealand	15	0.41
Israel/United States	15	0.41
Others (211 countries)	506	13.87
Total = 240	3,649	100.0%

prised researchers from the United States and Canada (121 articles), United
States and France (41), and United States and Israel (40).

TABLE 14.2 Origins of International Management Research by Country
(Consolidated), 1954-1994

Country	Number of Articles	Percentage
United States	1,365	37.41
United Kingdom	572	15.68
Canada	572	15.68
Germany	218	5.97
Israel	181	4.96
France	177	4.85
the Netherlands	144	3.95
Japan	94	2.58
Australia	86	2.36
India	82	2.25
Switzerland	68	1.86
Sweden	63	1.73
Belgium	58	1.59
Italy	52	1.43
Norway	35	0.01
Hong Kong	34	0.01
South Africa	33	0.01
Korea	27	0.01
Scotland	25	0.01
Finland	25	0.01
Austria	22	0.01
Ireland	22	0.01
Poland	19	0.01
New Zealand	17	0.00
Denmark	17	0.00

One conclusion is easy to reach. The United States plays the lead instrument in the IM orchestra, with a small supporting cast of predominantly European nations, while the rest of the voices are relegated to a barely heard chorus. In addition, a vast number of players never get to go on stage. Table 14.3 gives the long list of nations that find no representation whatsoever in the IM literature in terms of authorship.

This overwhelming domination has several implications for the field of IM. First, the demographics of the researchers publishing in this field ensure that IM

TABLE 14.3 Countries Not Participating in International Management Research

Afghanistan	Gabon	Niger
Albania	Gambia	Oman
Angola	Ghana	Panama
Antigua & Barbuda	Grenada	Papua New Guinea
Bahamas	Guatemala	Paraguay
Bahrain	Guinea	Peru
Barbados	Guinea-Bissau	Philippines
Belize	Guyana	Qatar
Benin	Haiti	Rwanda
Bhutan	Honduras	St Lucia
Bolivia	Iceland	St Vincent & Grenadines
Botswana	Iraq	Sao Tome & Principe
Brunei	Jamaica	Senegal
Bulgaria	Jordan	Seychelles
Burkina Faso	Kenya	Sierra Leone
Burundi	Korea (North)	Solomon Islands
Cambodia	Laos	Somalia
Cameroon	Lesotho	Sri Lanka
Cape Verde	Liberia	Suriname
Central African Republic	Madagascar	Swaziland
Chad	Malawi	Syria
Comoros	Maldives	Togo
Côte d'Ivoire	Mali	Trinidad & Tobago
Cuba	Malta	Tunisia
Cyprus	Mauritania	Uganda
Djibouti	Mauritius	United Arab Emirates
Dominica	Mongolia	Uruguay
Dominican Republic	Morocco	Vanuatu
Ecuador	Mozambique	Vietnam
El Salvador	Myanmar	Western Sahara
Equatorial Guinea	Namibia	Western Samoa
Ethiopia	Nepal	Zimbabwe
Fiji	Nicaragua	

NOTE: New nation states formed as of 1991 have not been included.

approaches its subject matter from a predominantly Western and Eurocentric perspective. Not only does the institutional affiliation of the researchers drive them to prioritize Western propensities and predilections, but the influence of academic values and norms imposes a relatively narrow epistemological terrain on the research process. Second, the process of knowledge production builds upon and is sustained by this narrow perspective, which then tends to acquire the weight of hegemonic self-evidence over a period of time, assigning other modes of inquiry to the margins. Third, the international character of IM becomes highly suspect with the voice of a select, relatively homogenous few attempting to define and dictate the nature of the field. Fourth, the domination of certain perspectives either relegates the occasional voices emerging from the sparsely represented parts of the world to the less privileged region of the periphery or exoticizes and fetishizes them in problematic ways. Fifth, the occasional murmurs from this periphery rarely get the opportunity to (re)present the diversity of the region they speak from, resulting in across-the-board romanticizations, essentializations, reifications, and generalizations. Finally, the silence from large parts of the world serves as a legitimating device for deemphasizing their importance and relevance to issues of IM.

Who Are the Subjects of Study in IM?

Although the asymmetry described above is revealing, the flip side of the question is just as important. If most of the research in IM is emanating from the West, who is the field studying? One might expect that even though the rest of the world does not have the privilege of theorizing about the field, it would find a place as the subject of its examination. However, this does not appear to be the case.

Tables 14.4 and 14.5 summarize the findings of our research into this issue. Table 14.4 presents the countries and the country combinations studied by the field, and Table 14.5 presents the consolidated frequency of appearance of some countries in the surveyed articles.

Of the articles we examined, 1,030 were coded under No Specified Nation. This category includes all articles that were written by international scholars on issues of management. The second most populous category we came across was Global, which includes all those articles that talk about IM without identifying the nation or region of study and those that attempt to examine several different nations and regions (eight or more) simultaneously. This classification includes 569 articles (15.59%).

Among the individual nation states, the United States was the most popular region of study, with over 15% of the articles featuring it (559 articles, 15.32%). Out of these, the United States was the exclusive subject of 232 articles (6.36%). The United Kingdom came second, finding a place in 334 (9.15%) articles. Japan

TABLE 14.4 Subjects of Study in International Management Research by
Countries and Country Combinations, 1954-1994

Country/ Country Combination	Number of Articles	Percentage of Articles
No Specified Nation	1,030	28.23
Global	569	15.59
United States	232	6.36
United Kingdom	184	5.04
Canada	134	3.67
Japan	114	3.12
Europe	94	2.58
Germany	74	2.03
India	63	1.73
Third World	55	1.51
United States/Japan	54	1.48
China	38	1.04
United States/Europe	34	0.93
Sweden	32	0.88
Israel	30	0.82
Italy	20	0.55
U.S.S.R.	18	0.49
Turkey	17	0.47
Norway	15	0.41
Ireland	14	0.38
Nigeria	13	0.36
Brazil	12	0.33
Korea	12	0.33
Belgium	10	0.27
Latin America	10	0.27
Mexico	10	0.27
South Africa	10	0.27
Switzerland	10	0.27
Others (327)	775	21.24
Totals = 355	3,649	100.0%

(266 articles), Canada (204), Germany (162), France (84), India (78), China
(53), and Sweden (53) followed in that order. The United States and Japan were
featured together in 54 of the articles, while the U.S.-Europe combination was
the subject of study in 34.

TABLE 14.5 Subjects of Study in International Management Research by Country (Consolidated), 1954-1994

Country	Number of Articles	Percentage of Articles
United States	559	15.32
United Kingdom	334	9.15
Japan	266	7.29
Canada	204	5.59
Germany	162	4.44
France	84	2.30
India	78	2.14
China	56	1.53
Sweden	53	1.45
Australia	43	1.18
Italy	42	1.15
the Netherlands	41	1.12
Israel	38	1.04
Korea	33	0.90
Russia	31	0.85
Mexico	28	0.77
Norway	26	0.71
Belgium	24	0.66
Turkey	22	0.60
Ireland	20	0.55
Brazil	18	0.49
Singapore	17	0.47
Switzerland	16	0.44
Hong Kong	15	0.41
South Africa	15	0.41
Taiwan	15	0.41

Some tentative conclusions can be reached from this analysis. To begin with, there is clearly more diversity and a broader spread among the subjects of the study than there was in the area of authorship. Yet this diversity is merely relative. While Third World nations such as Turkey (17 articles), Nigeria (12), and Brazil (12) were represented in the literature, their numbers continue to be small in comparison to those of the industrialized nations.

The No Specified Nation category is illustrative, too. It appears that many scholars writing from outside the national boundaries of the publishing nation treat management as an unsituated and therefore a universal discourse. The teleological and non-self-reflexive nature of these inquiries is a further indictment of the field as regards its diversity. The second-largest category of articles (Global) is yet another illustration of the limited nature of the IM discourse. A large number of researchers seem to believe that it is feasible to talk of IM in broad conceptual terms without any serious reference to its relationship with the social, economic, and political realities of the terrain in which it operates.

The economic and political domination of the West is reflected in the literature through the choice of nations that are seen as worthy of significant study. Although the frequent appearance of Western and industrialized nations as the subject of study is certainly a reflection of the dominance of Western authorship, it is also an indication of the reluctance of Western scholars to seriously engage with the problems and issues of peoples from large parts of the world. Whereas Tables 14.4 and 14.5 offer an indication of the paucity of diversity in terms of the subjects of study, Table 14.6 provides a list of the nations that have not been mentioned in the surveyed literature at all.

The small number of articles that speak about the less represented nations presents a further problem. In the absence of a significant literature on the subject, these articles assume the burden of speaking for these regions and thus end up providing a portrayal that once again essentializes and fetishizes the people and the practices of these parts of the world.

What Sources of Knowledge Does IM Research Draw upon?

If most scholarship in IM is carried out by researchers from the West and focuses on the issues of industrialized nations, what are the antecedents of this work? What does the literature draw upon to create this body of knowledge? Whose work is considered relevant by the field? Who are the researchers citing in order to legitimize their efforts? This section attempts to answer these questions by looking at the bibliographies of each of the 3,649 articles examined in this work.

Each citation from every article was examined to determine the journal or book it was drawn from. The location of the publishing source was then used as a surrogate to determine the national origin of the reference. Table 14.7 is a summary of our findings. The first column lists the nation-states that were the sources of the references, the second column gives the number of articles that cited at least one reference from the country in the corresponding row, and the third column lists the total number of cited references from this country.

TABLE 14.6 Countries Ignored in International Management Research

Afghanistan	Ecuador	Mozambique
Albania	El Salvador	Namibia
Algeria	Equatorial Guinea	Nicaragua
Angola	Ethiopia	Niger
Antigua & Barbuda	Fiji	Oman
Bahamas	Gabon	Panama
Bahrain	Gambia	Papua New Guinea
Barbados	Grenada	Rwanda
Belize	Guatemala	St Lucia
Benin	Guinea	St Vincent & Grenadines
Bhutan	Guinea-Bissau	Sao Tome & Principe
Bolivia	Haiti	Seychelles
Botswana	Honduras	Sierra Leone
Brunei	Iceland	Solomon Islands
Bulgaria	Iraq	Somalia
Burkina Faso	Jamaica	Sri Lanka
Burundi	Jordan	Sudan
Cambodia	Kenya	Suriname
Cameroon	Korea (North)	Swaziland
Cape Verde	Laos	Syria
Central African Republic	Lesotho	Togo
Chad	Liberia	Trinidad & Tobago
Comoros	Luxembourg	Tunisia
Congo	Madagascar	Uruguay
Côte d'Ivoire	Maldives	Vanuatu
Cuba	Mali	Western Sahara
Cyprus	Malta	Western Samoa
Djibouti	Mauritania	Yemen
Dominica	Mauritius	Zimbabwe
Dominican Republic	Mongolia	

NOTE: New nation states formed as of 1991 have not been included.

The results outlined in Table 14.7 speak quite forcefully for themselves. The United States emerges as the overwhelmingly dominant contributor to the discourse of this field. No references are cited by 375 of the surveyed articles. Out of the remaining 3,274 articles, 3,080—over 94%—cited at least one reference published in the United States. A total of 56,464 references from the United States were cited in these articles (an average of over 15 citations per

TABLE 14.7 Sources of References Used in International Management Research, 1954-1994

Sources of References	Number of Articles Citing References From This Country	Number of References Cited From This Country
United States	3,080	56,464
United Kingdom	2,010	9,714
Germany	602	2,582
Canada	453	1,061
France	417	1,162
the Netherlands	376	649
No References Used	375	0
Japan	212	688
Sweden	170	384
Belgium	126	213
Switzerland	116	184
Australia	89	228
India	82	224
Norway	64	125
Italy	59	254
Israel	58	109
Hong Kong	47	131
Finland	42	82
Austria	38	57
China	35	185
U.S.S.R.	33	152
Mexico	29	47
Ireland	28	62
Hungary	26	87
Spain	22	39
Denmark	21	27
Scotland	20	23
Turkey	19	58
Korea	19	39
New Zealand	19	26
Singapore	19	25
Poland	18	65
Nigeria	17	57

article surveyed). The United Kingdom was a distant second, with a total of 9,714 citations in 2,010 articles (an average of 2.67 per article surveyed). Germany (2,582 citations), Canada (1,061), and France (1,162) were other significant contributors to the citations. India, the highest contributor from the group of nonindustrialized nations, was the source of a mere 224 citations.

Again, the implications of these results are clear. First, knowledge production in this field is clearly the privilege of the United States and some other West European nations. Although the number of citations contributed by Western publishers is a reflection of the nature of the publishing industry itself, the degree of skew seems to go way beyond that explanation. Second, it appears that IM researchers are attempting to produce global and universal knowledge on the basis of narrow and limited sources. Third, the reading habits of the research scholars appear to be constrained by their institutional demands and the availability of literature, leading them to read and cite from a narrow range of writing. Fourth, the nature of the bibliographic distribution implies that IM researchers valorize works of Western authors. Not only do they privilege Western scholarship by deeming it worthy of reference, but by citing these sources repeatedly (and exclusively), they create a history of sedimented references which then demands the further citation of these works by future scholarship. Fifth, this valorization proceeds hand in hand with a simultaneous devalorization of non-Western scholarship. Drawing upon these nontraditional works, then, potentially becomes an act of transgression that runs the risk of delegitimizing the research process and denying it serious consideration. It is little surprise, then, that there are hardly any citations in the surveyed literature from Africa, South and Central America, and large parts of Asia. Finally, the field, through habit, runs the risk of becoming self-referential and closes itself off to outside influence.

LIMITATIONS OF THE STUDY

This section is meant to underscore both the constraints within which research of this kind must be conducted and the limitations that are imposed upon the validity of its conclusions by the categorizations and parameters it chooses to employ. It is meant to serve as a warning about the nature of results and attendant discussion in the hope that it would help the readers appreciate the insights this work offers without having to buy into the writers' arguments. It is also a reminder to ourselves about the tenuous and uncertain nature of the path we tread.

We have already commented on some of the limitations of the process of our journal selection. However, there are a couple of other issues that need to be highlighted. Journal rankings and ratings are determined by a set of criteria that are peculiar to the system of Western education. Issues of rigor, clarity, and writing style that determine the "quality" of journal articles are products of a specific educational system, training, and environment. Thus, the selection of journals and journal articles based upon these criteria loads the dice in favor of Western authors and those who are products of a Western education. In addition, our choice was limited to those journals that publish articles in English, which skews the sample further. Thus, our domain of study suffers from this predominant bias. It must therefore be kept in mind that the picture of IM that emerges from our research is one that has been taken from the specific vantage point of the United States.

The choice of the nation-state as a unit of analysis is extremely problematic. We would be hard put to justify the use of the nation-state as a surrogate for anything at all. All countries of the world are inhabited by people with diverse histories, cultures, habits, predispositions, and ideologies. Also, cultural differences within certain nations (say, China) can far exceed those across certain national boundaries (say Belgium and Luxembourg). Given this, we need to be very careful about interpreting what it means when we say that certain nationalities dominate certain discourses. However, although the problems faced when using countries as surrogates for culture are significant, we must point out that international management research has predominantly operationalized culture as something that is determined and separated by sovereign boundaries (Adler, 1983a; Sekaran, 1983).

The above problem is further compounded by our use of institutional affiliation as an indicator of the national origin of the research. Our work, for example, would classify an article written by someone born, raised, and educated in Kenya but writing while employed by a university in the United States as originating in the United States. Our classification of the nationality of the research must be interpreted in this light.

Furthermore, the origin of a research in a distant location of the world may not necessarily absolve it of a Western perspective. The case of India, for example, is fairly illustrative. India is the only non-Western nation that finds significant representation in the categories of Origin of research, Subject of study, and Sources of bibliographic references. The reason for this is not hard to figure out. Given its colonial legacy, India has a schooling system that ensures all its elite (and a significant part of its middle classes) a Westernized education in the English language. India's top business schools are all modeled after and mimic the curricula of prominent U.S. business schools. Many Indians come to the United States to obtain their Ph.D.s, and some stay on to accept jobs in U.S. business schools. Many Indian business school faculty members have a Ph.D. from a U.S. institution and continue to publish in Western journals. It is not surprising, then, that the output of these researchers is based upon Western paradigms, theories, research methodologies, and priorities.

Another limitation arises from the attempt to answer the question concerning the source of the bibliographic citations. The country of the publication of the journal is taken as an indicator of the source as opposed to the institutional affiliation of the authors of the cited works. Although the latter may have offered better data, the sheer number of references involved precluded this attempt. Again, it must be kept in mind that the issue being raised here is one of the control of knowledge production; the origin of the publication is being used in order to give us pointers and clues in this regard.

Despite these significant limitations, we believe that the data obtained makes its point very strongly. However, an informed reading would demand that the restrictions outlined in the above discussion be kept in mind while interpreting the significance of the results of this work.

CONCLUSIONS

We live in a world where issues of global diversity are becoming increasingly central to organizational inquiry. Finance and productive capital crosses nation-state boundaries with greater-than-ever frequencies. Labor, particularly of the skilled variety, is acquiring newer levels of mobility. Technological innovations such as telecommunication and computer networks are resulting in a space-time compression that is shrinking the international landscape within which big businesses and big governments act. The new organizational paradigm is acquiring truly international dimensions.

The traditional way of coping with diversity has typically involved attempts at force-fitting standardized practices and techniques in an effort to homogenize people and cultures in offices and factories across the world. This has resulted in managerial practices and theories that not only look the same but also acquire the aura of universality. Recent experiences have exposed the weakness of this approach. The success of alternate organizational systems (Sayer & Walker, 1992), the advent of what have been called New Social Movements (Escobar, 1994), and the enormous growth of the Newly Industrialized Countries (Waters, 1995) have thrown old formulations in much disarray. Any body of research and knowledge that wishes to retain legitimacy in this changing environment needs to pay more than mere lip service to the issue of diversity. The field of IM has even more responsibility toward the issue of diversity than most others, not just because of the nature of its inquiry but also because of its specific mandate.

In this chapter, we asked three questions:

1. Who is doing IM research?
2. Who are the subjects of study in IM?
3. What sources of knowledge does IM research draw upon?

Three corresponding conclusions can be reached as a result of our work: From the vantage point of scholars in the United States, who are primarily exposed to the literature that we have examined,

1. IM research is predominantly conducted by scholars from the United States and a small number of West European countries.
2. IM research focuses largely either on generalized and deterritorialized conceptual issues or on matters related to the United States, Western Europe, and Japan.
3. IM research draws overwhelmingly from sources published in the United States, and to a lesser degree on those coming out of Western Europe.

Let us revisit the tone on which we started this chapter. The nature of our results is hardly surprising. Explanations for the phenomena we talk about could come thick, fast, and easy. It may be instructive to indulge in some of these ourselves. Most management scholars of the world are products of a Western education and are affiliated with Western universities and institutions. The demands of a research profession in the Western world include the need to publish frequently, especially in journals of the kind we chose to examine. It follows then, that most of the articles published in these journals would have Western authorship.

The leeway afforded to researchers in terms of the subjects of their study ought to be fairly broad. Yet, it is not difficult to explain away the focus on industrialized nations. Most of the world's nongovernmental formal economic activity is centered in the industrialized nations or is carried out in other parts of the world under the economic control of agencies from these nations. The economic dominance of these countries makes them more relevant and worthy subjects of inquiry; the importance of other countries is merely proportional to their relationship with the industrialized ones. Furthermore, because most scholars are located in the West, logistics make it easier to study Western nations.

The large amount of attention paid to global and universal issues of IM is also understandable. Western inquiry has been accustomed to assuming universality, and Western paradigms, until recently at least, have seldom felt the need to situate themselves in spatial, temporal, or epistemological contexts. Finally, the wide use of bibliographic citations from the United States (and, to a lesser degree, England) can be seen as a reflection of a number of phenomena. The infrastructure of the publishing industry ensures that most books written in the English language are published in these two countries. The reluctance of people in the United States to learn and read different languages is a further hurdle. The legitimacy afforded to citing a reference written by a trained (read: Western) researcher cannot be obtained by citing writers who may be operating from a different set of paradigms and standards. The historic exoticization of large parts of the world and a corresponding distrust of the "scientific" validity of their work contributes to their marginalization.

Having said that, we must make certain observations. Given the nature of the results of our work, the claim of IM to being international rings hollow. IM comes across as a field where Western scholars study the economic activity of the West and justify their conclusions based upon the work of other Western researchers. This indictment is one that a community of responsible scholars cannot afford to ignore. If IM is to fulfill its mandate, it must demonstrate an urgent sense of purpose in expanding its agenda and shunning the exclusionary path. In their review of cross-cultural studies in the 1980s, Godkin et al. (1989) conclude that the "dangers inherent in remaining ignorant of our neighbors are disturbing: the ramifications of competing in ignorance even more so. The bliss proverbially associated with ignorance and the arrogance accompanying it have a down side" (p. 9).

Although these are valuable words of caution, there is surely more to it than just that. It is useful to realize here that IM accurately mirrors the unequal world it inhabits and reflects the huge imbalances of riches and power between nation-states and their corresponding inhabitants. Issues of voice and representation follow the dictates of this structure. The study of IM thus assumes the proportions of an ideological formation that imposes a near-hegemonic stranglehold on the discourse of this field. Breaking free is not merely a matter of recognizing the instrumental value of inclusiveness. We believe that this effort will involve a deeper understanding of the discipline that may require us to ask uncomfortable questions regarding our role as scholars in the field and demand certain paradigmatic shifts in our thinking.

In a book exploring the dilemmas of workplace diversity, we especially believe that the concerns raised here have special merit. Too often, discussions

of workplace diversity are restricted to North American concerns and issues
(e.g., affirmative action, the American women's movement, etc.) and fail to even
address some challenges raised by managing globally diverse populations. Even
when IM scholars look beyond North American boundaries, it is usually with
an espoused view to improve cross-cultural communication, and so on. This
chapter, however, suggests that the very way in which IM constructs and
structures the global Other is severely problematic and has consequences for the
practice of management in the new world of multinational and international
transactions.

In their widely read article, Boyacigiller and Adler (1991) offer one set of
recommendations for a more internationally relevant organizational science.
Apart from our immediately preceding thought, we are reluctant to suggest
further "solutions" to the "problems" discussed in this chapter. Where we go
from here is a matter for all of us to debate and to figure out. The community of
IM scholars is not unaware of the situation deliberated here. Critiques of a
similar nature have been heard from within the field in the past and are
continuing to surface with increasing frequency. Presumably, our work gives us
enough credibility to join this small chorus. The charge, then, that IM is not
international enough is not new; hopefully, our "bean-counting" efforts can help
persuade responsible scholars of the field to respond to it in a productive manner.

NOTES

1. The abbreviation, IM, will hereafter be used to refer to the academic discipline of
international management and the scholarship that forms part of its discourse.

2. The term *industrialized nations* is used to refer to the United States, Western Europe, and
Japan. The term *West* is used as a proxy for the geographical and the epistemological terrain of
the United States and Western Europe.

3. The year 1954 was chosen as our point of departure simply because it is the date of the first
publication of any of the 16 journals we examined.

4. We allowed ourselves to be influenced more by Ebrahimi et al. (1991) than by the others.
Ebrahimi and associates used feedback received from active scholars in the field of international
business to rank journals that published articles in this discipline. Of the 16 journals we selected,
13 rank highly in Ebrahimi et al.'s rating scheme. These 13 also constitute almost the entire set of
management journals (as opposed to journals of economics, law, marketing, etc.) in their list.
Harvard Business Review is a glaring omission; we did not examine this journal because of its
practitioner orientation. The other 3 of the 16 journals we examined (*Organization Studies, Journal
of Business Studies,* and *Journal of General Management*) were included on the basis of the other
reviews we looked at.

5. Despite attempts to use past ratings of journals and a judgment based upon several years
of familiarity with this field of study, we confess to a sense of inadequacy with our selection
process. We can engage in a criticism of our choices ourselves and have no doubt that the readers

will have their own misgivings about our preferences. Some of the limitations of our choice are articulated subsequently in the chapter.

6. It must be clarified that the source of each citation was not visited—that would have been too daunting a project to undertake. Only the bibliographic references were used to make this coding.

REFERENCES

Adler, N. J. (1983a). Cross-cultural management of research: The ostrich and the trend. *Academy of Management Research, 3*(2), 226-232.

Adler, N. J. (1983b). A typology of management studies involving culture. *Journal of International Business Studies, 3,* 29-48.

Blackburn, R. S. (1990). Organizational behavior: Whom do we talk to and who talks to us? *Journal of Management, 16*(2), 279-305.

Boyacigiller, N. A., & Adler, N. J. (1991). The parochial dinosaur: Organizational science in a global context. *Academy of Management Review, 16*(2), 262-290.

Coe, R., & Weinstock, I. (1984). Evaluating the management journals: A second look. *Academy of Management Journal, 27*(3), 660-666.

Daniels, J. D. (1991). Relevance in international business research: A need for more linkages. *Journal of International Business Studies, 22*(2), 177-186.

Davidson, A. R., Jaccard, J. J., Triandis, H. C., Morales, M. L., & Diaz-Guerrero, R. (1976). Cross-cultural model testing: Toward a solution of the etic-emic dilemma. *International Journal of Psychology, 11*(1), 1-13.

Doktor, R., Tung, R. L., & von Glinow, M. A. (1991). Incorporating international dimensions in management theory building. *Academy of Management Review, 16*(2), 259-261.

Dunning, J. H. (1989, Fall). The study of international business: A plea for a more interdisciplinary approach. *Journal of International Business Studies, 20,* 411-436.

Dymsza, W. A. (1984). Future international business research and multidisciplinary studies. *Journal of International Business Studies, 15,* 9-13.

Ebrahimi, B. Gamesh, C. K., & Chandy, P. R. (1991). International and noninternational business journal awareness and evaluation: Perceptions of active researchers. *Management International Review, 31*(4), 347–364.

Escobar, A. (1994). *Contesting development.* Princeton, NJ: Princeton University Press.

Extejt, M. M., & Smith, J. E. (1990). The behavioral sciences and management: An evaluation of relevant journals. *Journal of Management, 16*(3), 539-551.

Franke, R. H., Edlund, T. W., & Oster, F., III. (1990). The development of strategic management: Journal quality and article impact. *Strategic Management Journal, 11,* 243-253.

Godkin, L., Braye, C. E., & Caunch, C. L. (1989). U.S.-based cross-cultural management research in the eighties. *Journal of Business and Economic Perspectives, 15*(2), 37-45.

Hawkins, R. G. (1984, Winter). International business in academia: The state of the field. *Journal of International Business Studies, 15,* 13-18.

Hui, C. H., & Triandis, H. C. (1985). Measurement in cross-cultural psychology: A review and comparison of strategies. *Journal of Cross-Cultural Psychology, 16*(2), 131-152.

Kwok, C. C. Y., Arpan, J., & Folks, W. R. (1994). A global survey of international business education in the 1990s. *Journal of International Business Studies, 25,* Third Quarter, 605-623.

Macharzina, K., & Engelhard, J. (1991). Paradigm shift in international business research: From partist and eclectic approaches to the GAINS paradigm. *Management International Review, 31*, 23-43.

Macmillan, I. C. (1991). The emerging forum for business policy scholars. *Strategic Management Journal, 12*(1), 161-165.

Nasif, E. G., al-Daeaj, H., Ebrahimi, B., & Thibodeaux, M. S. (1991). Methodological problems in cross-cultural research: An updated review. *Management International Review, 31*(1), 79-91.

Negandhi, A. R. (1974). Cross-cultural management studies: Too many conclusions, not enough conceptualization. *Management International Review, 14*(6), 59-67.

Peng, T. K., Peterson, M. F., & Shyi, Y. P. (1991). Quantitative methods in cross-national management research: Trends and equivalence issues. *Journal of Organizational Behavior, 12*, 87-107.

Redding, S. G. (1994). Comparative management theory: Jungle, zoo, or fossil bed? *Organization Studies, 15*(3), 323-359.

Rieger, F., & Wong-Rieger, D. (1988). Model building in organizational/cross-cultural research: The need for multiple methods, indices, and cultures. *International Studies of Management and Organization, 18*(3), 19-30.

Roberts, K. H. (1970). On looking at elephant: An evaluation of cross-cultural research related to organizations. *Psychological Bulletin, 5*, 327-350.

Roberts, K. H. & Boyacigiller, N. A. (1983). Research review: A survey of cross-national organizational researchers; Their views and opinions. *Organization Studies, 4*(4), 375-386.

Roberts, K. H. & Boyacigiller, N. A. (1984). Cross-national organizational research: The grasp of the blind men. *Research in Organizational Behavior, 6*, 423-475.

Ronen, S., & Shenkar, O. (1985). Clustering countries on attitudinal dimensions: A review and synthesis. *Academy of Management Review, 10*(3), 435-454.

Sayer, A., & Walker, R. (1992). *The new social economy.* Cambridge, MA: Blackwell.

Schollhammer, H. (1973). Strategies and methodologies in international business and comparative management research. *Management International Review, 13*(6), 17-32.

Schollhammer, H. (1975). Current research on international and comparative management issues. *Management International Review, 15*(2/3), 29-45.

Sekaran, U. (1983). Methodological and theoretical issues and advancements in cross-cultural research. *Journal of International Business Studies, 2*, 61-74.

Sharplin, A., & Mabry, R. (1985). The relative importance of journals used in management research: An alternative ranking. *Human Relations, 38*, 139-149.

Tayeb, M. (1994). Organizations and national culture: Methodology considered. *Organization Studies, 15*(3), 429-446.

Waters, M. (1995). *Globalization.* London: Routledge.

PART

IV

CONCLUSION

Issues in the Management of Workplace Diversity

ANSHUMAN PRASAD

MICHAEL ELMES

The discourse of diversity management in the North American workplace is a phenomenon of relatively recent origins. This novelty of the phenomenon, however, sometimes tends to obscure the important fact that diversity as a "problem" has exercised the imagination of English-speaking North American elites for quite some time, going as far back as the 1940s, if not earlier (Menand, 1995). One of the early mentions of the "problems of diversity," for instance, is to be found in the report of a twelve-member committee on general education appointed during the Second World War years by James Conant,[1] the then President of Harvard University.

The report, entitled *General Education in a Free Society* (1945), has an interesting history (see Menand, 1995). One of Conant's primary concerns was to maintain social stability in a world which, in his opinion, was seriously imperilled by forces of Communism. Conant believed that only by ensuring social mobility could America avoid class stratification and thereby ward off the threat to its stability posed by Communism. Conant believed, moreover, that the best approach for ensuring social mobility required that meritocratic and specialized education be made "the only key to economic success" (Menand, 1995, p. 341). However, Conant's view of meritocratic education did not imply that all Americans would end up at the "top"; it only implied that going to the "top" would be governed solely on the basis of people's ranking and certification by institutions of specialized education, and that public access to such institutions of specialized education would be governed solely on grounds of merit (i.e., on the basis of standardized tests and scores like SAT, GMAT, LSAT and so on).

Conant recognized, therefore, that his system was not doing away with social stratification per se; it was only attempting to ensure that the movement from a lower social level to a higher one was governed by specialized education alone, and that the opportunity for such education was available to all on the basis of individual merit. Conant's America, therefore, was to remain a hierarchically stratified society, because, as he understood it, while the talented one-tenth of the nation joined the law school and went on to become lawyers, there would have to be people who could be "tracked" to become chauffeurs and cab drivers and who could "drive the lawyers to their meetings" (Menand, 1995, p. 341). Conant's committee was required to recommend a common core of general education for all which would ensure that class animosity in such a hierarchically segmented society would not endanger social stability.

It is while considering the threats to social stability that the Conant Committee report, *General Education in a Free Society*,[2] discusses what it refers to as the "problems of diversity". Diversity, according to this report, is a major problem (and a grave danger to stability) because it undermines the collective social belief in a common American destiny (Menand, 1995). What is interesting about this report's concern with diversity is the fact that the Conant Committee's notion of diversity has nothing to do with ideas of race, gender, ethnicity, etc. which crowd contemporary discussions of workplace diversity; the Committee sees diversity exclusively in terms of class. An important reason why the Conant Committee can ignore other forms of diversity along lines of race, gender, ethnicity, age, sexual preferences and so on, of course, is that it is still possible for this committee to conceive of a primarily homogeneous America.[3]

Since the days of the Conant Committee report, the demographic profile of the North American workforce has visibly changed (Carr-Ruffino, 1996; Johnston & Packer, 1987). One has to take due care here not to exaggerate the extent of these demographic changes, especially along the lines of race and ethnicity: for instance, as late as 1994, 85% of the civilians (sixteen years old and over) employed in the United States continued to be white (U.S. Bureau of Labor Statistics data). Nevertheless, certain important demographic changes did occur. In terms of civilian (sixteen years old and over) employment in the United States, the proportion of women, for example, increased from about 33% of those employed in 1960 to roughly 46% by 1994.[4] Similarly, by 1990, the ethnic and gender composition of the entire U.S. workforce had come to read as follows (Carr-Ruffino, 1996): white men (39%), white women (35%), men of color (13%), women of color (13%).

As a result of these changes, the white male establishment was forcibly made to bear witness to a situation in which, in 1990 for example, white men accounted for only 39% of the U.S. workforce, while 61% of this workforce consisted of women and members of various ethnic minorities. It is true that these demographic changes occurring in the workforce did not lead to any significant modification (along lines of gender and/or ethnicity) of the long-established power structure that characterizes the American workplace: as late as 1990, for instance, women and minorities, although accounting for 61% of the total U.S. workforce, constituted only 30% of middle management America, and only 5% of the top management ranks (Carr-Ruffino, 1996).[5] Notwithstanding such lack of significant change in the inner sanctums of private and public corporate power, however, in demographic terms, the North American organizational world of the 1980s and the 1990s is substantially different from that of the 1960s or the 1970s. Hence, in brief, the corporate desire to manage workplace diversity.

As we mentioned earlier, the Conant Committee viewed diversity exclusively in terms of class and, given the Committee's identification with the perspectives and the standpoints of the American elites, feared that the stratification of American society into diverse classes posed a grave threat to the existing status quo. Not surprisingly, therefore, the committee's principal concern was with smoothing over class differences with a view to maintaining social stability and, thereby, preserving the prevailing societal relationships of power, privilege and hierarchy. The "solution" suggested by the committee, as we saw, was a common core of education for the entire society in the hope that, by denying social differences and emphasizing social and cultural commonalities, such an education would result in the constitution of (com)pliant human subjectivities who would be unlikely to meaningfully threaten the status quo. Clearly, for the Conant Committee, (class) diversity represented a "problem" that needed to be "managed" in such a way that it would not seriously interfere with the country's pursuit of an elite-sponsored "collective" vision for America.

Despite its lack of concern with diversity stemming from differences of ethnicity, race, gender and so on, therefore, an understanding of the Conant Committee's approach to managing diversity is important for developing an overall historical perspective on diversity management in America. Following broadly in the footsteps of the Conant Committee, the current diversity management industry continues to mostly view diversity (of race, culture, gender, etc.) as a "problem" and continues to be primarily concerned with smoothing over these differences with a view to maintaining systemic stability (even at the expense of all other social considerations), and facilitating the pursuit of "corporate" goals which often only reflect the narrow sectional interests of the organizational/societal elites. It would appear as if the Conant Committee of the 1940s has provided America with an overall cultural script for dealing with "diversity" which the American society continues to enact even in the 1990s. But with one significant difference. Unlike the Conant Committee report which conceptualized diversity only in terms of class, current discussions of diversity management in North America carefully insulate themselves from the important issue of class.

In its investigation of workplace diversity, this book chooses not to remain silent on the issue of class. This is so not only because, given the prevailing environment of growing poverty and of rapidly accelerating disparity between the haves and the have-nots, class divisions continue to remain one of the starkest features of the North American social landscape, but also because the element of class frequently casts its shadow, in a number of different ways, on those inner dynamics of diversity (social and/or organizational) which are sometimes seen as driven solely by elements of gender, race, ethnicity, sexuality, age, disability and so on. In other words, the dimension of socio-economic class often interacts in unique ways with other aspects of the phenomenon of diversity to produce highly complex and intriguing effects. One of the important instances of the role of class, for example, is provided in Barbara Ehrenreich's (1989) classic analysis of (white) women's movement in America. In her best-selling book, *Fear of Falling: The Inner Life of the Middle Class,* Ehrenreich (1989) concludes that, in an economic environment of the 1970s which was characterized by declining real incomes for white, middle class American families, liberal feminism worked to "save the professional [white] middle class from economic decline" and, thus, to preserve the socio-economic status quo in America (p. 214; see also Carr-Ruffino, 1996, 149 ff.), while also gaining "dignity and self-esteem" (p. 214) for American women.[6] Thus, Ehrenreich's (1989) analysis highlights the salience of class dynamics in a social movement usually understood along lines of sex/gender differences alone.

Class, of course, is not the only frame of reference adopted in this book. As readers of the book may have noticed, individual contributions to this volume approach the issue of workplace diversity along a number of different dimensions such as gender, race, ethnicity, migrancy and immigration, colonialism, globalization, and so forth. Such multiplicity of approaches, however, does not imply that the book individually addresses the unique problems, concerns, and dilemmas of each of the many identity groups or "voices" which collectively constitute the phenomenon of workplace diversity in North America. To give just a few examples of the identity groups not receiving detailed and individualized attention in this book, mention may be made of such "voices" as gays and lesbians, people with disabilities, the elderly, Hispanics, and Native Americans/First Nations. Clearly, such "neglect"—if the above-noted absence of individualized, independent focus upon certain specific identity groups may be so categorized—of some of the voices from within the diversity phenomenon does not imply that the contributors to this volume do not consider the concerns of these groups to be important or unique enough to receive their analytic attention. What it does imply is that the overall approach adopted by this study does not mimic or imitate a somewhat conventional analytic strategy for understanding workplace diversity followed by many organizational researchers.

In sum, the approach followed in the present book is not one of providing chapter-length analyses of the dilemmas of diversity surrounding individual identity groups. Rather, the approach adopted here is somewhat more complex, and represents an attempt to go to the very roots of some of the key issues which invariably arise whenever diverse social and human groups are made to interact with one another within an overall matrix of power which accords a position of routine, unacknowledged, and frequently unchallenged privilege to one group (e.g., white males) at the expense of others. In some ways, therefore, our intent here is to identify and examine those fundamental issues which may help render the surface-level problems of diversity (revolving around race, gender, sexual orientation etc.) relatively more transparent. In many respects, this implies a deep concern with analyzing the overall dynamic of 'otherness' and of the center-periphery transactions.

Within such an overall approach, however, the individual chapters in this collection do display some interesting similarities and differences. So far as similarities among the chapters are concerned, a few things readily stand out. These may be summarized as concerns with: (a) critique, (b) emancipation, (c) context, history, and totality, and (d) social constructivism. First, all the chapters of this book bring with them a critical orientation either toward current scholarship or toward existing societal and organizational practices/arrangements, or toward both. Second, explicitly or implicitly, all chapters seem to be motivated by a commitment to the idea of emancipatory, praxic social/organizational change. Third, most of the contributions to this collection steer away from doing a decontextualized and ahistorical "reading" of workplace diversity, and seek to situate their analyses of diversity within the wider framework of socio-historical totality. And fourth, implicitly or explicitly, these chapters refuse to adopt a reified view of organizations/society/scholarship.

With respect to differences among individual contributions, the most obvious one, of course, relates to the specific focus of each chapter, which reaches into such diverse areas as (to mention only a few) the discursive constitution of the sexually specific subject (Oseen), the role of the micro-practices of Industrial Relations and Human Resource Management in the production of 'normal' behaviour (Marsden), the influence of the cultural traditions of Protestantism and the Myths of the Frontier on everyday organizational practices in North America (P. Prasad), the role of powerful "resisting" forces in hindering the emergence of pluralistic organizations (Elmes & Connelley), corporate imagery in the British airline industry (Mills), the Rodney King and Tailhook scandals (Caproni & Finley), the colonialist construction of "otherness" in the discourse of the Western oil industry (A. Prasad), and the sedimented parochialism of the International Management literature (Wong-MingJi & Mir). Another important difference among the individual chapters of the volume is with respect to their conceptual/epistemological foundations which cover a wide and varied range including (but not limited to) Feminism, Marxism, Postcolonialism, Institutional Theory, Social Identity Theory, Poststructuralism, and so forth. And finally, the chapters display a fair amount of methodological diversity as well. It is the shared belief of all the contributors to this collection that, by allowing us to approach the issue of workplace diversity from a number of distinct vantage points, these theoretical, methodological, and epistemological differences have helped us develop a more sophisticated understanding of the complexities surrounding the diversity phenomenon in North America.

In addition to some of the shared sentiments and viewpoints mentioned above which have lent unity and wholeness to this volume, what has also helped to turn this collection of unique and distinctive essays into an organic whole is a certain commonality of spirit which seems to have driven each individual contributor. To understand the common spirit in which this book has been conceptualized, written and produced, we may usefully borrow a passage from bell hooks (1989) in her book, *Talking Back: Thinking Feminist, Thinking Black*:

Moving from silence into speech is for the oppressed, the colonized, the exploited and those who stand in struggle side by side, a gesture of defiance that heals, that makes new life and new growth possible. It is that act of speech, of "talking back," that is no mere gesture of empty words, that is the expression of moving from object to subject—the liberated voice. (p. 9)

The authors in this book have tried to "talk back" in a similar way. They suggest that a discourse of diversity that fails to address the oppressed, the colonized, and the exploited in organizations, or to face the cultural forms, historical influences, dominant assumptions, and psycho-social processes that shape the construction and enactment of "otherness" in the workplace, can never bring about meaningful change. Only by examining the social, political, cultural, and historical context in which workplace diversity has evolved can academics and practitioners move beyond a managerialist discourse of diversity which all too frequently seeks to obscure, conceal, and deny the real human differences that inhabit today's organizations, and which seems to equate "diversity management" with "learning to get along" in organizations that have been theoretically sanitized.

Collectively, these chapters suggest that the persistence of tensions that exist around race and gender, among others, in organizations might represent a hopeful sign. Hopeful in the sense that success in efforts to homogenize differences in the workplace in the interest of "team work" and smooth organizational functioning has been significantly less than total. For now, at least. However, it would appear that the same ideological and cultural forces that have colonized the workplace have also turned diversity management into a growth industry. If diversity is the "problem," say the experts, effective management is the solution.

So where do the chapters appearing in this book leave us? In some ways, guardedly skeptical. If the road to hell—with its "diversity management" signposts—is paved with good intentions, the path to heaven—to subjectivity, agency, liberation, and radical change—is no piece of cake. They suggest that the ideologies and practices discussed in this book foster an allegiance to a managerialist view of the workplace, discouraging organizational members from probing beneath the surface of popular programs like "diversity management." Can practicing managers really use some of the theoretical and critical insights from this book to bring about meaningful change in their organizations? Yes, we believe that they can. However, to do so, they must be willing to critically examine what they see as being basic to the organization, namely, its dominant discourse, power relations, and so on. Many may not for fear that it will reveal what they already suspect: that the enterprise of diversity management is morally indefensible.

Mixed with our skepticism about the likelihood of meaningful change in "managerialist" diversity management practices, however, are certain joys. One is the joy of talking back to that segment of academic discourse on diversity which frequently arrogates to itself the label of "mainstream." Another is the joy associated with seeing a larger picture, of finding our own subjectivity and voice to oppose what is presumed to be commonsensical or normal. Just as academia as an organization has dominant discourses and rules by which academic behavior is sought to be controlled, regulated, and disciplined, so too this book marks an attempt at "resistance through persistence" (Collinson, 1994)—at challenging the putative center of the academy itself and at articulating some radically innovative metaphors for thinking about diversity in the workplace.

Most of this talking back is rigorously intellectual, drawing from a variety of theoretical perspectives to explain various dilemmas of diversity in the modern Western workplace. Some of it is quite personal, employing personal experience as a vehicle for exploring the topic. Some, on the other hand, relies upon conventional research to stir up conventional wisdom. Just as, in the process of developing and pulling together these chapters, we developed a deeper awareness of the various dimensions of diversity, so we believe that others, especially those in the academy and industry, can begin to understand workplace diversity —and its myriad dilemmas—from a fresh point of view. Given that the dilemmas of diversity in this "global economy" are unlikely to disappear anytime soon, we believe that this book offers a timely and important intellectual tool kit for understanding and responding to an organizational melting pot that may be close to boiling over.

NOTES

1. Menand (1995, p. 340) describes Conant as "a classic Cold Warrior" and "a principal figure in the decision to drop the [atom] bomb on Hiroshima and Nagasaki". Conant was extremely concerned about what he saw as the threat posed to the United States by forces of Communism, and openly argued that Communists should be barred from the teaching and scholarly professions. After leaving Harvard in 1953, he was appointed as the U.S. ambassador to West Germany.

2. Ironically, this report is sometimes called the Red Book.

3. According to data compiled by the U.S. Bureau of Labor Statistics, the number of civilians (sixteen years old and over) who were employed in America in 1960 stood at 66 million. Out of these 66 million, 89% were white, and 67% were men (the percentage of white men, of course, being much higher in managerial and executive positions, and in better-paying professional occupations). Similarly, as Menand (1995, 343 ff.) notes, as late as 1960, about 95% of college

students in America were white, 80% of faculty positions and 90% of new doctoral degrees were held by men, and several public and private universities did not admit African-Americans. As a result, the Conant Committee would have mostly "seen" America as white and male. In such an America, as far as the Committee was concerned, issues of race, gender, etc. simply did not exist.

4. A similar change took place in the Canadian workforce as well. On the basis of data reported in the *Labour Force Statistics,* a publication of the Organization for Economic Cooperation and Development (OECD), Paris, women in Canada accounted for about 31 percent of the labor force in 1965. The proportion of women in the Canadian labor force rose to about 44% by 1987.

5. Carr-Ruffino (1996; 146) points out that, in 1990, white males, while accounting for only 39% of the total workforce in the United States, continued to corner 95% of top management positions, 82.5% of the Forbes 400 list of wealthy (net worth of $265 million or more) persons, 77% of the U.S. Congress, 92% of state governorships, 70% of the ranks of tenured college faculty, 90% of daily newspaper editorships, and 77% of television news directorships.

6. See Ehrenreich (1989) for some of the major dilemmas and ambivalence experienced by the American feminist movement in its quest for empowerment. See also, in this connection, Chandra Talpade Mohanty (1991) for a celebrated and incisive critique of the hegemonic and universalistic pretensions of Western feminism.

REFERENCES

Carr-Ruffino, N. (1996). *Managing diversity*. San Francisco: Thomson Executive Press.

Collinson, D. (1994). Strategies of resistance. In J. Jermier, D. Knights, & W. Nord (eds.), *Resistance and power in organizations* (pp. 25-68). London: Routledge.

Ehrenreich, B. (1989). *Fear of falling: The inner life of the middle class*. New York: Harper Collins.

hooks, b. (1989). *Talking back: Thinking feminist, thinking Black*. Boston: South End Press.

Johnston, W. B., & Packer, A. H. (1987). *Workforce 2000*. Indianapolis, IN: Hudson.

Menand, L. (1995). Diversity. In F.Lentricchia & T. McLaughlin (eds.), *Critical terms for literary study* (2nd ed., pp. 336-353). Chicago: University of Chicago Press.

Mohanty, C. T. (1991). Under western eyes: Feminist scholarship and colonial discourse. In C. T. Mohanty, A. Russo, & L. Torres (eds.), *Third world women and the politics of feminism* (pp. 51-80). Bloomington: Indiana University Press.

Author Index

Pfeffer, J., 33, 36, 52
Phillips, K. P., 160, 167
Pierce, J. L., 203, 225
Polster, M., 215, 225
Porter, L. W., 203, 225
Powell, G., 82, 86, 106, 148, 167, 227, 254
Prakash, G., 286, 288, 290, 307, 311
Prasad, A., 23-24, 285-311, 365-373
Prasad, P., 3-27, 129-147, 370
Pringle, R., 176, 198
Prinz, A. M., 113, 128
Probyn, E., 222, 225
Pudney, J.195, 198
Pugh, M., 187, 196, 198

Rabinow, P.209, 225
Ragins, B. R., 33, 42, 52
Ramsey, R. D., 42, 47, 52
Ramsey, V. J., 40, 43, 52
Redding, S. G., 343, 364
Reza, H. G., 284
Ricks, T., 284
Rieger, F., 343, 364
Roberts, K. H., 343, 344, 364
Robinson, T., 217, 225
Rodgers, D. T., 133, 146
Rogers, W., 226, 228, 236, 238, 240, 242,
    244-246, 248, 249, 254
Roncaglia, A., 291, 307, 311
Ronen, S., 343, 364
Rose, N., 126, 128
Roseueau, P. M., 141, 146
Ross, L., 206, 215, 225
Ross, M. B., 32, 53
Rossett, A., 286, 311
Roosevelt, T., 135, 146
Roszak, T., 17, 27
Rothschild-Witt, J., 36, 53
Rourke, C., 134, 146
Ruddick, S., 232, 254

Sachs, W., 289, 311
Said, E., 73, 79, 286-290, 293, 299, 300, 304,
    307, 309, 311
Salholz, E., 284
Sampson, A., 291, 307, 308, 311
Sayer, A., 359, 364
Sayer, D., 128

Schaef, A. W., 227, 234, 251, 254
Schein, E., 15, 27
Schmitt, E., 284
Schneider, H. W., 133, 134, 147
Schollhammer, H., 343, 364
Scott, W. G., 38, 45, 53
Scott, R. W., 35, 53, 132, 147
Sekaran, U., 343, 358, 364
Semler, R., 64, 68, 69, 71, 75, 76, 78, 79
Sessa, V. T., 12, 27
Seward, S. B., 325, 338
Shain, B. A., 137, 147
Sharplin, A., 344, 364
Shrivastava, P., 257, 284
Sikula, A., 39, 45, 53
Simpson, P., 154, 159, 167
Sims, R. R., 32, 53
Sitaram, K. S., 140, 147
Slotkin, R., 131, 135-137, 147
Smith, B. H., 105, 106
Smith, D. E., 35, 53, 74, 79, 205, 225
Smolowe, J., 284
Sommers, C. H., 90, 106
Sowell, T., 33, 53
Spender, D., 227, 254
Spivak, G. C., 286, 289, 311
Spurr, D., 289, 290, 293, 302, 305, 306, 311
Starbuck, W. H., 131, 147, 240, 254, 282, 284
Starhawk, 210, 211, 213-215, 217, 225
Staub, E., 272, 284
Steinem, G., 217, 225
Stewart, P., 64, 66, 67, 71, 79
Stiehm, J., 35, 39, 40, 48, 53
Stinchcombe, A. L., 132, 147
Strenski, I., 131, 147
Strobel, F. R., 160, 167
Suleri, S., 289, 311
Summa, H., 40, 43, 53
Sumner, W. G., 159, 167
Swoboda, F., 105, 106

Tannen, D., 81, 102, 106
Tajfel, H., 155, 156, 167, 314, 339
Tannen, D., 232, 244, 246, 254
Tawney, R. H., 133, 147
Tayeb, M., 343, 364
Terzian, P., 291, 293, 296, 297, 311
Therborn, G., 131, 147
Thiederman, S., 42, 53

Subject Index

About the Authors

Patricia Bradshaw has her doctorate in organizational behavior from York University, where she is currently Associate Professor in the Faculty of Administrative Studies. At York, she teaches introductory organizational behavior, as well as elective courses on women and men in organizations and qualitative methods. Her research interests include organizational power and politics, governance of nonprofit organizations, and women in organizations and on boards of directors. Her publications appear in a number of journals including the *Journal of Applied Behavioral Science, Organizational Science, Nonprofit Management and Leadership,* and the *Nonprofit and Voluntary Sector Quarterly.* She has worked with a variety of organizations in the corporate and nonprofit sectors as a consultant and facilitator and has been an Associate of the Niagara Institute for 3 years.

Paula Caproni is on the organizational behavior/human resources management faculty at the University of Michigan School of Business Administration. She received her MBA degree from the University of Massachusetts and her PhD in organizational behavior from Yale University. In addition to teaching in the University of Michigan MBA program, she has taught in the University of Michigan Executive Education Program and at the Helsinki School of Economics. She has presented her research, currently focused on the moral dimensions of organizational life, at several conferences in the United States and abroad. She currently serves on the Editorial Board of the *Journal of Applied Behavioral Science* and on the Board of Directors of the Organizational Behavior Teaching Society.

J. Michael Cavanaugh received his PhD from the University of Massachusetts in 1992. He is currently Assistant Professor at Fairfield University, Connecticut, where he teaches organizational behavior and theory. His research revolves around the study of interorganizational relationships, especially between the university and the business community. His work has been published in the *Journal of Management Education* and *Organization Science*. Recently, his experiments in teaching and pedagogy have also been written up in the *Wall Street Journal*.

Debra L. Connelley is Assistant Professor of Organizational Behavior at the Jacobs School of Management, State University of New York at Buffalo. She holds a BA in psychology from the University of Texas, an MBA from Southern Illinois University, and a PhD in organizational behavior from the New York State School of Industrial and Labor Relations at Cornell University. She has taught organizational behavior, managing diversity, and organizational change at the undergraduate and graduate levels. She also teaches cross-cultural leadership in an international executive program. Her research involves intergroup cooperation and conflict, and she has written on the effects of intergroup conflict on diversity management. She has also consulted with both public and private institutions on managing a diverse workforce.

Michael Elmes is Assistant Professor in the Department of Management, Worcester Polytechnic Institute (WPI), Worcester, Massachusetts, Associate and a visiting scholar at MIT in the Spring of 1997. His research interests are in the areas of dissent, learning, and transformation in teams and organizations; interpretive approaches to organizational culture and change; and intergroup relations. His research appears in the *Academy of Management Review, Human Relations, Journal of Applied Behavioral Science, Journal of Management Inquiry, Journal of Engineering and Technology Management,* and *Small Group Research*. He has been a process consultant, management trainer, and career development counselor in several different organizations. He received his PhD in organizational behavior from Syracuse University in 1989.

Jocelyn A. Finley is Visiting Professor in the Management of Organization Behavior Department at Columbia Business School. Her primary research areas are cultural diversity, intergroup communication, crisis management, and organizational paradox. Currently, her research focuses on dilemmas of talk and silence about value-laden issues such as race, gender, and ethnicity.

Roy Jacques is Assistant Professor at the California School of Professional Psychology in Alameda, California. He received his PhD in organization studies from the University of Massachusetts, Amherst. His recent book with Sage, London, entitled *Manufacturing the Employee: Management Knowledge From the 19th to the 21st Centuries,* explores the coalescence of the institutions of management in the United States in the period 1870 to 1920. His primary gender-related interest is in better understanding the processes through which work practices related to caring, connection, emotion, and/or relationship come to be devalued. He is currently attempting to develop the concept of "women's work" as knowledge work.

Mark Maier is Associate Professor of Organizational Leadership and Director of the Organizational Leadership Program at Chapman University in Orange, California. A former Woodrow Wilson Fellow and holder of a 1991 GTE Lectureship in Technology and Ethics, he was among a group of prominent organizational scholars selected to participate in the 1989 watershed National Science Foundation Conference on the Relationship of Feminist Theory to Ethical and Value Issues in Organizational Science. He is best known in the OB/management education community for his creation of a pedagogical documentary on the Challenger disaster that is in use at over 600 universities and leading corporations around the world. His chapter won the Dorothy Harlow Award for best paper given by the Women in Management Division of the Academy of Management in 1996.

Richard Marsden is Associate Professor and coordinator of the Industrial Relations program at the Centre for Economics, Industrial Relations, and Organization Studies, Athabasca University, Canada's open and distance university. He holds a PhD from the University of Warwick. His research focuses on the relationship between the practice of IR/HRM and social theory. He has published in *Sociology, Journal of Historical Sociology, Organization Studies, Electronic Journal of Radical Organization Theory,* and the *Handbook of Organization Studies.*

E. Joy Mighty earned her PhD in organizational behavior from York University in Toronto. She is currently an Associate Professor in the Faculty of Administration at the University of New Brunswick (Fredericton), where she teaches organizational behavior and organization theory. Her research interests include issues related to the management of workplace diversity, women in management, the processes of institutionalization, and organizational change. She has published in several journals and in various proceedings of national and regional conferences. She is currently coordinating a multidisciplinary action research project on The Impact of Family Violence on the Workplace for the Atlantic Region Muriel McQueen Fergusson Centre for Family Violence Research.

Albert J. Mills is Professor of Management and the Associate Dean of the Faculty of Commerce at Saint Mary's University, Nova Scotia, Canada. His central research interest is gender and organization, and his publications have focused on sexuality, sexual harassment, organizational culture, the adult learner, employment equity, and gender and organizational communication. He has published books and articles and is a member of the Executive Board of the Women in Management Division of the Academy of Management and an Associate Editor of *The Canadian Review of Sociology and Anthropology*. He has taught management in the United Kingdom, United States, Canada, Holland, Slovenia, Macedonia, Hungary, Kuwait, and Vietnam.

Ali H. Mir is completing his PhD at the University of Massachusetts at Amherst and has a background that includes a bachelor's degree in mechanical engineering, an MBA, and 5 years of work experience in large transnational corporations. His research and publications have been concerned with issues of management education, the future of workplace governance, the epistemological dimensions of management discourse, and the ideologies of contemporary industrial paradigms. His current work focuses on the transformation of work in late 20th-century capitalism and its implications for the division of labor in domestic and international arenas.

Collette Oseen has a doctorate in Feminist/Postmodernist Organizational theory from the University of Alberta. Since completing her doctorate, she has worked as an organizational equity consultant. Previously, she taught in northern China at the University of Alberta. Her research focuses on the processes through which women are marginalized in organizations.

Anshuman Prasad (PhD, University of Massachusetts at Amherst) teaches Organization Theory and Behavior, Organizational Communication, and the

Management of Change in the Faculty of Management at the University of Calgary. His research is primarily concerned with understanding organizational processes from a critical, symbolic, and noninstrumental perspective. Within this broad framework, his publications and conference presentations have dealt with such themes as postcolonialism, organizational ideology, alienation, gender issues, aggression and resistance at the workplace, and epistemological considerations in management research. He also teaches at the Helsinki School of Economics and Business Administration.

Pushkala Prasad is Associate Professor in the Faculty of Management at the University of Calgary, Canada, where she teaches organization theory and organizational behavior. Her research interests include organizational culture and symbolism, gender issues in work computerization, and multiculturalism in the workplace, and she has published extensively on these topics. Her paper, "Life and Death in Career" was awarded the Best Experiential Paper Award at the Eastern Academy of Management in 1992. Last year, she was awarded the Outstanding New Scholar Award by the University of Calgary. She currently serves on several editorial boards including the *Journal of Management, Technology Studies,* and the *Journal of Management Inquiry.* She has also taught courses at the Helsinki School of Economics and at Lund University in Sweden.

David Wicks (PhD, York University) is Assistant Professor in the faculty of commerce at Saint Mary's University (Halifax, Canada) where he teaches strategic management and organizationl behavior. His research interests include compliant behavior in organizations, gender and organizational culture and organizational responses to institutional pressures. His paper (coauthored with Patricia Bradshaw) *Cycles of Resistance and Compliance* was awarded the Best Paper Award at the Administrative Sciences Association of Canada Conference in 1996. He serves as an academic reviewer for the organizational behavior, organizational theory, and women-in-management divisions of the Administrative Sciences Association of Canada and the Academy of Management.

Diana Wong-MingJi is a doctoral student at the University of Massachusetts at Amherst. Her research focuses on issues in international management, global competition, business-government relationships, and theory building. She is also a Research Fellow at the North American Policy Group of Dalhousie University in Halifax, Nova Scotia (Canada), where her work is concerned with economic development and trade policies, especially in relation to the U.S.-Canada Free Trade Agreement and the North American Free Trade Agreement.